LANTERNS
OVER DEMNER

LANTERNS
OVER DEMNER

A SCIENCE FICTION MURDER MYSTERY

DALE A. KAGAN

Cover by Jeff Mettler

This book was printed in the United States of America.

To order additional copies of this book, contact:
Xlibris Corporation
1-888-7-XLIBRIS
www.Xlibris.com
Orders@Xlibris.com

CONTENTS

to
Diana Lindsay Richard
United States Air Force, Retired

Her characters Councilwoman Lim Miusov,
Pasha Miusov, Westerman and Klemperer
are used with her permission

Slash marks (//) indicate the use of telepathy.

The Special Forces Council, Earth, is a military organization and
specializes in the use of extra-sensory perception and paranormal
abilities.

The characters in this book are fictional and bear no resemblance to
any person, living or dead.

Mystery CAST OF CHARACTERS

John Eccles—white-haired, Governor of Demner. He did not expect to have a murder on his property.

Hawken Eccles—his niece, business consultant

Lim—Black-rank Councilman, Special Forces Council. She came to investigate a murder.

Pasha (Patrick) Miusov—Lim's son, a child prodigy in telepathic ability, age 18, half-human, half-Sigma Draconian

Steve Winters—former first-in scout, Security Officer, assigned to protect the Councilmen

Renate Ramón y Cajal—diplomat from Eta Cassiopiae. Murder was not in his original game plan.

O'Connors—diplomatic aide to Ramón

Aargau—Eccles' grounds keeper, a young precocious inventor

Robert Moncrief—Council agent, Special Forces Council. He came to investigate a smuggler on Dauropa.

Aaron Tennyson—wealthy free trader from planet Jalug, under a curse, age 40

Wendnagel—his wife

Raymond Berquist—Black-rank Councilman

Michael Westerman—Black-rank Councilman, Leader of the Special Forces

Klemperer—Second in command, Special Forces Council, on Earth and in the field. He sent the Councilmen to investigate a murder.

Prologue

I

"What can you do about the communications breakdown?" The Ambassador from Dauropa eyed the people in the room, his gaze passing over a tall woman with long dark hair who wore a black Special Forces uniform, to her eighteen year old son, similarly dressed, to the teenage girl with long brown hair, to settle finally on a man in his 60's, showing his age, and wearing a Special Forces uniform.

The man in his sixties was the head of the Special Forces branch of the Space Force, based on Earth. They stood inside a small black building located in the suburbs of Moscow.

The man was Michael Westerman. "Let's get this straight. You received a message from an important Family on Dauropa that a Councilman was found dead. Then communications broke up?"

"That is correct," the blue-decked Ambassador replied.

"And this kind of mechanical break down is frequent on Dauropa?"

"Very."

"I want to send in two agents with E.S.P., both Special Forces Councilmen. How familiar are you with E.S.P.?"

"Well, I—"

"Let me help you," suggested Westerman. He gestured to the sixteen year old girl.

"Erin—"

"Yes. Mr. Ambassador, there are several kinds of E.S.P. or extra sensory perception. Lim will demonstrate clairvoyance." She gestured to the tall, woman with long black hair. The Councilwoman nodded to the Ambassador with only a touch of emotion. Keep it under control, second-in-command Klemperer had always instructed.

Erin Browne gave the cards to the Ambassador, "If you will choose one of the cards and place it face down before you?"

The Ambassador adjusted his collar, then hefted the deck suspiciously, as if about to discover a trick, and selected a card, put it in front of the deck, face down. The backs of the cards had a blue, navy and white geometric design.

Lim said stolidly, "It's an Ace of Spades."

The Ambassador from Dauropa turned it over. "Correct." Lim stated to speak and he held up his hand—"Wait. Another, if I may. That was much too quick. Don't you have to concentrate or something?"

Erin explained, "The Councilmen are noted for their speed and accuracy."

The Ambassador spread the cards, selected one, and gestured.

Lim demurred, "That's a moving card."

"Can you tell or can't you?"

"Yes, it's a Queen of Hearts."

He turned it over. Although it revealed a Queen of Hearts, the ink moved like liquid mercury and re-formed into a Jack of Hearts. After a pause it formed a Two of Clubs. Another pause. Then a scrambled set of ovals that re-formed into an Eight of Spades.

Lin Miusov picked up the cards. "That's Councilman Berquist's deck. He used it to test young sensitives. Here, Pasha, you hold them." She gave them to her son.

Westerman suggested, "How about a telepathy demonstration?" He turned to the Ambassador. "This is how we will circumvent your communications problem on Dauropa."

He nodded to Erin. She motioned for Lim's son. "Patrick will take you to the other room. Close the door and give him a message. Lim here will pick it up."

The Ambassador was unmoved but willing to give it a try. "After you, Patrick," he told the youth.

"Please call me Pasha." They entered the room together. "It's dark, of course," the Ambassador noticed the light was off, then decided, "How very apropos." Chairs lined the walls and an oval table could be discerned in the darkness.

Pasha spoke first. He said, "Give me a moment to clear my mind . . . go ahead."

The Ambassador spoke to Pasha . . .

Lim was waiting for them when they opened the door.

"Well?" stated the Ambassador smugly.

"It's a chess move. An old grand masters game. 'Black king castles. Checkmate.'"

The Ambassador was stunned. "It's an old game. I didn't think you'd recognize it." He made a quick recovery. "I should have known."

Lim smiled warmly. It was okay after the E.S.P. was over. She tossed her long black hair over her shoulders.

She mused to herself that the Special Forces Council was not about cards or playing radio. She could still remember a recent assignment to a break away colony once called Polaris VI. The job was to sit in the Federation Mission and do clairvoyant scans, looking for underground chemical warfare factories. She and her team found one–and the people on which they were being tested.

They were shaken. It had taken three weeks of debriefing before they could do a clairvoyant scan on anything.

No, the SFC was not about cards. She wondered what was really on Councilman Westerman's mind with this assignment and why the local authorities on Dauropa could not handle it.

She asked, ""Can you tell us something about Dauropa?"

"The Thok Dauropa/Thok Jalug system has two inhabitable planets: Dauropa and Jalug.

"Dauropa is a full Earth colony. Its cities were built by rich corporations and its countryside terraformed by rich individuals to mimic Earth's forests.

"Jalug is a whole different matter. Its natives are six-legged and the society resembles old India."

"Overpopulated and underfed?" asked Westerman.

"No. I meant two centuries earlier. Its Kings have absolute authority over life and death of their subjects. Only the work of the free trader named Aaron Tennyson brought trade contact with them and the main Terran Trade City."

Lim interposed. "When I said brief us, I meant the political situation."

"I'll get you the materials you need," he answered. "Let me gather my notes."

As the Ambassador departed Westerman turned to Lim. "I'm concerned about Klemperer. He's greatly overextended. The Daupora sector must be a mess. Whatever you do, don't give him an excuse to leave Earth and come to Dauropa. Understand?"

"Yes," Lim answered.

"Maybe we can help him with the workload," Pasha volunteered.

"Just remember what I said."

Pasha nodded and entered one of the side cubicles. He sat down in a plush arm chair. The non-emotional reserve dropped. Tears came to his green eyes. A Councilman was dead.

"Pasha—" Erin entered the room. Brown eyes met green and there was no need to speak. Her presence was enough.

Sitting on the arm of the chair, Erin removed her boot. She ran her toes down Pasha's leg. He welcomed her reassurance.

II

There was a feeling of a storm in the air. Wendnagel brushed her long blond hair over her shoulders and strode over the cedar bridge. Beneath the crunch of footfalls on leaves, the water splashed by cold with the swift current.

Its source was high on the Demner side of the mountain.

As she walked over the bridge the path wound on, partially obscured beneath the fallen leaves of red, yellow and orange. She pulled her long red cloak around her and came suddenly upon the chalet in the forest, hard to find because it was outwardly designed to blend into the forest.

Japanese prayer bells hung from a nearby tree bough and made a soft sound.

Beyond the tree was a stone-lined pool. She looked into the depths as if she could see through the water into the future, which she could do after a fashion, like a seer using a crystal.

She reached the cottage door when someone called her name.

Wendnagel waved on Eccles' niece who was at the wooden bridge, no doubt trying to find the exact spot of the chalet. The blond-haired tall woman was already inside.

Hawken Eccles entered with the feeling that was a cross between awe and reverence.

Wendnagel was one of the Family, whose line went back to the settlement of Dauropa. Every school child know the story. When the rich colonists came from Earth, they had found an invisible form of life on Dauropa called the Shades. They liked to eat electrical energy and many of their devices failed before colonists with high amounts of extra-sensory perception or E.S.P. could detect them. The Shades had been driven high into the mountains and the Family had acquired a great deal of land and fame as they intermarried. Wendnagel was still to this day called a Blue Witch.

There were three kinds of E.S.P: telepathy—transmission and reception of thought, clairvoyance—the seeing of objects not present in the room, precognition—seeing the future. The Family had all three.

Over time the fortunes of the Family had waned and that led Wendnagel to marry the fabulously rich trader from Jalug—Aaron Tennyson. They were very much in love.

Now they were waiting for the Councilmen, of the Special Forces Council.

Hawken Eccles followed Wendnagel inside and saw more cedar furniture, more wind chimes and felt an overall sense of warmth in the room. Prisms hung in the windows, splitting the light into a chorus of rainbow colors. A painting hung on the wall of oil lanterns hanging in the air as if they could levitate.

On another wall was a framed picture of stars, the Big Dipper and Small Dipper as seen from Earth. Between them wound the stars of Draco the Dragon, an inhabited star system of Sigma Draconis. Dauropa and Jalug, sister planets, were lost in the bowl of the Big Dipper, which could be seen from Earth only through a telescope or strong binoculars.

The Special Forces Council on Earth had such a telescope.

Wendnaged sized up Hawken. Eccles' niece was a local business consultant. Her uncle had recently been re-elected Governor of Demner and would re-inhabit the small castle. Only Eccles had really liked the place. Everyone else kept their offices in the village of Demner or the town of the same name. *Hawken was dating, let's see,* thought Wendnagel, *Renate Ramón.* The visiting diplomat from Eta Cassiopeae was currently staying at Eccles' castle, with an aide.

"Are you still seeing him?" she asked. She did not have to say who the "him" was.

"Of course."

Wendnagel thought she was too provincial to have a romantic attachment to a diplomat as well-traveled as Ramón. And he was far older than she. He would see an experienced business woman, but what did she see in him?

"Are you sleeping with him?"

"As if I will tell you that !"

She changed the subject.

"The visitors will be here soon."

"Yes, the Councilmen of the Special Forces."

"To investigate the death of one of the Councilmen on Dauropa. They will be staying at the castle. Their leader is a woman named Lim, a strong telepath," she added.

"No one is stronger than you are, Wendnagel."

"You are too provincial. She comes from Earth which is still the center of the Solar Federation. We are the frontier. Lim is to solve the mystery of who killed him. She is the most powerful telepath in the Special Forces Council."

"She is no one next to you. Everyone knows of you."

"You will have to get over that feeling." Wendnagel suddenly felt a chill. She almost did not hear her next question.

"Who comes with her?"

"Her son, Pasha Miusov. It's the taken Russian name of a part Sigma Draconian."

"How was this done? Does he look human?"

"He looks human." How was a secret. She knew but would not say.

Wendnagel turned suddenly, her red cloak billowing out. She hadn't taken it off.

She said, "She is accompanied by a Security Officer from the starship DISCOVERY. His name is Steve Winters and he will probably chafe at her restrictions."

She went on, "The Black-rank Councilmen can teletap objects." Black was the ultimate color rank. The others were white, yellow, green and brown in ascending order. "They can sensitize an object so that after that they can always "see" who is holding it and sometimes even what they are saying. By teletapping parts of the castle grounds they can watch who enters and exits better than any surveillance system. They may refuse to set up mechanical eyes or human watchers. There is also Bob Moncrief, a Council Agent on the staff—"

She stopped abruptly. Wendnagel smelled a Shade. It must have been attracted by Eccles' zoo, and small gauge railroad—it ran on electricity—that ran around the property. She always said it would attract a Shade. She could "see" it now.

All at once, time became non-sequential. She would "see" several images one after the other in her mind:

//Dark-haired Lim traveling on the omnicraft to the spaceport, Winters shouting at her.//

//A tall dark Councilman standing at night on the mountainside with a look of incredible surprise followed by an explosion.//

//Aaron lying motionless on the floor of a citadel on Jalug.//

//Pasha, dark-haired, his face mirrored by a violet light about to make an announcement.//

Past, present and future sorted itself out.

"It's a Shade," she told Hawken.

"Where?" She looked around as if she could see what could not be seen.

"It's in the mountains."

In a glide, Wendnagel was in front of the desk. On the desk were potted native flowers in Spanish vases that in older times held grain on Earth. She moved the vase aside to reveal a recessed area. Squares in the hidden area responded to the heat of her fingers. On the wall was the stylized outline of an atomic lantern. It was actually in the wall. When Wendnagel turned it on, it could be seen for a long distance.

Out the window on the same side, one could see that there was an opening in the trees. The deed to the chalet included the stipulation that she had permanent line-of-sight with the spaceport below. No one on any property could grow a tree high enough to obstruct the view.

The Lantern of Demner was on. Now it was up to the rangers.

III

The shipment is lost read the report.

"Mon Dieu," muttered Ramón y Cajal, Ambassador to Dauropa from the former Earth colony of Eta Cassiopiae. The envoy to Dauropa repeated his feeling in less politely acceptable French.

Ramón was tough of build with an air of elegance. These last orders from Eta Cassiopiae had all but undermined the goodwill he had built up with Governor Eccles here on Dauropa. He had expected a hefty aid package. Now he might be sent home in disgrace.

Even worse the powers to be had appointed O'Connors as his aide to see that the job got done. Although delicate in appearance, O'Connor was known to be a tough negotiator, tough but fair.

Ramón knew part of Dauropa had been build with funds from Switzerland on Earth, funds that investors spent to insure that Dauropa was a neutral planet. "This isn't exactly a neutral gesture," he murmured outloud.

"Everyone knows the famous trader, Aaron Tennyson left Earth to escape high regulations and tariffs. So we are violating a Dauropa tariff. It's in the same spirit."

"This is more than a tariff violation, "Ramón growled.

"The question is what are we to do? I have news that two Black Councilmen are due to arrive."

"So."

"Members of the Special Forces Council? Elite users of E.S.P.?" He prodded Ramón's memory.

"*Those* forces? Why?

"I don't know. I suggest we destroy certain documents and they can read our minds."

"No they can't. The telepaths only send to each other."

"What they have is clairvoyance or precognitions and can read the future?

"They can't read the future. That's a Dauropa specialty and only members of the Family have it and they need special conditions. Calm down.

"We must make a plan about the lost shipment."

Ramón sighed. He was hoping to see Hawken tonight. Better make it tomorrow. Can I take her to Eta? he wondered.

O'Connors was supposed to know this stuff. If only they had another week. Or these silly orders hadn't arrived. They weren't silly; he just would have protected Eta's interests in another way. Could O'Connor negotiate his way out?

"What's your plan?" Ramón wanted to know.

They changed languages and O'Connors briefed him.

When he was done, O'Connor switched back to French, the language of diplomacy in another era. "I'm concerned about you," O'Connors began, changing the subject. "And your love interest in Hawken. She could be a trained spy and the Dauropan government could have trained her. Don't you think they don't debrief her after every lengthy stay with you?"

Ramón thought about it. Spying was a common problem for a government. In the Cold War in the twentieth century the Soviet Union sent trained female spies to American embassies in the Eastern Bloc. American interests were compromised on several occasions.

During the colony war in the twenty-fourth century, Earth and Sirius sent trained spies of the opposite sex to warring colonies. They were

19

instructed to learn the codes of the colonies' relay comm-sats. Whoever knew the codes controlled the subspace radio relay in that sector. Since it was largely an economic war, spying had top priority.

Was that the case here? Ramón mused. Was she a spy? He thought for a minute and then replied in Standard, "I don't think so. Her interest is genuine. I don't think she is a spy."

"Count on it," O'Connors persisted.

Chapter 1

THE CRASH

It all happened in one second.

One moment Security Officer Steve Winters was piloting the omnicraft. The former first-in scout turned security officer had been detached from the Space Force starship DISCOVERY. The Councilman had turned down a larger security crew, preferring to rely on their own special abilities.

Winters glanced behind him at his passengers.

THE PROTECTIVE AGENT SHOULD PROVIDE ESCORT read the security manual.

Winters studied his charges.

The leader was tall, dark-haired Lim Miusov, resplendent in her black uniform. An extrovert, she sat in a manner that showed her to be aerobically fit.

Her last mission with her son Patrick had won praises. This was her second trip to the planet Dauropa, a system of twin planets—Dauropa and Jalog (sometimes spelled Jalug). Her last assignment in the Short War had been behind enemy lines and utilized clairvoyance, surprise and superior weapons.

Her son Patrick, called Pasha, was dark haired. Half-Draconian, his father had come from Sigma Draconis. His outward appearance was pensive, almost morose manner and introverted, but Winters had learned it merely meant he was thinking. His extra sensory perception potential was so high as to be unratable. His partner, Erin Browne, didn't accompany him on this trip. She had stayed on Earth. The third member of this investigation party was Bob Moncrief, a Councilman. He had done most of the liaison work.

Winters glanced at them and back to his console in all of a second. That was enough.

Without giving any warning the instrument panel blanked out.

With instant reflexes, Lim was at the control console, trying the emergency backup and reaching for the on button for the spaceport radio.

"Sit down and strap in!" Winters snapped. It took a lot of nerve to shout at a Councilman.

Lim gave him a look but quickly strapped into her seat. The others already had landing harnesses on.

Winters saw the mountains rushing up toward the craft and thumbed the spaceport radio. He gave his position and reported what had happened.

"By the Shades!" were the responses from the spaceport tower. Winters couldn't ferret that out and stated, "Mayday, Mayday."

"There's a clearing high up in the mountains. You might be able to land in that. Please give us the passenger list."

"Confirmed." He looked out the forward port and reported seeing a light.

The spaceport gave instructions after again exclaiming, "A Shade! You must be seeing a Lantern of the Blue Witch."

"This is Security Officer Steve Winters from the starship DISCOVERY. I am carrying Black-rank Councilman Lim Miusov, Patrick Miusov and Councilman Robert Moncrief."

"You aren't going to make it to the spaceport. You will have to try the clearing."

The trees looked larger. Suddenly Winters saw the opening.

He glided the ship down to it. The dorsal ridge on the bottom, designed to keep the ship gravity oriented in the atmosphere, dug a ditch into the ground and left a groove behind the fast moving ship. The right wing hit the ground as the ship rolled to starboard, and Winters made a correction that caused the left wing to dip but not hit the ground. Suddenly he had power on the board and he fired the ions in reverse. The ion grill on the wings squeaked in reverse. Crash foam webbing spewed into the cockpit and that was the last Winters saw before the ship ripped off its right wing and came to a stop.

The ship was still as a ghost.

He was grateful they weren't all dead.

Outside a bird-shaped thing passed between the sun and the downed ship. A high-pitched call was emitted. In the background something hummed.

Winters pulled out a knife and tore at the crash foam, cutting himself out. His first concern was the safety of the Councilmen. He had to see them safely to Eccles' castle. He cut them out one at a time.

Lim's first thought was that she had broken no bones. Then she waited for the Security Officers' assessment of the rest of them. Even her fear had not shaken her outward aura of reserve. Her black eyes met Pasha's green eyes as he was cut out.

Pasha's pulse was racing. It was said that when a car was speeding the driver was calm and the passengers had the heart attack. He appeared all right. He regained his appearance of being imperturbable.

Lim bolted out of the chair. "There are people outside. They may be our rescue."

"Or they may be kidnappers," returned Winters warily. "I'd like to know why our board went out. It could be a set-up."

He cut Moncrief out. He had slipped out of his harness and been held by the crash foam. Moncrief looked relieved. Moncrief had been assigned to Dauropa for two years and had sent to Earth himself for Lim and Pasha.

High in the Demner mountains there were answering high pitched bird calls.

Winters had been the first to explore many planets and he knew his job. Safety was uppermost in his mind. At the sound of another bird cry he opened the weapons locker. The computerized shelf popped out an energyzer. He hefted the weapon, hoping the Councilwoman was right. Their use of E.S.P. was frequently unsettling.

Outside, a man beneath a color-splashed hang glider landed by the wreck and pulled himself out of the harness. He ran over and wrenched open the omnicraft door using the manual override as the electric motor was not working. "Oh, Hullo!" he called.

Winters emerged first, to check out the newcomers.

"Are you the rescue party from the spaceport?"

"No. We're rangers from Demner. Wendnagel said there was a Shade."

Winters pulled out an energyzer and looked around.

The man in the colorful outfit looked amused. "You can't hit a Shade with an energyzer. It eats the energy."

The Councilmen were outside. Miusov remarked, "It also can't be seen. But I can sense it."

"Tell it to leave, telepathically, "Lim instructed.

The glider pilot was bemused, wondering if it could be done. "Sometimes they appear over electrical wire like round gaseous balls."

"I took care of it," said Muisov, who showed no sign of having expended energy.

Winters wanted to know, "How did you find us so fast?"

"We followed that line," he pointed.

The dorsal flap beneath the ship had left a scooped-out line that ran all the way to the horizon. Scrap that had been torn off the ship was strewn along the line for nearly one quarter of a mile.

The man put his hands to the sides of his mouth and gave a call "Kooaaaa!" that was echoed from the sky. Two more hang gliders descended. One bird-shaped object cut a path across the sun. As it spiraled down it became more clearly a motorized canard glider. One man sat in the open pilot's seat.

Lim told the pilot, "We were headed for the spaceport until the crash. We have a meeting with Governor Eccles."

Faces lit up among the flyers. "You're going to the castle!"

"Have you seen it before?"

"We could take you there," offered the third.

Their reactions made Winters secretly wonder what he had gotten into. The castle was apparently a well known sort for its unusual nature.

Winters hesitated to accept but Lim overruled him. They were in the middle of getting an explanation on the safety of the passengers when Miusov took a good look down the mountains. He was leaning against the omnicraft because of the exertion of telling the Shade to retreat. The long vista made him appreciate what a narrow scrape they had just had. Getting his strength back he took another look down at the tree-studded mountainside and trembled.

"If you don't mind, I'll stay with the ship until the launches from the spaceport show up. I'll go down with them."

Lim said, "But Pasha, it's perfectly safe."

"No." He did not explain why.

"Then Moncrief will have to stay also. You can meet us at the castle."

"Are you sure you're not in shock?" asked one of the hang glider pilots. "Maybe you'd better lie down. Put your feet up on a pillow."

"I'm fine, but Moncrief has a sprained wrist." Pasha gestured to Moncrief who was holding his wrist. The dark-haired youth checked the wrist with his E.S.P. "It might be broken," he added.

A pilot in bright white, yellow and blue unfastened a second harness from the glider and showed Lim how to strap it on. The tall, dark-haired Councilwoman hoped they weren't compromising security by taking this route down the mountain. She always expected to be a target on a new Special Forces Council mission.

A pilot in red and white did the same with Winters who had apparently done it before. A third glider would take their luggage. Lim moved the luggage and grabbed a red thermo jacket, slipped it on and adjusted the thermostat to a comfortable temperature.

The air was chilled and it might even snow.

They were towed by the powered glider into the sky. The pilots were familiar with the land below and easily guided them over the forest to the town of Demner and then onto Eccles' castle. Lim's guide gave her an enthusiastic running account, over her protests that she had been here before.

The air currents swept them along and Lim's breath was taken away at the vast panorama of sky and land.

The hang glider pilot, named Aarau, expounded, "The trees are pine, conifers, maple and oak, transported all the way from Earth, New England I believe. The mountains rival my former home in Switzerland. The river can be seen. Governor Eccles has a footpath along the mountains, made of wood, to overlook it. He also has a small gauge railroad that runs around the property. And cats! A million cats. Well, eleven, twelve or thirteen of them, all underfoot."

"I've seen his art gallery, don't forget to mention that." Lim agreed Eccles was something wonderful and eccentric. The pilot was so taken with the local legend of the castle he could not stop talking about it.

Winters was fuming from his vantage point.

THE SECURITY AGENT SHOULD BE FAMILIAR WITH THE MEET-ING SITE.

Not only was he denied a force in full, but he had no time to screen the castle before the entrance of the Councilmen. It had passed a cursory check, of course, but the people to assist him were at the spaceport.

To compensate he asked his red-and white-clothed rescuer to make a few circles over the property before landing.

They passed low over the railroad "Station House" and swung over the stone three story castle. A fire escape was on one side, and several stone porches. Beyond a circle of trees on the lawn, was a precipitous drop of at least one hundred feet.

The second pass showed a glimmer of water and gleam of coins from the bottom of the wishing well on an adjoining side. The castle had been moved from Earth stone by stone.

Coins sparkled in a pool, giving it the appearance of an enchanted body of water.

The sky filled half his vision like the vault of heaven. Scarcely a cloud was present. His breath came short. A flag tied to the strut fluttered. The rope which secured it rapped the pole—click, click, click. Wind tore against his face. It was exhilarating in its cold intensity. Possibly a storm was in the air. The chill heightened his awareness. Pine trees rushed by beneath him. He swept over the river until the pilot banked a turn. A wooden terrace spanned the side of the mountain and bridges arched over streams, but the view from the bridges wasn't as good as by the hang glider. Pockets of solid rocks had been deposited by glaciers in the last ice age. A winding road wound around them through the forest. It ended in a clearing. On the clearing there stood a three story castle.

The wind was right for them to come down on the lawn and Winters requested it. The first-in scout watched the pilot relay the message to his cohort by radio. That quote from his guidebook caused him to consult the blueprints from memory. As they descended he matched the view of the ground to his memory.

The vista from this sky perch was overwhelming, like a moment of quiet in a noisy city. The city of Zäringhen, home of the spaceport, was far away to the south. It could barely been seen from the air, then fell out of sight as the hang glider descended. The splashes of color on the glider could be seen from below.

As they made their descent, a white-haired old man ran out of one of the castle's many stone doorways and started waving his arms and shouting. Although it was too far to hear the actual words, they were not welcoming. In fact as he could hear the tonal inflection, down right threatening.

"Get out of here! You don't have any right to land on my lawn. What a fool stunt. Get off my property." Then, they landed, making a running stop.

The hang glider pilots were unruffled. They had known Eccles as boys. "John," said the pilot next to Lim, "I've brought your guests."

"You can't . . . WHAT?" Instead of relief, the Governor seemed almost terrified. He was white as a sheet. He calmed down when Lim disengaged from the harness to present herself, but not nearly like a man expecting a welcome guest.

Lim stripped off her thermo jacket, and stood shivering in uniform as she made formal introduction of herself and Security Officer Steve Winters from the DISCOVERY. She added, "Pasha and Special Forces agent Mr. Moncrief will be following."

"Not by hang glider!" Eccles protested.

"No, by spaceport launch." Only then did Eccles calm down.

He started to welcome the pilots but they made their excuses and headed for the precipice where they could continue their journey down the mountain over the river.

KAGA

THE SECURITY AGENT SHOULD EXHAUSTIVELY CHECK LIVING AND WORK AREAS.

Winters was still quoting in his mind from the security manual when Eccles led them inside, and allowed Winter to—finally—examine the rooms.

The castle was something of a vacation resort for the previous governors. It had been little used, but Eccles had moved right in and made use of it. Winters saw computers and robots but no sign of staff, human or otherwise. He didn't think Lim would go this far and decided to ask the governor when he calmed down.

The door to his "office" was made of wood. Eccles pulled a hammer-shaped lever. Wooden beams slid out of the wall, ceiling and floor. Winters was staring at the arrangement as Eccles pulled the door open. The windows also had strange wooden opening mechanisms. The table was on a track and could slide along the floor, as could a wooden, hand-carved chair.

Winters had just finished surveying the three floors, art gallery, servants area, "secret" passage, and the cottage outside before planning where to put the rooms of the Councilmen.

Eccles was still tense.

Two hours later Moncrief stormed in, Pasha in tow. He found Lim in the main living room and shouted at Pasha, as if finishing an argument. He turned to Lim and modulated his tone downward.

The room was dark and the way Lim liked it and it didn't improve his mood. Moncrief told her firmly. "I never want to travel in an omnicraft again with Pasha Miusov."

"What's the matter?" Normally Pasha's behavior was exemplary.

"My wrist wasn't broken, that's what the matter."

He marched out, leaving Pasha, and took off for the anteroom to find Winters.

Pasha said nothing, telepathically or verbally.

"Well-?" Lim asked.

"He opened his crash harness. He's up to something."

"You're paranoid," Lim told him.

Winters joined them with Eccles, distracting the moment.

The main room was open and two ceilings high. On the second floor was an interior balcony that ran parallel to the wall, ending in a staircase to the first floor. The second floor was their guest quarters.

Doors on the first floor were opened to a stone porch on one side and to a wishing well on the adjoining area.

Snowpaws, the cat, hugged his body around Miusov's legs. The feline had a sixth digit—an apposed thumb almost big enough to let the cat lift things. He had a telepathic awareness that made Miusov curious to find out if he could link up with the animal. The black and white feline told him that Eccles was uneasy.

In fact, Eccles was perceptibly shaking enough for Winters, Lim and Pasha to notice.

"Eccles, what's wrong?" "John, what's the matter?" "Are you okay?" they voiced at the same moment.

"What makes you think I'm nervous?" Eccles asked suspiciously. He had a telepathic block, previously taught to him by Lim.

"John, you're visibly shaking," Lim pointed out.

"If you were Governor, you'd have problems, too!" he snapped with uncharacteristic reticence.

Pasha and Lim's eyes met.

Lim thought //We'll find out about this.//

But it was a long while before Lim was to find out what was unsettling her host.

Snowpaws clicked in his throat and let out a meow as his latent telepathy picked up an awareness.

Pasha told Lim, //You'd think his white hair was from us.//

Eccles forced a smile, "We're not doing any work tonight. We're having a party."

Lim started to protest. Eccles insisted, "It's my house rule. There will be plenty of work to do tomorrow."

"Then we'll get ready," Lim took Pasha upstairs. "Speak out loud. Otherwise, you'll use up amputs and you might need them later."

"Will the free trader be there? He can help us a lot. The field sales office can tell us about the smugglers."

"I want to know why the vacation retreat is on automation. The

29

economists and staff must be in Demner or Zäringhen. I'm really puzzled over Eccles."

Pasha thought for a moment then transmitted his thoughts: //What could we see from the air?// the precocious youth asked. His thoughts burst in as a mental picture.

Winters followed Lim upstairs.

He stopped her at the door to her room.

"What's this about a party? We're here to investigate a death."

"It's John's house rule. I'd forgotten about it."

Winters went off fuming to himself and quoting from the security manual.

From the first floor, Eccles watches him go in the reflection in a mirror.

Chapter 2

THE PARTY

I

There was a feeling of storm in the air. Outside the castle rain clouds gathered. Inside, Aaron looked at the goblet and laughed. It had an intricate design. Eccles had passed out drinks at the party, and had insisted everyone attend, even Aaron and Wendnagel who were put up at a cottage.

His grounds keeper, Aargau, passed out additional rounds. Aargau was responsible for all the carved wood inventions.

The Special Forces Councilmen were there as were the diplomats.

"What's so funny, Aaron?" Wendnagel queried.

"I came from Earth to Jalug and saw a lot of fine craftware. On Dauropa I found planned cities and fine carved goods. And, here I am in the castle of a governor and the goblets are plastic." The young, blond-haired merchant put down the drinking vessel, "It's just funny, that's all."

Winters had been talking about anecdotes of his first-in scout days, including tracking beasts on Multi-Luna (the Planet of 100 Moons). The creatures could only be seen in the infra-red range and during storms.

Aaron's laughter interrupted his account. Ramón the diplomat continued to focus on Aaron.

Eccles called for more beer. Aargau poured Wendnagel's cup before she could refuse.

Pasha took it from her and downed it himself.

Outside rain began to beat on the door. The group was getting relaxed.

Ramón told the group in his soft voice, "Did you know that Aaron Tennyson is under a curse at Jalug? He entered the citadel and came out under a curse."

"It's true," the young blond-haired trader affirmed. He had turned surprisingly pale. "There is a citadel left to the natives of Jalug by an older group that previously occupied the planet. I entered the citadel and it is as if something inside is alive, something that knows me, as if it had my thumb prints and iris photo."

Lim started to say something about superstition.

"No, something is really there. I lost my jai' and something got hold of me. It was said if I returned there, I would die. The priest called me under a curse."

"What is a jai', Aaron?" Pasha inquired.

"It's a kind of gemstone only the priests wear. You have to wear one to get in and out of the Citadel. Mostly the place is closed off, but then L'rig's daughter ran in and I had to follow her . . . anyway that's a long story.

"This is curious," he reached toward a gem on a chain on his wife's neck. She took it off and handed it to Miusov. "This has been in Wendnagel's family for generations, yet I believe it is an exact duplicate of a jai'. Sometimes they are called jay'."

Pasha cupped it in his hand and wondered if he should do a clairvoyant probe. It looked like an ordinary white gem.

Wendnagel brushed her long blond tresses off her face, and offered, "You can keep it, no please do. Aaron has no intention of returning to Jalug."

He hung it on his neck.

"Not since I broke the hold of the smugglers there, "Aaron affirmed.

Lim said, "There's been no activity since."

"That's what I thought until recently. That's why we called you here."

Eccles twitched on his seat. Lightning lit up the room followed seconds later by thunder that shook the table. Hawken studied her drink. Eccles grabbed hold of his grounds keeper/inventor's sleeve.

"Aargau, more drinks."

"Certainly." He poured the pitcher. "Ay-ron." He called Aaron by a Dauropan accent. Sometimes it also came out "ay-uh-ron." He found Wendnagel's empty glass. She put her hand over it. "Oh, come on, Blue Witch," he urged, brushing it away and filling the glass.

She met Pasha's amused eyes. "That's too full for you."

He poured it into his own glass.

The senior diplomat cleared his throat. Unexpectedly, he called upon the free trader, "Aaron, tell us how you arrived on Jalug a mere free trader and rose to be one of the most powerful trade spokesman, a Captain of Industry, as we say on Eta."

Wendnagel added, "Not to mention one of the most powerful chieftains among the natives."

"War Lord's son-in-law, not chieftain… Khan, Supreme Ruler, Prince, margrave, governor magnate, but not chieftain. The Jalogans are no barbarians."

"Tell us," O'Connors urged. "Surely among such a culture there would be intrigue, politics and religion."

"Do not ask about the religion," Aaron begged, turning pale.

Wendnagel made the peace with, "And a story of a marriage."

"Yes," muttered Aaron sipping his wine. Other matters weighed on his mind much heavier than story telling. Nevertheless, he relived his past for them.

II

Aaron began: Kidnaping was not the best ending to a marriage offer. Or, so it unfolded until I learned of the smugglers. Jugpa! I remember that day.

The Warlord Prince of Jalug sat with his pine needle tea, shaking his head in the early evening, as Daleropa, which we call the planet Dauropa, swing in the purple sky. I could tell his plan was made.

The Prince was a being of brown hide, six legs, a head with a bone protruding in the back. Sunken areas over his eyes revealed his age. He had a long brown snout and sported a few silver hairs from his chin. The Jalogans age faster than humans. He wore brightly colored silk clothes, hand painted by artisans in their homes. The pieces hung together with pieces of leather and belt buckles in artistic arrangement. Over this, he wore a necklace of polished stones. Individual Jalogans can often be told apart by white stripes or spots on their hide. Prince Thai, Holder of Ibo the first jai', ruler of the Eastern Seaboard, could be told apart from the other Jalogans because he had none.

I steadied my cup in two hands while he balanced his brew in four. Fourteen retainers assisted the warlord and six Secret Society members stood in a courtyard patio.

A virtual estate, controlled by Prince Thai, spread across the fertile land between the sea to the east and the desert to the west. Small three story buildings with long eaves on each story were typical living quarters for the lesser princes. They dotted the landscape. Near the sea is a huge structure, a square base, capped with a smaller story with a dome over the decorative eaves or arches, and further back a larger structure, all told three stories. About 15 feet away, narrow spires encircle the building. From a sitting step, you can see the alignment bracket sun and stars at certain times of the year.

But I was in a living area of older design. Six stone castle-like towers, connected all around by six tilted walkways. We sat in the interior garden. I may as well tell you some of the Secret Society members were human.

"What!" gasped Ramón and O'Connors together.

Aaron's speech changed to more formal Standard. He continued: Centuries ago a multi-generation ship arrived on Jalug from Earth. They assimilated and took on the customs of the existing culture. It was only in this current century that a starship traveled through the new teleport boxes and founded Trade City. It was founded on the port of the only remaining tech culture on Jalug.

There are many humans in the Prince's court–singers, keepers of the verbal library, architects, holders of the calendar and festivals.

However, his fourteen retainers were Jalogan and as I said the Supreme Prince Magnate had a plan.

'You will marry my daughter, Queen of Jalac8ticote,' he said to me. His voice had the ring of an order. Ruler of thousands, his word was absolute. He had control of life and death over his subjects.

'Wait a minute,' I put down my cup on a tree stump. 'Kitara4-tia!' I repeated in Jalogan.

'Aaron'—my friend L'rig, is a non-human Jalogan, who was appointed the Prince's physician. He tried to intercept my protest to save my life.

I kept going. 'True, I'm a successful trader, mighty Prince. I like the woman, very much, however–'

'Aaron,' L'rig whispered, and his voice choked.

I had no idea how close to death I was. 'True,' I continued blithely, 'you have supported my ventures, even against other subservient Warlords.'

'I bought your first bicycles,' the Prince boasted. 'Your trade items from Earth brought us both profit and wealth. Thok warned us they were dangerous, the Terrans. You for advice I need. You will marry my daughter at noon rise at the end of the month.'

I did a rapid calculation. That was four weeks. 'Most aristocratic Lord, I can't.'

'You can, you will. Ordered it is.'

'Aaron,' L'rig pleaded. He finally got my attention. Taking my hands in his four, he joked at me in Jalogan.

Aaron stared at his audience. "More wine," he requested from Aargau.

Then, Aaron translated: He said something halfway between 'Now you've done it' and 'you're hooked!'

He gestured to me in signs, which, as a trader I had quickly learned to interpret. Then he dropped all four hands in the equivalent of a human shrug.

With that he walked off to go for his evening jog.

L'rig's confidence did not help me. I made my way to the tower room I had been given. The outside was round but the interior had six walls including a fireplace. I flung myself on the fine cloth hammock that was my bed. I had promised the Merchants Association to improve Class IV trade but what had I gotten into. Class IV–no higher technology can be imported from Earth or the Solar Federation except to the newly founded Trade City

There I carried a wristlet with ID computer with all-in-one comsat link, satellite geoposition computer, internet and bank trade computer. In the interior of Jalug I wore a dagger and a stun gun–energy weapons are banned. Why I wore the ID in a wristband I will never know–most of it had to be de-activated or blocked. Force of habit I guess. I wore it under my silk outfit, which the ancestors of the founding humans designed and updated after Jalogan garb. I never got used to having one of my hips exposed, however.

I could hear the Great Dane dogs, Gres and Dave, growling in their kennel in the courtyard, my gift to the Warlord.

My mind was ablaze. If I married Evan of Jalac8ticote, I would be the target of every subservient Warlord, not to mention the Prince's rivals in the next protectorate. Hidden Society members of the palace, Tog and Annog, non-human brothers, had already asked for her hand. They were allies today–but tomorrow?

O'Connor poured him the drink. "Thanks," Aaron said and sipped.

The free-trader continued: I jumped out of the hammock, decision made to speak to the Supreme Prince. L'rig was not there to stop me.

Wind Chimes rang in the doorway to the courtyard–drowned out occasionally by the dogs. Then I realized something was wrong. There were two glistening metal cages with atmospheric adjusting equipment. It took me a minute to realize they were contraband on Jalug. Then I wondered what else had come in and why.

Care of the dogs had been handed over to a native human called K8Kay, who spoke Terran Standard with an accent that was several centuries old.

'Where did they come from?' I asked.

'They are from the Daleropas,' he answered.

'From where?'

'Aw?'

'Never mind.'

'They like it,' he boasted.

'I'm not surprised,' I told him. Two of the Prince's retainers were in the doorway. I followed a line of them until I found the Prince.

'Ah, the betrothed has returned,' the Warlord spoke in passable centuries old Terran Standard and I did not miss the word 'betrothed'.

'A word–if I may, Oh, Supreme Margrave and Warlord.'

'The dogs–you like? I traded for this fine air device–without your advice. A good deal I make, did I?'

I told him it was a good deal, but not to buy anything more.

"Why not, Aaron?" asked Lim, for his audience.

"Because they did not have the technology to make the goods themselves. If they got dependent on them the Terrans would drain them of every trade good of value they possessed. Then the Prince would find himself in poverty."

Eccles cleared his throat but did not drink any more wine. Aaron went on after the interruption:

The elderly Prince drew himself up. He said, 'Find out where these things are coming from. I will give you unlimited authority.' He straightened his robe, which he carelessly drew aside to reveal a sword in a jeweled scabbard.

The proud Warlord waved his retainers to leave. 'Yes, Merchant Aaron?'

I hesitated. 'The arrangement cannot be made. I cannot be your son-in-law. There–there would be no children from the mating. Certainly, you would want–'

'Of course you can have a human consort. Wasn't that understood? Remember the singer's story of K2ALL and T'SOL. They were brother and sister–king and queen, but of course, KZALL, who we call K2ALL, had his own consort. You'll be an excellent father and husband. It's all been done before.'

I bowed. The retainers bowed. Then, I realized they were bowing at me, even the native humans.

I returned to my room, to find L'rig standing in front on my geometric red mandala tapestry and Novan a native human from the Festival Society, sitting in my easy chair from Earth–I can't sit in a Jalogan chair.

'I've got it,' I said.

-KAGA

'I'm sorry. Came back from my jog I, and is Terran Standard my not follow this.'

'I've got what I'll say to the Warlord!'

'You can't stop the marriage! Besides a good idea it is.'

'I think I can.'

'Then take a knife because your stun gun will never them stop.'

'I'll tell him I'm not worthy.'

There was a stunned silence. Then Novan, member of the Festival Hidden Society, bowed to me. L'rig said, 'I will tell him "yes" for you.'

I told L'rig about the atmospheric device used to acclimate the dogs. I tried several times to explain the economic problems. L'rig is very smart and he finally caught on and raised the ante by asking, 'Are inebriating drinks next?'

'Nothing we have will intoxicate a Jalogan.'

'I've heard stories from the native Terrans. What do you think is next?'

I said, 'Weapons. I hope these are only a trickle of class II tech goods from some merchant greedy for Jalogan tapestries. Unless your people have something more valuable than tapestries, L'rig?'

'Thok knows.' He says this when he will not talk. He says it with such conviction one would think Thok spoke to him directly.

'What's on the horizon?' I asked.

'You are now in a position of power, Prince Aaron. If it's weapons, someone will make a move.'

III

As nightfall passed into midnight over the dwelling, I was unable to sleep. I looked out the window. It was only an instant but I thought the stars cast their paltry light on black clothed figures scaling the wall. I blinked and they were lost in darkness. I woke up in a hurry as I saw the last one slide into a window–it was Evan's room. A shrill alien voice screamed. Grabbing my stun gun and knife, I ran out of the door and down the corridor between the adjoining towers. Retainers were running and calling out from the other passages. Twisted candles and ornamental kerosene lamps sent patterns of light and shadows dancing on the walls. Everything was in confusion. I rounded the corridor to the next tower. The lights were out and the air was sooty. A dark shape ran from the room and pinned me to the wall. I struggled to grip my stun gun and fired it.

As the alien collapsed, another non-human reached for my free arm. I recognized L'rig just in time. 'To the ground,' he pushed me hard. As I fell, another hooded assassin appeared. L'rig threw a knife.

'Aaron, get out of here.'

Then the retainers closed in.

I V

'She has been kidnaped,' Prince Thai, ruler of the Eastern Seaboard, moaned, 'My daughter Evan has been taken!'

He put a dagger flush on the lacquered table while another hand made sign gestures that I interpreted to mean this was a hidden or secret meeting. L'rig was always present. Four other Warlords–call them aristocratic princes–entered the room. I identified Hidden Society members Tog and Annog who were also military governors of the Condor. I also recognized the human military governor of the Cliffs Traphen Dnoces, but L'rig, had to sign me the name of the fourth Jolagan–a Warlord allied but not giving tribute to Thai–a woman, Princess of the Trees Jalal, Lady Holder of Aeinta second of the jai'. They all wore silk–like layers of sparkling clothing with their house symbols on them.

The background wall was a tapestry of Thok's Citadel. The walls were stone.

Exalted and proud Prince Thai, the Absolute Ruler of the Eastern Seaboard, intoned to me solemnly, 'This hearing to determine if kidnapper of Evan was you.'

'What!' I cried out. 'I was nowhere near–'

'Silence,' bade the Warlord. 'I want to discuss motives, not where you were.'

Even after five years, Jalogan logic eludes me. Painstakingly, the Warlord questioned my motives for being on Jalug and my feelings for his daughter.

The retainers, lined behind the table, all carried huge swords. My normal unshakable trading demeanor was undermined by a shudder.

'Appear you,' the Prince stated, 'not to have attempted to end the marriage by murder or kidnaping. Agree I you had nothing–null–to do with it. May you wait in the room I gave you.'

Everyone but the Warlord bowed to me.

I backed out through the door. L'rig followed me. I was afraid to speak out loud so I signed with my hands, 'Is that it? I am let off.'

'L'rig signed back, 'Leave while you can.'

Traphen Dnoces stomped out behind me. He was wearing a long blue cloak, which he threw over his shoulder. As he passed L'rig, he whispered, 'I have to get back to my estate, pressing matters.'

V

After a sleepless night in my room and a cold breakfast, a retainer entered and spoke to me and to L'rig that the Warlord Thai wanted to see us.

The retainer led us to a room with a large round table. Seated were several senior retainers, Tog, Annog, and several of the Prince Thai's relatives.

As we entered the retainers rose and bowed. When he saw me, the elderly Warlord said in a long, sad tone, 'We are here to seek out the hiddeness inside each person and declare who prescribed this act.' He pointed to a Terran chair. 'Be seated, Exalted Prince Aaron.'

I won't go into the discussion which was lengthy. Not everyone was sure what my marriage would do to the balance of power and wealth since I had, and still have, great influence in Trade City. I expended a great deal of that influence, now extending to Jalogan communities. What I learned was disquieting–more trade goods were trickling in–and they were not all coming from Trade City. That meant shuttles. Shuttles can get into the interior of Jalug, if upon leaving Dauropa they lose some of their electronics to the Shades. I still wasn't sure of the overall plan and none of the Hidden Society members would tell me what they had that was so valuable to trade.

If someone was merely trying to bring the Jalogans to the Solar Federation's technical level, the parade of goods was inconsistent with that goal. I just had not yet figured it out. I reported all this to the council. Prince Thai talked at length about the balance of wealth so I had to explain, again, why it would be disastrous to buy and depend on goods they could not make.

Not everyone was pleased. The conversation returned to Evan.

The Warlord continued solemnly, 'Tog and Annog were suitors for my daughter's vows. They in enmity came not. No motive it appears they have. The Lady Warlord Jalal, Princess of the Trees, comes from a rival province but not rival in wealth. Think she did it not. On the other balance of scales, Traphen Dnoces of the Cliffs has often sided against me. He opposed me in off-world Trade let in. Kidnaped Evan I believe. We will convene war counsel on his estate and take action. Bring him here. That is my word. That is my order. So, be it.'

No discussion. No opinions. It was to be done. The retainers got to their feet.

Did I tell you about Jalogan psychology? The wizened–faced Warlord held up two hands. 'More to be said.'

Everyone sat down.

'An island off the coast is source of off-world goods, it is said.'

Hawken broke in, "Aaron we know these fine people don't speak grammatically correct Standard but could you clean it up in your account? It might be important to remember this some time."

"Affirmative."

Rain continued to beat on the roof of Eccles' castle but soon only Aaron's words and translation were what everyone in the room heard. He said:

"That's when I found out about the crashed ship".

Aaron continued: Prince Thai's voice was clear despite his age and everyone heard him when he spoke, 'The Cottage Industry received a gift. When they inquired where it came from, they were told: a smashed Terran boat on the island of Demar10 in the Phi Phi Islands. The word was passed to me by the Architects Society. This may be Aaron's shuttle.'

I said, 'If it is smashed, it may have crashed.' I hit my palm with my fist. L'rig signed me something but it was so fast I could not understand.

Annog stood up. 'Then you, my Emir Aaron should go and find out.'

The Warlord agreed. 'The wise young Annog has made a good proposal. You will supply the boat, Annog. Also, as Keeper of the Record, you must go in order to provide eyewitness testimony.'

'Agreed.' He sat down with a hand sign that could only be interpreted as smug.

Tog of Condor stood up and folded his four upper arms, a sign of reverence. 'Perhaps we should think about consulting Thok.'

Nobody made a sound.

Tog repeated, 'Perhaps we should think about it.' He sat down.

VI

Kidnaping has a strange face of turn about and so does Jalogan logic. The next day the Warlord summoned me to his private quarters in his adjoining buildings. Private that is, with four retainers in gold trimmed clothing.

The Jalogan Warlord wore grey and a grey cloak fastened to his hip on one side. I wore a similar outfit designed by the native humans. Mine was brown. I've never seen a Jolagon wear grey before.

The Prince told me, 'I will confide in you. Evan is not kidnapped.'

'What?'

'She is in hiding. I needed to see who would throw their dice. Traphen has offered an alliance with Tog of Condor. I do not know the outcome, wise trader. We cannot conquer Traphen's estate but we may force a stalemate.'

'She's safe. Thank God.'

'Thok be praised. The attempt may have been made to force new alliances with the Terrans or with one of us. The Terrans are mere annoyances to our great powers, so I suspect I am the target of this new alignment. You may go to her, if you wish.'

'I will.'

'Here are the instructions on how to find her. You will say what I tell you to say to the retainer.'

An hour later I found myself in a two story wooden tower with a roof of elegant eaves and gargoyle–like glyphs. Two female guards were posted in the room. I ignored them.

As I drew near, she drew away. For ten minutes we did a series of postures that was a type of dance of re-acquaintance. Finally she permitted the lightest touch. Only then did we speak in words.

After five years, I can speak the Jolagan tongue. It translates thus: 'Evan, I'm glad to see you alive.' 'Thank Thok. And,' she added, 'Thanks to those who came to my assistance.'

We talked for a while. I offered to marry her in secret but she said to wait until I got back from the island. The next thing I said would change my life. The use of *Thok* never coincided exactly with the Terran concept of God. It had always been my hobby to try to crack the concept.

I tested the waters with, 'Thok, who is everywhere and hears everything.'

'No one knows where Thok is,' she asserted.

'Only Thok knows, I suppose. And those who say they speak Thok's word.'

'No one can say they speak Thok's word. Only Thok can say,' she countered.

'On Earth, a prophet has an insight and speaks the will of God. Is it so here?'

'None speak with an insight.'

'Yet you speak of the will of Thok, as if he has spoken words.'

'People can commune with Thok at Jalog City that you call Trade City.'

I was amazed. This was my first clue that Thok could be a person rather than a deity.

She asked me, 'Confide in me. What are your thoughts?'

'I will go to Trade City to learn about Thok.'

Her face held an expression I had never seen before. I should have been warned when she changed the subject.

Then she said, 'Find your shuttle ship.'

VII

The army of Prince Thai of the Eastern Seaboard was to assemble in the desert to meet the army of Military Governor Dnoces of the Cliffs. I expected a battle. But, Jalogans are short-lived compared to humans and they are less fond of war.

Instead they raided a village, and they brought Traphen Dnoces and five human free traders to Lord Thai's court.

I was there, at the same table, where the war had been ordered by the proud Prince.

Several Jalogans brought in the captives. The Jalogans could have been from any Hidden Society, but now they were dressed for war.

Prince Thai gave a commendable speech which showed the old Jalogan understood at least partly that which I had told him about unbalanced trade. He sentenced them to death.

'Hold!' I cried before he could say 'so ordered'. 'Let me speak,' I implored.

L'rig gasped, 'Aaron!' Sometimes I think he is more worried about me than the Prince who is his patient.

'Can't you send them to prison or a dungeon?'

'What's a dungeon?'

I explained.

'We have no such things. I am Supreme Ruler. What's the problem?'

I couldn't believe I was doing this, but I could not let him put people to death over a trade issue, not even Jalogans. Traphen probably deserved it but I just could not do it.

I stammered, then said, using the most formal Jalogan, 'Prince and Warlord of the Eastern Seaboard, there is a book some of my Terran ancestors used for the law. In it, it says if a man steals, he must repay everything he stole plus twenty percent. Then they can be restituted into the community'—I did not know how to say "and to God" in Jalogan—'The goods were contraband and our people paid for them. The value of the goods should be returned plus twenty percent.'

The Prince touched his chin in a very human gesture. The captives were brought forward. He spoke slowly in carefully enunciated Terran Standard.

'Our people paid 10,000 kilo credits worth of goods to you. The merchandise we received was illegal. You will hereby instruct your fellow traders in Trade City the following:

'We have in total 32 fingers and toes. Thirty-two is our key numbering system. You will pay us in trade goods 32 times the value of what you took. You will pay it in one month's time or you will all die.'

I gasped. The humans all nodded and bowed. The price would wipe most of them out so I had no idea why they were bowing. I was so confused; I did not get to ask what would happen to Traphen. This time L'rig did not have to tell me to make an exit.

VIII

Tog, Novan and I journeyed to the coast by animal drawn wagon, then by foot. L'rig told me he could not go. After he treated the royal court, he ministered to everyone else, especially, the poorer Jalogans in the Hidden Societies. I had not expected him to go.

The ocean side had no beach. There was a sudden cliff covered with purple-tinted moss. We rappelled down to a small wooden boat that awaited us. This trip was clandestine but in case we failed, Prince Thai had larger sailing Yachts down the coast ready to land on Damar10.

Tog and Novan sat in the back, with Annog as pilot and two oarsmen. I sat in the front with the map. The boat slid easily through the chartreuse water, colored by underwater vegetation. We rowed past an island surrounded by cliffs. Indeed, it appeared to be a chunk of the mainland that had broken off. Then the water turned olive, then deep olive green. As we entered deeper water, it reflected the color of the purple sky.

45

The time of day was pre-dawn. It seemed like a good idea when I planned it. Now I was not so sure. The sea was dead calm. There was barely a breeze. I had aloe on my skin to prevent burn and the Jalogans were prepared to wear tinted spectacles of some kind. Novan said the skill came from the First Ships.

I opened a parchment Tog had given me. Although the light was dim, I knew what it contained: the tides for the area, based on the phases of the moon. At the top of the paper was a map of the neighboring islands.

The pre-dawn light created mirages in the mist. The first islands were obscured by fog. In the distance to my incredulity I saw a horizontal stone hanging over the water with water vapor beneath. It was several minutes before we had paddled close enough for us to see the two standing stones rising out of the sea, and holding up the capstone. The illusion of the stone floating on its own power was broken, as the morning fog cleared away. We paddled on.

Before landing on Damar10, we had a plan. Traphen's flotilla was in front of another island. We rowed for the island, careful to arrive up current. As we neared the area, we drew in the oars and let the current push us toward the five native sailing ships.

They were anchored, and this was the first time I had ever seen them up close. They were all sloops, with a central cabin, below deck area, and a tent behind the cabin where the crew slept. The ships were of varying sizes, but in the mist, I could not see well enough to estimate their length. A watchman kept a lookout on the largest ship but his back was to us. Our fancy silks had been discarded for dark leather in the hope they would be less visible.

We continued to drift past the first four ships, all according to plan. As we came upon the fifth ship, we stopped our forward motion by breaking with the oars very gently.

Tog pulled a very sharp knife from a sheath. The plan was to cut the anchor line of each ship. He would let them ride the current until each sailing ship beached on the next island or went aground on a sandbar.

Unfortunately, the anchor lines go through a chock on the foredeck, where they are then tied down on a klete. Constant wave motion makes the rope chafe in the chock, usually until it breaks. To prevent this, a protective rubber hose is placed around the rope at the point of pressure.

On this ship, the tubing extended several feet to the water. Tog was trying to cut through both the rubber tubing and the rope inside.

I bent over Tog to gesture that he try at water level where the rubber ended. His reaction was sudden. With surprising force he pushed me away and slammed me against the prow of our small ship.

I had forgotten—Jalogans from the Prince's area hate to be crowded. It must be a cultural thing because Jalogans in the Trade City have no trouble with crowds. As far as he was concerned, I had invaded his personal space.

Trade sign language failed me.

We did not dare to speak. For an instant we held each other's gaze, then Tog went back to cutting through the tubing.

All at once the rope parted. We help our position not daring to breath. Traphen's ship slowly slid backwards but it was so gradual the crew did not awaken.

As quietly as possible we rowed to the next four ships. The protective tubing on these ships did not protrude very far. Cutting the anchor lines was easy.

The fifth and largest sailing ship was cut loose and my comrades quietly rowed toward the cliffs. Water lapped against the fifth ship but there was still no wind to carry sound.

The watchman turned and saw us.

He must have recognized us as a rival Warlord's ship. However, he had not yet perceived that the anchor line had been cut nor did he perceive his danger. He turned away from us and our ship disappeared into the fog.

As the pre-dawn light increased, Novan and the Jalogans donned their rectangular sun Shades. Now out of sight of the ships, we changed course, still not daring to speak.

The next island I came to was Damar10. There was a beach beleaguered with water-polished stones. Trees, all with purple-tinted leaves and bark, were broken halfway down, their tops littering the landscape.

'By Thok!' the Jologans gasped.

I signed them to be quiet and made sure they all saw my motions.

We beached the boat and climbed out. Tog, Novan and I walked inland. The pilot Annog told his oarsman crew to hide the boat and they agreed to wait for us.

'What are we looking for?' Annog signed.

I gestured something large.

We kept walking. Beyond the rim of trees was a desert interior, its sand burned to glass by anti-gravs. The ship had crashed and broken upon impact, but it was not in pieces scattered over the landscape. The cargo bay was intact.

It was a small ship, larger than a shuttle. I wished fervently for an unblocked ID-card, radio or internet, and a techcorder.

As Keeper of the Records, Annog observed and studied everything. So he could testify to what he saw.

Obviously, someone was either trying to smuggle something in or was looting a deserted ship and selling it to their Jalogan neighbors.

Sounds could carry for miles on the island. We dared go no further because I saw tents staked out by the ship. No one was awake yet. Then we heard sounds behind us, coming from the beach.

'They must have had sentries posted,' Annog signed.

'Right to.' I signed back.

Tog intervened, 'We must hide. Perhaps further inland where the trees are less broken.'

The three Jalogans conferred. I looked at the map and indicated a direction to them. It took us about fifteen minutes to see what would change the whole picture.

Aaron told his audience in Eccles' castle, "I didn't want to wait. Lord Thai had to land his flotilla and I had to make an emergency trip to Trade City."

Lim interrupted, "Don't end the story there. Tell us what you saw."

O'Connors leaned forward to listen.

Aaron did not look happy.

He swallowed and went on:"It was a small military transport, a bit archaic for it had wheels. But, it was carrying a modern energyzer canon. It only weighed about 10 pounds and was small for its firepower but the vehicle is needed to transport the super batteries and the solar panels to power it. I had never seen one before but I knew what it was. The vehicle was small enough and light enough to be carried to the mainland by a Jalogan sailing ship.

I told Novan, Annog and Tog, 'Whoever has this can destroy your homes, Thai's entire palace and your crops.'

Annog turned to Novan, 'Climb up a tree and set off a flare that we brought.' He passed Novan a long small stick that was a Roman candle.

To make a long story short, the Great Thai arrived with his flotilla ships. There was a short battle, which he won. I advised him to toss the energyzer canon in the sea. I hope he did but I'll never know.

Several days later I'm back at my room in Thai's living quarters building. Novan and L'rig are seated in the only chairs so I sit in a cloth recliner hung from the ceiling, a gift from a cottage weaver.

Anyway, something started beeping. L'rig looks at me and says I knocked into the piano harp. The instrument is untouched by the wall. I finally realized it was my ID card in my wristlet holder. The internet was sounding.

I pulled the card out of its holder on my wrist and it was the Trade Board. From Jalog City.

'Jeesus, Tennyson, what are you up to out there?'

Chief of Staff Brittel knows me well.

'Chief, is there a lot of activity among traders to buy trade goods for the interior–for the Jalogans?'

'Tons of it. Listen, I'm on this emergency channel because—'

'Chief, listen to *me*. Anyone who buys good for Traphen Dnoces, let the goods go through, then arrest them, arrest all of them!'

'I don't have the authority. Aaron, I'm getting reports of changes in the balance of power all over the East Coast and you're the center of it.'

'Chief, I'm not a military expert but I just found an energyzer canon complete with batteries and solar power supply earmarked for the Jalogans. If you can't start arresting people, find out—' The line went dead.

The signal came on again about 30 seconds later.

'Aaron, this is a secure line. Tell me all this again.'

I did, and I added, 'But you have to give amnesty to 10 free traders.'

49

'Aaron, you better come to Trade City to report this to the Trade Commission.'

'I will. After my wedding.'

'Jeesus, your what?'

'I'm marrying Evan, daughter of the Supreme Warlord Prince Thai.'

'Can you get into any more trouble, Your Highness, I suppose it is now.'

'Just Aaron. See you shortly. Call me if—'

The line went dead again.

Aaron sighed. He commented: The marriage was beautiful.

We both wore silk robes. It took place in the huge palace I described earlier. The Singers' Society sang selections of traditional epic poems. The Librarians read or recited ancient Jalogan history including the story of the First Ships. We danced.

We were in high spirits for weeks.

Then Trade City sent a messenger to formally request my appearance. The Jalogan leaders held a conclave.

Prince Thai said solemnly to me, 'We have decided to send someone to commune with Thok. L'rig Esol and his daughter will go to Trade City with you and he will enter the Citadel. And Aaron, such a thing has not occurred in three generations.'

He waved to a retainer who signed for me to follow. I was led to Evan's private guest chambers. Evan was dressed in her finest jewelry and a fine gown with a ceremonial dagger on a strap that ran from her upper shoulder to the opposite hip. Two attendants in gold trimmed robes were asked to leave.

She had a parchment in her hand that was rolled up on a wooden spindle. She unrolled it for me and I could discern the Jalogan script, hanging below the lines instead of on top.

'It looks like a very formal request but the language is too archaic for me, Evan.'

'It is a request from me to the priests of the Citadel of Thok to let you in as an observer. You must follow their instructions *exactly*. There are human acolytes there, so get the rules in the Terran tongue. Be *very* careful.' She added, 'No human has ever done this.'

'It is an honor.'

'Whatever happens, always send me news.'

We talked about things that are more personal, then I departed for Trade City.

Prince Thai sent an armed detachment of Hidden Society members as escort for his son-in-law. Everyone knew who I was by the time I reached Trade City.

It was said later how that very night as Dauropa swung in the evening sky he made his plan. But, this time to plan would become undone.

What I did not learn about until later was a conversation between L'rig and his daughter Enid Esol.

It was very lengthy but it can be summed up like this. Enid spoke these things: 'You are too old, father, and you are a healer and the prince needs you. He will always need you.

'I am a weaver. Send me. Or if you will not send me because I am a weaver, remember: Lord Thai is Supreme Ruler because his father was. But, in the old times the men of the clans each selected their chief. And in more ancient days the women of the tribe chose the male leader.

'In memory of those great ancestors, let me make the pilgrimage.'

And so it was decided that Enid would run into the Citadel after but without a jai'. But, this I did not know at the time.

I already told you a little of what happened at the Citadel. I won't repeat myself.

When I came out, Enid appeared on a balcony of the Citadel and everyone was clamoring, 'A sign, a sign!'

She spoke to them, about a new age for Jalogans. I don't know where she got all these instructions–she was giving orders in subjects in which she had no background–sociology, economic changes to Jalug, political changes, warning about other races besides the Terrans. She spoke for nearly an hour. Then she went inside and never came out.

Then priests asked me where was my jai? I told them what Thok had said and they called it a curse.

L'rig, my very reliable friend, told me to pack my bags and leave for Dauropa as fast as I could go. It is said that he stayed in Trade City but had frequent reports from the Prince.

KAGA

So here I am on Dauropa, but the story of the smugglers had one last act to play out.

Meanwhile I still think of the Warlord of Jalug as he was, sipping his pine needle drink, shaking his head. In the early evening as Dauropa swings across the sky, he will make his next plan.

IX

Aaron brought those in the room up to date, with the last installment of his story: As a rather famous and wealthy free trader from Jalug, I found myself invited to Governor Zool's social events in Zäringhen valley. At that time, he governed this part of Dauropa through the Demner mountains and beyond. Eccles now has that post.

Whenever I could, I enjoyed hiking up the mountains. The trees remind me of Earth. I do get homesick once in awhile. There I met Wendnagel of the First Family.

We were only married for a year when a group of free traders invited me to a meeting near a town on the mountainside. I was with Wendy at her cottage and she started staring into the pool of water and she's seeing things clairvoyantly, but I don't know what.

Wendnagel spoke up, "I told him to hit the right corner of his ID card just before he went into the meeting to set it to a Patrol frequency and to carry a stun gun."

Aaron told them: The meeting directions were to go to the space ferry dock, then to walk down one of the side streets to the meeting place. The subject was a trade proposal. I get hundreds and listen to a few every few months.

The space ferry travels from Demner to Zähringhen. It does not really go into space, although it used to.

The meeting place was near the old path that winds around the mountain, overlooking the river. I nearly forgot to set my ID, but I did it just before going in.

When I got there refreshments were served at a table, and I sipped a cup of tea. Nobody was in a particular hurry and I finished the tea.

I sat down in an area that was once used for hologram calls. The empty chair where the other party appears as a hologram was still there.

The men ranged in height and sizes, obviously born on different planets. The sun weathered them all. I tried to match their faces to the names on the proposal.

The tallest free trader removed the hologram seat and then said, 'You better not sit down, Tennyson.'

'Why? What better way to listen to the proposal?'

'We have a new one. We didn't send our aides because we want to handle this ourselves.'

They moved in on me in a ring. I got up from the chair and suddenly felt light headed.

He said, 'You're coming with me.''

'Why?' A trader never agrees to anything that's not clearly spelled out.

'You spoiled our plans on Jalug.'

I stopped smiling. 'You mean the portable canon.'

'There's much more to this that you don't see–and never will.'

'''I'm sorry you feel that way.' I was on my way out but my legs suddenly felt rickety. 'What was in the tea?'

'Guess.'

The leader gestured to two of his fellow businessmen. They took me by the arms, led me outside to a mountain walk. The path is on a ledge and the drop to the river is steep.

'Over the side with him.'

I started to struggle. I took self-defense in school but it had been a long time. But, there was an old trick I had learned to pop out of a hold. They were grasping me by the wrists and suddenly I freed myself.

They came after me. I pulled out the stun gun and the first three fell unconscious. The fourth wrestled it out of my hand. The leader took a look at the odds and ran.

I tried to back against the mountain. My knees got weak and I passed out. The last thing I remembered was my wrist ID card buzzing.

Wendnagel was there when I woke up. Nothing could have made me happier.

KAGA

X

That brought them back to the present. The diplomats had refills of sweet vermouth. O'Connors sipped it. Hawken had politely refused Pasha's friendly conversation and moved to sit alone. Agent Bob Moncrief moved next to Miusov to keep both eyes on the youth.

The patter of rain gave way to a downpour.

Lim waited. She gazed at Aaron with an alert expression. "That was a few years ago. I think it's time you tell us what caused you to call for us to come here today."

Aaron cleared his throat. "Several months ago there was renewed smuggling activity in the Demner mountains. A shipment usually goes from Jalug to Dauropa, but recently something special came down. It was carried across the mountain by hand. One of the carrying capsules was rigged with a bomb. It went off halfway across. Wendnagel and I found the remains.

"The carrying capsules were moved to one of her sanctuaries on the Demner side of the mountain. We couldn't open them. She locked them behind a force field.

"One of the dead men was carrying this."

He handed Lim a unique Special Forces Council ID card. The name on it was RAYMOND BERQUIST, Black-rank COUNCILMAN, SPECIAL FORCES COUNCIL.

Lim gasped in recognition.

A burst of brilliant white light filled Lim's and Pasha's minds. It was followed by what appeared to be bright concentric circles rushing toward them. It was over. Lim confirmed, "It's authentic."

Winters said to Lim, "I take it he's important."

"I know him."

Pasha nodded. "He has a high telepathic rating. He helped me to develop mine."

Lim studied the card, vowing, "We'll work on this tomorrow."

Miusov promised, "I'll get out my equipment."

Aargau exuberantly refilled the drinks. The hang glider pilots had mockingly called him the mad cobbler for all of the inventions which he turned out for Eccles in the basement. The young man looked happy. Eccles continued to look like a sheet.

"What sort of equipment, Pasha?" Hawken questioned him.

Miusov pulled from his pocket something that looked like a tall pencil. "This is a sub-space com unit. It is relayed through teleport gates in space. You turn it on by wishing. Here, try it."

Hawken look at the object. "Wishing, you said?" She laughed self-consciously and made a wish. "I don't hear anything."

"That's the telepathic frequency. Here." He touched it and wished on the sub-space channel. Official voices could be heard. "That's radio chatter from incoming starships to the Zäringhen spaceport."

He wished it off.

"That's what we presently hear. A powerful enough receiver could hear sounds from the past—faint lingering vibrations. Telepathic and old thoughts are harder to pick up."

"But you can?" She glanced at Wendnagel uncertainly.

Ramón piped up, "Do you know this young man has a cat brain among his devices?"

Hawken gave a sharp intake of breath and put a hand over her mouth.

"It's used to amplify E.S.P.," Pasha explained to Wendnagel.

There was another flash of lightning followed by the squeal of a cat, and the pitter patter of many feet.

"If you'll excuse me for a minute," Lim got up to leave.

Eccles said, "When—"

"I'll be right back."

She heard a sound upstairs. She walked upstairs to the inner balcony, turned down a dark hallway to an unlit room. Rain pounded against the window as it came down in sheets. Droplets formed on the window, gleaming from a light on the outside.

She heard an intake of breath behind her and moved.

In a blur she assumed a fighting stance, then grabbed the arm of her unknown assailant. It was a man and he gave a yell as he fell over his head onto his back. Lim edged along the wall and found the light switch—another of Eccles' strange gadgets. She thumbed it on.

"Steve!"

It was Winters.

Lim exclaimed, "Never sneak up behind me like that."

Winters got up, rubbing his neck. "Aaron wanted to call one of his sales offices. I was going to screen the phone. It's noon on Jalug."

"I'm jumpy over what happened to Berquist."

"We'll know more tomorrow when he takes us to the spot."

"You better believe we will," she said firmly. And Lim took charge.

Chapter 3

SORCERY IN THE CASTLE

I

Leaves were piled high on the footpath and the sky was so clean it was postcard clear. Lim was being guided by Aargau to the cottage where Eccles had put up Wendnagel. Aargau spoke unending praise about the couple.

"And that was a marriage made in heaven. Wealthy free-trader marries famous member of the Family and a Blue Witch besides."

One of the lawns which Lim had teletapped now appeared in her mind. In a flash she saw in her mind's eyes something overhead. She missed a step, grabbed Aargau by the arm and peered skyward.

A hang glider was coming down.

They ran to an open meadow and the glider pilot made a running landing. It was heavy laden. The pilot, Aarau, was the yellow-and blue-dressed rescuer from yesterday.

"Hi, it's me, Aarau. I brought your boxes from the wreck. I didn't want John Eccles to see me come down. How did you know I was landing?"

Aargau interjected, "This is a member of the Special Forces Council. Of course she'd know you were overhead, Aarau." He pronounced it Ay-uh-row.

Lim added, "Thank you, Aarau, we'll take it to the castle. We can manage further."

"Then I better leave before John sees me." He started folding up the struts to carry the glider back up the mountain.

I I

Winters stood on the interior balcony over the main room. He had discreetly set up his own monitoring system, despite Lim's protests. He was finally getting things to his high standards of security.

The Security Officer thought he heard Lim calling him. He turned abruptly. The only person there was Bob Moncrief.

"Good day, Councilman."

"You don't have to address me as 'councilman'; I don't sit on the Black council. My rank is agent and you can just call me Moncrief."

"What can I—"

Moncrief jumped on his words. "I want you to keep a special eye on Miusov."

"You mean Pasha?"

"He came back from his last mission under a cloud. He created a disturbance for the whole northern hemisphere of the planet we were on."

That didn't jibe with what Winters had seen of Pasha. The Captain of the DISCOVERY had described his job as a liaison between the Special Forces and civilians. It now looked like he was going to have to liaison between different council members.

Moncrief reinforced his words. "If you're not with him, make sure I am."

I I I

Aide O'Connors was with Ramón when Hawken entered the outer suite of the diplomats' rooms in the castle.

O'Connors smiled in a most correct fashion but said, "Mademoiselle Hawken, this is not a good time . . ."

Ramón waved him aside. "Come in, Hawken, come in."

"Renate, if this is not a good time—it's not my strong suit to—"

"Nonsense, mon amie." He switched to French. "Ce vas? How is it going?"

"Ce vas. It goes all right." Ramón put a hand on one of her delicate palms and waved the smaller man, O'Connors, to leave.

IV

Everything was completely still in Miusov's room. Boxes were carefully unpacked. Beside the boxes on the table was a container holding the cat brain.

Wooden latches on the door slid out of the ceiling, floor and wall. In the dim lights a small, slim thin-fingered hand reached out with a vial and poured something into the cat brain container.

A moment later it withdrew and everything was quiet, as before.

V

Lim had her red thermo jacket back on and she turned up the thermostat as she walked with Lt. Winters. The pair strode on leaves underfoot, exchanging speech at a low murmur. They trod past trees bare of leaves and up a steep incline lined with glacier rocks. It was a short cut to the place where Aaron and Wendnagel had found the body. Miusov, Moncrief and Aaron were ahead.

Lim breathed in the fresh air just as there was a distant call from the trio ahead. Both Lim and Lt. Winters carried boxes.

The grass ramp leveled off. In front of the leaders, the grass was blackened for a long distance.

"Must have been quite an explosion, Councilwoman." Winters commented.

"What do your first-in scout eyes see, Steve?"

Winters looked at the bodies. They were in shadow and frozen by the cold. Blackened grass and tree stumps went on for some distance. He thought he could describe the type of explosive used. There were grooves in the ground and a heavily trampled are. "Something was moved from here."

Aaron cut in. "That was Wendnagel and me. We dragged the carrying capsules away."

Lim heightened the energy in her mind. There was a quanta jump and she clairvoyantly scanned the area. If Berquist had been here, there was nothing left to see now.

She gestured to Miusov to take the boxes. He produced a small slide, like a slide for a microscope, and set it on the ground.

They stood at opposite sides of the meadow and focused their clair-voyant energy on the slide. It would register an interference pattern, slightly distorted by emanations from previous events. They would study those later, through another clairvoyant frequency. They then did the same for telepathic energy.

"It's a hologram of sorts," Lim explained to Winters, "but uses E.S.P. waves instead of laser light."

Pasha carefully packed it in a box. The dark-haired half-Draconian was trying to piece it all together. He wondered what was in the carrying capsules.

"Are you done?" Moncrief questioned Lim. His breath was white with cold but he stood his ground, keeping an eye on Miusov.

"We've done all we can here."

"By the code," Pasha exhaled roughly.

Pasha stared at Moncrief, pondering to himself. Moncrief had sprained his wrist because the agent had opened his harness during the crash. No one in his right mind did that unless he was trying to signal somebody with his comm unit. The half-Draconian wondered if there were more of these canisters. He had lied about the broken wrist to keep Moncrief from making an air surveillance by hang glider, until he found out what was going on.

Eccles, too, was concerned about what could be seen from the air.

Pasha hoped his E.S.P. sweep into the past would provide some answers.

When Aaron had found Berquist's charred body, Moncrief had been posted already at Dauropa. Pasha wondered what possessed him to tell Winters to keep an eye on him. It was true he had created a disturbance on a planet in his previous assignment. However, he had been ordered by Westerman to create a diversion for the Special Forces on the other side of the planet. He had received a commendation for not creating any bloodshed. He would talk to Winters when the opportunity came.

It was a long time before he got that opportunity.

VI

The mood was set by violet light streaming through the window on one continuous beam, from the sun's nonstop source of energy. Thick cellulose wrap of violet color adhered to the window, changing normal yellow light to the more subdued tone. Miusov had put it up, and his attachment to the light was like a teenager to a favorite poster or an adult to some adored painting.

The half-human had set up the same equipment on many planets under different conditions of climate, atmosphere and gravity.

Always he hung the violet plastic on the windows so that no matter where he was he always had the same comfortable work conditions.

The slide was on the stand.

First he reached for his comm unit to file a report. He wished it on. The telepath at the other end was one he recognized. He preferred to work with people he know. The specialist on the other end had a rating of 4 amputs so he would have to compress the message.

//Receivedreport. FromTennyson. Berquistdead. Miusov.//

Four amputs was a message about the length of his full name four times. He personally could use up to 34, then the clarity got weaker. If he went further than that he'd hear false echoes, then would go telepathically deaf until he recharged his E.S.P. His latent potential, yet to be tapped, was considered to be much higher.

//Message received.//

E.S.P. waves weakened back and forth in time which stymied researchers for centuries until the mathematics were finally worked out.

The wish switch in the comm unit was a singularly simple design. Making a decision caused energy to drop in the brain. A sensor picked up the drop and automatically turned on the unit. Miusov put the comm unit on a timer for his next report. Too much use of the wish switch had the unwanted side effect of emptying the bladder.

His face and black uniform were bathed in violet as he bent over the slide. He adjusted its position and mentally prepared himself.

Winters found him in this pensive posture as he entered the room.

The Security Officer called out, "I'm here, Councilman." He had learned not to walk up behind a Councilman unannounced more than once.

"Call me Pasha. It's a Russian nick-name, but I'm North American. You can stand in the doorway."

"What should I do?"

"Let no one in. Whatever you do, and whatever you see, don't touch me or the apparatus."

Pasha concentrated on the slide. He saw a mental picture that was nebulous and unclear. There was a time lag as the different parts of his mind processed the data at different speeds. All at once he could see Lim in his mind's eye instructing him where to place the slide. The picture grew clear but it was too close to the present. He needed to back up without losing the thread of continuity that led to the explosion.

He grimaced and closed his eyes but time would not go back any further. Ever so gently he touched the awareness in the cat brain container. Energy reached a level of ecstasy and suddenly he had more power at his disposal.

The scene in the mountains was of Berquist, standing alive. It was so real it threatened to overpower the vision of the room in subdued violet twilight. Berquist was talking to someone and his voice had risen to an argument. Thoughts were about concern for their canisters. The tall dark-haired Councilman was arguing further and louder. He was wearing contemporary Dauropan garb. The smuggler pulled out a modified stun gun and shot the Councilman. Berquist was warning him of interrelated smuggling agreements when he fell.

Gingerly, the smuggler rifled through his clothes looking for a weapon. He found the comm unit and threw it away. Then he found the ID, RAYMOND BERQUIST, SPECIAL FORCES COUNCIL. The smuggler dropped it as if it burned. He looked around at the capsules. Frightened, he snapped up the ID and put it in his own coat.

He left Berquist where he was and started yelling to his followers to take as many canisters as they could carry and run. They were leaving the Demner side of the mountain as fast as they could when they were set upon by another group of smugglers. There was hand-to-hand fighting. In the confusion the explosion went off. Two smugglers were not caught in the explosion directly. They were blown off their feet. One of them started jabbering to the other, as they ran off with a container.

A look of surprise was on Muisov's face as the whole plan unfolded.

His eyes were open but otherwhere as he looked somewhere else and somewhen. Miusov's green eyes then refocused on the container of the cat brain. Light framed his face in silhouette. As he glanced down it sunk into his consciousness that he was seeing in the room. A slow acting acid had been placed in the container and now it was starting to bubble.

Awareness dropped all at once. Energy in the equipment's system ran back into his mind. He gave voice to a long, tortured scream. The slide shattered.

Winters took an alarmed step forward.

Miusov waved him back. He was an outsider and didn't understand, Miusov thought warily.

The dark-haired Councilman backed up from the equipment and blacked out.

Winters rushed to the recumbent form.

//Wait for me. Don't touch him. Lim.// The words burst in Winter's mind and the feminine sound echoed in his head over and over. Had he really heard that?

Fast moving footsteps on the stairs turned into Lim who rushed in from the doorway. The strong, lithe woman breathed, "Pasha!"

She knelt down and took a pulse. She put a hand over his mouth and felt a faint breath, very faint. He remained still.

//Pasha?//

There was no answer.

Winters gestured at the cat brain, afraid to touch anything. "There's some kind of acid in the container."

"Oh my God, and with his senses extended. He's withdrawn." Lim did not know what to do. She concentrated and used all her 36 amputs to try to revive him.

Not getting anywhere she looked up at the Security Officer.

She demanded urgently, "What did you see?"

Winters was confused. "Pasha was here in the room. He appeared trance-like. Then he screamed."

"You don't understand. The nature of these tools are so powerful, you might have seen the E.S.P. image."

"No."

Lim made fists.

Winters wanted to know, "Did you contact me with telepathy just before?"

"Yes, it was necessary."

She knelt by the Black Councilman. "No one on Dauropa has the power to revive him."

"The facilities are better on the DISCOVERY."

"We'll do it. For now, we'll take him to his room. There's a subspace radio in the basement. I think they're still in orbit. I don't dare take my attention off of him. Then, assemble everyone downstairs. I want to question them," Lim ordered. She'd take Pasha to the spaceport by special air ferry from Demner village. "Moncrief will stay with the equipment. He is to make sure no one leaves."

Wendnagel and Hawken were the first to arrive in the main room. The yellow-blond woman was supposed to have high E.S.P. Lim solicited her help. "The cat brain was destroyed by acid and Pasha has passed out. Do you know anything about this?"

Hawken stammered, "How dare you accuse Wendnagel!" Hawken fumed.

"You're an off-worlder. She's a member of the Family!"

"I'm a member of the Special Forces Council and someone just tried to kill Pasha."

Soon everyone residing in the castle was there in the room. Lim repeated, "Someone poured a delayed reaction powerful acid in the cat brain container. I don't know whether this was done maliciously or just out of dislike for the thing in the container. But I would like whoever did it to come forward so I know what was poured in the container. It might save his life."

Everyone started talking at once. No one came forward.

Winters observed, "Everyone at the party heard about the cat brain. It could have been anyone."

It could have been done at any time, Lim thought to herself. She decided to conduct an on-the-spot interrogation of everyone who was at the party.

Everyone who had been at the party was present—Eccles, Ramón, O'Connors, Aaron, Wendnagel, Hawken, Aargau, Winters, and Moncrief.

Without preliminary Lim bore into Eccles, "John, you've been very nervous lately. Did you pour acid in the cat brain container?"

"No, Lim. I first heard of it at the party and I wouldn't know where to look."

Lim turned to Ramón. "Renate Ramón y Cajal," she used his full name. "You brought up the cat brain at the party. Did you have a double motive? You shocked the guests. Did you also plan to hurt Pasha? The cat brain had sentience and when their minds are in a linkup there is great energy exchange. Did you do it? Where were you this morning?"

"Mais non. No, I did not, Councilwoman. I meant to bring it up only as a conversation piece. Besides I was with Hawken all morning. I have an alibi."

"Aaron, I've never seen a trader so even-handed as you, but I have to ask, did you—"

"No, I did not, Lim. I already came here to notify you of the death of one Councilman."

"*Hawken*—"

"Now this is getting ridiculous . . ."

Lim persisted. "You registered alarm over the cat brain. Maybe you just wanted to get rid of it."

"I'm a business consultant, not a teenager."

Lim tried a different tactic. "Aargau, you served the drinks."

"Yes, Councilwoman."

"What else do you do?"

"I take care of the grounds and maintain in kitchen computers. I also carve door latches in the basement and other shop projects."

"The cat brain could have been tampered with any time yesterday morning. Most of us—Steve, Moncrief, Aaron—were on the mountain slope. Where were you?"

"In the basement, carving wooden light switches."

"Alone?"

"Afraid so."

"Did you do it? You could have gone upstairs with acid from an etch set in the basement. You do your own inventory. It would never turn up missing."

"No!" Aargau said with great vehemence. "You've been here before and you know I don't touch your things. They are beyond my understanding, most of it. What did he see on the 'time slide'?"

"I don't know. Don't try to change the conversation."

"I'm not in one, Councilwoman."

There were only three others in the room and they also drew negative responses.

Councilwoman surmised, "This is a murder attempt and I won't let it rest here."

Winters said, "I have a chemical analysis here of what we believe was poured in the container." Winters held up an techcorder, "It's agrenometric acid."

Lim asked Aargau, "Does that sound familiar?"

"It's a slow acting acid. It's what I use to etch wood. It takes about forty or fifty minutes to work."

"Somebody found the time to stroll down to the basement and steal some of it. And they would have had time to leave the cat brain container before anyone knew what happened. Bob Moncrief, where were you when we returned from the mountain?"

"In my room—most of the time."

"Did you-?"

"You know I didn't, but get the formality over with. I don't know who tried to kill Patrick but it chills me to think he—or she—still walks among us, and may try again. Why haven't you arrested Aargau? The circumstantial evidence is—"

"Only circumstantial, "Lim finished.

"I'm innocent," Aargau protested.

"I believe you," said the telepath.

Lim left instructions to Moncrief. "Seal the equipment room. Let no one leave the castle while we are gone. Lt. Winters and I are taking Pasha."

"Then everyone's still under suspicion-?"

"Everyone." Her black eyes flashed her strong intent to find a suspect.

Chapter 4

The Unknown Past

I

The soft dripping of water in Eccles' wishing well was replaced by the sound of the starship DISCOVERY'S medical computer, which beeped out pulse and other monitored functions.

Pasha lay awake on the medical bed, his green eyes fastened on Lim. "It's gone," he moaned.

"Your E.S.P.? Sometimes there are peaks and valleys. It will come back."

"I mean the memory of what was on the time slide. I had everything. I can remember feeling it! Everything fell into place and—it's all blank."

"How do you feel besides that?"

"Not too good. I know I cannot telepathically interrogate someone because of the code but sometimes people's thoughts leak into mine. Now there is not even that."

"Can you remember what did it?"

"The cat brain died . . ." He closed his eyes. ". . . while I was linked to it . . ."

"Klemperer revived you."

Councilman Westerman was the highest man in the Council. Just beneath him with overlapping responsibilities was Councilman Klemperer, who was often in the field. Klemperer had come by teleport gate, an expensive but speedy way to travel. He had arrived by starship from the teleport gate in sector three.

Miusov said urgently, "We have to find out what was on that slide."

"You smashed it. We can't make another one until your E.S.P. returns."

"What makes you so sure that it will?"

"You had a shock. It is normal to go telepathically deaf after such a shock."

"I wonder who did it?"

So do I, Lim thought. She encircled her son with her arms.

II

Winters was in his own element on the ship. He know most of the crew and he thought it would give him moral support. Instead he found the Council members treating him like an outsider. A pep talk from the Captain did not help him too much.

Then, Councilman Klemperer had requested an interview with him. Klemperer was wearing a white scientist's lab coat over his uniform and was carrying a briefcase. He was to the point and did not take the time for niceties of casual conversation.

Klemperer started by telling him, "I am sending Patrick Miusov back to Demner. Familiar surroundings may help him get his memory back. And his E.S.P. ability, which is too valuable to lose. I want you to make the appropriate securing arrangements."

"Yes, sir."

"And, Mr. Winters, if this works out, we may make this liaison officer job permanent."

Klemperer took stock of Winters and the reports he had received, then added, "Keep watch over Councilwoman Lim. She's too valuable to replace."

Miusov sat on the side of the bed with his legs dangling down the side. He brushed his dark hair out of his hazel eyes.

He was thinking about Berquist. The tall Councilman's words came back to him from an early training session. SOME TELEPATHS ARE NATURAL SENDERS. SOME ARE NATURAL RECEIVERS. WHEN YOU ARE TRAINED YOU CAN DO BOTH, EQUALLY WELL.

It was incomprehensible to think that Berquist was gone.

With his E.S.P. absent, he found himself concentrating on his other senses. He heard footsteps and Lt. Winters appeared in the doorway.

"We'll be leaving soon. I wondered if you'd like to spend some time discussing Xyltan."

"That's Draconian philosophy and I'm unfamiliar with it. I was brought up on Earth. You might try my mother Lim on it."

Winters was disappointed. While Pasha was formally comfortable in many social situations he remained uncommonly aloof from everyone except the Council staff. He was hoping that with his first-in scout experience on many planets, he could find a common ground with the Councilman, some sort of friendship.

He also still wondered why Moncrief said to watch him.

Chapter 5

FIRE IN THE SKY

I

Renate Ramón's quarters included a window view of the forest. Ramón had closed the window to the fresh air and closed the door with its latches in the floor, ceiling and sides, to assure no one overheard his conversation with his aide, O'Connors.

Ramón was speaking in Standard and his tone was one of berating. "How could you have done such a thing! I understand your feelings about the Councilman. But, after all of the trust we have been trying to build up with Governor Eccles, to go out and tamper with Councilman Miusov's equipment—it's out of line!"

"There is just one thing. I didn't do it."

Ramón sputtered, "Then who did?"

"I don't know. Someone is lying."

11

The Councilmen returned to Zäringhen spaceport by omnicraft, then took the anti-grav ferry over the river. Ground transport provided the rest of the trip to the castle.

Once there, Councilwoman Lim carried out the first step in her plan which was to re-interrogate John Eccles.

The Governor asked after Pasha.

"He is back with me to see if familiarity with the castle area will recover his memory of what happened to Councilman Berquist."

"But other than that he is all right?"

"Basically."

"I did not do it, if that is any reassurance to you, Lim."

The information that Pasha was safe did not seem to calm Eccles down in the slightest.

Lim challenged him, " John, what is the matter?"

"I am naturally worried about Pasha."

"You have been unnaturally jumpy since we first arrived—"

"Natural concern for—"

Lim interrupted. "The smugglers operations were largely destroyed by Aaron Tennyson. I've been briefed on this planet. Something has been upsetting you and it's something that affects you personally. So out with it,"

"Nothing. Really."

"John, I'm a friend of yours. Certainly you can tell me . . ."

Eccles shook his head. He looked around, really frightened. His thoughts were so forceful, they cut through his telepathic block. He thought, //I CAN'T TELL YOU!//

*   *   *

Step two of Lim's plan was to re-question trader Aaron Tennyson. She listened to him repeat his account in front of Lt. Winters.

The free trader was noted for his honesty and he repeated basically the same story.

"There must have been a bomb in one of the canisters. Everyone seems to have died at once."

Lim felt impelled to say, "I checked with Council Leader Klemperer. Raymond Berquist had been assigned to infiltrate the smugglers and assess their activities. If this bomb means a resurgence of the smugglers, would this put your life in danger?"

"It could. They could put a price on my head. Is there any evidence that they have?"

"No."

"Let me also add I had nothing to do with the accident with Pasha Miusov. Wendnagel says Pasha is telepathically deaf and asks after him."

"Thank you. That's all I have to ask you, Aaron."

The trader left the room. Lim drummed on the table with her fingers.

"I got nowhere with Governor Eccles. And I'm sure he knows something more than he's saying."

Winters asked succinctly, "Can't you read his mind?"

"Not if he's not sending. And there's the code. Besides, John has a telepathic block that we—Pasha and I—taught him to use."

She walked to the window. "Pasha seemed to think John was worried about something being seen from the air."

"I could ask Zäringhen to authorize a satellite scan."

"I tried that. They don't have a satellite in the right position."

"The DISCOVERY could use its sensors to scan the area."

"I can't get the authority to change their orbit. Can you?"

"I can try."

Winters radioed the starship and was surprised to receive a blanket NO. He was beginning to see why the Councilmen relied on their own abilities instead of his mechanical security. He also wondered if a bribe had been paid somewhere.

Then a fantastic idea came to him on this frontier planet. "Why don't I go up in a hang glider." Before Lim could protest, he added, "There are some stored in the cottage where Governor Eccles put up Aaron and Wendnagel."

"I advise you to go armed."

An attempt had been made on Miusov and someone had killed Berquist. Whatever was stored in the capsules of Wendnagel's sanctuary had to be very hot and very coveted.

III

The cliff was edged with solid rock, deposited by melting glaciers. Winters took the hang glider over the cliff's edge. It caught an updraft of wind that caused him to sail higher up on the mountain. He was glad he wore a thermo jacket over his navy uniform because the air was cold.

He flew directly over the castle and started a spiral, each turn wider than the next. He saw nothing he had not seen on the first trip.

In one hand he carried an techcorder that he had readjusted for long distance scans. He would play it back later.

He followed Eccles' small gauge railroad tracks and picked up an infa-red light in a tunnel. He was puzzled but couldn't do another sweep because the wind wasn't right.

Fenced enclosures held Eccles' zoo, a few animals from other planets which he could identify from his travels.

An updraft took him out of range of Eccles' property line. He followed the forest to the timberline, wondering if he could reach there on the other side of the mountain where Berquist had been killed. If the air currents held . . . —a down draft dropped the glider. Winters made a hasty adjustment in his weight. The wind picked up in velocity and tore at his face.

He flexed the wing and dumped wind off it to cut his speed, like a sailor luffing his sails.

Below him was an opening in the trees. It ran along the mountainside and appeared man-made. At one end he saw the Zäringhen spaceport. He looked the other way and saw a blue light aimed for the sky.

Winters steered toward it.

His techcorder hissed. That was all the warning there was.

A narrow green laser beam cut across the hang glider fabric and right through a strut.

Winters looked up from the techcorder, saw the burned edges of the wing, just as the glider came apart. The former first-in scout yelled as he fell out of the sky.

The ground rushed toward him. Interlaced pine branches caught the cloth and broke his fall. The branches split from the impact. A rope dangled and threatened to wrap around Winters' neck. He unwound it as another branch broke. It was another ten feet to the ground, and the impact stunned him.

Winters groaned. His ribs ached. It was a minute before he could unstrap from the harness that attached him to the hang glider.

He rolled behind a tree, pulled out his stun gun and looked around. He heard a brook flowing over stones not far away, and the tinkling of copper bells. There was a sound like the sea. He looked up and saw it was the wind rustling in the leaves in the trees.

His head hurt.

He put down the weapon. Winters closed his eyes. Taking his thumbs, he pressed them against the outer corners of his eyelids very gently. At first lights danced. Then as the pressure continued he saw a bright white light—white boxes ran towards him. Winters let go. None of the lines were broken. He had no damage to his skull. The *phosphene* light faded. His vision returned to normal. He had learned this trick while on the Planet of 100 Moons.

Slowly he got to his feet. Following the sound of the bells he came to one of Wendnagel's sanctuaries. An atomic Lantern beamed a blue light in the sky.

Anger arose within him. That thing had severed his hang glider! Winters had a temper he turned against hostile planets and he raged for several minutes before he realized the beam was too wide to have cut through his hang glider. It was also not hot enough.

He walked around the building, incredulous that he had not seen the chalet from the air.

The doorway was open. Inside were stacked carrying capsules, upright like bowling pins. There were at least ten of the canisters. Winters stopped before entering.

He stooped to pick up a stone. He tossed it toward the doorway. It deflected off a force field and hit the ground outside the sanctuary. The doorway was very secure.

These were the capsules taken by Aaron and Wendnagel.

Winters pondered for a few minutes. It came to him that there could have been more capsules that these. Was that the answer to Pasha's riddle of what could be seen from the sky?

Warily, he hiked back to the pieces of the hang glider. The techcorder had survived the fall. He set it for short range and scanned for electromagnetic disturbances that might indicate a Shade. He was afraid of the things since the omnicraft instruments had gone out.

He folded the wing and wrapped the ultra light weight poles. It was going to be a long walk back. His ribs were sore and bruised. He kept his stun gun out.

Chapter 6

WENDNAGEL

"Table, move to the left," Wendnagel ordered the computer.

The table slid on its track. This was Eccles' work room. The tall, blond-haired woman of Demner was using it to detect a Shade.

Her E.S.P. worked very differently from the Councilman's. She cleared her mind and sat calmly, hands on the table.

Nothing came. Then instead of a Shade, she got a clear instantaneous image of a man. He was thinking of Berquist. The man was a stranger to her.

In a second it was over.

"By the Shades, what was that?" she said softly.

She left the room, walked around the inner balcony, feet soft on the carpet to the stairs. Descending the stairs to the first floor, she paced through the main living room and out an open door.

Before her was the wishing well. She picked out a triangular coin from her pocket and tossed it in.

Steve Winters stomped into the doorway just as it hit the water. Coins glimmered beneath the surface.

"Have you seen the Councilwoman?"

"She's upstairs . . . what's the matter?"

Winters hesitated, then remembered Wendnagel was one of the revered personages on this planet.

"My hang glider was cut in two by a laser. The trees broke my fall. I saw your sanctuary and the atomic Lantern is pointed at the sky. Is it supposed to do that?"

"No, it is supposed to be pointed at Zäringhen."

"Well, you better fix it. The distraction nearly broke my neck."

"There may come a time when you may want those Lanterns," she retorted. His temper was disrespectful.

"I'm sorry. I had a bad scare. And another thought occurred to me. Are there more of these carrying canisters?"

"We took all that there were."

"Could some have been removed earlier?"

"Isn't that what Pasha was trying to find out?"

"Are they trying to encourage his memory—ouch."

"Are you all right?"

"Just had the wind knocked out of me. Can you tell if my rib is broken?"

"I don't have that ability."

It was well past sunset when Lim, Pasha and Moncrief were finished. Lim had tried all kinds of subtle questioning to pick up pieces of Pasha's memory of the time slide. To no avail.

Moncrief was losing his patience. "Patrick, try cooperating."

"I remember nothing."

"What about your E.S.P.? You had no trouble on the omnicraft."

"Are you jealous of my abilities?"

Lim cut in. "Stop. I want to examine Pasha's workroom now."

They walked over to the room. Lim ordered Moncrief, "Stand in the doorway."

"Be careful, Councilwoman."

Lim walked the perimeter. Violet light came through the window. "Ah, Pasha's preferred light." She looked down to the ground story below. It was lit by a porch light.

Continuing to move, she stepped up to the table. The cat brain had been removed and buried. The time slide pieces were still on the table, as were several boxes of apparatus.

She concentrated. She had some precognition. Theoretically, someone with precognition could also see the past.

She concentrated on the slide. Pain! She got a vivid image of Miusov seeing the container bubbling with acid. She backed up from the table until her elbow hit the window. One more step and she'd be through it.

She "saw" a mental image of Berquist standing over the canisters. It was intense, but suddenly blotted out by Pasha screaming.

Lim gasped and ran from the room.

She stood in the hallway, breathing hard. The memory alternately receded then re-echoed.

The arcane E.S.P. equipment sat abandoned, never to give up its secrets.

Aargau was in the basement. The young cobbler put the finishing touches on a door latch which Eccles had commissioned. All of his work was hand carved.

His exertion was so focused he had not realized it was after dark. The top of the cellar had windows and he was not operating by porch light. He glanced up at a window and realized it was dark.

He reached for the light switch, another Eccles invention.

As he did, he looked back at the window. A tool had been placed diagonally across the window.

"By the Shades," he gulped. That hadn't been there before.

Then a face came to the window and stared in from the outside.

Aargau screamed and ran out, yelling. "A face! There's someone outside. Maybe it's the murderer! Help!"

He ran upstairs into the main room, attracting the attention of Lim, Moncrief, Pasha, Winters and the diplomats.

Aargau was still screaming, "Murderer! Help!"

Lim asked, "Where?"

"Downstairs. There's a face in the window. But don't you go down there."

Winters pulled out his stun gun. "I'll take a look outside."

Agent Moncrief agreed, adding, "I'll look downstairs."

He descended the stairs and reappeared a moment later. "There's some kind of tool across the window. It's not supernatural, just calculated to surprise." He turned to the cobbler.

"Aargau, what did he look like?"

"It was hard to see features. He had dark-brown hair, a narrow face, and was bent way over like he was tall." He tried to describe the nose and eyes. "Eyes like a hawk."

Pasha piped up, "That description would fit Berquist!"

Lim said quickly, "That description would fit many people."

Winters had returned. "The ground's partly frozen, so I'm not sure about footprints. The ground was disturbed by the window. How did he get by my surveillance?"

"A clairvoyant could do it."

"Then, how did he get past yours?"

"I don't know. He bypassed my teletapped areas. His thoughts are shielded. If he's that good, I want to recruit him for the Special Forces." The teletapped areas were especially tuned to strangers. She ignored movements from people from the castle.

She turned up the thermostat on her red thermo jacket. "Let's have a look outside. Bring flashlights."

"By the Shades!" Aargau said vehemently.

"That wasn't a Shade, "Lim returned. "It was a man."

*   *   *

Hawken Eccles sat alone in her room. It had been a boring day. The diplomats were alone in their quarters, except one when O'Connors had called for her. The Council people were all in their rooms. Aargau was downstairs. Aaron Tennyson the free trader was in the cottage.

Aaron had hired her to advise him on local customs, for a sales office he wanted to set up on Dauropa. Although she was young, just out of school, she had made few mistakes in advising him. Now Ramón wanted to hire her for similar advice in setting up a consulate in Zäringhen.

She had warm thoughts for Renate Ramòn but he had been busy today.

Voices drifting in from the window distracted her. She doused the room light and peered out. Far below, Winter's flashlight and Lim's lit up her red thermo jacket. Hawken stared at her with a strange intensity.

What was the Outworlder doing outside! Hawken had not liked her attitude toward Wendnagel.

Whatever was going on, Hawken was going to follow her.

The Councilwoman had been busy all day using E.S.P. Hawken knew no telepath could broadcast continually. She might be able to follow unnoticed.

Hawken grabbed her fur-lined coat and, throwing it over her shoulders, ran out without a flashlight.

Ramón and O'Connors roused Eccles out of his study.

Ramón spoke softly, "There's been some kind of disturbance downstairs."

O'Connors added, "Everyone is outside. It's too dangerous. I suggest you get everyone back in *vite!* Quickly."

Eccles appeared frightened.

The moon had risen over Wendnagel's sanctuary. She looked up and saw the triangle of lights from a starhip passing overhead.

Wendnagel pulled her red cloak around her, against the night chill. She had corrected the angle of the Lantern. It now pointed at Zäringhen. She was puzzled as to how it had shifted position. The capsules were untouched. She had assumed a bird had hit it, but now she wondered if it had been knocked aside by someone trying to get into the sanctuary.

With this thought, she walked back over the cedar bridge and she looked behind her. Aaron would be furious when he found out she went out at night alone.

She kicked aside the leaves to find the dirt path. It led to a wider stream, and spanned a bridge with lights at either end.

Wendnagel stepped with the confidence of one who knows no one on Dauropa would knowingly assault her. She was the Family.

Beneath the bridge, the river ran swift and cold. Boulders could be seen and spray glinted in the light as water spilled down a small fall.

The red cloak billowed in the wind and disappeared into black, as she walked across the bridge. She stopped in the middle and clung to the railing.

A silhouetted figure ran out from behind a bush. It ran across the bridge, and pushed Wendnagel, who half-turned at the sound.

She screamed as she went over the railing.

Wendnagel was dead when she hit the rocks, a look of incredible surprise on her face.

Chapter 7

AARON'S CURSE

Dawn found Winters and Lim bending over Wendnagel by the stream bank.

"I told you I thought something was wrong," Lim told him.

//Wendnagel,// she thought softly. There was no answer.

Before she could stop him, Winters took a pulse. "She's been dead a while. Someone obviously surprised her on the bridge. Look at her expression." Winters blinked from several hours of lost sleep.

"Don't touch Wendnagel. Lim won't be able to read who was here." Moncrief's warning came too late.

Lim stepped back and concentrated on the cold stream. Her awareness touched the banks, the bridge: nothing.

Around Wendnagel were the awareness auras of Winters and Moncrief.

She thought silently for a few minutes. Something about Winters' words about surprise tugged at her mind.

"I think," she said after a minute, "she looked surprised because she recognized her assailant."

"Someone from the castle?"

"Or someone she knew."

"That lets out our mystery visitor," Winters observed.

Lim felt very sad. "How will I break the news to Aaron?"

One of Wendnagel's relatives came to claim the body. The Lantern was shut off. Councilwoman Lim Miusov had gotten permission from the authorities to conduct the investigation herself. After notifying Aaron the next step was to open the capsules. They were still in the sanctuary. The death of Wendnagel had caused an unforseen delay.

Aaron Tennyson did not take the news well. Lim met him at Eccles' cottage.

"But who would do such a thing? Wendnagel is revered all over Demner. All over Dauropa. Even the smugglers deferred to her. And, if it is a smuggler, am I next?"

Lim told him her theory that it was someone from the castle or nearby.

"I'm getting out of here."

"No, if you run, you'll be out of our protection. They'll follow you."

"Are these the same people who killed Councilman Berquist?"

"I don't know."

"Wendnagel's death couldn't have been an accident, could it? A fall?"

"She was pushed,"

Aaron fell silent.

Lim went on, "The diplomat, Mr. O'Connors, wants to talk to you about employing Hawken. I told him to wait."

"Have you seen her yet?"

"I'm about to."

Lim and Moncrief approached Hawken in her room.

Hawken looked blankly at Lim.

Then she took it worse than Aaron.

Hawken protested, "This is impossible. Wendnagel is venerated throughout Demner and the whole of the planet. You've got to be wrong."

Moncrief said slowly, "We're not wrong. Someone—"

"No one could have done this." Hawken pointed at Moncrief. "You don't know what you are saying. Maybe on some other planet of yours. Not on Dauropa. You *offworlders* don't know how things are here!"

She stared at Lim, "What are you doing here!" Hawken sat down. "This can't be!"

Lim said persistantly, "I have to ask this again . Are you sure you know nothing about what happened to the cat brain?"

"I didn't do it . . ."

Lim started to tell her theory when Hawken cut her off. "Are you suggesting the same person might have killed Wendnagel?" Hawken looked upset.

Then, she remembered she was a consultant now. She took a breath and said evenly, "I think you better leave."

Lim nodded, but before she left she told Hawken, "We'll be opening those stolen capsules, soon."

When they were gone, Hawken threw herself on the bed and cried. Her anguish and fear could be "heard" by Lim even through the wall.

Aaron walked out of the cottage, glancing over his shoulder. He stepped on the wide leaves growing on the side of the cottage and peered up at the castle. He had never been so frightened.

Upstairs in the castle, Pasha Miusov was pacing the hallways, oblivious to the paintings on display boards. His feet made no sound on the soft, intricately designed carpet.

None of the outsiders were making any sense. The diplomats were in their room, refusing to see Eccles. Aargau was with Winters trying to make a sketch of the stranger. Winters spent most of the time berating himself for not catching a man who obviously had superior abilities.

Hawken was in her room with the door closed when she should have been consoling Aaron or something.

Just when he thought he could understand those outside the Council, everyone was acting strangely. He wished he had the missing piece that would make the puzzle clear.

Eccles hailed him.

Pasha answered. "How are you, John?"

"I'm a survivor," the Governor replied.

"I'm puzzled about these Outsiders."

Eccles put an arm around him. "People handle stress and strain differently. Try not to think of people outside your service as 'Outsiders'. They're just people. You can't keep them outside forever. Always remember

85

that when you deal with them, they have lives beyond the immediate work and you're seeing only a piece of them."

"That still doesn't explain the puzzles."

"When it's you, Pasha, talking about a puzzle, I believe it's there. Keep working on it."

"What can I see out this window?"

"That's the Station House for the small railroad. I call it Grand Central Station."

"What's beyond it?"

"Er-I have to leave."

So, Pasha thought, that's another puzzle I can't solve: what's bothering Eccles.

He stared out the window. Nothing happened with his E.S.P. It was still blank. He'd have to depend on his other senses. He saw trees and broad-leafed lilies of the valley on the grounds. It was the wrong season for flowers.

And now . . . without warning he saw Aaron running. He crossed Eccles' small gauge railroad tracks and ran by the station house. Another crazy Outsider.

He should have been heading for the road. It was miles long and wound down the mountain, but Aaron headed for neither road nor ground car.

Suddenly Miusov remembered there was a wide gorge that was used as a footpath to the base of the mountain. It was a short cut that led to the river and the air ferry to Zäringhen.

Lim had said she told Aaron not to leave. Here he was running as if for his life.

Miusov ran for his room and grabbed up his thermo jacket. In no time he was out the door and in a breath he was across the lawn and running for the Station House.

Somewhere his foot triggered Winters' surveillance equipment. Before Pasha could reach the station house, Winters was running hard behind him and caught his jacket just as Pasha found the opening to the footpath.

The Security Officer snapped, "Where do you think you're going?"

"It's Aaron. He's going to fulfill the curse," Pasha panted. "Let go of me."

"What are you talking about?"

"There's going to be another murder. Winters, I can't stop to explain. He has to be stopped. Follow me if you wish."

Pasha pulled out of Winters' grasp and ran down the wide footpath.

Winters stood momentarily paralyzed. Councilman Klemperer had ordered him not to leave Councilwoman Lim. Agent Moncrief had warned him not to let Miusov out of his sight. Winters didn't know what to do. He had to choose.

The former first-in scout reminded himself that Pasha was the one without E.S.P. and decided to follow him for his own protection. He ran down the footpath gorge.

By the time he made the decision, Pasha was out of sight.

The moment Winters stepped off the grounds the trap was sprung on Lim.

*　　*　　*

The stars were more numerous in space than could be seen from Dauropa. The Milky Way, also visible from Earth, stood out in all its glory of pearly stars.

Councilman Pasha Miusov watched the display through the ship's window. He felt a tension all through his body.

Aaron had taken the anti-grav ferry ahead of him, crossed the river to Zäringhen and apparently booked a starship shuttle to Jalug. Pasha had ceased thinking of him as an Outsider and considered him instead, as a friend in trouble. He followed on the next starship shuttle, using his Special Forces ID.

From his seat, he asked the computer for information about Jalug. Both Dauropa and Jalug had a star, listed as catalog number HR1182. There was no name for this insignificant star on Earth, only the number.

It wasn't listed in the local computer. Then, he found it under the Thok Jalug/Thok Dauropa system. He punched for a definition of Thok.

The computer gave him:

Thok: 1) a local Jalug deity

2) possibly an ancient personage on Jalug

3) a Jalogan philosophy on how to conduct oneself

He tried to find out more information but the definitions ran around in circles. There was a reference to Thok's Citadel. He punched it up.

It was located in the Trade City and was cited as the place where philosophers of Thok emerged. Repeated requests for maps and data got the flashing sign NO DATA and OFF-LIMITS.

He was sure this was Aaron's goal. He wished he had the trader's notes.

*   *   *

It was late evening when he arrived. The temperature was thirty degrees higher than Demner. He folded up his thermo jacket and put it in his back pocket where it bulged. He walked around in his black uniform.

The human quarter of the city was not what he wanted. He desired to enter the native quarter with its local architecture, bicycle and push-cart traffic, and Citadel of Thok.

His mind whirled from the activities of the last few hours. It was seven hours later on Jalug, due to a time zone difference and he still had plenty of energy.

Back at Zäringhen he had tried to get the authorities to stop Aaron's ship. Since his actual rank could not be confirmed until his next birthday, he had called Councilman Klemperer's temporary headquarters at the spaceport.

The shuttle to Jalug did not have passenger lists. Tickets could even be bought on shipboard after liftoff. By the time he had permission to stop a shuttle, one had already entered Jalug atmosphere. They told him the ship was out of Dauropan jurisdiction.

"Pasha, do you have to create another incident!" grumbled a Green-rank councilman at Zäringhen. The voice came over his communit.

Miusov also filed a report with Council Leader Westerman, but without his E.S.P. the message would take hours to reach Earth, even through the teleport gates.

The Green-rank Councilman relayed an order from Klemperer, "Check for smuggling activity."

Pasha put away the communit, brushed his black bangs out of his eyes, and surveyed his first glimpse of Trade City at night.

*　　*　　*

Halfway between the native and human quarters of the city was a small spaceport, much smaller than the spaceport in the Terran Zone where incoming ships normally landed.

Ships and shuttles were parked in a row next to an airport landing strip. A dark figure in silhouette climbed the fence and landed next to an anti-grav shuttle. It probably transported cargo between spaceports.

Further down the line the short figure hugged the shadow of a space-worthy craft.

A regular inspection through the front door would have led Miusov to carefully correct documents and forged flight certificates. He would have learned nothing.

He looked over the starship and found a meter standing three feet off the ground on a pole in front of the landing ramp. The meter was filled with native stones with numbers on them, all the same. Miusov copied the number on the meter onto his communit computer. He wrote 86351790A.

An instant later a powerful search beam bathed the ship, narrowly missing him.

"Who goes there?"

Pasha ran for the fence.

The high powered spotlight moved to the area where he was standing, played across the meter, and on to the next ship.

Several seconds later the dark outline of Miusov was over the fence and to safety.

He planned to ask about that ship number in the morning.

The dark-haired half-human tried Aaron's offices in the trade zone. They were closed and locked.

He wandered into the native quarter, trying to get his bearings. The

KAGA

streets were well lit and he could see the wide eaves of the rooftops. Many buildings were also flat-roofed. The humidity was higher than he was used to and he felt it in every breath.

He saw natives that were six-footed like short centipedes, a few of them on bicycles with extra handle bars or peddles. There were ground cars, mostly driven by humans. They wore the same mode of brightly colored dress as the centipedes. The women wore intricate jewelry.

Pasha walked into a drinking establishment. He was the only one in uniform.

The Terrans, those of human descent, were sitting among themselves. They had a variety of complexions. The centipede-like Jalogan natives sat around a table.

Pasha could be charming when he wanted to be. Soon he had engaged several of the Terrans in conversation.

"My name is Traphen Dnoces, but you can call me Trap," the Terran told Miusov.

"I noticed a lot of bicycles."

"Those were introduced by Aaron Tennyson many years ago. They are only now catching on with the natives."

Another Terran said, "He had to get special permission to import them legally."

"Where can I find Aaron Tennyson? His offices were closed."

"He's gone. Married some princess on Thok Dauropa."

"He's back on Jalug," Miusov asserted.

"No, he won't be back. He's under a curse."

"Thok's Citadel?"

"We only call it *the* Citadel."

"Tell me about Thok."

It was the wrong question. "Thok is everywhere, especially in the Citadel." The answer was cryptic.

Then he said, "It is said Aaron Tennyson asked this question of a Jalogan prince who told him 'It can take many years to understand Thok.'"

Three of the centipedal Jalogans walked in a crawling fashion to Miusov. The Leader rose on its back legs. The spokesman had a red head and brown and green body, covered partially by a robe. The other two had brown heads with twin green ridges across the back.

He took great pains to speak grammatically correct Standard. He spoke with a British accent. "You ask about Thok," the first one said evenly. "In the last revelation Thok wanted us to welcome offworlders. I bid you welcome, as our philosophy dictates."

"I thank you. Who is your philosopher?"

"Our last philosopher was L'rig Esol's daughter, Enid. She entered the Citadel and communed with Thok. She brought us the latest understanding."

"How can I get to this Citadel?"

"No one is allowed inside. It is guarded by Thok's priests and their acolytes. Even they don't go inside."

"Enid went inside."

"Enid Esol, blessed by Thok, is dead."

"Aaron Tennyson himself walked inside."

"He was allowed by the priests."

"Where is he now?"

The Terran answered for him. "Probably on Thok Dauropa. Try the Merchants Association. And don't think, offworlder, that you can walk into the Citadel. You wouldn't come out alive."

Miusov pulled out the jewel Wendnagel gave him so long ago at the party. "I have this." It was still on a chain around his neck.

One of the Jalogan natives cried out, "He's got a jai'. One of the Seven. He must have stolen it from the priests!"

Chaos reigned.

Trap tried to protect Pasha as one native reached for the crystal. The chain would not break. Pasha made a fist and deflected the centipede-like being's arm with his free hand. Pasha opened his hand, prepared to strike with the bone beneath his palms. It was harder than a fist, and he could still use his hands.

The Jalogans moved to ring him in. Pasha picked up a chair and yelled. They backed off uncertainly. He threw the chairs aside and ran out the door.

He heard a howl go up and he could hear them, Jalogan and Terran, running after him.

91

Pasha ran past a line of shops and came to a residential area. The eaves of the roof of each building arched almost to the ground. Pasha ran up to it and took to the roof, leaped from the angled roof to a flat one, and then from one rooftop to another. Beneath him he heard the crowd from the bar dashing down the alleys and surrounding buildings.

As he stopped for breath he heard an uproar and saw lights in the distance. Old style oil torches had been lit. It took him an instant to realize the shouting was not directed at him.

The cries sounded like, "A sign, a sign!" And then, "The curse! He's coming to fulfill the curse."

Pasha jumped from a flat roof to an angled one with long eaves. He climbed down an arch and dropped to the ground.

He followed the shouts and he was led deep into the native quarter.

With his short stature he found it hard to see anything, especially over the huge Jalogan natives. In the distance rose the walls of the Citadel. It had the magnificence of a Tibetan temple.

He saw that it was made of native materials. It had several stories and a stepped flat roof, running along part of each story. There were towers for a bell in the corners of the first story. Every corner had a carved gargoyle.

Someone jostled him for room to see. He heard the Terrans shouting, "The curse!"

He heard the natives yelling on the other side, "A sign, a sign! We want a Sign! Speak to Thok then speak to us!"

Miusov pushed forward. "Let me through. I'm Patrick Miusov of the Special Forces Council. Let me through!"

He pushed his way to the front.

The Citadel had a stone pathway to the double doors. Before the pathway was a courtyard. The priests and acolytes, some of them human, warned the crowd not to go further than the courtyard.

Aaron Tennyson walked out from the crowd followed by an old Jalogan native, who was imploring, "It's L'rig. You don't have to do this, Aaron. It's not our way. And, it's not your way. You don't have to walk into the Citadel."

Pasha fought his way out of the crowd and ran to the trader.

"Aaron. It's me, Pasha. Don't go in—" He stopped suddenly. Aaron wasn't even looking at him. His eyes were glazed over, and staring ahead of him. He brushed past Miusov without even acknowledging his existence. Pasha thought, he's in some kind of trance.

Pasha felt something wet. He had put up his hands when the trader brushed them. Pasha looked down and found them covered with blood.

Someone from the crowd grabbed Pasha and drew him back to the courtyard. Others began pulling at him. "It's the curse coming to claim him."

"No. It's not a curse. Let me go."

"You can't enter the Citadel with him!"

The priests opened the doors for Aaron.

Pasha's protesting alto voice was drowned out by native cries of "A sign, a sign!"

A black arm reached out and a six digit hand grasped Pasha's forearm.

"The priests have seen you. There is no way you can get close again. Come with me, please."

It was the old Jalogan native. Up close he looked even older. His face had silver hairs. The centipedal native led him inside an herb shop. A human assistant drew the curtains. Two Jalogans were in the shadows behind them. Even in the dark their iridescent silk clothes sparkled.

"I can see you don't believe the curse had drawn back my friend Aaron Tennyson. I am L'rig Esol, a friend of his. This is Tog Ev'uoy. His brother Annog is outside watching. If you are brave enough to enter the Citadel, you have to elude the priests."

"My name is Patrick Miusov. You can call me Pasha. What do you have in mind?"

"You need native clothing." The Jalogan addressed Tog in his Jalogan language. The native seemed to understand.

Pasha let fall, "Is there somewhere I can wash my hands?"

Once he had freshened up, Pasha asked, "Can you tell me precisely what is happening?"

"Tennyson is supposed to commune with Thok then come to a balcony and give us a discourse on Thok's will. But he can't. Tennyson told me if he returns he'll die. Thok said so. He can only enter with a jai'."

"Aaron gave me something which he says is identical to a jai'. It's of Dauropa." He paused, then drew it out.

"A jai'" L'rig breathed.

"It's not one of the Seven, L'rig." Quickly he explained events on Dauropa.

"Aaron is very knowledgeable. Here put this on your face and hands."

"What does it do?"

"It bends light. You will look older. Here, let me do it."

Ev'uoy brought in a cup. L'rig took it. "Here, drink this," L'rig instructed.

Pasha hesitated, "Is it safe for Draconians?"

"Drink it!" L'rig ordered.

Miusov drank it down.

L'rig explained, "It will lower your vocal range." He looked around. "Where is the outfit, Tog?"

Miusov needed help getting into it. It was a tunic with 2/3 sleeves and a cloak that fastened to one wrist. The tunic buckled at the sides. He took the communit and Special Forces ID card out of his discarded uniform and put them in a pocket inside the tunic. The outfit was dull brown.

"Most of the Jalogan garments I've seen are brightly colored." His voice was strangely baritone.

"You are trying to stay out of sight, Pasha. When you get outdoors, circle around to the side of the Citadel. And good luck, brave one."

Miusov stared at what he took to be a photograph on the wall. Pictured was a man with flat features in his mid-twenties. With a start, he realized it was a mirror. He felt his face for his high cheek bones. The face in the mirror stayed stubbornly flat boned, and several degrees of weathered tan.

Full night met him when he tread outside. As he traveled he faded into the shadows. Walking away from the torches, he circled the building.

An area was unlit from torches. Miusov, a dark silent figure, leaped to the bottom of the gargoyle. He pulled himself over the contorted statue and then slid onto the roof. It sloped and acted as a ramp to the next higher level. He inched around a corner tower. Next, he found an open window and pulled himself inside.

Miusov was later to describe it as dropping into another world. The air was warm and dry. Light spilled yellow from slabs in the floor, wall or cciling. No dust was on the floor but the place felt old. The interior walls were wood or wood-like, and covered with a mandala.

All at once a white light surrounded him. He felt a shock. The crystal warmed against his skin. Miusov took it out. The crystal given to him by Wendnagel was brightly lit.

Something with awareness was trying to talk to him but it couldn't get past the light around him. Miusov felt that rather than heard it.

Now he rued his lack of E.S.P. He should have done that clairvoyant scan on the crystal. It might contain a microelectronic circuit.

The Jalogan native culture had nothing like this! Little was stopping whatever was in here from stepping up the electrical power, enough to kill him.

Miusov wondered if Thok was a computer.

The narrow hallway led to a double staircase. He took the down steps and then another set of steps. He was below ground level. The stairs gave out to a large room. There was a bricked wall on one side. On the far wall was another stair. On the right was an alcove and a hallway. Along the wall he saw unlit torches. An embroidered curtain was across one wall. The air smelled of orange spice. Along the brick wall was an altar that hadn't been used in a long time.

In the center of the floor Aaron Tennyson lay sprawled on his back. Very faintly Miusov could hear the crowd outside.

Miusov ran toward the trader. He was staring at the ceiling with a look of incredible surprise.

The half-Draconian fingered the lit crystal sadly. "And all they had to do was give you one of these."

He remembered the blood and opened the trader's jacket. He saw that Aaron had been stabbed seven times! Miusov grimaced and dropped the jacket closed. He was shaken but he refused to give up his examination.

The blond trader's hands were clenched. Prying them open, Miusov found in one, a piece of torn brown cloth and a stone. The stone was painted with the number 86351790A.

Miusov pulled out his communit and wished on the computer. The numbers matched.

"Good man!" he breathed.

Cool-headed through trade ups and downs, Aaron Tennyson had stayed cool-headed through his own murder. He had struggled with his assailant.

Carefully, Miusov put the stone and cloth in a pocket and zipped it closed.

Outside below a balcony, expectant Jalogans chanted, "A sign, a sign!" The voices could be heard inside by Miusov. But no life stirred in the body of trader Aaron Tennyson and he never spoke to the crowd.

Leaving Aaron where he was, the half-human prowled the perimeter looking for more clues.

Three steps led to a lower level. The dark-haired Councilman found a heavily ornamented trunk.

Something touched the youth. It touched his face and he felt pressure against his green eyes. Miusov held up his hand, expecting to find a force field but there was none.

A figure in white sprang up between him and the trunk. It was a Jalogan native dressed in gleaming armor and carrying a sword. The creature took a swing at him and Miusov ducked.

A voice rang out in Standard, "What is the source of all knowledge?"

The half-Draconian tried answering with Zen. "It is found within."

"And what is the source of that?"

He took a wild guess. "Thok."

The figure disappeared.

Miusov tried paraphrasing John Locke, from the 1700's on Earth. "Knowledge comes to us through our senses—sight, touch, hearing, feeling and smelling. We use our intellect to study it."

"What is beyond that?" the voice boomed.

"God," he said in his new baritone.

The discussion went on into succeeding generations of Earth Western philosophy. They started with representative government.

Then, the voice touched him inside his head. "Offworlder. New offworlder. Not of Jalug." The voice had bypassed his hearing and had used a nerve as a receptor.

He wished for his E.S.P., an techcorder and a piece of his equipment.

Something was alive in the room!

Miusov abandoned his theory about a computer. He had a new, wild idea. "Among humanity, evolution is toward larger brains. Scientists have speculated that future evolution would lead to a larger brain and mind that had a smaller and smaller body.

"Here on Jalug is a being that needed no body at all!"

The dark-haired half-human remembered back at the party about Aaron describing that the Citadel might have been left by an advanced race that had deserted Jalug. He was also right that something here was alive.

The being that was Thok touched his mind and sent queries through his nervous system in words Miusov didn't understand. The air was charged with static electricity and Miusov felt several small pricks of a shock.

He tried to frame a question about the trader. "What did you do to Aaron Tennyson?" he asked aloud.

The voice in his head responded, "He was told he would come back and he did."

Miusov's pulse raced. Here was a chance to talk to an incredibly ancient, venerable being. One who was apparently guiding the civilization of Jalug.

He looked for a place to sit down. The half-human tripped over the edge of the Jalogan cloak. In the same instant the chain of the necklace around his neck parted. He caught it in his hand. The clasp was broken.

He felt an indrawn breath from the evolved being, or a mental equivalent: silence.

Chilled, Miusov realized he was about to duplicate the disaster that long ago befell Aaron. He put the jewel back around his neck and tied the chain. Then he waited.

The unseen being touched the stone. Inside his mind, Miusov heard, "This is to identify a seeker of knowledge." It was not E.S.P. Rather the being was tapping directly into a nerve in his head.

The subject switched from philosophy to science. Thok asked, "What is information theory? How is information stored?"

A few additional questions told Miusov that Thok wanted to know how an techcorder worked. The youth had written a paper on it in high school. When he wrote it, he never expected such intense questioning. He answered from the data in his paper.

Miusov realized he had no knowledge of Jalogan history. He had not even expected to visit the planet. He didn't know if it held a seat in the Solar Federation. The Thok Jalug/Thok Dauropa designation of the system might indicate that Dauropa held that seat.

Miusov said out loud, "You're a being like myself, only more evolved."

A gentle touch pushed him back. Miusov allowed himself to be led by touch to where Aaron Tennyson was lying.

And Thok said, "Find out who did this."

In the next moment the jai' became cool. The light went out and the thin white light that had surrounded the half-human diminished. Thok became silent and the Councilman realized he had a ferocious headache.

The interview was over.

The youth walked up a flight of stairs. He cracked open one of a double set of doors. Most of the Jalogan population had moved under a balcony somewhere on the side. There were thousands. No one was in this section of the courtyard. He tucked the jai' under his Jalogan tunic, then slid out.

Miusov had only walked a few steps when acolytes appeared as if from nowhere. Two Terran acolytes, wearing a great deal of jewelry, seized him by each arm. They were very strong.

"A smuggler. Trying to get into the Citadel."

"Did you jump customs, smuggler?"

"Don't touch his hands, he's probably not medically cleared."

"I'm Patrick Miusov, of the Special Forces Co—"

"I don't care who you are. I want to see your medical clearance."

He had none. There was no stamp because he had entered on his Special Forces ID. Miusov freed a hand and tried to unzipper the pocket.

The taller acolyte took his arm while the other kicked him. "Get him out of here."

"I'm not a smuggler—"

His voice was drowned out by a new crowd yelling, "Thok, Thok!" in the courtyard.

Miusov spied a familiar blue uniform. It had the white, four-pointed star of the Solar Federation on one breast. "Steve!" he recognized the Security Officer. "Lt. Winters," he called. "Lt. Winters, tell them who I am!"

The two acolytes glanced at each other, then beckoned a Jalogan native, also a heavily jeweled acolyte.

He brought Winters over. The acolyte said in too-perfect Standard, "Can you identify this man?"

Miusov struggled against the hold of the two powerful humans. In a thick baritone, he cried out, "Lt. Winters, tell them who I am."

Winters stared at the captive in Jalogan clothing. The flat cheeks, large wrinkled hands, someone around twenty-five. Winters couldn't place him nor the voice.

"I've never seen this man before," Winters declared.

Miusov groaned.

The Jalogan acolyte said, "Take him to medical. Quick! He might have something catching. Then we'll arrest him."

Twenty minutes later, Miusov found himself on his back on a table. His arms were held by telepathically locked pinions. The room was spartan by Earth medical standards.

Miusov read the manufacturer's label on the restraints and grinned. That manufacturer was known for its defective work. He struggled for a while and his smile faded into a frown. Finally he stopped. Apparently, the only working pair the manufacturer ever made was around his wrists.

The doctor was examining Miusov's cells under a microscope. He had taken a blood sample.

"By Thok!" the doctor cried out.

Miusov had forgotten what he would see.

The medic looked up at Miusov. "These are 'pressed' cells. One cell has been superimposed over another. I've never head of this being done on non-dentritic life. I've got to study this."

Miusov strained at the restraints. The last thing he wanted was to be held as a scientific guinea pig. He was a test tube child. All of his records were held by the Special Forces Council, who would probably never release them. In fact, he had been brought up within the Council.

Just then the door opened. A tall man in Jalogan tunic entered. He flashed a card at the doctor. "From the bureau. I want to talk to the captive."

The doctor waved him at Miusov.

The stranger's back was to Miusov but the face was in profile. Miusov gave a start of surprise and recognition. Berquist! He was alive.

Thoughts raced through his mind. Words of praise from Westerman's office on Earth. Rumors from Klemperer's local office that Berquist had gone renegade.

Quickly he assumed a neutral expression. Only the knowledge that Berquist couldn't possibly recognize him kept him quiet while he sorted things out. Berquist might also be under cover.

Councilman Berquist, a black rank, walked over to him. Berquist pulled out an elongated object.

Berquist told him, "This is a sound umbrella. It shields our conversation. I am seeking to recruit you as a smuggler."

Miusov blinked. Berquist went on, "You're good. You entered Jalug's Trade City without medical clearance. You made it all way to the native quarter undetected. You made it all the way to the Citadel. Would you like to try it again with a real organization?"

"Your organization?"

Berquist held up a rod and flashed a light in Miusov's eyes. "I just took an iris photo of your eyes. I can find your name in the planet's files. It will detail any criminal activity. Perhaps you'd rather join us?"

Berquist grew impatient. "I suggest you make up your mind. I can leave you to the mercy of the authorities."

Miusov realized that if Berquist were alive, he could have been the face at the window at the castle. That meant Berquist had been present for both the murders of Wendnagel and Aaron. Miusov felt a chill as he stared at his friend.

The doctor exclaimed, "I've got to study this! By Thok!"

Berquist put the sound umbrella down. "What is it?"

"These cells. I took a sample." the doctor exclaimed. "They're 'pressed'. There have been experiments on native plants."

"What are you talking about?" Only one human in the known galaxy had cells like that!

"The human cells have been superimposed over Draconian."

Berquist studied the captive. The voice was too old even allowing for the lapse of years, since he'd seen Pasha. What had he done to himself?

The tall renegade reached for Miusov's face, turned it. Long black hair parted to reveal an unusually shaped ear. He stared at Miusov's hands.

"Pasha Miusov," he breathed. "I don't know how you've done this trick. Maybe we should renegotiate this offer."

"Leave me out of your intrigues, Berquist."

A smile lit up the renegade's face. Miusov had played his cards too soon. Now the identity was certain.

His gaze shifted to the shackles. A questioning expression slid across the renegade's face. "Why haven't you opened these? They can't hold a true telepath . . . could it be you have lost your unique abilities?"

Berquist turned his gaze to Miusov and brown eyes met green. //Can you hear this?// Berquist asked.

Miusov guessed what he had done. He felt fear. He asserted, "You know I have a good telepathic block, Berquist."

"I don't think so. I don't think you have the E.S.P. to open these locks.

"I can get out of them any time I want."

"Try."

Miusov exerted a pressure but the normally defective locks refused to open.

Berquist held his hand over one of them. With a powerful burst of telepathy he overrode the ID and the shackles burst open. It was a show of power.

Miusov proposed, "If you are having a disagreement with Council policy, I have a plan for reorganization that—"

"Not now." Berquist interrupted.

"Klemperer is overloaded. If we could shift—"

"I want him for study."

"I'm taking him," Berquist repeated. "If you have any questions, contact the bureau."

To Miusov the renegade asked, "How do I restore your features and get your voice to normal?"

"I don't know," Miusov answered.

"Then it'll have to wear off." He hauled Miusov to his feet. "Where's your uniform?"

Miusov told him.

"By the way," Berquist announced. He felt for the communit and found it. Miusov had wished it on. Berquist wished it off and confiscated it.

Hours later Miusov was held on a ship destined for Dauropa. Berquist jumped customs on the way out.

Chapter 8

SKULLDUGGERY IN THE CASTLE

Moncrief had been gone no more than ten minutes when Lim strode toward his room. She pushed her long dark hair over her shoulders to keep it out of her eyes.

"Moncrief," she called. "May I walk in?"

She came in and the room was empty.

Puzzled, the tall Councilwoman exited and stood in the hallway. A clairvoyant sweep didn't find him. Eccles appeared to her second sight.

She spun around and saw the silver-haired gentleman climbing the stairs on the other side of the interior balcony.

His footfalls spoke of haste. His voice was sotto voce low, "I have to talk with you, Lim."

He glanced over the balcony rail and checked a mirror. Nodding satisfactorily that no one was present, he said swiftly, "Not here, in the workroom. Otherwise they'll hear."

The duo entered the workroom, previously used by Wendnagel. Eccles ordered the computer, "Table, to the right." At the sound, it slid slowly on its tracks.

"What—"

"Wait," Eccles interrupted her.

Lim appeared puzzled as Eccles melodramatically checked outside the door, then shut it. "We don't have much time."

"What—"

It's the diplomats. They're holding us hostage. Or rather, I'm being held. Possibly Hawken, too, although she slipped out once."

"I don't follow you. Why would they want—"

"It's those carrying capsules. There are two on the property. When I won the election, they didn't have a way to retrieve them. They made a deal—"

Door latches moved out of the ceiling, floor and side panel. O'Connors entered followed by Ramón.

"Don't move," said O'Connors warningly. He pulled out a small energyzer. "Especially you, Councilwoman Miusov, don't move. Don't come within an arm's length of this weapon. I am aware of your special abilities with hand-to-hand combat."

Lim said contritely, "You'll attract a Shade with that weapon."

"I'll take the risk."

Lim looked at Ramón. To the chief diplomat she demanded, "Did you kill Wendnagel Tennyson? Or Councilman Berquist?"

"Believe me, Councilwoman, murder is not in my game plan," Ramón answered.

Lim looked puzzled. "More denials."

O'Connors said to Ramón in French, "I don't trust her telepathy. Can't I stun her?"

"Non," Ramón countermanded. "Leave Governor Eccles here. We'll lock the Councilwoman in her room."

"Where's Moncrief?" Lim said insistently.

"We can't and won't answer your questions. Will you come this way?" O'Connors directed. "Maintain your distance."

A minute later Lim found herself back in the room Eccles had given her. A force field had been rigged just inside the door. The moment she entered it lit up, fully operable. The controls were on the outside in the hall. O'Connors slammed the door shut and the latch slid into the floor, ceiling and side. Lim reached for the inside handle that worked the door. Her hand was stopped three inches away by the force field.

She touched all around the doorway and found the force field blocked her hands from touching the source of the field.

She concentrated. Pasha was not on the castle grounds. Neither were Lt. Winters or Moncrief. Her awareness touched the cottage Eccles had given Aaron and Wendnagel. It, too, stood empty. Lim felt echoes and had to stop. She had put everything into trying to revive Pasha and she needed more time to recharge.

The music player was performing Beethoven's Pastoral Symphony. Lim turned it off. The recording collection included an old recording of Pasha playing the violin.

After shutting down the player, she moved in a swift stride to the window. She pondered what to do next. Jumping would not be fatal.. Or, if she could climb to the servants' side, there was another way down. Although the stones were irregular, there was not enough tilt for handholds.

She feared Tennyson's absence meant more skullduggery. With Ramón's denial of guilt, she was even beginning to suspect the reliable Lt. Winters. And where was Moncrief?

All in an instant the force field collapsed. Latches opened on the door. The latter was opened wide. Hawken stood in the doorway.

She had washed her face and stood staring at the dark-haired Councilwoman.

Hesitantly, Hawken began, "Wendnagel said we would come to be friends. I don't know how that can be but I will try. O'Connors thinks he can hide smuggled weapons on my uncle's property. Renate loves me and I don't think he will let O'Connors go through with his plan. Something went wrong with their shipment."

Councilwoman Lim thought fast. "You can't stay here any longer. It's no longer safe. Council Leader Klemperer had a temporary headquarters at Zäringhen. I will take you there. He's a Black-rank Councilman and wields great power."

Hawken looked forlorn. She spoke, "I confess I don't know how to get us out of the castle unobserved. Uncle John watches everything in those mirrors on the wall, downstairs."

"I've been here before. Upstairs, there's a hidden entrance to the servants' side of the building. The servants have long since been replaced by computers, but there's still another way out."

Lim stood outside the room. She shut the door and re-activated the force field. "It'll look like I walked through a wall."

She led Hawken down the hall toward the upper level staircase. Lim's delicate frame made no sound. She scanned ahead clairvoyantly. "The diplomats' rooms are empty," Lim whispered. Hawken ran on ahead.

Then Lim's foot hit something on the floor. She picked it up. It was a cylinder-shape. Her E.S.P. was still too weak to figure out who it resonated to. All she could tell was that many hands had touched it. She turned it on. A light flickered at one end with a hypnotic glow. Quickly she shut it off. She dropped it in her pocket for further thought. "Lt. Winters," she murmured to herself, "when I get back, it's time to unpack your equipment." She knew he would be delighted.

Lim swiftly caught up to Hawken and showed her the hidden panel.

Some time later, Lim and Hawken surreptitiously boarded the anti-grav ferry at the river. Lim secretly approved of Hawken's new attitude.

The ferry was very old. Lim observed that it had once been used in orbit and still had fuel for launch and re-entry. The new employment as shuttle to Zäringhen spaceport didn't require the seals and locks it was built with.

The anti-grav ferry parked at Zaringhen. Hawken ran out with the crowd, separating herself from Lim. The Councilwoman was afraid to call out to her, for fear of attracting attention. She waited for everyone to leave. As she walked to the exit, she spied Hawken waiting at the landing dock, fists on hips.

Councilwoman Lim had a premonition of danger. The two attendants on either side of the door held her from leaving. One held her by the wrist. "Wait a minute, Councilwoman."

Lim shouted to Hawken through the closing door, "Run, Hawken! Go to Klemperer!"

The other slammed the door shut. "You are being kidnaped."

Inside the leader shouted to the computer in the cockpit. Minutes later the ferry shook and took off for space with the bewildered Lim on board.

Chapter 9

THE MOUNTAINS

High in the mountains on the Runick side, was a labyrinth of caves. They had been cut by machine by the early settlers of Dauropa. They were now used by smugglers.

Across the mouth of the entrance was an opaque field that slowed the exchange of molecules. It kept heat in the caves and screened electrical machinery from the Shades. Humans could walk in and out of it undisturbed, however,

Miusov found himself deep inside the caves with Berquist and two other smugglers, apparently guards. A portable heater kept the temperature constant.

Berquist produced two large carrying capsules. He contended, "These are closed by telepathic lock. The cover on this one is broken. I need your help to open the other one. The rest are in the sanctuary of the Blue Witch. Open it." He pointed.

"I can't," Miusov replied.

Berquist looked stubborn, "You've had plenty of time to rest, now. Open it."

"I can't. As you already observed I have no E.S.P. whatsoever."

"That's a strangely long period to stay weak, Pasha. We'll try again, later."

Miusov regarded him. His green eyes studied the renegade.

Miusov ventured, "Do you know anything about the death of Wendnagel Tennyson?"

"Who?" Then he caught the significance of the name. "You mean Wendnagel of the Family is dead?"

The smugglers started whispering among themselves.

Miusov put forth, "That was you on Eccles' property. You peered through the castle window."

"I had two carrying capsules stolen from me. But I didn't know she was dead. No one would dare."

"She was murdered. So was Aaron Tennyson."

"Tennyson was under a curse. He walked into the Citadel on Jalug. Thok took him."

"He was murdered. Stabbed seven times by the look of the body."

"How would you know?"

"I was in the Citadel."

Berquist couldn't believe what he was hearing. "You wouldn't be able to get in."

"I got in with this." He pulled forth the necklace. "Aaron gave this to me. It's some kind of identification symbol."

Berquist was amazed.

Miusov tucked the jewel back under his shirt. "I wonder what will become of mankind," he said thoughtfully.

"You are strangely solemn. You have grown since we last met."

"I communed with Thok," Miusov told him.

"There's nothing in the Citadel. You sound like the natives."

"You are wrong. Aaron had the right of it. Something's alive in there beyond what we can possibly understand."

"This is superstitious nonsense," the renegade raged.

He turned to the two smugglers. "I'm taking him down to Eccles' railroad line. Follow us but don't cross his property line. Come with me, Pasha."

Travel by groundcar ceased at Eccles' property line. Berquist ordered Miusov to walk in front of him. The road was bordered by walls of glacier rock. They filed past the tall boulders and Berquist told him to detour into the forest. His feet crunched on brown pine needles. Berquist pushed him aside.

"This area's been teletapped by a clairvoyant. Walk over here."

"What's your rating now, Berquist?"

"32 amputs."

"The rating is low. I'm sure it's higher than that."

"Spoken by someone with the highest potential rating on this world." Berquist looked amused.

Shortly they picked up small gauge railroad tracks. They paralleled them a distance and finally came to a tall tunnel. The roof arched at 20 feet. Berquist signaled him to go in.

The ambient light quickly dropped. A few paces later the renegade ordered him to stop.

"Wait here," Berquist said.

Miusov looked baffled. He turned to the dim figure that was Berquist.

Suddenly, an infra-red light flashed on in the tunnel. Miusov yelled, "What is that?"

Across the top of the tunnel he saw the outline of a backbone. Eight pair of insect-like arms were dug into the sides of the tunnel.

Miusov got over his fright and peered curiously at the animal. Twenty feet to the ceiling meant the creature was taller than a house.

The infra-red lights, arranged at the base of the tunnel, clicked off. The outline of the animal vanished.

Berquist explained, "That's a little surprise Governor Eccles has for his guests. It can only be seen under infra-red light. That light's on a 3-minute timer. It can also be triggered by our entrance. That's a beast from the Planet of 100 Moons."

"Multi-Luna," Miusov identified.

"You've heard of them?"

"Our security officer talked about them. How does John hold it here?"

"Listen."

Miusov did. "I hear a hum."

"That's a sleep trancer. It's holding the creature asleep. If you 'listen' with your E.S.P., you can hear the beast's awareness. It's relatively easy—"

Miusov was amazed at his ingenuity. He tried it, then shook his head. "I hear nothing."

"I don't understand."

"There was an accident."

"Your mind is using the word deliberately. Why don't you start at the beginning. Why are you on Dauropa at all?"

Miusov told him.

Berquist uttered, "So they got a time slide to work."

"I don't remember what I saw."

Sabotage with a linkup. Berquist wanted to cradle Miusov in his arms but the youth was too old. Infra-red light outlined the youth's face. The light had come back for another minute.

Then Berquist admitted, "I have an ulterior reason for bringing you here. We can talk privately here. I have to warn you not to let the smugglers know I am a Councilman. I will be strung up on the nearest tree, and hung. Do you hear me?" He grabbed Miusov by the arm.

The half-Draconian was relieved. It was like the old Berquist to have four or five reasons for doing something. Berquist was a complicated person. Perhaps the rumors he'd gone renegade were not true.

The half-Draconian said, "You were posted here after Polaris VI."

"That's correct. My back-up never showed up on Polaris and I got marooned there. Murder is legal on Polaris. I had to file an intent-to-murder and escape a few taken out on me."

"Klemperer should have had a better back-up."

"It wasn't his fault."

"What did you do?"

"I got out of it—no thanks to Klemperer's office. Then I was assigned here to infiltrate the smugglers."

"I thought Aaron Tennyson had destroyed them all."

"He did. There was little activity for a long time. I worked my way up fast. I am now near the top of this branch of the operations and very vulnerable. Klemperer has refused to recall me."

"But you could be stuck, and arrested one night as the leader of the smugglers."

"I wish you could remember who stole my ID."

"He could be dead from the explosion."

"He could have told someone. Anyway, my original cover was of a trader from Earth with trade ties to Jalug. I have to go there periodically to renew that cover. Most illicit shipments are small until one came through for the diplomats from Eta."

"Eta?"

"What? Oh, Eta Cassiopiae."

"What?"

"Most of the capsules are in the Blue Witch sanctuary. I need a strong telepath to open them but I think I can get them open without you."

"What's in them?"

"I don't know. Someone in administration closed his eyes to the shipment."

"There's a force field on the door."

"I can get around it."

That last was too smug to suit Miusov. "You're becoming a smuggler. As a Black-rank Councilman, I'll issue recall orders."

Berquist started to reply, then did a double-take. "When's your birth date, Pasha?"

Miusov told him.

"I thought so. You're three weeks short of being confirmed in that rank."

"Go to the castle. My mother, Lim, will issue that order."

Berquist's eyes glazed over. He did a clairvoyant scan. "She's not in the castle."

"She can 'hear' you when you do that."

"She thinks I'm dead. It will only puzzle her." Berquist explained.

"What can you do now?"

"I'm taking you back to the mountains. I told my men—and women—that you were a telepath and could open the capsules. I can't go back without you." He paused to scan. "Besides, the two men that I posted outside are getting restless. I don't want them to enter the castle grounds. To be arrested would be an embarrassment."

"You haven't violated the code have you?"

"No. No more talk on this subject. I have to get back and I have to get rough."

Berquist pulled Miusov out of the tunnel. The infra-red light flashed its trick.

He hauled Miusov back to the groundcar. Berquist took tighter hold on his shirt. Miusov decided to escape.

Miusov relaxed his resistance and fell forward. Berquist fell on his back. The half-human scrambled for Berquist's weapon.

In a lightning move Berquist was on cat feet. He kicked the weapon out of Miusov's hand. In an instant the two smugglers appeared and covered him with stun guns.

Berquist was angry. He said pointedly, "Pasha Miusov, look at those guns well. They are not stun guns. They have been modified to kill."

Back at the cave, two women smugglers brought Berquist a second carrying capsule. The cover was broken and gave at repeated tugs. From the inside of the container Berquist removed a flat object with a handle.

Miusov watched with cat eyes. He was unhappy. Berquist had found something that would get him inside Wendnagel's sanctuary.

Chapter 10

THE OUTSIDER

Miusov could hear a smuggler calling for a meeting through the cave wall. He sat alone with the same two guards, and pondered the mystery that had unfolded.

Someone had sabotaged his equipment. Someone had killed Wendnagel. Thok had demanded he find the killer of Aaron.

Berquist had been in the right places. But his friend had no motivation. He did not even seem to know about Wendnagel's death. His outrage seemed genuine.

One by one Miusov went down his mental list of those in the castle.

Moncrief had been posted on Dauropa. Although he was sure since the crash that the Council agent was up to something, he could not see Moncrief trying to destroy the cat brain.

The diplomats seemed connected with the smuggled shipment. It was already in Wendnagel's possession. Killing her would not get the capsules back. In fact the death made no sense at all from their point of view.

That left Eccles, who Pasha had known for a long time. Although the Governor was hiding something, the half-human couldn't see him involving himself in the murders of Wendnagel nor Aaron. For that matter,

Eccles would know that sabotaging the cat brain could kill him. He could not see his friend John doing that to him.

Hawken might have hidden motives. Winters had cleared her for contact with the Councilmen and the security officer was thorough. Besides she was devoted to Wendnagel. That let her out.

He was left with Winters as a suspect. He had the opportunity to go after all three. His position gave him access to his equipment. The former first-in scout had been handpicked by the Captain of the DISCOVERY, though.

Miusov was left with a puzzle. He had dismissed Aargau.

One of the guards spoke up. "Is it true Wendnagel of the Family is dead?"

"It's true."

"She saw in the water for my uncle. And she warned us of a Shade at our settlement. We are very grateful to her. How did this happen?"

"She was pushed off a bridge."

"You must be mistaken. No one would do anything to her." He turned to his companion. "We'll eventually find out."

"If I hear this again, I'm going to start doubting that it happened, too." Miusov muttered.

"Let's get some light in here," said the first smuggler, squinting. "This one can see in twilight, but we can't."

He reached for the switch on the wall. Without warning he fell forward. The other jumped to his feet as his companion collapsed on the floor. Seconds later the other one fell to the floor.

Miusov pulled his hands out of his pockets and slid along the wall, arms in a fighting stance palms open.

"Winters!" he identified as the security officer walked in the doorway, stun gun in hand. "Steve, how did you find me?"

"I traced you from Jalug." Winters surveyed the two stunned smugglers. He relieved one of his energyzer.

"Come on, Pasha. I don't know where everyone went, but—"

"They're at a meeting."

"Shhh."

Miusov whispered, "The least you could have done was identify me to the acolytes."

"What are you talking about?"

"Never mind."

"Be quiet."

They passed three more stunned smugglers in the hallway.

Winters led him to a side entrance, not the one Miusov came in. It, too, had an opaque field. Miusov felt tingles as he climbed through it.

Winters warned him, "We'll have to climb down. There's no roadway at this entrance. Anyway stealing a groundcar would rouse the whole hive." He picked up coils of rope and put them across his shoulder. The ground in shadow was white with snow.

Winters produced two pairs of short skis, carved by energyzer from wood. "These were cut by spec from my techcorder. I learned how to do this on Sunex. See if they fit. Can you ski?"

"Somewhat."

The skis fit well to his boots. Winters had also cut poles. The pair used them to glide down a path in the trees. They came out of it to a clearing and Winters turned, kicking up snow as he stopped. There was an awesome view of the valley between Demner and the next peak. The snowline stopped about halfway down the mountain. Tree tops looked small at the base of the mountain.

Miusov looked down and then at Winters. "I can't do this. I'm afraid of heights."

"When did you find this out!" Winters exploded.

"Just now." Miusov added, "Since the omnicraft crash."

Then Winters remembered Miusov had refused to fly in a hang glider. "Maybe the glider men had the right idea when they talked about crash shock."

"I'll get down," Miusov determinedly set his jaw.

"Not that way, you won't. You have to go straight down before you execute your first turn."

Miusov was game but his legs wouldn't stop trembling. The half-human asked, "How did you get up here? Isn't there a road?"

"It's on the other side of the mountain. I flew up by motorized hang glider, but I crashed the plane. Look here—" he pondered how to get

Miusov over his phobia. He wanted to get beneath the Councilman's reserve, but not this way. Winters pointed, "There's ice on this slope."

"I see it."

"To get down you have to take out your aggressions on the slope. Vent your anger on it. Parallel ski on the snow but turn your edges in on the ice. You may slide a little, but keep pouring your anger and aggressions out at it. Feel that you'd like to rip the slope apart."

That was Winters' normal speech to landing parties, but with Miusov's special problem, Winters added some insults to his worthiness to be a Councilman.

"That's enough, Winters," Miusov cautioned. He thought Steve would eventually learn not to talk this way to a Councilman.

Winters pressed on even to a veiled suggestion Miusov had faked his own injury and murdered Wendnagel.

Then, he skied down the mountain, executing elegant turns, the back of the skis throwing snow in the air as he braked.

Miusov felt heat beneath his thermo jacket and poled off toward the slope that would take him straight down. Winters kept up the tirade until he was out of earshot.

Miusove initiated a turn, swinging the back of a ski wide, then pushing them parallel as he rounded the turn. He would never forget Winters' manner. The Councilman was afraid to look anywhere except the nearest snow. He almost lost his balance when the skis hit a mogul, a snow hill.

Gradually the snow bed got thinner. Further down he saw Winters with his skis off. Miusov kicked off his own skis and ran toward him. It had the spontaneity of a hockey game fight. One moment they were looking at each other and the next moment they were shouting and throwing snow.

Miusov shouted, "How dare you accuse me of sabotaging my own equipment."

"Pasha, I—"

"Did you kill Wendnagel?"

"Pasha—"

"You were there when Aaron died!"

"Pasha, look up. Look how far you've skied."

"What?" He surveyed the slope above, squinting at the brightness. An inner light awakened. "It's back! My E.S.P. is back."

Miusov put down the ice ball.

Winters stuffed snow down Pasha's shirt and they laughed.

Miusov suddenly saw a clairvoyant picture. "There are hang gliders further down the mountain." He was looking pensive.

"I'm an Outsider again. Must you keep up this wall of reserve. With your E.S.P. even the expression on your face is different. I serve on a sister service. We should be friends."

"It's not a matter of friendship. It's the code. I have to keep a barrier so I'm not constantly hearing your thoughts. Of course, sometimes they leak."

"Can you hear them now?"

"No. Only the clairvoyance has come on. I'm sure the rest will come."

"The way you saw the hang gliders—is your E.S.P. always this erratic?"

"No, only an untrained person is erratic. You can say I'm at the level of the untrained. It's not all back yet."

"What about your memory?"

"Still blocked. But let me bring you up to date." He talked about Tennyson and then about Berquist.

Winters emphasized, "If he's acting under cover, he'll make sure you escape. We may have more time."

"I think he's near the edge."

"I hope not. There are too many people conveniently on hand for a murder."

"I want to know who sabotaged my equipment. I can't—"

"And I want those hang gliders. If you don't mind, we have some climbing to do."

Winters commented, "By the way, Mr. Moncrief said I should keep an eye on you. Nothing I've seen of you justifies his story that you created a crisis on your last assignment."

"I did create one, under orders. That story has been repeated wrong and I'm not sure what Moncrief has to gain by it. He has been on Dauropa for two years."

"Do you think he killed Wendnagel?"

"I can't see why anyone would. And as a Councilman, he certainly wouldn't enter my equipment room."

"But he could do the most damage."

"He's up to something. He didn't expect the omnicraft to crash and tried to signal someone." The Councilman explained about the open harness.

"That doesn't prove anything."

"For a Council member, his behavior is baffling. We get to know each other well in the Council and opening a shock harness is not like Bob Moncrief."

Miusov and Winters started though the trees along a path that got narrower and narrower.

It led them to a clearing. Beyond it was a drop of one hundred fifty feet.

Winters stood looking at it. He said, "I'd hate to do this to your fear of heights, but the only way down is to rappel."

"I think I'm over that . . . thanks to you."

"I wouldn't count on it. An omnicraft crash phobia is not something to get over easily."

Miusov paused several times to "look" with his sixth sense, but he didn't report anything. Winters started to get used to the intenseness of the Councilman.

Winters took the rope from his shoulder and cut a length off of it. Winters fastened it into a harness around the youth's hips. "This is high-gauge rated rope. It won't break."

"That gives me an idea." Miusov asked Winters to rig a safety rope around his waist and then put the rope in a double loop around a tree. He tugged hard against the rope. "It is one thing to say it, and another to have an emotional confidence in the rope." He leaned against the rope and put his weight on it. The rope held.

The Security Officer looped a second rope through the makeshift harness and put one side in Miusov's hand. The rest he dropped over the cliff. "You first," he told Pasha.

"What will you use as a safety rope for *your* descent?"

"Don't worry about me," said the former explorer of worlds.

Miusov stood at the edge, facing the tree, his back to the drop. He didn't look down. He let the rope out slowly through the harness at his hips.

"Ready to rappel."

"Ready," Winters grunted. "Don't try anything fancy. Don't try to stand up and down; you'll fall."

"Rappelling."

Miusov leaned out over the cliff. There was one bad moment where he thought he'd fall over backwards. He let out more line and took a step. He was perpendicular to the wall. As he let out the rope, his hand was shaking, and he descended like a fly.

Winters had told him not to jump. It was a faster way down but the harness could not take it.

Miusov had a memory flashback of the omnicraft crash. He could see the tree tops with his clairvoyance, then, and now. He started to sweat. He couldn't reach the thermostat on his thermo jacket to turn it down. Instead he paid out more line and walked downward in jerks.

All at once he was at the bottom. He righted himself and fell two feet to the path below.

"Rappelling stop," he called up to Winters and removed the rope harness and the safety line from his waist.

Winters cut another length as a harness of his own. He wrapped the rope around a tree, tied it, then fed the other end behind his back and through the rope harness. He would be doing this without a safety line.

Walking over the side of the cliff was the worst moment. Winters sighted Miusov at the base and waved for him to provide room. Then he jumped, paying out rope quickly. It did not work well. Winters stopped, paid the rope out more slowly, and walked down the side of the rock face.

A few short minutes later he was down. Miusov and Winters shook hands.

As Winters pulled off the harness he inquired, "Where are the hang gliders?"

"Over this way. They're under some kind of cover."

Miusov found them. A brown tarpaulin covered the bound poles and multi-colored fabric.

Winters assembled the first one. "Can you fly one of these?" he wanted to know.

"I've had lessons."

Winters expressed his surprise. "Have you ever flown as high as this one is going to take you?"

"No."

Winters gave some instructions. Miusov had the "far away" look he had when studying something clairvoyantly.

Winters piped up, "Hey! Don't do that when you're flying. You have to watch where you are going."

"I'll be careful. If you can make for Zäringhen, Council Leader Klemperer has a temporary headquarters."

"What about the castle?"

"I thought a smuggler already took an energyzer shot at you there."

"If I am right, these hang gliders belong to the smugglers."

"Be careful that John Eccles doesn't take a shot at you."

"I will. Are you ready?"

Miusov lowered the setting on his jacket. "Ready."

The Councilman leaped off the cliff and sailed in a graceful circle.

Winters started one hundred paces from the edge. He tightened his hold on the harness bar and ran forward. At step ninety-nine the wind caught the wing and lifted it upwards. He was soon high enough to fly around the mountain, to the Demner side.

He looked down. Miusov was dumping air from the wing and heading down in a spiral for the Runick Valley on the Runick side of the mountain.

Miusov watched Winters pass overhead. The youth didn't have the skill to catch the updraft. A last clairvoyant scan on the ground told him neither Lim nor Moncrief were inside the castle. He wasn't steady enough to check the castle grounds yet.

The Councilman used his eyes to study the plateau below. He was searching for signs of smugglers and he found it: an omnicraft.

Miusov landed at a run and unfastened the harness of the hang glider quickly. He hid the poles over the branches of a tree and crept forward toward the craft. The door was open and voices drifted out. One was recognizably Moncrief. The other had to be a smuggler. He stood very still, so still he could hear his own breathing.

Chapter 11

MONCRIEF

The blue-eyed smuggler stood alone with Moncrief in the red aft room of the omnicraft. The airlock was open.

The smuggler professed, "We haven't found the two capsules yet. But we found the man who planted the bomb. He's part of a rival group of smugglers. They don't want to deal with Eta. Politics." He supplied a name.

"I thought he was arrested when Tennyson broke the back of their smuggling ring."

"He was one of the few who wasn't."

"This is the last time I want to ship anything for Eta."

"It's relatively close to our star, HR1182, and Sigma Draconis. It's easy to smuggle stuff to Draconis."

"I'll find those other capsules."

The smuggler was relieved and sat down. "How?"

Moncrief peered out the door at the beautiful autumn scenery. "Easy. With my E.S.P.," he said glibly.

The smuggler stiffened and rose to his feet. From the folds of his jacket he produced a knife. "Turn around Moncrief."

The Councilman did and the smile disappeared from his face. "What's this?"

The smuggler held up his knife. "I'm from Eta Cassiopiae. We rid thought controllers from Eta. It was once legal to kill telepaths."

He lunged forward. Moncrief ducked, then grabbed the knife arm, and the wrist. They wrestled and Moncrief squeezed. The knife fell from the smuggler's hand.

Moncrief kicked it toward the doorway.

The smuggler grinned. "That will do you no good." He put a hand around Moncrief's neck. The Councilman started choking.

"I lied," he gasped. "Reinhold, I lied. I don't—gasp—have E.S.P. I don't have any at all. I have a natural block of point nine. I lied. No telepath can hear me! I'll never make Black color rank because of it."

"I don't believe you." The smuggler did not relax his grip. Moncrief's struggles got weaker.

Suddenly there was a blur of motion outside the doorway. A figure waded out of the shadows. In a fluid motion Miusov picked up the knife and threw it at the smuggler.

The knife caught the folds of the smuggler's shirt jacket then buried itself in the wall. The smuggler was pinned.

All in a moment Reinhold let go of Moncrief and reached for the knife. He pulled at it, got it out.

Miusov produced a modified stun gun and fired it at a very low setting at the smuggler. He fell down like an empty bag.

The telepathic Councilman turned toward Moncrief.

"I will try to get you out of this, Mr. Moncrief, but your days with the Special Forces Council are over."

Miusov did some rapid thinking. He played over his conversation with Berquist in his mind. Berquist had said the last smuggled shipment was approved by an administrator.

Miusov waved the stun gun. "You've been posted here for two years. Did you approve the smuggled shipment that we thought cost Berquist his life?"

Moncrief beheld Miusov the child E.S.P. prodigy for a while before answering, "Yes."

"Why?"

"The embassy from Eta Cassiopiae offered to lobby for me for higher rank. I want to change the way the Council is structured."

"So do I but not this way."

"After that stunt you pulled on your last assignment, I'm surprised you want to work with the Council at all."

"What I did was under orders."

"Klemperer's office circulated newspaper accounts. They were embarrassing."

"I believe you didn't get the full story. Something's wrong at Council Leader Klemperer's end. I think it's this new reorganization. I'm going to push for a lot of changes when I get my color rank. I could have helped you if you had approached me as a friend."

"You and Councilman Lim were at Earth, the center of activity. This out-of-the-way post—"

"Any post is important." Miusov couldn't believe what he was hearing. Thok's *"find out who did this."* echoed in his mind.

"Did you kill Wendnagel and Aaron Tennyson?"

"No."

"Don't lie to me. I'll find out how good that block of point nine is."

"You don't have any E.S.P.!"

"It's come back. Do I owe this bad experience to you?"

"No . . . remember the code!"

"I'll get a warrant. Did you do all this? Tell me."

"No, Patrick. I'm a Councilman."

"Then who did?" Miusov pushed.

"I don't know."

The dark-haired Councilman made a decision. "Something's wrong at the temporary headquarters and I'm going there. I'm taking this omnicraft."

"Did your memory of the time slide also come back? What happened to Berquist?"

"No. He isn't—" Miusov stopped. Berquist had pleaded with him not to reveal to the smugglers that he was a Councilman. Moncrief was a leak to the smugglers. "Look, I don't have rank so I can't hold you and I can't advise you. I'm setting you off this ship with this smuggler. Make up your mind what you want to tell Council Leader Klemperer to his face. I'm taking this omnicraft there."

Moncrief turned white. Klemperer was known to be a frightful disciplinarian. Miusov didn't envy him. He remembered Klemperer's reaction to his own shortcomings when he was younger. Thankfully Michael Westerman had taken over his learning and he still reported to Westerman on a dotted line basis.

Miusov held up the weapon. "Okay. Get off. And take him with you."

"What'll I do then? He'll kill me."

Miusov tossed him the stun gun. "Use a low setting. A high one will kill."

Could he trust a Councilman? Miusov held his breath. Lim and he had trusted Moncrief to get them to Governor Eccles' castle. Instead he had betrayed them to the smugglers. Was he now to be murdered, too?

With a sigh Moncrief pocketed the gun.

Miusov breathed relief. "I'd like to hear the rest of this story but I have more pressing business." He wanted Klemperer to recall Berquist before he wound up dead. Also the way he had slandered Miusov made him wonder what else was wrong with that office.

"What's in the capsules?" Miusov interrogated Moncrief.

"I don't know."

"That's the first time you lied to me."

"Some kind of weapon."

"What kind?"

"I'm not certain. Something new."

"Well then, let's try this," Miusov wanted to know. "Why did you open your shock harness on the omnicraft during the emergency landing. Who were you trying to signal?"

"We had two carrying canisters on Eccles' property. If you flew over the area, you'd see our men looking for them."

"Do you realize how dangerous it was to open your harness at a time like that? You could have gotten yourself killed. Everything we do revolves around safety. Only Lt. Steve Winters' handling of the landing got us down in one piece."

"Don't quote me regs. I knew the clearing and was sure he could get us down."

"So I was right. You could have seen something by hang glider and not told us. I short circuited your plan by saying your wrist was broken."

The youth asked, "One last question. Where's my mother, Lim?"

"At the castle."

"She's not."

"How do you know? She was when I left."

"I did a clairvoyant scan. That's how I found you, although it took me a while."

"It's really back?"

"Yes, it is."

"Can you really break a point nine shield?"

Miusov backed down. "I might hurt you. But anyone who lives with telepaths, especially Councilmen, frequently develop a few amputs of his own. Think about it. Now get off this ship."

"I'm coming with you."

"I can't have you and this smuggler jump me while I'm piloting."

"I'll watch him."

Miusov reluctantly assented to his request, and closed the airlock. Then he made his way forward to the piloting station. He strapped in and looked for the knobs marked, "Superconductors." They were next to the ion drive.

Chapter 12

THE RANSOM

The inner balcony of Eccles' castle gave Ramón command view of the main living room. He turned from the view to the lithe Councilwoman's quarters. He posed within an arm's length of the door.

He was speaking through the door, "Lim, I believe I have diplomatic immunity for what I have done. However, I don't want to extend this to a murder or a kidnapping. I'm letting you out. Please stand away from the door."

O'Connors had the unlikely idea that she would escape and had posted an alternative plan. Fortunately, Ramón found the force field in place. He put a confident hand on the heat sensitive panel and it shut off.

Several cats were attracted by the activity. The diplomat vowed to lock them up. Snowpaws purred, sensed Lim was not present, and padded away, looking for more interesting humans.

The force field light winked out and stayed out. The diplomat had respect for the Councilwoman. She had come from Earth on a difficult assignment. The explosion had ruined all his plans. Aaron's arrival, requesting Eccles to call the Special Forces Council, had ruined his attenpt to retrieve the two missing capsules.

Ramón scanned Eccles' complicated door handle then found the right motion. Latches retreated from the floor, ceiling and side. The door opened inward.

The music player had been shut down and an unnatural silence hung in the room.

"Councilman?" Lim was gone. He walked to the window. "Mon Dieu!" he muttered. He was confounded. How had she gotten out?

II

"This is Zäringhen spaceport tower. You have made an unauthorized lift off without a flight plan. Please respond to our messages. We have given you emergency clearance. File an orbit plan," repeated the tower.

The space ferry lifted on anti-gravs. At 10,000 feet, ion drive switched on.

Lim sat in the cockpit next to the two smugglers. One was short and stocky. The other was tall and thin, and spoke with a more refined word choice. The latter held Lim's ID and communit.

The smuggler finally answered the radio requests. "Zäringhen, this is the space ferry. We have hijacked the ferry and are holding a hostage. We have kidnaped Special Forces Council member Lim Miusov," he read the name off the card. "We are asking for a hundred thousand credits and clear passage. I'd like to speak directly to the Special Forces Council."

He held the communit. At the bottom was a rectangular box that served as a computer. The hijacker couldn't figure out how to turn on the computer.

His partner read lights off the radar board. "They must've notified someone. Those are interceptors being launched."

The more cultured smuggler switched on the radio. "Zäringhen tower, get rid of those missiles. We have a hostage."

A second voice with an accent from Earth spoke. "This is the Special Forces Council temporary headquarters spokesman. Let me speak to Councilwoman Lim Miusov."

The smuggler put down the pocket computer, put aside his puzzlement over it, and held up a modified stun gun. He motioned Lim to speak.

Lim assured the Council spokesman, "This is Councilwoman Lim Miusov. I am being held by two hijackers. I am uninjured."

"We'll divert the missiles," the stentorian radio voice said in return.

After a long pause lights went out on the radar board.

The short, stocky man reassured his partner, "They've grounded them."

Lim "heard" a telepathic recognition signal and "saw" an image of a Green-rank Councilman. //Lim, are you all right? We've got your position.// The thoughts popped in with echoes. She was still in an E.S.P. low.

She answered, //So far. They are armed with stun guns.//

//Watch out// came the reply. //They might be modified to kill. Can you transmit pictures of their faces? Can you echo their speech into telepathy?//

While she was memorizing their features, the next telepathy from the Green Councilman arrived out of time phase. A message, yet to be sent for another ten minutes, filled her awareness. //You're heading for a dead man's zone in the asteroids. There will be no navigational signal.//

Lim wondered what that meant. "Why are we heading for an asteroid path?"

Both hijackers looked startled. "I heard they can read the future," the short one said.

"No one can do that. It was a lucky guess."

The Councilwoman remembered from her briefing that Dauropa had an asteroid belt, probably a former moon, that would give any orbiting navigator pause. Signal beacons from key chunks were used to navigate well-known flight paths. The only way to interpret that out-of-time telepathy message would be to assume there was a smuggler's channel that was out of navigation range of Zäringhen tower's instruments.

The tall hijacker reopened the radio channel. "Special Forces Council, will you tell Zäringhen tower to signal for safe passage in the asteroid belt. We want a flight path for a wider orbit."

"This is Zäringhen tower. You're not space-worthy."

"Let us worry about that," the hijacker said smugly.

Perturbed to learn the ship wasn't safe, Lim thought she knew what they had in mind. There had to be a ship hiding in the asteroid belt on the smuggler's lane.

Lights on the board indicated computer signals from the asteroids.

The tall one told his partner, "Steer this course. We'll lose their signal but they'll also lose ours. I know how to navigate this path."

Lim spoke outloud. "A ship. You're going to rendez-vous with a starship."

"Yes, they'll be taking you to Polaris VI."

The Green Councilman again spoke out of time phase. //Lim. I spent ten minutes checking. Polaris VI is a nefarious planet. I'll be back in five minutes.//

The space ferry followed the communications beacon from one of the asteroids. Then, instead of continuing, the ship swung around to a new course behind the same asteroid, blocking the ship's signals to Dauropa.

The last message from Zäringhen tower was, "They've gone off our monitors. Damn. A smuggler's route. We lost them."

Inside the cockpit, Lim and the hijackers heard a loud bang followed by crumpling metal. "The hull's ruptured!" Lim warned.

The hijackers heard air escaping.

Lim stood up and pushed a button on her belt. An emergency environmental field and personna field were activated. An envelope of air surrounded her.

Responding to the sudden motion, the tall hijacker reached up with the gun. He stood up. "Council'man, stay where—ack." Lim grappled with him, then put a foot behind him, reached for the gun arm and pulled, throwing the hijacker off his feet. The other stood gasping and flexing hands that were getting cold.

The tall one was on his back in Lim's pocket of air. She had her foot on the arm holding the stun gun.

She told him, "Your friend will die if you don't relinquish the gun. I'm the only one with air. That's the integrity of that hull that blew. I'm wearing a personna belt."

She scooped the gun out of his hand and motioned for the stocky one to sit in a chair. She stood behind it, putting both of them in the protective field. She relieved him of his weapon. She motioned for his tall, more educated friend to face the instrument panel, palms down.

The field wasn't designed for three and she turned the settings up to maximum.

Lim reached for the navigation board and ordered the computer to automatic emergency orbit and re-entry. She also activated the computer simulator and re-entry simulations.

"Open the radio to Zäringhen tower and leave it there. If you try anything, I'll step back and you'll asphyxiate." The stocky one found the correct switch.

Lim announced on the radio, "This is Special Forces Councilwoman Lim Miusov. I've regained control of the ship. We should be registering on your instruments. We're out of the smugglers' corridor. Sending computer simulations for orbit and landing. It's coming at speed 50 to 1. Pick one simulation and get us down. The integrity of the ship is broken."

The words were monitored by the Special Forces Council temporary headquarters.

//Congratulations, Lim.// The telepathic voice was back in time phase. Then, the voice faded out. The telepath had run out of amputs.

Lim hefted a stun gun and told the hijackers, "Now we shall have some answers. To whom do you report?"

"Raymond Berquist," both replied.

"He's dead."

"He's alive," said the tall one.

"He was killed in an explosion on the mountainside. I have his ID."

"He escaped."

"He ordered this kidnaping?"

"No. A connection to the smugglers is responsible."

"Start slowly. I want to hear the whole tale."

Just then, the space ferry responded to computer control and swung into an emergency re-entry orbit to Zäringhen spaceport.

Chapter 13

WENDNAGEL'S SANCTUARY

Edir Tiket, a human dressed in a native Jalogan colored robe, sat behind a table. He was the leader of the smugglers in the caves between Demner and Runick. Unexpectedly, the smuggler's caves erupted with noise and shouts. He ran to the main cavern, calling "Yad!" His brother Yad Tiket, also dressed in colorful Jalogan robe, this one blue, darted to his side.

"Yad," Edir directed. "Prepare to keep order."

Edir waded into the crowd of smugglers. In the knot in the middle, smugglers had surrounded Berquist. "All right, what's going on? Somebody speak up!"

Silence met his entrance.

Yad pulled two men away from Berquist. A smuggler at the center explained, "The captive has escaped."

"The one who can open the capsules!" several angry voices cried in unison.

"He had help," said the first.

Edir shook his head. "Berquist didn't help him."

He walked over to the tall renegade. "Thank you, Ed," Berquist expressed his relief.

"Can we get those capsules out of Wendnagel's sanctuary?"

Berquist held up the flat weapon with a handle. He answered, "I have found a way."

Several angry voices spoke at once. "What about opening the capsules?" They were on the verge of a riot.

"Order!" yelled Yad.

Berquist held up the tool. "I can get into the sanctuary and I can get the capsules out. They'll be back in our possession!"

Berquist turned to Edir the leader. "I have some telepathy. I can override the ID's on the capsules and open the telepathic locks. Our rivals have Eta Cassiopians in their midst. They must never learn this."

"We'll protect your back."

People were shouting at once. In the excitement of retrieving the canisters, Miusov's escape was forgotten. Selling the carrying canisters meant money. Keeping them meant power. Opening them and placing the contents in new containers would lose the identity of the original owner and designated destination, throwing the police off their trail.

One smuggler yelled slogans and waved his arms in the air. One of the smugglers who had surrounded Berquist smiled from ear to ear.

"Forget the boy," Berquist told Edir. "I picked him up on Jalug before I knew he could open the capsules. We can do just as well on our own."

"Where does this device come from?"

"The carrying capsule with the broken cover."

"How does it work?"

"It compresses matter. I'll literally slide under the force field."

"The wonders of modern science."

"Now, Berquist!" exclaimed the noisy smuggler who had been waving his arms. "Now, now!"

Berquist hesitated, the memory of the ill-fated trip clear in his mind. There had been a traitor, who had fired a stun gun at him. Although the smuggler had died in the explosion, Berquist was still worried about his identity being secret.

"Now, Berquist," Edir echoed. "Take twenty people and go to the sanctuary that holds the capsules."

"I don't need that many."

"There are many capsules." Edir made a Jalogan motion with his arms that meant his word was final.

Early evening heralded sunset. Berquist carried a personal electric torch, as did several of his followers.

They crept up to the sanctuary. There were no guards on it. Berquist was sure Lim would have removed the canisters if she could. Yet there they were inside the doorway.

Several men walked over the cedar bridge to take up the rear. One by one, they reached the other side and the path that led to the hidden sanctuary.

Berquist looked in the stone-lined pool with one of his followers.

"She can see the future in the pool, and images far away. I won't touch it," the smuggler told him. "Maybe they don't hear of such things on Earth where you're from."

No wind disturbed the Japanese prayer bells on the tree.

The only movement not caused by the smuggling party was a burst of static across the door—the force field.

Berquist motioned everyone back. He held up the tool, grasped the handle and faced the door and force field. He squeezed the handle.

Seconds later Berquist stood inside the building facing the other direction, exactly the same distance from the force field. He was inside! His pulse quickened as he adjusted the device to a wider field so he could get the carrying canisters out.

No alarm rang out as the tall Councilman squeezed the handle. Exactly two seconds later he appeared outside the door, the carrying canisters stacked up behind him.

One smuggler went wild. His shouts were stifled by two companions.

With discipline and efficiency, Berquist had the crew pick up the canisters. The air of celebration was catching and he scooped up a canister.

There was a long walk to the ground cars. The crew marched single file over the cedar bridge. The stream reflected a trail of lights from the electric torches.

Halfway back, Berquist stopped. The previous illicit shipment for the diplomats had contained perfumes from Jalug and quantities of jewels. This shipment should contain weapons.

134

The appearance of the flat tool in the capsule with the broken cover was a bad sign.

He wanted to see what else was being shipped. The renegade put down his carrying capsule.

Signaling the men and one woman to keep walking with their cargo, he put his hand on the cover. Closing his eyes, he concentrated.

The lock appeared as a mental image in his mind. //Open.// he commanded.

His powerful E.S.P. overrode the telepathically-sensitive lock.

The cover twisted off in his hand.

It was dark out and Berquist had trouble seeing with the electric torch. He reached in. Empty! In the bottom were three grains of sand.

The torch flickered and went out. "By the Shades!" he gave an oath. "Hand me another torch," he ordered a smuggler.

Berquist tossed the old torch to the ground. He caught the new one that the smuggler threw, and turned it on. He held it over the almost empty capsule interior. Shortly, it began flickering and it, too, went out.

"What the—" Berquist cursed, then thoughtfully picked up the capsule cover. It was strangely quiet and it took several minutes for Berquist to realize what was missing. Eccles' sleep trancer. Its steady hum carried for miles. He should be hearing it. Instead, things were deathly silent.

A strange look of recognition crossed Berquist's face. He examined the cover. Perhaps part of the mechanism was in the cover, in addition to the grains of sand. It had turned on when he opened the cover. The thing was designed like the Shades and dampened electrical power. Some kind of field was operating, or non-field, and it was expanding.

The tall renegade screwed the cover back on and ordered telepathically, //Close! Lock!//

The cover came off in his hand. He didn't have the telepathic strength to close it! If he couldn't, it wouldn't shut off.

Pinpoints of lights from the village of Demner started to flicker.

Berquist was frightened. //Close. Lock!// he tried a second time. It didn't work.

A line of blue lights was all the light on the mountainside. They were atomically powered, not electric. The Lanterns of Demner.

Berquist was near panic. Between breaths he clairvoyantly scanned for a Councilman. The first two he touched had weak ability and upon "seeing" his image insisted he was dead. The last person he found was Lim.

Her feminine voice echoed, //Berquist, thank God you're alive.//

//Councilman Pasha Miusov strongly recommends you issue recall order.//

//Isn't that Klemperer's area?//

//Do it, please.//

//Okay. This is Black-rank Councilwoman Lim Miusov ordering you recalled from your assignment.//

//As a fellow Black-rank Councilman, I need your aid immediately. Where are you?//

//At Zäringhen. Describe the problem.//

//I need your presence to close a telepathically-keyed cover.// Berquist hoped that her presence wouldn't mean his own death from the smugglers.

//Query. Is Aaron Tennyson with you?//

//He's dead on Jalug.//

//What?//

//Don't waste amputs. Just get here. Notify the Police Patrol. Eccles' zoo is loose. The sleep trancer is off. Here's a picture of where I am. Watch out for smugglers.//

The lights of the village of Demner went off. Further away, the lights of New Essex began to flicker.

Chapter 14

LANTERNS OVER DEMNER

Councilman Klemperer sat at his desk in a building near the Zäringhen spaceport. Information from all over the Solar Federation flooded his desk.

The holographic computer built into the table displayed reports on the table top from Sunex (the planet of 7 moons) and Sunev. A holographic screen on the desktop contained assignments of Special Forces Councilmen from Earth.

The artificial intelligence computer behind him reported data from Polaris VI, Sigma Draconis and Jalug. At last report, the Draconians were stopping smuggled shipments.

On top of the pile on his desk was Lim's report. It contained the attempt on Patrick Miusov's life, and the murder of Wendnagel; by Miusov, was a report on the impending death of Aaron Tennyson. A report by Wendnagel and Aaron on the apparent death of Berquist was on top of the stack.

Somehow the Tennysons had become targets by reporting Berquist's death.

On the other hand, there was no motive strong enough for the death of Wendnagel. On the third hand, but the fourth part. Klemperer stopped.

He had so many items on his desk requiring action, it threatened to overwhelm him. Maybe he should delegate—but no, Lim already prepared the report on everyone in the castle.

The news that Lim had overcome her kidnappers had removed one file from his desk.

Klemperer paused. Other assignments flashed on maps behind him or on 3D globes. He could not take on one more thing.

For a long time, Klemperer had his head in his hands. Then, slowly he straightened up and looked once more at Lim's report. Something had stuck in his mind. With a new burst of enthusiasm and energy he attacked the problem from a fifth angle.

A look of incredible surprise crossed his face.

He turned on the intercom. "Send Hawken Eccles up here."

Then he waited, digesting the facts one more time.

Several minutes later Hawken entered.

Klemperer stood up. Without preliminary he said, "Miss Eccles, I want you to help me catch a murderer."

"I don't follow you."

"Just bear with me. I've gone through these facts over and over again. Berquist in an explosion. Patrick Miusov in sabotage with the cat brain. Wendnagel on a bridge. And, Aaron in the Citadel of Jalug (we don't know if that was a murder). And—"

"The death of Wendnagel serves no purpose."

"Miss Eccles—may I call you Hawken to avoid confusion with your uncle—Hawken, that is what puzzled me. Aaron had stopped the smuggling operation. Although he was supposedly secure, no one would have been surprised if an ex-smuggler pushed *him* off a bridge. But Wendnagel was held in reverence, and she was the one pushed. That's where my facts stood until I realized we were looking at the matter in the wrong light—literally."

Klemperer's dark brown eyes bored into Hawken as he pursued his line of reasoning. He went on, "It was dark. No one could have possibly seen her. The target was Lim. A sick psychotic with jealousy as her motive thought she saw Lim in a red thermo jacket. All the assailant saw was the red clothing. And you pushed her—"

"It was only a warning. Then I found out, my God, it was Wendnagel."
She was trembling.

On sudden impulse, Hawken turned and ran out of the room.

Klemperer stood behind the desk, his line of reasoning unfinished.
She wouldn't go far. He waited. Then he switched on the intercom, "Send
Patrick Miusov in here."

He had underestimated Hawken. Two minutes later she ran into his
office brandishing a power gun.

His mouth dropped open to speak when she pulled the trigger. A line
of fire burned the desk then hit Klemperer. He screamed.

"They'll never find out. They'll never find out because you'll never
tell them!" Hawken proclaimed. Her eyes were glazed over.

She dropped the gun and ran out of the room.

Klemperer fell forward, then fell to the floor, badly burned.

In another part of the temporary headquarters, Hawken found herself
a stun gun and fled.

A figure in a black uniform entered Klemperer's office, with a premonition of trouble. His carefully prepared words about Klemperer being
overloaded and needing to delegate went unsaid. His argument about the
dangerous misinformation being generated by his condition fell aside.
He saw the power gun on the floor, knelt down and picked it up. Then
Miusov saw Klemperer and the burn marks on the table. He let out a
whistle of surprise.

Before he could go to Klemperer's side and assist, a Green-rank Councilman ran in. "I thought I heard gun fire. I saw a mental picture of fire.
What's going on—*Miusov*!"

The Green Councilman gasped as he took in the scene. Shakily he
pulled out his own weapon. "Miusov, you're under arrest for trying to kill
Council Leader Klemperer."

"He may be alive. I suggest you get aid—quickly."

The green uniformed Councilman ordered emergency medical
assistance over the intercom.

To Miusov, he said, "Don't move. I don't know what possessed you to
do this but I recommend you remain silent."

Outside the headquarters building, Hawken slowed her pace from a run to a fast walk. Her pulse raced and she felt her heart thumping. She concealed the weapon.

She was almost out of the area of the spaceport when a green uni-formed man stopped her. "Ms. Eccles, I'm Green-rank Councilman Drury. You may be unaware that all Council stun guns are teletapped. The minute you picked it up I received a mental image of hands touching the gun. It only took a few minutes to realize whose hands they belonged to. An Outsider. Will you come with me, please."

He located the gun and took it from her.

He said, "I'll have to insist."

Inside another room in the temporary headquarters, Miusov sat in handcuffs before Green-rank Councilman McIntyre. They had thoughtfully not used ones with telepathic locks.

"Why, Patrick, just tell me why? Was it those training sessions—were they too harsh? You came back from your last assignment under a cloud. What you did to the northern hemisphere of that planet was in the press for weeks."

"I was under orders."

"Were you under orders for this, too?"

"Is Klemperer going to be all right?"

"I don't know. Do you want to make a statement?"

Miusov was silent. This man, McIntyre, was the only man in the Special Forces Council he hadn't gotten along with.

Then Miusov was quiet for another reason. Messages sent between telepaths were leaking into his mind.

Green-rank Councilman Drury carried the stolen stun gun back with him in the corridor. He bumped into the only active Brown-rank in the headquarters.

"Did you hear?" he asked Drury. "Someone tried to kill Klemperer. Pasha Miusov has been arrested for it."

"By whom?"

"By Green-rank McIntyre."

"He used to discipline Pasha when he was a boy. Isn't that a conflict of—wait a minute. I just relieved a stun gun from a young woman. I want to hear this whole story."

"Where is she?"

"With Browne."

"Get her under better security. I'll talk to Pasha."

Miusov squirmed in his seat.

"What's the matter, now?" asked McIntyre.

Nothing was the matter. Miusov suddenly heard a personal message that only resonated to kin and near friends.

//Pasha, come quickly. This is Lim. The Multi-Luna beast is loose and I need your help. I'm trying to telepathically close one of the carrying capsules. I'm in Demner.//

Miusov stood up. "I can't!" He repeated it telepathically.

Miusov looked up at McIntyre who had figured out he was "hearing" something telepathically. Miusov told him, "You have to let me go. I'm needed in Demner."

"What are you talking about. The—"

"Go find a window and look out!" Miusov demanded.

The Brown-rank Councilman entered the room. "Did you look out the window at the mountain tonight? There are blue lights like lanterns in a line on the Demner side of the mountain. They're all over the mountain. All over Demner!"

McIntyre tried to remember the Dauropan folklore. "It means danger to Demner and Dauropa."

They both looked at Miusov.

"Better let me go," Miusov warned.

The Brown-rank Councilman gave the order. "Release him."

"Are you sure?"

"He has rank in three weeks over yours. You might remember that."

McIntyre looked uncomfortable as the truth dawned.

Miusov held up his wrists. The Green Councilman opened them.

The Brown Councilman told the Green, "Keep them. We have the real murderer."

"You're still under arrest," McIntyre cautioned Miusov.

The night was darker than he remembered it. As Miusov climbed out of the ground car it occurred to him he should have been seeing lights by now.

Winters climbed out of the car behind him, as did McIntyre.

The night was unusually dark. Stars were more prominent. Landmarks such as houses and water towers, normally lit, were murky black.

A susserating sound pierced the night. Lightning lit up the sky. A tall beast flickered in and out of his vision. The Multi-Luna beast had telescoped his legs. It had grown from twenty to fifty feet high.

Several more ground cars landed without lights. Police Patrol officers got out, stun guns held high.

Miusov was still hearing telepathic messages from Lim. She had been unable to find Berquist. Faintly he could "hear" the tall Councilman's attempt to close the carrying capsules by telepathy. Several other "voices" competed for attention.

Strange. Stranger.

It was the Shade who had crashed the omnicraft. It was forming words in its mind the way he had experienced Pasha's telepathic messages. Miusov could read it.

Stranger is here.

It was referring to the Multi-Luna beast. The humans were no longer strange to Shades.

Four white lights circled each other in the clouds then came together. They dropped down next to Miusov all exclaiming, "Stranger is awake."

The first Shade passed around Miusov. The gaseous form had an interior that clicked, popped and whistled and made sounds no human had heard before. It was trying to communicate.

//Pasha, over here,// came Lim's telepathic voice.

Miusov ran across the darkened footpath. "I'm here!"

"Careful. I'm holding the Multi-Luna beast with my mind, but only for an instant."

Winters ran up behind him. "How can there be a Multi-Luna rómol here? With the atmosphere alone, it would be insane."

"Eccles kept it under a sleep trancer in the railroad tunnel. He lit it with infra-red light. It was a surprise for his guests. It was part of his zoo."

"He'd have to use infra-red. Try these visors," Winters offered.

Miusov did. The beast lit up as a dark red image, with several fifty-foot long legs encased in a crab-like exoskeleton. The legs ended in points that buried in the ground as it walked. The exoskeleton of the backbone contained several brains. If it kept its present path, it would trample houses in the village of Demner.

Miusov asked Winters, "Check your stun gun."

"It's at half charge."

"Is the reading steady or flickering?"

"Flickering."

Lim told him warningly, "Whatever Berquist turned on is effecting everything. Lights are out as far as New Essex. The blackouts are on a straight line for Zäringhen."

The Multi-Luna rómol hissed. Miusov telepathically ordered it to stop its forward movement. The half-Draconian's head spun as he made contact. He felt himself high in the air, trying to move legs, leaden in gravity that was higher than it was used to, and breathing air that was too heavy with oxygen. The thoughts of the rómol were confused and with a growing fear of where it was. It wanted its companions. It was going to run.

Miusov fought his fear of heights and ordered it to stop its flight.

A talon came down withing a half-foot of him. Miusov stood stock still.

The leg flickered into the sight of Winters and the Patrol. Winters fired his weapon. Energyzers were the weapon of choice with a rómol. It would sting them and drive them away. The stun gun slowed the beast but did not stop it.

Miusov broke contact. He got his orientation as several Patrol officers fired stun guns upwards at the flickering rómol. The Councilman picked out the Sergeant and called out to her, "There are smugglers on the mountainside. Concentrate your efforts on arresting them. They're well concealed in this darkness so make sure they don't get away. I can stop the rómol beast."

She frowned at him. "Who are you and how can you stop this thing? Stunners barely slow it down."

"I am Patrick Miusov of the Special Forces Council. I can stop it with a telepathic linkup. I can override its brain commands. This is Lt. Steve Winters, my security chief."

"Are the smugglers active again?"

"Very. They're up by Wendnagel's sanctuary."

"She has several."

He gave her the location. Then he spun on his heel and made out Winters in the starlight. For an instant lightning lit their faces. Thunder resounded. "Steve, guard my back. I may not be able to move or answer your questions. Don't let anyone touch me."

"This is like with the time slide?"

"Hopefully not."

Winters moved to a stance where he could use the stun gun. For the first time he comprehended his role as security officer. His job was to protect the Councilmen in this delicate state. He moved to another hillock, feeling part of the team.

Winters put on a night visor. The Multi-Luna rómol lit up in infra-red. The trees lit up in green. All of a sudden the image flickered. The silent weapon was even effecting the visors.

"Pasha, the visors are intermittent. Be careful."

//Acknowledged.// Had he heard that?

The Sergeant stated, "I'm leaving two men with you with orders to stun the beast if you can't stop it."

Miusov stepped out into the center of the footpath. He was in a wide area clear of trees. Leaves, pine needles and grass were under his feet. He almost stepped in a hole left by the rómol's foot.

Stranger is here, Pasha. Stranger-thing is here.

That was the same Shade. It was learning Standard. Clairvoyantly he saw bright spherical lights of several more. Something was attracting them. He received clairvoyant pictures of their point-of-view from the sky. It was like being in the mountains before skiing—very high.

Quickly, Miusov turned his attention to the rómol. The visor gave him one last look of it stepping along the footpath, then went dark. The Patrol officers were running up the footpath, looking for the stream to the cedar bridge and the smugglers. Two smugglers fired modified stun guns from behind large canisters. Four more gave themselves up. They ducked as stun gun fire came from the ground car. The Patrol officers dodged behind trees and returned the fire, stunning the driver. The beams were almost invisible but the hum of the modified guns was almost shrill.

The Sergeant ordered her force in at closer range. Two more smugglers gave themselves up by throwing away their guns and lying prone.

Back at the footpath, Miusov took the energy in his mind and increased its intensity. All at once he was in contact with the rómol. //Stop! Go back.// he ordered. //You are in a strange place. Don't move.//

Several minutes ticked by. He started to sweat. He knew he was exceeding 34 amputs. He continued to hold the rómol.

The Multi-Luna denizen was quiet at first, then became fretful. It expanded its telescoping legs another meter. It dragged one foot along the ground, leaving a furrow three feet deep. Winters fired the stun gun.

Miusov winced as he felt the numbing effect it had on the rómol. His potential E.S.P. was so high that it had measured unlimited on Council scales. Now he began tapping into that potential.

The rómol hissed at the renewed input of energy but made no intelligent reply. Hunger, anger and confusion, partially soothed by repeated contact, hit Miusov's mind. He screened out Lim and Berquist and then Winters' voice telling him to get out of the way and that he was in the creature's path. Miusov hesitated, then screened out the Shades, although he knew their messages were important.

His mind, which had become one with the rómol, now disentangled himself. He was on the ground with a fifty-foot rómol towering over his head. He gained the upper hand. //Don't move.//

Two Patrol officers who the Sergeant had left behind lowered their weapons.

Lim ran up a stony path. She found Berquist with the carrying capsules. The cover was in his hand. Once again he screwed it on.

"Allow me, Raymond," Lim told him. She reached out and touched the cover. At full telepathy power she thought //Lock, close.// She scanned the personal code to which it was attuned to respond, then overrode it. // This is a Special Forces Council order to keep this closed and locked.// She left that message on it for any potential telepath to read. It would give any telepathic smuggler pause. //Lock, close.//

The cover clicked. It was locked shut.

In the distance the lights of the town of New Essex came on. The lights of the village of Demner began flickering on.

A gentle hum resonated across the palisade and dales. It started in a railroad tunnel and filtered back to a footpath. The Multi-Luna rómol retracted its legs until it was twenty feet high. Then it fell asleep.

Miusov slowly and tentatively ceased telepathic signals.

He turned to Winters. "Good job, Steve . . ." He closed his eyes, received a message, then opened them. "She shut off the device."

The hum could be faintly heard for a fleeting instant as far as Wendnagel's sanctuary. Berquist and Lim stood over the capsules, their eyes adjusted to the astonishing absence of light. As lights along the Family's footpath came on, white lines on Lim's jet black uniform reflected brightly.

A man rose from the shrubbery. He had eluded the Patrol and had run back to the sanctuary, keeping a low profile as he ran from shrub to tree. Now he stood upright, holding a modified stun gun trained on Lim.

The smuggler sneered, "Berquist, you're too familiar with these Councilmen."

"She shut off the device. The Lanterns cued her—"

"Quiet, traitor!" the smuggler snapped, as he pointed his weapon at Berquist.

The hum of a stun gun could be heard clearly. Berquist flinched. This was his nightmare—to be shot by the smugglers as a traitor.

But he didn't fall.

The smuggler dropped to his knees and passed out.

Behind the smuggler the Patrol Sergeant was standing. She lowered her stun gun, still hot from being used on the smuggler. She squinted through night goggles.

"Councilman Patrick Miusov said there were smugglers up here." She eyed Berquist's clothing. "I believe you are under arrest."

"Wait," Lim intoned. "This is Raymond Berquist of the Special Forces Council."

"Do you have ID?"

Berquist said, "No, I don't."

"I have ID," Lim said quickly. "I am Lim Miusov of the Special Forces Council, Earth." As she fumbled for her own ID, she rediscovered a second card. She stared at it, unable to read it in the dark. She read it clairvoyantly and saw the image of three concentric circles—Berquist's symbol. "This is Berquist's ID," she said. A flood of memories came with it.

A Patrolman strode up to the Sergeant. "Our flashlights are working." He gave her one.

She looked over the ID in the light and saluted. "All's in order, ma'am."

"Not quite. Governor John Eccles is being held in a room in the castle. Two diplomats there are responsible for smuggling these canisters. They are to be escorted to the spaceport and shown the first ship off Dauropa."

"What about these canisters?" She touched one and "heard" a telepathic request for an ID.

"Stop—" Lim warned.

A voice spoke by telepathy in the Sergeant's mind. //This is a Special Forces Council order to keep this closed and locked!// boomed out of the canister mentally.

The Sergeant jumped back. "By the Shades!" she cursed.

Lim gave the order, "These are to be taken under heavy escort to Special Forces Council HQ at Zäringhen."

The Sergeant's voice shook, "This is highly irregular. We take contraband to—never mind. Do you want all of them? I'll order my men."

Lim walked down the path back to Eccles' property line. She found the short-cut footpath to the space ferry by the river. Halfway there she met Miusov standing in front of the motionless rómol.

For several minutes they spoke in a conversation no one else, except the Councilmen, could hear. The information exchange was rapid and in code.

Chapter 15

MYSTERY SOLVED

McIntyre said, "Patrick, I sense something alive present in the area."

"Those are the mythical Shades," Miusov explained. Then he added brusquely, "I have to go to the castle. They want me to talk to Governor Eccles."

"I have to take you back to headquarters."

"This won't wait. Remember, one of them crashed our omnicraft."

The Patrol arrived ahead of them, locating Eccles and unlocking him from his work room and escorting away the diplomats.

Miusov spoke to Eccles who was thanking them. "I have to talk to you, outside, John. Will you come with us, Steve?"

Eccles looked puzzled but followed him out a doorway. The stone castle had several lights that were back on, shining on the front lawn. The lawn was carefully surrounded by tall trees to keep the unwary from falling off a glacier rock, a sudden drop on the edge of the property.

Eccles suddenly noted movement. "Pasha, check with your E.S.P. Something is moving out there."

"Yes, they're Shades. May I present Scout-1 who wishes me to address you with grievances."

Eccles laughed. "Pasha, the Shades are animals. They don't think. Please send them away. I'll call the rangers. Are the Lanterns on?"

"Calm down and wait," Miusov urged. "This one next to me who you can't see is really a scout and he really represents the Shades. There are four more behind me. I made them promise not to drain the electricity from your lights or stall an omnicraft. They are intelligent. What do you really know about Shades?"

"They live off solar energy and are gaseous."

"Yes, and they also float up to the atmosphere and live off the ions in the clouds. There's a natural flow of electricity in the clouds. You chased them off their favorite valley and into the shadows of the mountains. The air in their favorite valley has been polluted by a substance that neutralizes ions. They ventured out because they are getting—" He looked for the word and translated it as "—anemic. Also, because they met me who can talk to them via telepathy. They are gaseous," he agreed, "but they have an inner core of bipolar gases that is magnetic. That is, they can think in binary patterns. This one has learned some Standard from contact with me."

Steve Winters lit up. "I served with a Sunevian on board the DISCOVERY. If he learned this, he could petition the Solar Federation to take away the colonists' seat in the Federation and award it to the Shades."

"Or, if you put it that way," Miusov said thoughtfully, "the Draconians might be interested in giving the seat to the Shades, also. If you want to avoid this, I suggest you bargain with them."

"I'm a survivor," said Eccles, "but this is really a surprise blow. We always thought of them as animals. We've killed hundreds of them over the century. What is this favorite valley?"

"I'm having trouble translating—ah, I've got it, it's the valley Zäringhen spaceport was built over."

"Pasha, we can't give them Zäringhen back!"

"No, but you could authorize they travel unmolested to another valley."

"This is really the province of the President of the planet."

"You have the authority within Demner and I suggest you grant it. I've asked them not to drain your electricity but there may be a maverick in the group. I suggest you treat them as you would any group of diplomats and entertain them. They'd like to see your railroad run."

149

AGA

"Pasha, this is ridiculous. Entertain a Shade. Something I can't see . . . ?"

"You entertain the diplomats from Eta Cassiopiae. You entertain visitors from Earth and Jalug. Solar Federation soldiers stand in your yard. If a dignitary came from Bluen, who lives only under water, would you entertain them? You, too, are too provincial. The Shades can't stay *Outsiders* forever."

He threw back the words concerning Outsiders that Eccles had given him.

Miusov continued, "Scout-1 has to report back to his Leader or Leaders. What should I tell them?"

Eccles was quick on the uptake. "I'll give them a valley but I'll have to consult my maps. Pasha, are you going to upset the balance on Dauropa! My home will never be the same. You've made this mountain seem different. Shades coming and going—please don't let them shut down my computers!"

Miusov was silent several minutes while he talked to the Shade.

The dark-haired Draconian waited for the Shades to recede into the distance then strode with Winters and Eccles back to the castle's main room.

McIntyre told him straight off, "I heard all this and I'm taking you back to headquarters—now!"

"Wait," Lim extolled him. "We are going to the spaceport. Quickly. Call HQ and ask the Brown Councilman,"–she asked for him by name— "to join us. It's urgent." A look of surprise was on her face.

II

Renate Ramón y Cajal and his aid, O'Connors, were about to board a starship headed for Eta Cassiopiae.

As they were on the verge of walking up the ramp, a ground car pulled up. Lim alighted from it, followed by the Brown Councilman, McIntyre, Winters, Miusov and the Patrol Sergeant.

"What's this?" asked Ramón. "I thought we had diplomatic immunity."

"You, Ramón, have diplomatic immunity and are free to go. O'Connors, however, is under arrest."

O'Connors sputtered, "What is the charge?"

"Murder. The attempted murder of Patrick Miusov, the murder of Wendnagel, the murder of Aaron Tennyson, and the attempted murder of Council Leader Klemperer."

McIntyre tried to interrupt, "Lim, Pasha is—"

The Brown-rank Councilman intervened, "Lim, we think Hawken Eccles is the one who killed Wendnagel and tried to kill—"

"No, there's been a terrible miscarriage of justice. Hawken is innocent. You are the murderer, O'Connors," Lim pointed at him and held up a long cylinder. "And this is the murder weapon."

Lim said breathlessly, "*You* poured acid in the cat brain container. This cylinder is a cyber-jammer. You hacked into Hawken's mind and ordered her to kill me. Somehow Wendnagel was killed instead. To cover the crime, you tried to kill Aaron and made it look like the smugglers did it. You hacked into Aaron and ordered him to go to Jalug to fulfill the curse. You didn't trust the native superstitions so you went ahead and met him on Jalug and stabbed him."

"Mere conjecture," O'Connors said, flustered.

"No, Aaron tore the pocket of your jacket. Here is the cloth which still matches the missing pocket on the jacket you are still wearing. Inside the pocket was this stone with a number on it that matches the native markers at a spaceport on Jalug. The vessel with this number is registered openly in your name. Here is the stone." She held it up.

"Mon Dieu!" cried Ramón, "what have you done? I was going to marry the girl."

"You are much too old for her."

"How would you know? Our enemies are thought controllers, not free traders. Free traders are essential to our economy!"

Ramón turned to Lim. "What about Klemperer?" he said in defense of his countryman.

Lim assured him, "When we are done debriefing Hawken, I am sure

151

we will find a cyber-jam order for this also. You have been very thorough, Mr. O'Connors. Thoroughly wicked." To the Patrol officer she gestured, "Arrest him. Ramón, you may board your ship."

"I will be back to visit Hawken."

"You will have to wait until the Council is done with her. There's also the matter of these capsules."

"You have them all."

Miusov said to McIntyre, "Do you still want to take me to headquarters?"

McIntyre looked unhappy. "I have to."

Chapter 16

EPILOGUE

Lt. Winters stood before the doorway, at the Special Forces Council temporary HQ changers. Black Councilman Berquist, Lim, a Brown Councilman, and a Green-rank Councilman were already inside. All but Lim had looked at him in his navy Solar Federation uniform as an Outsider. He would work on all of them to rid them of this attitude if he had to.

Without warning, Miusov and a Green-rank Councilman, McIntyre, came down the corridor. Miusov said nothing. The Green Councilman told Winters, "Let no one in, unless the Council Leader himself comes."

Lim was next in command after Klemperer but because the person under arrest was her son, she had to defer the proceeding to Berquist.

Everyone maintained a neutral expression and all had their minds barricaded and blocked so no thought could be read.

Berquist told Miusov, "Step forward and give your name to the Hearing."

"Patrick Miusov."

Berquist said to McIntyre, "What are the charges?"

"Attempt to kill Council Leader Klemperer. Attempted murder. The suspect came in with anger on his mind over the structure of the Council."

Berquist asked him, "How do you plea?"

Miusov answered, "Innocent."

Berquist pressed on, "What do you have to say about these charges?"

Miusov stammered. He had come in with anger and he couldn't deny it at these proceedings with so many telepaths present. "It's true that—I came in—"

Berquist interrupted him. "The charges are untrue in the eyes of the Council. I see there are two Black-rank Councilmen present and one Brown-rank, so I can begin other proceedings. It is still three weeks from your nineteenth birthday, but I think we can overlook the protocol."

Miusov was so lost in thought with dread and it took him a moment to realize Berquist was initiating the ceremony to give him full Black rank in the Council.

The door opened and Berquist looked up. "I thought we weren't supposed to be disturbed." He stopped. The man in the doorway was obviously in pain but standing on his feet: Klemperer.

The Council Leader said, "I'd like the honor of doing this ceremony, if you don't mind."

Klemperer started, "State your name for the record."

"Patrick Miusov."

"Also known as Pasha. On this day of . . ."

The ceremony took only fifteen minutes.

At the end Miusov's communit wished on and a message came through telepathically from Council Leader Westerman. //Congratulations, Pasha.//

Chapter 17

THE CAPSULES

Lim closed the log of the report she was writing. Wendnagel's body had
been put in deep freeze against the day she could be revived. Aaron's
body was unrecoverable from Thok's Citadel. A dispute had arisen with
the natives of Jalug when she tried to gain information from the priests.
"It's in Thok's hands," said Pasha and wouldn't explain.

   She wrote . . . Two capsules remain lost on Eccles' property, containing whatever they secretly contain. Lt. Steve Winters, Security Officer, to
be dispatched to try to locate them.

*   *   *

Afterword—Inspiration for "Lanterns Over Demner"

Around 1967 there was an art show on Long Island that featured an artist with three sets of strange and wondrous paintings.

The first set were paintings of kerosene lanterns hanging in the air as if some power had lifted them off the ground. The pictures had a sense of phenomenon. The second set featured vases and ceramic cups lifted in the air. Some power was causing the cups to corrode or dissolve. The third set showed battered metal pots and pans sitting on a low stone wall somewhere in New England or New York. All sets had the same sense of strangeness.

I went home and tried to draw objects in the air, such as quill pens. It was tougher than it looked—the eye keeps correcting the image in one's mind, so it appears on the ground.

Not knowing the name of the artist, I have been unsuccessful in finding any of these paintings in order to buy one.

Instead I decided to write a story whose work would portray the same sense of mystery, wonder, and power. "Lanterns Over Demner" is this story. I share it with you in the hopes you will enjoy it with me.

The "wish switch" is a real device. It is based on an invention described in a circa 1968 POPULAR SCIENCE article. In the article the device was hard-wired to a helmet which in turn was hard-wired to a TV set. The TV set went on whenever the helmet wearer made a decision. It was extrapolated that this device could be designed without wire sensors and that it could learn to differentiate the desire to turn on a device from other desires or wishes.

The description of E.S.P. fade, as well as the two systems— Wendnagel's system of relaxing—and Lim's system of concentrating— are described in a book called E.S.P.

John Locke's philosophy comes from the Encyclopedia of Philosophy, Free Press, 1976.

There are several good books on information theory. A specialized use of it—pulse code modulation—is written up in a 1970 issue of SCIENTIFIC AMERICAN.

The *phosphene* lights that Winters sees after he crashes his hang glider come from a February 1970 article in the SCIENTIFIC AMERICAN. They refer to lights that a person can see when a brain area is stimulated, or when parts of the eye are stimulated. Long periods of prolonged darkness can also make a person see these brilliant lights. They have many shapes, all very bright and white—concentric circles, mountain-like shapes, broken circles, concentric squares, etc. Winters assumes that a break in the pattern of the lights would indicate damage to his skull, so he takes a look at them. This use that Winters makes of these lights after his hang glider crash are from the imagination of the author.

The Councilmen use the typical light patterns for identification symbols in their ID cards.

MANAGING
IMITATION
STRATEGIES

MANAGING IMITATION STRATEGIES _____

HOW LATER ENTRANTS
SEIZE MARKETS FROM PIONEERS

Steven P. Schnaars

THE FREE PRESS
A Division of Macmillan, Inc.
NEW YORK

Maxwell Macmillan Canada
TORONTO

Maxwell Macmillan International
NEW YORK   OXFORD   SINGAPORE   SYDNEY

THE FREE PRESS
Rockefeller Center
1230 Avenue of the Americas
New York, NY 10020

Manufactured in the United States of America

10 9 8 7 6 5 4 3 2 1

Library of Congress Cataloging-In-Publication Data

ISBN 0-7432-4265-3

For information regarding the special discounts for bulk purchases, please contact Simon &
Schuster Special Sales at 1-800-456-6798 or business@simonandschuster.com

CONTENTS _____

MANAGING
IMITATION
STRATEGIES _____

Introduction
The Argument for Imitation

Imitation is not only more abundant than innovation, it is actually a much more prevalent road to business growth and profits. I wish I could claim credit for that insightful observation, but it was first made more than twenty-five years ago by Theodore Levitt, the noted Harvard professor.[1] I simply paraphrase his original statement because the idea it conveys is as applicable today as it was then. Imitation is *still* more commonplace than innovation, and it is still a viable marketing strategy.

That is not to say that imitation is preferable to innovation in all, or even the majority of, instances. The merits of innovation are indisputable. Firms that develop and bring to market innovative products before competitors often build and sustain commanding leads in market share—the so-called first-mover advantages or order-of-entry effect. But innovation is not the only choice of market entry, and in many instances it may not even be the best choice. Just as often, innovators end up worse off than those who follow.

The basic thesis of this book is that the benefits of innovation and early market entry have been grossly oversold. So much has been written about the benefits of innovation, and so little about imitation, that it has become a one-sided argument. A search of *ABI/Inform*—a computerized business database that tracks articles published in more than seven hundred leading business journals—lists a total of 9,006 articles on the subject of "innovation" but only 145 on "imitation." A more specific set of delimiters yields not a single article containing the terms "product imitation" anywhere in the title or abstract, and only one article contains the term "product copying." Likewise, the database lists 17,940 articles on "engineering," but only 93 on "reverse engineering," and almost all of those deal solely with a specific computer software issue. On the basis of sheer proportions someone might conclude that imitating the innovations of others is an ineffectual, infrequent, and economically unimportant exercise. That conclusion would be dead wrong.

1

For a variety of reasons, the evidence in favor of imitation is often hidden from public view. Whereas firms are often eager to trumpet the occasions when they were the "first" to discover something, they are often less willing to publicize their skills at imitation. Still, examples of successful imitation can be found in nearly every nook and cranny of the economy. Imitation is no fad, nor is it restricted to a few unique industries.

- In soft drinks, for example, a marketing manager for Coca-Cola explained his firm's marketing strategy to a *Business Week* reporter in 1983 as follows: "The high ground is that we should be leading the way, but that's not our style. We let others come out, stand back and watch, and then see what it takes to take the category over."[2] A historical analysis of Coke's action suggests that that policy has been in place for some time.
- Pepsi obviously holds similar views. The CEO of North American operations was quoted in 1993 as saying: "I'm very much in the camp of thinking stealing ideas is one of the most honorable things you can do."[3]
- In breakfast cereals, the *Wall Street Journal* observed a change in competitive patterns in 1991: "Whereas in the past the rivals seldom copied each other, both [Kellogg and General Mills] are now blatantly using knockoffs to win points."[4]
- A 1987 *Business Week* article examined new product introductions in the distilled spirits industry. The magazine concluded that Hiram Walker "has often allowed others to test new markets first, and only when [the firm's president, H. Clifford] Hatch is satisfied that demand is solidly in place will Hiram Walker move in."[5] Following that time-honored pattern, the firm entered the fastest-growing markets for vodka, gin, rum, and tequila through imitation and later entry.
- More than a decade later, little had changed. In 1989 *Business Week* noted that "liquor has always been a 'me-too' business."[6] After the market success of DeKuyper Peachtree, a sweet cordial introduced in 1985, a flood of competitors entered and eventually surpassed that innovative brand with imitative entries.
- In 1984, *Business Week* observed that the large chemical and pharmaceutical firms were beginning to enter the emerging biotechnology business. The industry giants were expected to overwhelm the smaller firms that pioneered the market. As one manager noted: "It's becoming the waltz of the elephants, and the fleas are going to get squashed."[7]
- None of this is new. In 1933 the *New York Times* reported that competition for television sets—an incubating technology—was likely to follow a time-honored pattern: "[It] has usually been the practice since 1927 to let

smaller organizations take the first bow, and if well received the larger manufacturers come upon stage."[8]

• Other examples of successful product copying go back even farther than that. In the 1500s, Dutch sailors discovered Chinese porcelain in the course of their explorations. That innovative new product created a huge growth market when introduced in Europe. Demand exceeded supply. As one author concluded: "[S]o the Dutch began to knock-off the porcelain. They even went so far as to copy the Chinese symbols and used similar colors. The technique is still used today and the product is known as Delftware."[9]

• Sometimes small firms succeed with copies of larger firms' products. In recreational vehicles, for example, Rexhall Industries muscled its way into the market by selling a cheaper version of the all-chrome, bubble-shaped Airstream trailer. According to *Business Week*: "Rex [the entrepreneurial founder] got his idea the old-fashioned way: he copied it."[10] He copied Airstream's innovative design but substituted less expensive fiberglass for chrome. Rexhall's president summed up industry practice this way: "In this industry, we call it R&C: research and copy."

• Copying is common in retailing. Sam Walton, the immensely successful retailing entrepreneur, whose Wal-Mart discount stores have surpassed $44 billion in sales and continue to storm across America, admits in his autobiography that "most everything I've done I've copied from somebody else."[11]

• Copying is especially common in the fashion industry. In 1990, for example, the *New York Times* observed that the Limited, the incredibly successful retailing wonder, had "built its success on its ability to quickly turn the latest runway fashion into less expensive merchandise."[12] The Limited would imitate emerging fashion trends and then rush less expensive versions of those fashions to market before the innovators themselves.

• In software development, the market leader, Microsoft, has often been accused of benefiting economically from inventions made by others. In 1991 the *New York Times* observed that competitors "have long complained that the rest of the industry has served as Microsoft's R&D lab." As one embittered competitor noted: "You will have a hard time finding anything that Microsoft pioneered."[13] Specific examples of product copying include Windows, which was based on Apple's Macintosh operating system and MS-DOS itself, which, according to the *Times*, was acquired from another company.

• Another example of product copying by Microsoft occurred in the case of "pen-based" computer software. Critics contend that after the Go Corpo-

ration tried to interest Microsoft in its innovative "pen" software, Microsoft stole the idea and put the person in charge of dealing with the Go Corporation on its own development team, which introduced its own pen-based product. It was all perfectly legal.

- Sometimes even the copycats get copies. In the early 1980s, Franklin Computer made its living by making exact copies of Apple's then popular personal computer. That is, until Apple enforced its patents and put Franklin out of the cloning business. So Franklin repositioned itself. By 1989, Franklin Electronic Publishers had remade itself into the leading seller of electronic reference manuals—such as language translators. That is, until larger, lower-cost producers such as Texas Instruments, Seiko, and others jumped into Franklin's market and trounced the leader. The successful, but illegal, cloner had become a successful, but short-lived, pioneer.[14]

- As a final case, consider the crazy world of dictionary publishing. Every important dictionary in the United States carries the name Webster (an unprotected trademark). Since every brand carries the same trademark, product copying has become more subtle. *Webster's Ninth New Collegiate Dictionary*, for example, has a bright red cover with the Webster's name boldly printed in white on the book's spine. That dictionary has been published by Merriam-Webster since 1973. A competitive entry by Random House, a much larger company, also has a red cover and a white-lettered spine, as does Simon & Schuster's *Webster's New World Dictionary*. But in 1991, the Random House dictionary switched its name from the *Random House College Dictionary* to *Webster's College Dictionary*. Although there are many red Webster's dictionaries with white letters on the spine, Random House was the first to copy the word "College." It was more than Merriam-Webster could stand. The original copy of Webster's dictionary sued the copied copy for violation of "trade dress."[15]

  The anecdotal evidence in favor of imitation is nearly endless. Taken as a whole, it illustrates that imitation is neither rare nor ineffective. It is in fact a powerful and frequently used entry strategy that, like a long-term spouse, is often unappreciated and taken for granted. This book tries to rekindle the romance in that relationship.

The Elements of Imitation

Not all copies are created equal. This chapter examines the different kinds of imitations that are frequently found in the business world and categorizes possible later entry strategies.

KINDS OF COPIES

Imitation runs the gamut from surreptitious and illegal duplicates of popular products to truly innovative new products that are merely inspired by a pioneering brand.

Counterfeits or Product Pirates

On the streets of New York, third-world entrepreneurs hawk counterfeit Gucci and Cartier watches to unsuspecting (or uncaring) tourists. They are engaged in the darker side of imitation. Counterfeits are copies that carry the same brand name or trademark as the original. They are an attempt to rob the innovator of due profits. Counterfeits are strictly illegal. They trade on the protected brand name or trademark of an established seller.

Counterfeits are usually low-quality, shoddy goods, sold under the guise of a premium-priced seller's respected brand name. They typically carry a much lower price than the original. Counterfeits are the least creative attempt at imitation. What sets them apart from other forms of imitative products is their illegality.

The consumer may or may not be aware of the intended deception. The cachet of a prestigious brand name at a much lower price may entice consumers inadvertently to support a counterfeiter's copy.

Counterfeits are big business. *Business Week* estimates that pirates steal

$20 billion a year from U.S. businesses.[1] Rolex and Cartier watches, Izod shirts, Gucci and Vuitton handbags, Jordache jeans, and Nintendo video games are examples of products that have all been subjected to widespread counterfeiting. Often, counterfeiters operate out of Korea, Taiwan, and Hong Kong. In recent years counterfeiting has become so widespread that sellers of popular brand products have been forced to track down and prosecute the counterfeiters. Search and seizure tactics are often used to slow the international flow of counterfeit products.

Much of the negative image attached to imitative products results from the illicit actions of counterfeiters. Their illegality is obvious, and the impression is widespread that all imitations are of a similar ilk. It is no wonder that imitators are reluctant to crow about their successes.

Knockoffs or Clones

When the IBM personal computer was introduced in 1981, it became an immediate success. That success, and the open architecture of the PC, created a secondary market for IBM-PC clones. The clones were close copies of the IBM product but carried their own brand names, not the brand name of the original. Eventually the copies surpassed the original.

Clones are often legal products in their own right. The absence or expiration of patents, copyrights, and trademarks makes many of them legal. But often there is a dispute, which the courts must resolve. Typically, clones sell the same basic product as the innovator but at a lower price and without the prestigious brand name.

Outside the computer industry, clones are usually called knockoffs. Knockoffs are legal copies of a competitor's product. Consider the case of Tyco Toys, which has succeeded on numerous occasions by copying the innovations of others. In 1984 Tyco introduced Super Blocks, a children's plastic building block that is nearly identical to those sold by Lego, the market leader from Denmark. Lego sued to protect its product from imitation, but its case was weakened by the fact that its patent had expired in 1981. Furthermore, as a *Forbes* reporter discovered in 1988, "Lego itself had copied the product from an English firm in the 1940s."[2] Lego lost. By the late 1980s, Tyco was selling $20 million a year worth of "Super Blocks."

Tyco repeated the strategy with Super Dough, a direct copy of Kenner Parker's Play-Doh. Kenner Parker also sued. It also lost. For Tyco, copying proved to be a potent strategy. It sells knockoffs of established products at significantly lower prices.

Design Copies or Trade Dress

Design copies trade on the style, design, or fashion of a competitor's popular product. In instances where fashion or design is the most important part of the product, design copies mimic clones. But in instances where design plays a lesser role, design copies may be based on a unique and innovative technology. Design copies then combine aspects of innovation and imitation.

Consider, for example, the case of Japanese luxury cars. In the late 1980s the Japanese auto sellers moved up-market to challenge the German luxury auto makers Mercedes and BMW with prestige models of their own: Lexus (Toyota), Infiniti (Nissan), and Acura (Honda). The Germans assert that the Japanese are using a familiar marketing strategy—they emulate the innovator and sell at a lower price. In this case the Japanese are accused of copying the coveted German design features. A BMW marketing executive is quoted by *Business Week* as saying: "Look at the shape of the Lexus, it's almost a blatant copy of Mercedes."[3] The product carries it own brand name and possesses its own unique engineering specifications. It merely mimics the design of the market leader.

A nearly identical situation occurred with the Mazda Miata. A lengthy analysis of that product's entry in the *New York Times* concluded that the Miata is a design copy of the popular English sports cars of the 1960s and 1970s, especially the Triumph Spitfire. Mazda produced a classic British sports car without the attending quality problems that plagued the originals.[4]

Creative Adaptations

Creative adaptations are the most innovative kind of copy. They take an existing product and either improve upon it or adapt it to a new arena of competition. They are what Theodore Levitt calls "innovative imitations."

Creative adaptations of existing products are often more in tune with the innovation process than the glorified notion of the breakthrough invention. There is myth in American culture that innovation springs from the creative genius of heroic inventors. But few innovations actually develop in that way. Most innovations are deeply rooted in existing ideas and current practices. They are more accurately viewed as creative adaptations of existing ideas to new applications or incremental improvements. Innovation, in short, is often more incremental than revolutionary. Ideas rarely appear out of nowhere. Typically, new products build on old products. Stated differently, innovation often entails a great deal of imitation and extension.

Conversely, imitation often entails large degree of innovation. That is especially true in business, where the motivation for imitation is not necessarily to produce exact copies of original works but to earn profits. Art forgers may seek to profit by creating exact copies, but in business copiers have other motives. Richard Nelson and Sidney Winter conclude that "the imitator [in business] is not directly concerned with creating a good likeness, but with achieving an economic success."[5] That is, copying is a means to an end, not an end in itself. As a result, the best business imitations often combine copying with creativity. In that way, technological development moves forward a small step at a time.

Creative adaptations often take the form of either copying and then making incremental improvements on existing products or adapting existing products to new situations.

Technological Leapfrogging

Firms that enter a growing market after an innovator sometimes have access to newer technology. Sometimes the later entrant is able to read the market more accurately than the innovator solely because of the passage of time. Rarely does the innovator fully understand the form the market will ultimately take. That allows the imitator to "leapfrog" the innovator with a superior product.

Adaptation to Another Industry

Creative imitation often takes the form of recognizing the potential of an innovation developed in one industry for use in another. It applies innovation elsewhere. Arthur Bartlett, for example, who started the Century 21 real estate brokerage franchise, succeeded by using the idea of converting existing agencies to his system rather than relying on startups. John Fanning imitated the same idea to expand his Uniforce Temporary Personnel Services. He recalled: "We didn't reinvent the wheel . . . we try to leapfrog from someone else's ideas."[6] Well, not exactly. Actually, he applied an innovation from one industry to another.

WHAT TO IMITATE

The four types of copies listed above apply mostly to products and services, but imitation is not restricted to products and services. It is also possible to copy procedures, processes, or strategies.

Products

Japanese competitors have excelled at copying American products and selling them on world markets at lower prices. The popular press is loaded with examples of how American firms have failed to reap the economic benefits of innovations made here in America.

In recent years, many authors have argued that Japan has switched from a product imitator to a product innovator. It has. But it would be a mistake to conclude that the Japanese have sworn off imitation and embraced innovation. Instead, they have embraced the benefits of both approaches to new product introduction, applying each where appropriate.

American competitors have been less successful in copying Japanese products. Nathan Rosenberg and Edward Steinmueller attribute that shortcoming to an overemphasis on innovation. They observe: "American thinking about the innovation process has focused excessively upon the earliest stages" of R&D. The focus of American firms on basic research in pursuit of "creative leaps" results in a "preoccupation with discontinuities and creative destruction, and its neglect of the cumulative power of small, incremental changes."[7]

Procedures, Processes, and Strategies

It is also possible to imitate the procedures, processes, and strategies of competitors. In recent years American firms have been especially interested in copying the procedures that have made Japanese firms so competitive on world markets. For a variety of reasons, however, it is more difficult to reverse-engineer intangible processes than it is to copy physical products. Not only are process innovations intangible and rooted in culture and organizational design, they are also easier to keep secret. Edwin Mansfield, for example, found that process technology leaks out more slowly than product innovations.[8]

The results are as might be expected: The Japanese generally have had more success in copying Western product innovations than American firms have had in copying Japanese processes and operational innovations.

Processes, procedures, and strategies are often culturally bound. Consequently, imitations of them often must be tailored to fit a particular society. That means such imitations must entail a healthy degree of innovation.

When Japanese organizations have copied American procedures they have usually adapted those innovations to fit their own culture. An insightful book by D. Eleanor Westney examined Japanese imitation of Western ideas between 1868 and 1912, the Meiji period, when Japan sought to transform itself quickly from a feudal society to a modern industrial nation.[9] She stud-

ied in great detail a small number of case histories where the Japanese conscientiously copied European practices. What she found was that imitation and innovation are inextricably intertwined. In the case of creating a modern police force, for example, the Japanese first conducted a ten-month study of the Paris police force. They then copied the idea, but found that it could not be applied without adapting it to their own peculiar needs and culture. She concludes that successful imitation of procedures almost always requires innovation.

Competitive Benchmarking

In recent years the rush to improve the quality of American products has created an almost faddish interest in competitive benchmarking—the legal and explicit practice of copying the best business practices of successful competitors. The idea is that quality can be improved by doing at least as well as the best in the business. The popularity of this newly discovered form of imitation is characterized by Roger Milliken, the textile firm chairman, who summed up his firm's interest in competitive benchmarking this way: "We borrow shamelessly."[10]

Probably the most widely publicized example of copying came with the development of the extremely successful Ford Taurus. Ford officials readily admit that they scoured the world to find the most smartly designed components and best practices and then incorporated them, or better yet improved upon them, to build their innovative auto.

Gerald Nadler, a management expert, opposes the practice of competitive benchmarking.[11] He argues that making exact copies of procedural innovations is a recipe for disaster. He takes issue with the practice of imitating the procedures of successful firms. When the Japanese once again "borrowed" American manufacturing know-how in the 1950s, Nadler argues, they did not copy verbatim. Instead, they adapted American manufacturing procedures to fit their own peculiar model. He calls such imitative adaptations "breakthrough thinking."

There are numerous examples of American firms that copied and adapted the strategies of other firms to fit their own needs. Retailers often take an idea that has been successful in one field and apply it to another. Home Depot, for example, has served as a model for many other retailers. In 1991 *Forbes* reported that the Pep Boys—the once old-fashioned auto parts retailer—adapted Home Depot's ideas to its own operation. Its president, Mitchell Leibovitz, said: "I consider myself a student and Bernie Marcus [of Home Depot] a teacher."[12] In the early 1990s Pep Boys changed its promotional

programs and merchandising strategy to match those used by the Home Depot.

Sometimes firms even copy each other's promotions. Radio stations often do so. Nationwide Communications, which owns a successful group of radio stations around the country, has raised imitation to a high art. In 1991 *Forbes* reported that Nationwide often copies promotions from competitors and then claims them as its own.[13] In one particularly memorable instance in Columbus, Ohio, the Nationwide radio station started a drive to help a local family burned out its house within twenty minutes of a competitor who initiated the campaign.

THE MOTIVATION FOR IMITATION

Firms imitate for at least two reasons.

Playing Catch-up

Some firms are caught off guard by the introduction of new and innovative products. They fail to recognize the potential of a new product introduced by a small, entrepreneurial firm until demand for that product explodes. Even then, they might view its initial success as a fad that will quickly dissipate. Often they are right. There may be a long history of similar types of new products that have entered and failed. The current may simply be viewed as yet another in a long string of inevitable product failures. But the product may suddenly show signs of staying around for a while. Still, the incumbent firm may be reluctant to cannibalize its existing lines, or be forced to split sales between two entries with no net gain. But at some point the incumbent is forced to react to a trend that it did not see coming and that has now passed it by. Typically, the incumbent is forced to catch up and catch up quickly. It copies because it has no other choice. There is a decided sense of urgency to this motivation for imitators.

Watchful Waiting

In other cases, firms consciously prefer to wait patiently on the sidelines until the fog clears. They seek benefits from moving slowly. Typically, watchful waiting is a game played by industry leaders with strong competitive skills in distribution and advertising, and the funds to fight and win. When the market proves to be attractive, and the pioneer makes the inevitable mistakes

that pioneers almost always make, the imitators enter and regain what, in their view, is rightfully theirs. There is a calculated patience, using the passage of time to one's advantage, that is part of a strategy of watchful waiting.

IMITATION VERSUS LATER MARKET ENTRY

The concept of imitation is related to, but distinct from, the concept of later market entry. Imitation implies copying, where the imitator consciously mimics the pioneer's product. Later entry, in contrast, implies only that the firm has entered the market after the pioneer, often with an innovative product of its own.

Likewise, the concept of innovation differs from pioneering. Innovation conveys a strong hint of invention—the process whereby a firm develops a radically new product. Pioneering, in contrast, implies commercialization, where a firm is the first to bring a product to market.

Table 1.1 illustrates the possible combinations of innovation/imitation and pioneering/later entry.

Typically, *imitation implies later entry*. Lacking an innovation of its own, the imitator enters the market after the pioneer's entry with products that are "imitative" or improved versions "inspired" by the pioneer's innovation. In

TABLE 1.1
IMITATION VERSUS LATER ENTRY

	Innovator	**Imitator**
Pioneer	The innovator is first to market with an innovative product. Rollerblades introduced the first in-line roller skates.	An imitator beats the innovator to market with an imitative product, typically while the innovator lingers in test marketing. Reynolds introduced the first ballpoint pen, which it copied from the innovator.
Later Entrant	One innovator is beaten to market by another innovator. Each has developed its new product independently. Matsushita's VCR entered after Sony's, but it was an innovative product in its own right.	The imitator enters the market after the innovator with a copy of the innovator's product. Diet Coke did it in low-calorie soft drinks.

diet soft drinks, for example, Coke and Pepsi may have copied Royal Crown's innovative idea (which Royal Crown, in turn, probably had copied from others).

But *later entry does not necessarily imply imitation.* Often firms simultaneously, but independently, pursue similar innovative products. When one firm rushes its entry to market, the later entrant perforce must introduce its own innovative product after the innovator's entry. Consider, for example, the case of Sony's Betamax VCR versus Matsushita's VHS format. Sony pioneered the market for videocassette recorders. Matsushita was a later entrant. But VHS was not an imitation of Beta; it was developed independently. Matsushita was working on an innovative product that just happened to be brought to market after Sony's Betamax. Consequently, Matsushita was a later entrant but not an imitator.

In some cases, the distinction between copycats and later entrants is clear. In others, however, it is difficult to assess the motivation for product entry. DeHavilland, for example, was the pioneer in jet aircraft, and Boeing was a later entrant. But while Boeing had an innovative design of its own derived from its work on jet bombers, it clearly learned much from deHavilland's mistakes.

Although it is sometimes difficult to distinguish between imitators and later entrants in practice, there are clear conceptual differences:

An *imitator* copies at least some aspect of a pioneer's product.

A *later entrant* enters the market after a pioneer's successful entry.

CLASSIFYING LATER ENTRANTS

Later entrants can be classified in two ways: according to the sequence in which they enter the market after the pioneer, and according to the amount of time that has elapsed between entries.

Order-of-entry effects tabulate the sequence of market entry—the pioneer, by definition, enters first, followed by the second, third, and subsequent entrants.

Early versus late followers are classified according to whether a firm reacts immediately to a pioneer's entry or waits until much later to enter.

The distinction between early and late followers was illustrated metaphorically back in the mid-1960s by Theodore Levitt with the "used apple policy." He described early followers as follows:

Instead of being the first company to see and seize an opportunity, they systematically avoid being first. They let others do the pioneering. If the idea works they quickly follow suit. . . . [Early followers say:] We don't have to get the first bite of the apple. The second bite is good enough. . . . they at least get the second big bite, not the tenth skimpy one.[14]

The implication is that, in many instances, there is such a thing as being too early or too late. The pioneers bear undue risk, while the much later entrant misses most of the opportunity. The early entrant, in contrast, earns most of the economic rewards.

DECIDING WHO IS THE PIONEER

Defining a pioneer seems simple—it is the first firm to introduce a new product. But a problem is often encountered when that definition is applied to actual case histories. Typically, many firms enter and leave, sometimes over a period of decades, before the pioneer finally cracks the market and achieves commercial success. In light beers, videocassette recorders, personal computers, and a host of other innovative product categories that are now commonplace, there was not one single pioneer but a sequence of potential pioneers that entered and left the market before someone actually succeeded. Who was the pioneer? Was it the earliest explorers, who were killed on their unsuccessful quest? Or, was it the first firm actually to achieve commercial success?

Complicating the issue is the fact that in many cases the successful pioneer learned much about the market form the efforts of its unsuccessful predecessors. That is, many pioneers rely heavily on imitation and product improvement to pioneer new markets. In this study the following definition is used:

A *pioneer* is defined as any of those firms introducing a product to the market, *up to and including* the first to sell it successfully.

With those definitions and categorizations in mind, it is time to turn to the advantages proposed for both pioneers and later entrants.

First-Mover Advantages Versus Free-Rider Effects

Pioneers benefit from "first-mover" advantages, which result from their being the first firms to establish themselves in the market. But pioneers do not possess all of the competitive advantages. "First-mover" advantages are counterbalanced by "free-rider" effects, which accrue to imitators and later entrants. Which effect is stronger? Rhetorically, the outcome of that argument depends on which metaphor is used to describe each set of advantages.

Proponents of pioneering explain "first-mover" advantages by imagining a 5-kilometer footrace in which the pioneer leaves the starting line before the other contestants. The greater the length of the pioneer's lead, the less likely it is that later entrants will ever catch up. In fact, the very last entrants have almost no chance of placing anywhere near the front of the pack. Only in those rare cases where the later entrant possesses outstanding physical talents or reacts quickly to the pioneer's entry can the horrendous odds of leaving the starting line after the first entrant be overcome to win the footrace.

Proponents of later entry illustrate "free-rider" effects with a metaphor drawn from geographic exploration. According to this view, pioneers took on enormous personal risks to explore uncharted lands in the Western United States. They opened up the wilderness for the settlers who followed. Some pioneers are immortalized in history textbooks, but most were not enriched monetarily for their trail-blazing explorations. That benefit went to the settlers who created economic wealth. The pioneers may have gotten the glory, but it was the followers who reaped the largest economic rewards.

FIRST-MOVER ADVANTAGES

Many authors speak glowingly of the benefits of pioneering. Pioneers, they claim, are the beneficiaries of numerous first-mover advantages, which are unavailable to later entrants. The most important are summarized here.

Image and Reputation

Pioneers benefit from important reputation advantages that derive from their innovative products and early entry. Pioneers bask in the warm glow of a positive image infused with innovativeness and progressiveness, while later entrants are stuck with a copycat image, which tarnishes the appeal of their products and hinders the firm's performance.

Brand Loyalty

Pioneers have an opportunity to create loyal customers for their innovative products. Consumers become familiar with—and even form habits around—the first product they try. If the innovative product is designed correctly and priced competitively, there is no reason for consumers to experiment with similar products sold by imitators and later entrants.

Support for that advantage comes from a number of studies that show long-lived market share advantages for established brand names. One study found that nineteen of the leading twenty-five brands in 1923 were still number one in their product categories in 1981 (four others were strong number twos, and none was less than fifth in its product category).[1] Proponents of pioneering argue that the first brand has the opportunity to establish itself as the leading brand, which leads to long-term market share advantages.

Additional support comes from two studies, one by Joe Bain (which is discussed in greater detail at the end of this chapter) and another by Richard Schmalensee, who picked up on Bain's original finding that brand loyalty accrues to the pioneer. Schmalensee presents a *theoretical* model that incorporates product differentiation advantages for the pioneer. Although the model he proposes is packed with what the author admits are implausible assumptions, he concludes that

> . . . brands enter sequentially, and consumers are initially skeptical about their quality. When consumers become convinced that the first brand in any product class performs satisfactorily, that brand becomes the standard against which subsequent brands are rationally judged. It thus becomes harder for later entrants to persuade consumers to invest in learning about their qualities than it was for the first brand.[2]

It is important to note that Schmalensee's model does not test that hypothesis. It merely incorporates it into a mathematical representation. The model has been widely cited as an illustration of product differentiation advantages that accrue to pioneers.

An Opportunity to Pick the Best Market Position

Pioneers have the first opportunity at product positioning. If they understand the market correctly and can correctly predict which product attributes will ultimately be most important to consumers, they can preempt the most favorable market position before later entrants even have a product on the market. Later entrants will then be forced to pick between two unappealing choices: (1) They can adopt an inferior product position, or (2) they can copy the pioneer's product position and be saddled with the perception that their product is a "me-too," second-rate entry. Both strategic choices place the later entrant at a competitive disadvantage. By moving first, the pioneer preempts the premier positioning strategy, forcing the later entrant into an unfavorable, and often untenable, market position.

Technological Leadership

Because it starts first, the pioneer is likely to have a head start in technology as well as market position. While competitors play catch-up, the innovator can pursue the next technological generation, staying one step ahead of lagging entrants.

An Opportunity to Set Product Standards

Pioneers have an opportunity to define an emerging product category in terms of their own products. They can set industry standards, which later entrants are forced to follow. The first group of customers becomes familiar with the pioneer's product. As that established base of users grows, it becomes harder and harder for later entrants to switch the market to its own proprietary standard. The later entrant is forced to imitate the pioneer's product and adopt a subservient position.

Access to Distribution

In many cases, there is room for only a limited number of brands in distribution channels. By virtue of being first, pioneers ensure that their products have access to preferential distribution. Later entrants are less fortunate. They may find themselves shut out of the distribution network simply because of their later entry. In the early days of personal computers, for example, there were nearly 150 different brands, only a handful of which found their way into the computer-store retailing chains, which were the dominant form of distribution in the early 1980s. Many technologically worthy brands perished for lack of distribution caused by later entry.

Experience Effects

Experience effects are cost advantages that accrue to the firm that has produced the largest accumulated volume. Since the pioneer is the first entrant, it is most likely to slide down the experience curve faster than later entrants. These cost advantages place later entrants with less experience at a competitive disadvantage. That gives the pioneer a price advantage that cannot be matched by later entrants. Typical of such claims is the comment that "the initial price advantage for an established brand gives it a market share advantage over time and may enable it to enjoy a monopoly in the market."[3]

Patents as a Barrier to Entry

Patents granted on innovative products can be used to lock out later entrants. Innovative pioneers are able to gain control over the essence of innovative products, which allows them to reap the economic benefits.

Switching Costs as a Barrier to Entry

Pioneers can also raise barriers to entry by building mutually beneficial relationships with their customers. Those relationships keep customers loyal to the pioneer's product and keep competitors at bay. Long-term contracts, familiarity with the first supplier's product, a lack of incentive to switch, and other intentional and unintentional inhibitors serve to bind the buyer to the first seller.

Support for First-Mover Advantages

Numerous empirical studies claim to have found that first-mover advantages result in long-lived market share advantages for pioneers. Table 2.1 lists some of the studies that have found in favor of pioneering.

FREE-RIDER EFFECTS

Critics contend that the benefits of pioneering have been grossly oversold. While in theory first-mover advantages appear to be strong and immutable, in practice they prove to be weak and vulnerable to the actions of crafty later entrants.

Criticisms of Studies Supporting First-Mover Advantages

Criticisms of pioneering have been made for decades, but in recent years the voices of critics have gained strength. Consider some of the criticisms that have been leveled against pioneering.

TABLE 2.1
EMPIRICAL STUDIES THAT FOUND FOR PIONEERING

Study	Sample	Conclusion
Bond and Lean (1977)[a]	Two prescription drugs	"The advantage to firms of being first to offer a new type of drug is considerable, and physicians' first brands appear to insulate firms from competition even more effectively than do patents." (p. 77)
Whitten (1979)[b]	Seven cigarette product categories	". . . the first entry brand received a substantial and enduring sales advantage." (p. 41)
Robinson and Fornell (1985)[c]	371 mature consumer goods manufacturing businesses in the PIMS database	"In a broad cross section of consumer goods businesses, market pioneers generally have substantially higher market shares than later entrants." (p. 305)
Urban et al. (1986)[d]	24 frequently purchased consumer products	"The results of our analysis imply a significant market share penalty for later entrants." (p. 655)
Lambkin (1988)[e]	129 start-up and 187 adolescent businesses in the PIMS database	". . . these results confirm the general tendency observed in previous research for pioneers to out-perform all later entrants . . ." (p. 137)
Robinson (1988)[f]	1,209 mature industrial goods manufacturing businesses and 584 mature consumer goods businesses (an update of Robinson and Fornell 1985) in the PIMS database	"In a broad cross-section of mature industrial goods businesses, market pioneers have important market share advantages over later entrants." (p. 93)
Carpenter and Nakamoto (1989)[g]	Two experiments using a total of 103 MBA students	". . . the pioneer occupies a favorable perceptual position that is difficult to imitate and costly to compete against, yielding a powerful competitive advantage." (p. 298)

TABLE 2.1 (CONTINUED)
EMPIRICAL STUDIES THAT FOUND FOR PIONEERING

Study	Sample	Conclusion
Kardes and Kalyanaram (1992)[h]	Two longitudinal experiments using a total of 86 MBA students	". . . judgmental processes lead to a long-run pioneering advantage . . ." (p. 356)

[a] Ronald Bond and David Lean, *Sales, Promotion, and Product Differentiation in Two Prescription Drug Markets* (Washington, D.C.: Federal Trade Commission, Bureau of Economics, February 1977).

[b] Ira Whitten, *Brand Performance in the Cigarette Industry and the Advantage of Early Entry, 1913–1974* (Washington, D.C.: Federal Trade Commission, Bureau of Economics, 1979).

[c] William Robinson and Claes Fornell, "Sources of Market Pioneer Advantages: The Case of Consumer Goods Industries," *Journal of Marketing Research*, August 1985, pp. 305–17.

[d] Glen Urban, Theresa Carter, Steve Gaskin, and Zofia Mucha, "Market Share Rewards to Pioneering Brands: An Empirical Analysis and Strategic Implications," *Management Science*, June 1986, pp. 645–59.

[e] Mary Lambkin, "Order of Entry and Performances in New Markets," *Strategic Management Journal*, Summer 1988, pp. 127–40.

[f] William Robinson, "Sources of Market Pioneer Advantages: The Case of Industrial Goods Industries," *Journal of Marketing Research*, February 1988, pp. 87–94.

[g] Gregory Carpenter and Kent Nakamoto, "Consumer Preference Formation and Pioneering Advantage," *Journal of Marketing Research*, August 1989, pp. 285–98.

[h] Frank Kardes and Gurumurthy Kalyanaram, "Order-of-Entry Effects on Consumer Memory and Judgment: An Information Integration Perspective," *Journal of Marketing Research*, August 1992, pp. 343–57.

The trouble with being a pioneer is that the pioneers get killed by the Indians.[4]

. . . the belief that entry order automatically endows first movers with immutable competitive advantages and later entrants with overwhelming disadvantages in naïve in light of conceptual and empirical evidence[5]

The fundamental question of when a firm should enter a market, and the profits it can expect to accrue from that decision, remain unanswered.[6]

What about the empirical studies that support pioneering? Don't they *prove* that pioneering is preferable? Critics claim that the studies listed in Table 2.1 are biased in favor of pioneers.

Much of the empirical evidence on the market share advantages of pioneering comes from studies that use the PIMS database. PIMS is a computerized database of the business experience of hundreds of large, diversified companies competing in literally thousands of individual businesses. It has been used to answer many strategic questions. The PIMS database is a godsend for researchers in that it facilitates data collection and analysis, but it is burdened by two key limitations.

First, PIMS tallies data only on successful pioneers. It includes no data on pioneers who failed. In essence, PIMS studies conclude that pioneering is successful after studying only successful pioneers. That implies that pioneer-

ing is much less risky than it actually is. Most PIMS studies recognize this shortcoming; for example:

> Because failures in creating new markets are not recognized . . . the results clearly overstate the returns for attempting to pioneer the market.[7]

However, proponents tend to downplay those limitations.

A second criticism is that PIMS businesses are not representative of those typically found in most competitive encounters. The database consists almost solely of large firms, many of which are members of the Fortune 500. It is competition solely among giants. As such, it provides few clues as to how small, entrepreneurial pioneers fare against large, later entrants with tremendous competitive advantages in distribution, marketing, and finance. Again, the researchers themselves speak freely about these limitations but downplay their importance:

> . . . there is an upward bias in the performance of the businesses studied here, because they are all subsidiaries of large successful operations (many in the Fortune 500) which have clearly survived their early attempts.[8]

> . . .the findings do *not* necessarily apply when a relatively weak pioneer is challenged by established giants. The outcome of this competitive battle hinges on the force of brute strength strategies versus the pioneer's first-mover advantages.[9]

In conclusion, the evidence in favor of pioneering advantages based solely on the PIMS database is subject to a number of severe criticisms that cast considerable doubt on the findings.

A second criticism of empirical studies that find in favor of pioneering is that they use unrepresentative student samples. In Table 2.1, two of the studies are subject to this criticism. The authors of one of those studies freely admits that the results are questionable. In their own words, "The limitations of our laboratory setting are obvious and our conclusions must be, to a certain extent, speculative.[10]

A second criticism of pro-pioneering studies is that some are based on peculiar products. Two studies stand out in that regard—one that claims first-mover advantages in cigarettes, another that makes similar claims for pioneers in prescription drugs. Critics argue that these product categories are not representative of other markets. What they say about first-mover advantages is difficult to generalize.

In fact, one study that is widely cited as support for first-mover advantages actually shows something quite different when examined closely. Ira Whit-

ten looked at the advantages of pioneering cigarette brands in seven newly created product categories between 1913 and 1974. He claims to have found support for pioneering in six of seven cigarette submarkets, but in fact pioneers earned an indisputable long-term market share lead in only two of the seven markets studied:

1. *Regular non-filters*. Camel, which was introduced in 1913, held a long-term market share advantage over later entrants, although it lost its lead for a few years to Lucky Strike, the second entrant, and Chesterfield, a later entrant.
2. *King-size non-filters:* Pall Mall was the first and long-term market leader.

Later entrants surpassed the pioneer in three markets:

1. *Plain filters:* Parliament was first introduced in 1931, but distribution was limited. Viceroy was the first nationally distributed pioneer, introduced in 1936. When the market soared in the early 1950s, many other entrants followed. By the mid-1950s, Winston and then Marlboro outpaced Viceroy.
3. *Menthol:* Kool menthol non-filters were introduced in the 1930s. By the 1950s the market had changed. Salem (the pioneer according to Whitten) was the first menthol filter. Salem took the clear lead. Kool, however, retaliated with a filter of its own, more menthol flavor, and a clever advertising campaign. Kool surpassed Salem in 1973 after Salem's fifteen-year lead.
4. *Low-tar:* True was introduced in 1966. Many other entrants followed. Vantage, a much later entrant, was introduced in 1970. Vantage surpassed True in 1974 by spending more on advertising.

The two remaining markets studied by Whitten turned out to be short-lived specialty segments. Both segments were dominated by a single pioneering brand:

1. *High filtration:* a short-lived segment created by Kent.
6. *Charcoal filters:* "the latest fad" (p. 35) in the mid-1960s fad dominated by Tareyton.

In sum, of the seven markets Whitten studied, pioneers earned a long-term market share advantage in two, later entrants prevailed in three, and pioneers dominated in two short-lived fads. Depending on how the results

are tallied, either pioneers or later entrants prevailed. Under any interpretation, later entrants did better than researchers give them credit for.

The evidence in favor of later entry becomes even more compelling because Whitten stacked the deck in favor of pioneers. To be classified as a pioneer in Whitten's study, a brand had to do more than merely enter the market first. The pioneer also had to "promote, and widely distribute a brand for which there was a favorable market trend."[11] That definition, along with the high level of industry concentration, ignored the role played by small entrepreneurial firms that lack national distribution in pioneering new markets. Whitten considered only large, well-financed, successful pioneers.

Whitten also failed to consider product failures. No categories were studied for "ethnic" cigarettes, such as "Uptown," or smokeless cigarettes, which failed to create growth markets and served as traps for unsuspecting pioneers.

Finally, pioneers in the cigarette industry had a peculiar advantage. They could not be challenged by later entrants who sold at lower prices. Until recently, there was no price competition among major brands. All brands carried the same price, a practice that had been in effect since the 1920s.

Support for Free-Rider Effects

Critics argue that constructing actual case histories of sequential market entry is a more realistic approach than that employed by supporters of pioneering. Analyses based on historical profiles of actual competitive entries have proved much more supportive of imitation and later entry, and much less supportive of pioneering. Some of the more important studies are listed in Table 2.2

Numerous benefits have been proposed for later entrants. Some of the more important ones are described here.

Avoiding Products That Have No Potential

Later entrants avoid spending time and money on products for which later there turns out to be no demand. Their strategy is to sit back and watch. Only when the market potential becomes clearly favorable do they move in and gain a viable, and often commanding, lead. That reduces their risks and lowers their costs considerably, although they may have to spend heavily during the later stages of market development to overcome their later start.

TABLE 2.2
EMPIRICAL STUDIES THAT FOUND FOR LATER ENTRY

Study	Sample	Conclusion
Cooper (1979)[a]	a survey of executives concerning 195 new product projects in Canadian firms	". . . the advantages of being 'first in' are almost equally balanced by the many pitfalls and disadvantages." (p. 102)
Glazer (1985)[b]	"a careful study of entry and exit in several dozen markets" for daily newspapers in Iowa. (p. 474)	"Observers who look only at the performance of early entrants in successful markets will overestimate the advantages of innovation." (p. 479)
Schnaars (1986)[c]	detailed case histories of 12 product categories	"Pioneering, early entry, and late entry—each has produced its share of winners and losers . . . blanket statements such as *pioneering is best* cannot be supported." (p. 36)
Sullivan (1991)[d]	historical profiles of 11 consumer nondurable product categories	". . . late-entering brand extensions have been able to attain large market shares, even in the face of competition from strong incumbents." (from the summary)
Golder and Tellis (1992)[e]	detailed historical analysis of 50 consumer products	". . . being first in a new market may not confer automatic long-term rewards. An alternative strategy worth considering may be to let other firms pioneer and explore markets, and enter after learning more about the structure and dynamics of the market." (p. 26)

[a] Robert Cooper, "The Dimensions of Industrial New Product Success and Failure," *Journal of Marketing,* Summer 1979, pp. 93–102.

[b] A. Glazer, "The Advantages of Being First," *American Economic Review,* June 1985, pp. 473–80.

[c] Steven Schnaars, "When Entering Growth Markets, Are Pioneers Better Than Poachers?" *Business Horizons,* March–April 1986, pp. 27–36.

[d] Mary Sullivan, *Brand Extension and Order of Entry* (Cambridge, Mass: Marketing Science Institute, Report no. 91-105, March 1991).

[e] Peter Golder and Gerard Tellis, *Do Pioneers Really Have Long-Term Advantages? A Historical Analysis,* (Cambridge Mass: Marketing Science Institute, Report no. 92-124, September 1992).

Survivor Bias

Advocates who claim powerful and long-lasting benefits for pioneering often fail to consider the risk inherent in pioneering new and unproven markets. They fall victim to sample bias. Most studies of first-mover advantages focus solely on markets that started small and ended up large. They do not consider markets that started small and ended up even smaller. As a result, those studies minimize the extent to which money and effort are wasted on products for which there is no demand. They eliminate much of the risk of pioneering from the analysis. Those advocates inadvertently ignore the fact that many pioneers simply are not around to study at a later date. If a similar methodology were applied to assess the characteristics of big slot machine winners, it might conclude that big winners tend to bet big and play often. That would be because the study examined only large winners. But in gambling, playing often is likely to lead to large losses as well as that one large win.

The failure to consider forecasting errors can drastically influence the results. Consider the findings of a study that examined the success of Iowa newspapers over a 140-year period. It reasoned that if two newspapers sequentially entered an Iowa market, the pioneer should survive longer than the second entrant. Initially, that reasoning appeared sound. In thirteen of the eighteen markets that contained a successful first and second entrant, the first entrant did indeed survive longer. The author concludes: "It appeared that in a competition between first and second entrants, the first entrant possesses a significant advantage."[12]

The results were radically different, however, when markets where demand failed to materialize were included in the analysis. The results showed that "first and later entrants earn identical expected profits." The advantage of pioneering may be ensured by the failure to consider pioneers who failed and disappeared.

A more recent study by Golder and Tellis examined patterns of pioneering and later entry in 50 product categories.[13] Pioneering proved fairly risky. Overall, 47 percent of pioneers failed. Furthermore, market pioneers maintained leadership in only 11 percent of thirty-six cases. The authors conclude that previous studies did not adequately consider survival bias.

Estimates of New Product Failure Rates

Although the business press is chock full of *post hoc* reviews of emerging technologies and successful new products, the fact is that many new products, especially radically new products, fail to generate much interest among

buyers. Expectations for demand typically turn out to be much higher than actual sales. For every cellular telephone there is a picture telephone. For every Polaroid camera there is a "Nimslo," a three-dimensional camera—a sort of late-twentieth-century update of the hand-held stereoscopic devices found in antique stores. For every Nylon there are innumerable Corfams. The fact is, many pioneers introduce new products for which there is no demand. That means they spend time, effort, and money on opportunities that do not exist.

If survivor bias inflates the advantages of pioneering, then the key question becomes: How likely is it that the pioneer will pursue an opportunity that will not pan out? Some indication of those odds can be gleaned from the surprisingly small body of research of new product success and failure rates.

There are actually two ways to measure product success and failure. The first way is to assess the likelihood that a new product idea, once conceived, will eventually make its way to market. Studies that have looked at that issue conclude that the majority of new product ideas are killed before ever being sold to actual consumers. That is, money is spent on ideas that never reach the market. The second way to measure product success and failure is to assess the likelihood that once a product is brought to market it will be either accepted or rejected by consumers. The relationship between those two measures is illustrated graphically as follows:

The highest rate of product failure occurs during the first stage—the time between an idea's conception and its introduction in the market. Although precise estimates vary greatly, there is general agreement that the majority of new product ideas never make it to market. They are terminated at some stage of the development process. The innovative firm spends time and money on such products only to conclude that there is little chance of market success.

There is less agreement over how often products fail once they are actually placed on the market. Some experts claim that between 70 and 90 percent of all new products fail in the marketplace. One recent study, which surveyed 166 managers from 112 leading manufacturers and retailers, found that only 8 percent of new product projects actually made it to market and, *of those*, 83 percent failed when they were introduced.[14] All told, the managers felt that 99 percent of all new product effort is wasted on products that ultimately fail.

A widely cited study by C. Merle Crawford claims that such figures are

inflated. He looked at all of the *properly* conducted empirical studies on the topic of new product failure and concluded: "The best estimate from available studies is around 35% of new products fail."[15]

No matter which set of figures is correct, one point is clear: New products must run a gauntlet of risks before "success" can be claimed. A 1975 study by Edwin Mansfield and Samuel Wagner tried to capture the *overall* likelihood of success by assigning, and then combining, individual probability estimates at each stage of the new product development process—from a product idea to market success.[16] In 1987, Glenn Urban, John Hauser, and Nikhilesh Dholakia adapted that idea, changed the estimates to match their personal experiences, and extended it to consumer products.[17] They concluded that new consumer products have only a 16 percent chance of eventual market success. Fully 84 percent of new product ideas fail somewhere along the line.

Probability of Successful Design		Probability of Successful Test Market Given Design		Probability of Market Success Given Successful Test Market		Overall Probability of Success
50%	X	45%	X	70%	=	16%

A similar set of estimates concluded that new industrial goods have a 27 percent chance of success.

Probability of Technical Completion		Probability of Commericalization Given Technical Completion		Probability of Economic Success Given Commericalization		Overall Probability of Success
57%	X	65%	X	74%	=	27%

Clearly, there is a tremendous amount of financial risk in new product development. The chances of failure are especially high for radically new technological products and products that establish entirely new categories. As Crawford notes: "The higher a project's financial return, the higher the risk of failure associated with it."[18] But he also notes, "nothing ventured, nothing gained." Only by accepting high risks can a firm hope to earn high returns. As a random-walker might note: "There is no such thing as a free lunch."

Or is there? The nothing ventured, nothing gained argument assumes a strong bond between the bearer of high risks and the recipient of high rewards. The strength of that bond rests solely on the extent to which the

pioneer is able to hold on to the fruits of its product development process. If a later entrant is able to partake in the rewards without having to partake in the risks, which are borne solely by the pioneer, then the risks of innovation are raised considerably, while the rewards are lowered. The risks fall solely to the pioneer, while the rewards spread to others. From the perspective of the later entrant, that adage can be twisted to state: "much gained with little ventured." No wonder proponents of free-rider effects claim that later entrants benefit greatly by avoiding product failures.

Lower R&D Expenditures

Imitation is less expensive than innovation. It avoids many of the costs that must be borne solely by the first entrant. The innovator, for example, is forced to spend heavily on research and development and educating wary consumers as to the desirable benefits of the new product. The question is not whether imitation is less expensive than innovation—it clearly is—but whether sustainable benefits accrue to the pioneer who takes on those enormous expenses. That point is debatable.

Innovators are forced to spend heavily on research and development in order to identify and bring to market new products. That expanse is justified by the assumption that innovators gain a long lead on imitators, who are simply unable to catch up. How likely is that scenario? An empirical study by Edwin Mansfield found that the opposite outcome is more probable. The study examined data from one hundred firms and found that imitation often occurs quickly. It concluded that new product R&D projects typically found their way into the hands of competitors within twelve to eighteen months. In 20 percent of the cases, competitors knew of new product development projects within six months of their inception. Since it takes about three years for a new product to make its way from an idea to the marketplace, "there is a better-than-even chance that the decision will leak out before the innovation is half completed."[19] That leakage weakens the allure of purported first-mover advantages and enhances the appeal of free-rider effects. It also explains why imitation occurs so quickly in many applications.

Companies learn about each other's new product development projects (1) by monitoring each other's patent applications, which require going public with the firm's innovative ideas, (2) through papers and presentations at professional and academic conferences attended by scientists and engineers, and (3) when technical and marketing personnel switch jobs, taking with them inside information that, if not maliciously, then unintentionally, spreads knowledge.

A subsequent study by Mansfield, Schwartz, and Wagner found that it

typically takes the imitator only 70 percent of the time it takes the innovator to get a product to market.[20] The reason is simple: The imitator does not have to slog through the same arduous innovation process as the innovator.

Relative Costs of Innovation Versus Copying

It is clearly cheaper to imitate than to innovate. The imitator avoids many of the costs incurred by the innovator. Support for that proposition also comes primarily from Mansfield, Schwartz, and Wagner. They examined forty-eight product innovations in the chemical, ethical drug, electronics, and machinery industries and found that, on average, imitation costs were only 65 percent of innovation costs. The authors note that imitation is less expensive for the following reason:

> An imitator frequently can spend much less time and money on research than the innovator because the product's existence and characteristics provide the imitator with a great deal of information that the innovator had to obtain through its own research.[21]

If anything, the findings of that study *understate* the cost advantages of the imitator. First, 70 percent of the products they studied were patented. Second, nearly 40 percent were ethical drugs, in an industry where, in the authors' own words, "patents had a bigger impact on imitation costs."[22] Even so, within four years, 60 percent of the patented products have been copied. Patents did not stop copycats from entering. They simply drove up the costs of imitation, by an average of 11 percent.

The authors found that patents were most protective in the ethical drug industry, where patents increased imitation costs by 30 percent. That suggests that ethical drugs are peculiar rather than representative of the likelihood of imitation in the majority of markets.

It is also at odds with a study that is often held up as an example of the power of first-mover advantages. In 1977, Bond and Lean studied order-of-entry effects for two prescription drug markets: oral diuretics and antianginals. They found strong advantages for pioneering in both markets.

Oral diuretics are drugs used to treat edema and hypertension. In late 1957 Merck introduced Diuril, the pioneering product. Ciba entered second in early 1959 with Esidrix, a superior product with a clear therapeutic advantage. Within two weeks, however, Merck retaliated with HydroDiuril, a reformulated product that incorporated the same therapeutic advances as Ciba's Esidrix. The results were clear: The innovator won, and the second entrant failed. By 1971 Merck had swamped its competitors with a 52 percent market share. Pioneering paid off for Merck.

The latest entrants fared worst of all. Eli Lilly entered the diuretics market with Anhydron—a "me-too" product—six years after pioneer Merck, with a strategy based solely on heavy promotion. The copycat product failed to gain share. Bond and Lean conclude: "Brands that are the first to offer some therapeutic advantage should fare better in the marketplace than brands that merely duplicate existing therapy."[23]

Strong first-mover advantages were also observed for antianginals, an ethical drug that relieves the pain of blocked coronary arteries. Warner-Lambert introduced Peritrate in 1952. By 1956, Peritrate (and variations) held more than 70 percent of the market. Later entrants entered in droves. By 1971, ninety-seven firms were selling 229 brands of antianginals. Still, Warner-Lambert maintained a 30 percent share. Why did Peritrate succeed? In this case, patents played no part: Peritrate was not patented. Bond and Lean attribute success to two factors: (1) Peritrate was the pioneer and, as a result, (2) doctors were reluctant to switch from the first brand with which they had become familiar.

To what extent do the Bond and Lean results apply to other industries? Very little. In fact, the authors themselves question whether their results apply even to *other ethical drugs*. They note: "The coronary vasodilator market is peculiar."[24] They are on the right track; the entire ethical drug industry is peculiar. It is characterized by conditions that favor pioneering. First, it is doctors, not consumers, who decide on the brand (especially at the time the study was conducted). Second, price is less important, because physicians, and in many cases the patients themselves, do not pay for the product. Third, patients have little knowledge of competitive products and even less opportunity for comparison shopping. In essence, the consumer buys what the doctor orders (especially at that time). Finally, patents are more protective in ethical drugs than in most other industries. Overall, few other markets offer the peculiar combination of conditions found in ethical drugs. What the Bond and Lean study really indicates is that pioneering leads to clear advantages in some very selective instances.

An Opportunity to Gain Share with Heavy Promotion

Later entrants may also be able to make up for their slow start by spending heavily on marketing. In other words, they may be able to trade up-front R&D expenditures for later promotional spending, thereby nurturing what they are unable to conceive. A study of the new product practices of two hundred firms by Robert Cooper offers support for that contention.[25] It found that heavy spending on R&D did not increase the likelihood of new product success. In fact, it found: "Marketing resources appear to be the

most critical in deciding a successful new product program." The strength of the marketing areas—market research, advertising, promotion, sales force, and distribution prowess—were far more influential than expertise in the technological areas—engineering, R&D, and production. Cooper found that some firms relied more heavily on marketing to push their products than on R&D to gain a dominant position.

One of the most widely cited studies in support of first-mover advantages was conducted by Urban, Carter, Gaskin, and Mucha. It examined the effect of four variables—order of entry, lag between entry, positioning, and advertising—on market share. Overall, the authors conclude: "The results of our analysis imply a significant market share penalty for later entrants." Upon closer examination, however, the study actually concludes something quite different. More specifically, the authors note that "the second brand will . . . earn less than three quarters of the share of the pioneering brand *if its advertising and positioning are equal.*"[26] That turns out to be a big "if." It suggests that later entrants can overcome pioneering advantages *if* they have a better product and more advertising. In fact, the study found that "advertising" and "positioning" have stronger effects on market share than "order of entry," which implies that a focus on those variables, rather than on pioneering, will result in higher long-term market share. The authors themselves state this point clearly: "If the pioneer does not carefully design its product and an improved product is subsequently introduced and aggressively promoted by a competitor, the market share reward for innovation may be lost."[27] In sum, rather than unqualified support for later entry, Urban and colleagues found a *tendency* for pioneering to lead to market success. Their study actually shows that promotional expenditures can often be used to counteract first-mover advantages.

Lower Costs of Educating Consumers

By being first, pioneers must spend heavily to inform and persuade consumers as to the merits of a new product. That is especially true for radical innovations with which consumers are unfamiliar. In such instances the innovator must spend heavily, over long periods of time, to incubate a technology before it attracts large numbers of paying customers. During that incubation period, costs are high and revenues are low as the product prepares for life outside the pioneer's womb. Once again, the merits of such heavy up-front expenditures to incubate the market are defendable only if the rewards accrue to the early spender. If the pioneer is forced to spend heavily to convince the public of the product's promise only to lose its early lead, then waiting may be a preferable strategy to pioneering.

Technological Leapfrog

When a major new product is introduced, one that creates a huge growth market, it is never quite clear what the innovation will ultimately look like. Rarely do innovations spring forth from the laboratory fully formed. Instead, they are often crudely formed devices, based on first-generation technologies that evolve with the markets they seek to serve. The question is: What happens when the first-generation technology falls by the wayside?

Proponents claim technology leadership is a key benefit of pioneering. The pioneer is able to update its technology to stay current with the latest development. Later entrants are not so lucky. As a result of their later entry, they are perpetually one step behind the pioneer. Or are they?

In many cases, first-generation technology presents both a risk and an opportunity for pioneers. Typically, the pioneer picks the most modern technology available at the time of first entry. But that choice can quickly become dated. The pioneers may then find it difficult to switch technologies once they have invested so much in the first generation. The switch from 8-bit to 16-bit personal computers, Wordstar to WordPerfect in word processing software, and CP/M to MS-DOS in operating systems was anything but smooth. In each case, as well as in many others, the change in technology favored later entrants over pioneers. The pioneers were worse off than those who entered later. As the technology evolved, later entrants had an opportunity to leapfrog pioneers.

Sticking the Pioneer with an Obsolete Standard

Proponents of pioneering argue that the very first entrant has the advantage when it comes to setting standards. By being first, the pioneer is able to impose its standard on the market, forcing followers into the subservient position of imitating its innovative design. Once again, practice is often at odds with the theory.

It is true that a product standard eventually emerges, which defines the entire product category. Many sellers then rally around that standard. In personal computers, for example, there were competing and proprietary operating systems until IBM largely standardized the design of a personal computer around the MS-DOS standard in 1981. Matsushita likewise set the VHS standard for VCRs. Abernathy and Utterback refer to this process as the emergence of a "dominant design."[28]

But standards are not necessarily set by first-generation technology. That, too, creates an opportunity for later entrants. In the case of VCRs and per-

sonal computer operating systems, as well as many others, later entrants were unencumbered by investments and reputation in first-generation designs. By adopting a wait-and-see attitude, they are able to enter at a point where the market has grown larger and more appealing with a product targeted specifically at the most attractive segments. As a result, standards are often set by larger, more powerful later entrants, who enter later but with a superior product.

One point is clear: It is nearly impossible for the pioneer to get everything right on the first try. To do so would require an ability to forecast changes in the market and technology that is simply not possible with today's tools. It is incorrect to assume that early market moves automatically bestow long-lived first-mover advantages on the pioneer. In fact, the exact opposite may be more likely.

An Opportunity to Benefit from Market Changes

Not only are products not fully formed when they are first brought to market, but the market for those products is often poorly formed as well. The kinds of consumers who purchase at the beginning often differ in their needs from those who enter later in larger numbers. The earliest customers for personal computers and computer software, for example, were technically oriented hobbyists who needed little customer service and support. That changed when the market turned mainstream, attracting business users lacking technical skills. Then distribution turned to high-service, high-cost computer stores, where the product could be demonstrated and skills taught. The final turn came when the product became so widespread as to be virtually generic. At that time, mail order sales boomed, price became the most important criterion, and the power of prestigious brand names to command higher margins declined.

As a result of changes in the market served, the pioneer's product is often transformed from a mainstream design targeted to a small embryonic market to an obsolete design targeted to a small, fringe segment of a much larger market. In large-screen projection television, for example, the pioneer's early design hurt rather than helped. Its crude design was shunted to the sidelines by mainstream entries targeted directly to a larger new market.

If pioneers are able to garner the best market position, it is a temporary reward at best. What may have been the premier product-positioning strategy at the beginning is often an inferior market position later on. When the ultimate form of the market becomes clearer, the later entrant has an opportunity to design its product to fit that larger market more closely.

An Opportunity to Use Shared Experience

Once the potential of a market becomes clear, the later entrant has an opportunity to leap ahead of the pioneer by using "shared experience." Shared experience occurs when a firm has or does something closely related to what the pioneer claims as new. The later entrant may, for example, sell products that are similar, have experience with similar production methods, or distribute its products through similar channels. In addition, the later entrant may possess the marketing skills to sell similar products, which can be used to develop the market created by the pioneer. In short, the pioneer may be moving into a market where a dominant market leader holds all the cards.

Evidence from Entry into Existing Versus Growth Markets

Proponents of first-mover advantages claim that pioneers are often able to establish fortified positions in emerging markets. They are able to raise barriers to entry that keep latecomers out. Much of the evidence in support of that proposition comes from studies that examined the entry of firms into *existing* industries, not new markets. That raises questions about the true magnitude of first-mover advantages.

One of the most widely cited studies on the power of entry barriers was published by Joe Bain in 1956. He examined the conditions of entry faced by new competitors into twenty *established* industries. His results indicate that entry barriers place new entrants at a severe disadvantage. Economies of scale and absolute cost advantage were found to be important barriers, but the reputation benefits held by incumbent firms were found to be most important. Bain notes that "the advantage to established sellers accruing from buyer preferences for their products as opposed to potential entrant products is on average larger and more frequent in occurrence at larger values than any other barrier to entry.[29]

Proponents have interpreted Bain's findings as support for pioneering. Clearly, they reason, later entrants face the same barriers as those put up by the incumbent firms in Bain's study. On the face of it, the argument makes sense. But when examined more closely, the data support exactly the opposite conclusion.

The crux of the argument hinges on who is considered the pioneer, who is considered the incumbent, and who is considered the later entrant. The definitional differences between Bain's study and advocates of first-mover advantages are profound.

First, consider the nature of Bain's sample. Even a cursory glance at the

twenty industries he examined reveals that it consists solely of mature industries populated by strong, established sellers.

1. automobiles	11. meat packing
2. canned fruits and vegetables	12. metal containers
3. cement	13. petroleum refining
4. cigarettes	14. rayon
5. copper	15. shoes
6. farm machine	16. soap
7. flour	17. steel
8. fountain pens	18. tractors
9. gypsum products	19. typewriters
10. liquor	20. tires and tubes

Now consider a concrete example. Consider the beer industry, where Anheuser-Busch is the clear market leader. Using Bain's formulation, Anheuser-Busch would be classified as the incumbent, which has raised barriers to entry, making it difficult for new entrants to gain market share. New entrants would have a tough time introducing a parity product positioned directly against Busch's products. Proponents of first-mover advantages would interpret that case as an example in favor of pioneering.

But change the definitions slightly, and a completely different conclusion emerges. This time focus on markets rather than industries. Specifically, take the "light" beer segment, one of the longest-growing and fastest-growing product categories in the industry's history. Anheuser-Busch was one of the last entrants in that important category. A series of pioneers—ranging from Rheingold's Gablinger's to Miller Brewing's Lite beer—entered and dominated the market before Anheuser-Busch responded. But when Anheuser-Busch finally did enter with a "Bud-labeled" product, it was able to win back a significant share of the market even though it had entered much later than the pioneers.

In the first case, Anheuser-Busch is the industry incumbent and an early entrant. In the second case, it is the incumbent and a later entrant.

Bain was absolutely correct. Industry incumbents possess tremendous competitive advantages. But those advantages have little to do with pioneering. They arise from the power of shared experience—experience in reputation benefits from powerful brand names on related products, experience in distribution, experience in knowing how to advertise and having the money to do so. It was the industry incumbents who possessed the reputation benefits, not the innovative pioneers.

Bain was not studying the benefits of pioneering versus later entry in emerging growth markets. He was interested in how successful a firm would be when it tried to diversify from its own industry into another established industry. That is a different issue from assessing the likelihood of success of a later entrant who quickly follows a pioneer into a brand-new growth market.

The next chapter considers cases where later entrants prevailed against pioneers in emerging growth markets.

Imitators Who Surpassed Pioneers

In order to examine the relative power of free-rider effects, twenty-eight detailed case histories were constructed for situations where imitators surpassed pioneers in emerging markets:

1. 35mm cameras
2. Automated teller machines
3. Ballpoint pens
4. Caffeine-free soft drinks
5. CAT scanners
6. Commercial jet aircraft
7. Computerized ticketing services
8. Credit/charge cards
9. Diet soft drinks
10. Dry beer
11. Food processors
12. Light beer
13. Mainframe computers
14. Microwave ovens
15. Money-market mutual funds
16. MRIs
17. Nonalcoholic beer
18. Operating systems for personal computers
19. Paperback books
20. Personal computers
21. Pocket calculators
22. Projection television
23. Spreadsheets
24. Telephone answering machines
25. VCRs
26. Videogames
27. Warehouse clubs
28. Word-processing software

Table 3.1 (pp. 38–43) provides a more detailed summary. It lists the pioneers and the imitative later entrants, along with the dates they entered and the reasons for the imitators' success.

CHARACTERISTICS OF THE CASES

The twenty-eight cases were selected with the following specific criteria in mind.

TABLE 3.1
28 CASES WHERE IMITATORS SURPASSED PIONEERS

Product	Pioneer(s)	Imitator/Later Entrant(s)	Comments
1. 35mm cameras	Leica (1925) Contrax (1932) Exacta (1936)	Canon (1934) Nikon (1946) Nikon SLR (1959)	The pioneer was the technology and market leader for decades until the Japanese copied German technology, improved upon it, and lowered prices. The pioneer then failed to react and ended up as an incidental player.
2. Automated teller machines (ATMs)	Britain's DeLaRue (1967) Docutel (1969)	Diebold (1971) IBM (1973) NCR (1974)	The pioneer was a small, entrepreneurial upstart that faced two types of competitors: (1) larger firms with experience selling to banks and (2) the computer giants. The pioneer did not survive.
3. Ballpoint pens	Reynolds (1945) Eversharp (1946)	Parker "Jotter" (1954) Bic (1960)	The pioneers disappeared when the fad first ended in the late 1940s. Parker entered eight years later. Bic entered last and sold pens as cheap disposables.
4. Caffeine-free soft drinks	Canada Dry's "Sport" (1967) Royal Crown's RC100 (1980)	Pepsi Free (1982) Caffeine-free Coke, Diet Coke, Tab (1983)	The pioneer had a three-year head start on Coke but could not hope to match the distribution and promotional advantages of the giants.
5. CAT scanners (Computed Axial Tomography)	EMI (1972)	Pfizer (1974) Technicare (1975) GE (1976) Johnson & Johnson (1978)	The pioneer had no experience in the medical equipment industry. Copycats ignored its patents and drove the pioneer out of business with marketing, distribution, and financial advantages, as well as extensive industry experience.
6. Commercial jet aircraft	deHavilland Comet 1 (1952)	Boeing 707 (1958) Douglas DC-8	The British pioneer rushed to market with a jet that crashed frequently. Boeing followed with safer, larger, and more powerful jets unsullied by tragic crashes.

Product	Pioneer(s)	Imitator/Later Entrant(s)	Comments
7. Computerized ticketing services	Ticketron (1968)	Ticketmaster (1982)	A small, aggressive upstart with a better product displaced the arrogant pioneer whose parent was in deep financial trouble.
8. Credit/charge cards	Diners Club (1950)	Visa/Mastercard (1966) American Express (1958)	The pioneer was undercapitalized in a business where money is the key resource. AMEX entered last with funds from traveler's checks.
9. Diet soft drinks	Kirsch's No-Cal (1952) Royal Crown's Diet Rite Cola (1962)	Pepsi's Patio Cola (1963) Coke's Tab (1963) Diet Pepsi (1964) Diet Coke (1982)	The pioneer could not match the distribution advantages of Coke and Pepsi. Nor did it have the money needed for massive promotional campaigns.
10. Dry Beer	Asahi (1987)	Kirin, Sapporo, and Suntory in Japan (1988) Michelob Dry (1988) Bud Dry (1989)	The Japanese pioneer could not match Anheuser-Busch's financial, marketing, and distribution advantages in the U.S. market.
11. Food processors	Cuisinart (1973)	Lower-priced copies by Black & Decker (late-1970s) Sunbeam "Oskar" (1984)	The pioneer failed to sell lower-priced models. A leveraged buyout drove it into bankruptcy when the market became price-sensitive.
12. Light beer	Rheingold's Gablinger's (1966) Meister Brau Lite (1967)	Miller Lite (1975) Natural Light (1977) Coors Light (1978) Bud Light (1982)	The pioneers entered nine years before Miller and sixteen years before Bud Light, but financial problems drove both out of business. Marketing and distribution determined the outcome. Costly legal battles were commonplace.

TABLE 3.1 (CONTINUED)
28 CASES WHERE IMITATORS SURPASSED PIONEERS

Product	Pioneer(s)	Imitator/Later Entrant(s)	Comments
13. Mainframe computers	Atanasoff's ABC computer (1939) Eckert-Mauchly's ENIAC/UNIVAC (1946)	IBM (1953)	The marketing muscle of IBM, in particular its powerful sales force, proved no match for the tiny upstart. When the giant entered, it moved quickly to the forefront.
14. Microwave ovens	Raytheon "Radarange" for commercial market (1946) Tappan (1955) Amana (1968) Litton (1971)	Panasonic (early 1970s) Sharp (mid-1970s) Samsung (1980)	The pioneers spent two decades perfecting the product and developing the market. They sold premium products at premium prices. The Japanese, and then the Koreans, sold equal quality at much lower prices, which the pioneers could not match.
15. Money-market mutual funds	Reserve Fund of New York (1973)	Dreyfus Liquid Assets (1974) Fidelity Daily Income Trust (1974) Merrill Lynch Ready Assets (1975)	The tiny pioneer could not match the marketing, distribution, and financial advantages, as well as the reputation benefits, held by the imitators. Size mattered more than first entry. The later entrants swamped the pioneer with product variety.
16. MRI (magnetic resonance imaging)	Fonar (1978)	Johnson & Johnson's Technicare (1981) General Electric (1982)	The tiny pioneer faced the huge medical equipment suppliers, which easily expanded into MRIs. The pioneer could not hope to match their tremendous market power.
17. Nonalcoholic beer	G. Heileman's Kingsbuy (early 1980s) Switzerland's Moussy (1983)	Miller's Sharp's (1989) Anheuser-Busch's O'Doul's (1989) Coor's Cutter (1991)	The innovators had a six-year head start, but first-mover advantages were no match for the marketing and distribution advantages of the later entrants. Heileman was in bankruptcy by the time the imitators entered.

Product	Pioneer(s)	Imitator/Later Entrant(s)	Comments
18. Operating systems for personal computers	CP/M (1974)	MS-DOS (1981) Microsoft Windows (1985)	The pioneer created the early standard but did not upgrade for the IBM-PC. Microsoft bought an imitative upgrade and became the new standard. Windows entered later and borrowed heavily from predecessors, then emerged as the leading interface.
19. Paperback books	Penguin (1935 in England) (1939 in the U.S.) Modern Age Books (1937) Pocket Books (1939)	Avon (1941) Popular Library (1942) Dell (1943) Bantam (1946)	The first successful American entrant learned much from its predecessors. Although it remains a paperback powerhouse, the last major entrant is generally considered to be the mass market leader. It had rich corporate parents and easy access to titles.
20. Personal computers	MITS Altair 8800 (1975) Apple II (1977) Radio Shack (1977)	IBM-PC (1981) Compaq (1982) Dell (1984) Gateway (1985)	The pioneers created computers for hobbyists, but when the market turned to business uses, IBM entered and quickly dominated, using its reputation and its marketing and distribution skills. The cloners then copied IBM's standard and sold at lower prices.
21. Pocket calculators	Bowmar (1971)	Texas Instruments (1972)	The pioneer assembled calculators using TI's integrated circuits. TI controlled Bowmar's costs, which rose as calculator prices fell. Vertical integration was the key.
22. Projection television	Advent (1973) Sony (1973 with an industrial model) Kloss Video (1977)	Panasonic (1978) Mitsubishi (1980)	Everything seemed to be arrayed against the pioneer. It had no money and was beset by internal strife. It also faced Japanese giants who lowered prices and introduced a new design that rendered the pioneer's product obsolete. The pioneer went bankrupt.

TABLE 3.1 (CONTINUED)
28 CASES WHERE IMITATORS SURPASSED PIONEERS

Product	Pioneer(s)	Imitator/Later Entrant(s)	Comments
23. Spreadsheets	VisiCalc (1979)	Lotus 1-2-3 (1983)	The pioneer entered with a simple spreadsheet for primitive personal computers. Internal strife tore the firm apart while the imitator, who had developed part of VisiCalc's program, introduced a superior product for the IBM-PC.
24. Telephone answering machines	Code-A-Phone (1958)	Panasonic (mid-1970s) AT&T (1983)	The pioneer was late to move production overseas. It could not match the low-cost production of the later entrants with shared experience in related products.
25. VCRs	Ampex (1956) CBS-EVR (1970) Sony U-matic (1971) Cartrivision (1972) Sony Betamax (1975)	JVC VHS (1976) RCA Selectra Vision (1977) made by Matsushita	The pioneer focused on selling to broadcasters while Sony pursued the home market for more than a decade. Financial problems killed the pioneer. Sony Betamax was the first successful home VCR but was quickly supplanted by VHS, a late follower, which recorded for twice as long.
26. Videogames	Magnavox's Odyssey (1972), the first home game Atari's Pong (1972), the first coin-operated arcade game	Nintendo's Home Entertainment System (1985) Sega "Genesis" (1989) NEC "TurboGrafx" (1989)	The market went from boom to bust to boom. The bust occurred when home computers seemed likely to make game players obsolete. Kids lost interest when games lacked challenge. Price competition ruled. Nintendo rekindled interest with better games and restored market order with managed competition.
27. Warehouse clubs	Price Club (1976)	Sam's Club, Costco, Pace, and BJ's Wholesale Club (all entered in 1983)	The pioneer stuck to the Southern California market and could not match the financial resources of Wal-Mart's Sam's Club when it came to national expansion.

Product	Pioneer(s)	Imitator/Later Entrant(s)	Comments
28. Word-processing software	Wordstar (1979)	WordPerfect (1982) Microsoft Word (1983)	The pioneer was stuck with an obsolete standard when it failed to update. When it did update, Wordstar abandoned loyal users, offered no technical support, and fought internally. The follower took advantage.

Major Product Innovations

Most of the cases focus on major new products. In some instances they are the kinds of innovations that have changed the way we live. The intent was to avoid minor brand extensions of the type typically found on supermarket shelves. New cake and cookie preparations, for example, which change the size of the item or use a new flavored filling, were not considered. For the most part, the goal was to study competitive behavior in markets for important innovations that make a significant economic impact.

A Bias Toward High-Technology Products

More than half of the products listed qualify as high-technology products. Some are now so commonplace that they are no longer considered hi-tech, although they were when first introduced. Again, the intent was to focus on the types of innovations that are often perceived as the engines of economic growth.

A Bias Toward Consumer-oriented Products

My goal was to focus on products with which consumers have some direct experience. Some, like 35mm cameras and telephone answering machines, are items that consumers purchase directly for their own use. Commercial jet aircraft and CAT scanners, on the other hand, are examples of products that consumers do not purchase themselves but use through intermediaries. The intent was to avoid strictly industrial producs with which general readers would be unfamiliar. Previous studies of innovation, such as the one published by Jewkes, Sawers, and Stillerman more than a generation ago, which also relied on an analysis of case histories, have investigated such industrial products as tungsten carbide and continuous hot strip rolling in addition to consumer products like safety razors.[1]

Surpassed Rather than Merely Gained Share

There are different ways to measure the success of imitative later entries. Assessing whether the later entrant was able to gain a viable share of the market would be one way, or whether the imitator earned a profit. This study relies on the strictest measure of marketplace success. In every one of the cases considered in this chapter, the imitator *replaced* the pioneer as the market leader. Not only did the imitator gain a foothold in the market, it dominated the pioneer. In many cases, the pioneer was forced out of existence after the competitive battle had ended.

Competition in Emerging Versus Existing Markets

Every one of the cases listed above examines competitive market entry in an emerging growth market. None of them examines the entry of an outsider into a mature business dominated by a standing incumbent. Typically, the cases unfolded as follows: A pioneer would recognize a brand new opportunity, then later entrants would follow with an imitative product. What all the cases have in common is a high level of market growth.

That is different from competition in mature markets. Consider, for example, the automobile industry. When the Japanese auto sellers started to gain a significant share of the American automobile market from the Big Three American auto giants in the 1970s, it was not a case of pioneers and later entrants. Neither is the case of a firm that introduces a new kitchen cleanser in the 1990s and gains share on a dominant seller who entered in the late nineteenth century. Such cases are interesting examples of market share gains in mature markets, but they are hardly examples of competitive market entry strategies in new and emerging markets. Consequently, they are not considered.

HOW THE LIST WAS COMPILED

The cases listed in Table 3.1 were identified over a ten-year period from personal interviews, literature searches, mentions in other studies on pioneering and later entry, articles clipped and saved over the years, and just about anywhere else information could be found. The cases do not represent a random sample. They are more like a census of those important instances where later entrants with imitative products displaced pioneers with innovative products.

Selection was also restricted with respect to timing. Only entries that took

place in the post-World War II period were considered. It seemed unreasonable to draw contemporary conclusions from century-old cases, such as later entrant Goodyear's dominance in rubber tires over an even earlier entrant toward the end of the last century or Kodak's win over Daguerreotype. Besides, an excellent review of such cases is provided elsewhere, also using historical analysis.[2]

HOW THE CASES WERE CONSTRUCTED

The case histories were constructed from data drawn from multiple sources. In most cases, that entailed consulting then current newspaper reports, trade association data, articles in business magazines, in-depth industry analyses, and expert opinions. The *Wall Street Journal*, *New York Times*, *Business Week*, *Forbes*, and *Fortune* were particularly helpful, as were case histories constructed by other authors for other purposes. Citations of important works are noted in the cases themselves.

Specific attention was paid to dates of entry (and exit) as they were reported in the business press. The overriding goal was to reconstruct the events as they occurred. Researching the cases was a fascinating process that at times seemed like detective work. Little by little the pieces of the puzzle fell into place.

The cases themselves vary in length, the longest totaling fourteen typewritten pages. The length of any one case depends on the details needed to tell the story. In some instances, it is a relatively simple and unadorned tale of the rise and fall of sequential entrants. In others, there are complications and nuances that require greater length. The intent is to relate the events that characterized the emergence of the market and the competitive battle for dominance that ensued as the product category evolved.

1. 35mm CAMERAS

The development of the 35mm camera followed the development of 35mm film. An assistant to Thomas Edison may have been responsible for the creation of 35mm film. In the late 1800s, that assistant was working on a movie camera to supplement Edison's phonograph. According to industry lore, the 35mm standard was forever set in stone when that assistant ripped a roll of George Eastman's 70mm movie film lengthwise into two 35mm strips.[3] From that moment on, the 35mm camera was inextricably tied to refinements in 35mm film.

During the first few decades of the twentieth century, many inventors toyed with still-picture cameras using the 35mm format. At the time, it was a radical idea. If detailed negatives could be made on smaller-than-usual film, then images could be enlarged into full-size prints. That technology eventually replaced the huge box cameras of the past, which were built around huge negative plates that were turned directly into prints. The 35mm camera was the first major step toward miniaturization in photography. But smaller negatives required more sophisticated film, which was unavailable during those early years. Better 35mm cameras had to await better film.

Some experts consider the "Tourist Multiple" camera of 1913 by Herbert & Hugesson of New York to be the first 35mm camera offered commercially, but, like many failed pioneering innovations, it "came at the wrong time."[4] Its price was outrageously high ($175 in 1913), film quality was still notoriously poor, and World War I put a damper on European travel by American tourists, the target market for this pioneering innovation. Needless to say, sales were abysmal, and the camera hurried quickly back into the obscurity from which it had briefly emerged.

About the same time, Oskar Barnack, an optical engineer at Ernst Leitz Optische Werke, a leading German manufacturer of microscopes, telescopes, and other optical devices, developed a hand-made, precision-tooled, but still crude 35mm camera. His company was not in the camera business. Consequently, its owners were leery of the machinist's 1913 invention. But as film technology advanced during the next decade, Ernst Leitz agreed to invest in what might be an emerging market for hand-held 35mm cameras. In 1923, Leitz approved a preproduction run of thirty-one prototype cameras, then decided to enter the market in earnest.

The first 35mm "Leica" camera (Leica is a contraction from Leitz camera) was offered to the public in the spring of 1925. It was a stunning success. In 1926, more than 1,600 cameras were produced. Production doubled to more than 3,000 in 1927, then more than doubled—to 7,000—in 1928. By 1930 production had skyrocketed to more than 38,000 units. Throughout the depression, Leica averaged between 30,000 and 35,000 a year.

Leica's Leitz was a master of subtle promotion. He made sure that such high-profile personalities as Charles Lindbergh and Admiral Byrd carried Leicas with them on their travels. That conveyed an image of prestige and rugged superiority. Leitz also understood that the opinions of professional photographers carried considerable weight among hobbyists. He therefore curried favor with famous photographers like Alfred Eisenstaedt and Henri Cartier-Bresson, who, by simply using their Leicas, presold them to an upscale public.

But Leica was more than mere hype. Its sustained success was due largely

to the quality of its lenses and the precision of its construction. Leica was the "Mercedes" of the photographic world. And its strategy remained the same from the first day it was placed on the market: Leica sold the highest-quality cameras in the world, for which it charged premium prices.

During its first seven years on the market, Leica had virtually no competition. Its first serious challenge came from another German camera, the Contrax, which was introduced by Zeiss-Ikon in March 1932. Throughout the 1930s, 35mm technology advanced rapidly as both competitors provided consumers with additional features, such as interchangeable lenses and built-in light meters. Contrax often took the lead in innovation as the two sellers seemed to introduce more sequels than a "Rocky" movie—the Contrax II, III and the Leica IIIa, b, c, d.

The success of the Germans spawned a veritable flood of copycats in the years that followed. One of the first copies came from Japan. In 1934 Takeshi Mitarai, a gynecologist by training, put together an imitation "closely patterned after the German Leica 35-millimeter camera, the industry standard."[5] The camera was called the Kwanon in honor of the Buddhist god of mercy. The name was later changed to Canon, probably in honor of the god of export. Canon cameras were sold in Europe starting in 1937.

Even the Russians entered the fray. Starting in 1941, they produced a line of 35mm cameras for the home market that were virtual clones of the Leica line. The Russian copies were sold under the brand name Fed.

World War II put a damper on the competition, especially for the Germans and the Japanese. When the war was over, Leica resumed its dominant position, but competition crept in from Japan in the 1950s. The Japanese now seemed intent on replacing the German pioneers through an imitate-and-improve strategy.

The Germans had unwittingly sowed the seeds of their own destruction years earlier. Just after World War I, a newly formed company named Nikon sought the advice of the German optical industry—at the time the world's technological leaders.[6] In 1919 Nikon hired eight German optical engineers to help upgrade its technical knowledge. During World War II the Germans provided substantial technical advice in optics to its wartime ally. After the war Nikon shifted from military applications to consumer products. Its move into binoculars, microscopes, and 35mm cameras brought the student into direct competition with its tutor.

Nikon introduced its first camera in 1946 with what one historical review of the company calls "the advantage of German lens technology."[7] Nikon gradually perfected its innovative imitation and started selling it in the Japanese market, where it attracted the attention of U.S. soldiers of the Occupation forces. Just as Leica's reputation had been built on word-of-mouth

advertising, so too was Nikon's. As soldiers returned home with their inexpensive, high-quality Nikons they presold the product to an eager American public.

The Nikon S2 was introduced in 1954. It, too, borrowed heavily from German design and technology. One of the definitive histories of cameras judges Nikon's new product to be "very reminiscent of the pre-war Zeiss Contrax II."[8]

Two years earlier, in 1952, Canon had introduced the "IID," which, in addition to copying the lettering/numbering system used by Leica, was recognized as "showing strong pre-natal influence from Leica . . . Even the lens is Leica-ish."[9]

According to published sources, Minolta also had deep roots in German technology. In fact, it was originally called the Japan–German Camera Company. In 1928 two Germans brought state-of-the-art German technology to Japan. The firm sold a variety of cameras throughout the 1930s and 1940s. After the war, Minolta began to design and produce camera lenses that were serious competitors to Leica.

Suddenly, in the 1950s, all of the Japanese firms started to focus on single-lens reflex (SLR) 35mm cameras, a move that eventually pushed them past the Germans. The SLR was not a Japanese innovation. It, too, was pioneered in Germany. In 1936, Ihagee of Dresden introduced the Kine Exacta, which combined single-lens reflex (SLR) technology with the 35mm format. Now, more than twenty years later, the Japanese camera manufacturers saw an opportunity to leapfrog Leica, the market leader, with superior technology.

The Leica was a "rangefinder" camera. There were two separate lenses, one for the photographer's eye, the other for the film itself. The picture taker had to "line up" the two images before taking the shot. The SLR, in contrast, used a single lens for both the film and the photographer's eye. The difference is more than mere engineering detail. As 35mm cameras offered more features, in particular more interchangeable lenses, it became more and more difficult for users of rangefinder cameras to see the same sight as the film saw. In 1954, Leica introduced the M-3, which reconciled the rangefinder with up to four lenses. However, as the choice of lenses skyrocketed, it could not adapt the technology to every available option. SLR cameras now proved to have many advantages over rangefinder cameras.

In 1959 Nikon introduced the extremely successful Nikon "F" SLR. Minolta introduced its first SLR 35mm camera in 1958. Canon, Konica, and Asahi-Pentax followed shortly after.

Leica's response to the Japanese challenge was neither quick nor decisive. In fact, it was virtually nonexistent. Leica seemed blinded by its long-term market leadership. In 1965, about the same time that consumers started

switching to Japanese cameras in droves, Business Week noted ominously that Leica was reacting "calmly to the competition from Nikon" and seemed unworried.[10]

There are at least three reasons why Leica seemed in no rush to react to Nikon's aggressive entry.

- First, Leica had high standards. It felt compelled to introduce a camera that was vastly superior to the Japanese, not just a parity product.
- Second, there was a serious labor shortage in Germany during the mid-1960s. Producing a new camera meant shifting workers from current production to something new and unproven.
- Third, there was a backlog of production orders for current Leica cameras. It seemed foolish to take on a new task when the old task could barely be completed.

In hindsight, the Japanese onslaught seemed obvious. At the time, however, it seemed to make little sense to react to a potential threat to future sales at the expense of losing current sales.

Leica did not introduce its "Leicaflex" SLR camera to compete with the immensely successful Nikons until March 1965, six years after Nikon's first competitive entry. But by that time, it was too little, too late. The Japanese now held the performance advantage. Business Week noted at the time that "the consensus seems to be that Leitz had missed the boat, that the Leicaflex is an amateur rather than a professional camera."[11] It was less than a parity product.

During the first forty years of its existence, Leica stood out as the symbol of technological excellence in photography. It defined quality picture-taking. Between the first and second world wars, photos found in such picture-packed magazines as Life and National Geographic were almost always taken with a Leica. It seemed no other seller even came close to Leica in technical performance. The combination of quality and market dominance built up a near cult of brand loyalty for the Leica 35mm camera.

But Leica ended up paying a heavy price for its long-lived dominance. Its problem was diagnosed years later by one of Leica's marketing executives as follows: "The company is too proud of its history and forgets all about the present and the future."[12]

Leica ended up being pummeled by its own prominence. According to Forbes, by the late 1980s the best-selling Leica was virtually identical to the popular rangefinder camera it had introduced in 1954.[13] The failure to react quickly opened up the autobahn to the Japanese speed demons.

Not only did the Japanese pull a technological leapfrog on the Germans,

but they offered much lower prices to boot. In the mid-1960s, Nikon held a slight price advantage. At the time, a full-featured Nikon sold for $413 while a Leica sold for $599. But that was only the beginning. Prices of Japanese cameras fell drastically while Leica's costs skyrocketed. By the late 1980s, a Leica rangefinder sold for $3,800, while a full-featured Nikon could be had for less than one-third that amount.

Leica tried to cut costs by offshoring production to Portugal, but that strategy proved unsuccessful. Consumers were unwilling to pay very high prices for a non-German camera.[14]

For all practical purposes, the contest between the Japanese and Leica was over by the mid-1960s. By the end of the 1980s Leica was hopelessly out of the running. In 1988 it sold a mere 20,000 cameras while Minolta, only one of the later entrants, sold 2.5 million. In the United States, fewer than 10 percent of all camera sellers now carry the Leica line.

Leica still has a stellar reputation, but it no longer poses a potent challenge to the Japanese giants. Even the loyal professionals who once blanketed magazines with Leica photos have switched. A review of *National Geographic* and other picture-perfect magazines indicates that for many years now the Japanese cameras have dominated the professional market.

The Japanese rocketed past the Germans for two powerful reasons: superior performance and lower prices. Propelling them even faster forward was the fact that the leader did not retaliate quickly. That potent combination of an aggressive later entrant following an imitate-and-improve strategy with a submissive pioneer spelled the end of a powerful market leader, even though that leader had a generation head start and a virtual lock on the high end of the market. Copying, coupled with innovation, worked well for the Japanese camera giants.

2. AUTOMATED TELLER MACHINES (ATMs)

Automated teller machines (ATMs) revolutionized retail banking. Whereas consumers once had to interact exclusively with human tellers who worked bankers' hours, ATMs gave consumers access to their cash at their convenience. The machines also provided bankers with a key benefit—lower labor costs. In retrospect, such a stunning innovation seemed certain to succeed. But when it was first proposed, there was considerable doubt as to whether there would be any market for these high-tech marvels. The market for ATMs evolved as follows.

Experimental work on ATMs started in the mid-1960s. Developmental work was conducted by many different firms in many different countries,

but Europe seems to have the lead in the early years. The first commercial cash dispenser was developed by Britain's DeLaRue Instruments in conjunction with Barclay's Bank. On June 27, 1967, a "Barclaycash" machine was installed in a Barclay's Bank in Enfield, England. A year later DeLaRue set out to conquer America. In 1968 it installed ten of its cash dispensers at branches of the First Pennsylvania Bank in Philadelphia.

But the DeLaRue cash dispensers were crude punchcard devices that were poorly designed and lacked adequate security. Thieves were no less enchanted with the cash dispensers than were the proponents of the new technology. Thomas DeLaRue was slightly ahead of his time. The cash dispensers were soon withdrawn from the American market, and the firm faded back into obscurity.

The first commercially successful cash dispenser was developed by the Docutel Corporation, a small entrepreneurial upstart from Texas. Docutel was formed in May 1967 by Recognition Equipment Inc. (REI), a high-technology firm that specialized in optical character recognition machines. ATMs were a sideline for REI.

Docutel's first ATM was created with a considerable amount of imitation. It has been reported that REI sent Don Wetzel, a Docutel executive, to England "to study the DeLaRue" machine.[15] After examining the competition, Docutel was convinced it could improve upon the pioneer's design. Don Wetzel is generally recognized as the inventor of the ATM.[16]

Docutel's innovation in ATMs was to solve the security problem inherent in twenty-four-hour remote banking. Consumers were given "bank" cards with a magnetic stripe on the back encoded with scrambled information. Docutel also pioneered the use of personal identification (PIN) numbers. Its developers were granted a patent for their technical advances. The firm then set out to commercialize its innovation.

There were actually two pioneers of ATMs. In addition to Docutel, Chemical Bank was a pioneering user. It was the first bank to adopt the new technology *successfully* in the United States.

Chemical Bank of New York, a customer for REI's other products, agreed to try out the new Docutel device at one of its branch banks. Fearful of big-city crime, the bank tested the first cash dispenser in September 1969 in a Long Island suburb. Like a newborn baby, the infant technology required round-the-clock parenting.

REI would not, or could not, make the long-term commitment to develop the ATM market, so it sold Docutel to a small Texas outfit, which also had limited resources, in 1970.

ATMs started to catch on in the early 1970s. Sales went from nearly nothing in 1970 to nearly two thousand machines installed by the end of 1973.

By 1974, a year later, the number of installed units had better than doubled to more than four thousand. Docutel had stumbled upon a stunning *market* success.

Docutel's financial success was much less stunning. The pioneer was perpetually short of cash in the early 1970s. Its president remarked during that period: "We have spent most of the last eighteen months just trying to survive."[17] The future would turn out to be even more trying for the fledgling upstart. The firm was bracing for severe competition from larger, later entrants with potent competitive advantages that Docutel could not match.

By the end of 1972 there were seven manufacturers of ATMs in the U.S. market. As Table 3-2 illustrates, Docutel clearly dominated the market.

Waiting on the sidelines was NCR, which reported to *Banking* that it was "looking into automated teller manufacture and marketing."[18]

By the mid-1970s Docutel increased its market share to an astronomical 96 percent. Chemical Bank, the pioneering user, was also the market leader, with more than forty machines installed by 1975.

Docutel's competitors fell into two key groups. First, there were the computer companies, IBM and NCR. Unlike Docutel, these giants sold systems rather than individual machines. IBM was integrating forward into ATMs, while NCR was integrating backward from cash registers to computer-connected ATMs. The second group of competitiors compromised firms like Diebold and Mosler, which had sold security systems, including vaults, to banks for decades. Like Docutel, Diebold was the only other independent seller of ATMs in a market dominated by industry giants with highly diversified product lines.

In 1973 Docutel responded to the competitive onslaught with technolog-

TABLE 3.2
INSTALLED ATMs BY COMPANY IN 1972

Company	Units Installed by Late 1972
Docutel	850
Money Machine Inc.	150
Diebold	50
Mosler	6
LeFebure	delivery expected in late 1973
Burroughs	delivery expected in late 1973
IBM	no machines installed but orders pending

Source: Data adapted from "24-Hour Automatic Tellers: How Big a Boom?" *Banking*, February 1973, pp. 17–19, 78.

ical innovation. It upgraded its cash dispenser to perform a host of banking actions besides merely giving out money. Its ATMs were attached to mainframes, which allowed users to perform many other important banking functions. It also enabled banks to spot stolen cards. The first Docutel ATM was installed at the Citizens and Southern National Bank in Atlanta.

Chemical Bank, the pioneering user, was also pursued by later entrants with greater financial resources. In 1977 Citibank, the New York banking powerhouse, decided that it wanted to build a retail banking empire. A key component of that empire was ATMs. So, eight years after Chemical had installed its first cash dispenser, Citibank's John Reed decreed that it was time to enter the ATM market. As one expert noted, Citibank "had deliberately not rushed into major development of its own."[19] But when it decided to enter, Citibank spent heavily to deploy ATMs. It started by ordering Docutel machines, just as the other banks had done, but after gaining experience with the underlying technology it decided to design its own ATMs and have them built by someone else.

Citibank moved later, but it moved massively with lots of money and a determination to gain the lead. Rather than spend heavily on R&D before the market had formed, Citibank decided to spend its money later to muscle its way into the market. Its ad campaign—"The Citi Never Sleeps"—is still etched deeply in consumers' minds.

The defection of Citibank and the entrance of more powerful rivals spelled the end of Docutel's dominance. The market was now too big for the pioneering upstart. By the end of the 1970s Docutel had relinquished it role as market leader. Diebold emerged as the clear market leader. By 1990 it held 39 percent of the U.S. market. NCR, the very latest entrant, was in second place with a 38 percent share and was threatening to take over the leadership role. NCR's share had risen rapidly with Docutel's decline. In 1985, only five years earlier, NCR held only a 15 percent share. NCR's gain came largely at the expense of IBM, its longtime archrival. In 1985 IBM held 22 percent of the market. By 1990, its share had shriveled to a mere 9 percent.

Docutel's days were numbered. It merged with Olivetti, which promised to rejuvenate the declining firm. But the downward spiral could not be reversed. By 1986 it was all over for the pioneer. In that year, Docutel stopped manufacturing ATMs and left the business for good. Servicing the installed base of Docutel ATMs was relinquished to TRW. Seventeen years after it had created an entire market for ATMs, Docutel was no more.

Docutel's demise meant market share gains for others. But by the 1990s competition in ATMs had become global. In fact, growth in the United States was slowing, while worldwide sales were soaring. That gave the advantage to suppliers with global reach, which was not Diebold's strength. NCR was the

clear market leader in worldwide sales with a 29 percent share. Japan's Fujitsu was number two. Diebold came in third with a 12 percent share. IBM was an embarrassing number eight, with only 5 percent of the world market.

In July 1990 Diebold and IBM announced that they were forming a joint venture named Interbold, which gave them a combined share of nearly 50 percent of the U.S. market. Worldwide, the joint venture catapulted Interbold into second place, behind NCR but ahead of Japan's Fujitsu.

Citibank's leapfrog over Chemical was short-lived. Chemical led a consortium of other banks to form the New York Cash Exchange (NYCE), a cooperative agreement to connect independent banks into an ATM network. National networks, such as CIRRUS, followed. They became so successful with banks and customers alike that the networks quickly grew larger than Citibank's massive system. The networks allowed banks to spread costs through sharing. Citibank was reluctant to join competitors' networks after making its tremendous investment.

In the end, first-mover advantages seemed to count for little in ATMs. They were easily overcome by later entrants who entered with powerful competitive advantages. None of that was a surprise to the pioneer. Docutel itself expressed concern about the severity of competition at the end of 1974, just as the market was starting to grow large: "Some of these firms have historic relationships with the banking industry as suppliers of automated equipment and have substantially greater research and development efforts and financial resources."[20] It was an insightful and highly predictive statement. Those advantages proved decisive. Marketing and money quickly overwhelmed early entry. In the case of ATMs, not only did Docutel not succeed in the marketplace, it did not even survive to reap the benefits of the market it had created.

3. BALLPOINT PENS

The invention and commercialization of the ballpoint pen is a classic case of product copying and the success of later entrants. In fact, there is almost a perfect correlation between order of entry and market success—albeit a negative correlation. Neither of the first-round innovators remains in business today. The earlier copycats, who bettered the product after many years of watchful waiting, were forced into a minor role as sellers of pens as gift items and expensive special purchases by the very latest entrants. As the product catetory evolved, it was the very latest entrants that gained the greatest benefit. They succeeded by selling bags and boxes of low-priced throwaway ballpoints to the masses. It was an idea that horrified the industry leaders and did not mesh with historical patterns of selling in the industry.

For nearly two thousand years writing was a cumbersome chore accomplished by dipping a goose quill into a dark liquid. For centuries innovation in the pen business took the form of figuring out how to lengthen the time between dips. It was very slow going. Not until the 1800s were various patents issued for designs of pens that could hold their own ink. A breakthrough came in 1884, when L. E. Waterman, a New York City insurance salesman, designed the first workable fountain pen. His invention ensured that the fountain pen would become the dominant writing instrument for the first half of the twentieth century. Throughout those years the performance and styling of fountain pens improved incrementally. Four firms emerged as the dominant sellers: Parker, Sheaffer, Waterman, and Wahl-Eversharp.

The ballpoint pen made its first commercial appearance just after World War II. It came not from the "big four" fountain pen companies but from two Hungarian inventors, Ladislao and Georg Biro. Both brothers worked on the pen and applied for patents in 1938. When the war broke out they moved to Buenos Aires, Argentina, where their Biro pen was commercialized by the newly formed Eterpen Co.

How did a pen invented by two Hungarians living in South America end up in American department stores? It took two routes. In May 1945 Eversharp, a sort of "Chrysler" of fountain pens in that it was one of the major sellers but clearly the weakest player, teamed up with another firm, Eberhard Faber, to acquire the exclusive rights to manufacture and sell the Argentine Biro ballpoint in the United States. Eversharp's pen was branded the "Eversharp CA," which stood for capillary action. Its innovative design was shown to the press months before being sold to the public. The press hailed Eversharp's pen as a major technological breakthrough that could write for a year without refilling. Eversharp, it seemed at first, had pulled a tremendous coup on the rest of the industry. By acquiring the rights to the Biro pen before anyone else, Eversharp was sure to reap the economic benefits of being first to market.

But that did not happen. Instead, events took an unexpected turn. In June 1945, less than a month after Eversharp/Eberhard had closed the deal with Eterpen, a Chicago businessman named Milton Reynolds just happened to be visiting Buenos Aires on a business trip unrelated to the pen trade. While there, he saw the Biro pen for sale in retail stores. He instantly discerned its potential and bought a few as samples. When he returned home he immediately started the Reynolds International Pen Company. Milton Reynolds was unconcerned with Eversharp's formal deal. He copied the product in only four months and on October 29, 1945, had his pen for sale in Gimbel's department store in New York City. Reynolds's pen was an overnight success. Priced at $12.50, it sold a stunning $100,000 worth its first day on the

market. Reynolds, the copier, had beaten Eversharp, the innovator, to market. The ballpoint made Milton Reynolds a wealthy man almost overnight.

Reynolds's strategy was based on moving quickly and advertising heavily. His ads stressed the advantages of ballpoint technology over old-fashioned fountain pens. Unlike fountain pens, his ballpoints would not smear and were guaranteed to write for two years without refilling. A subsequent model, which was introduced in 1946, featured the now common, but then innovative, retractable point that clicked in and out of the barrel with the press of a button. Ads crowed that the Reynolds pens would write for five years without a refill. The advantage over fountain pens was clear and incontestable. The public was bitten by the bug of a new gadget.

Eversharp was furious at Reynolds's first entry and sought redress in the courts. Eversharp sued Reynolds for copying a design that it had acquired legally, but the suit was doomed. There was no patent protection for the Biro pen. The rotating writing ball that was the essence of the ballpoint had been previously patented by John Loud all the way back in 1888, and his rights had expired long ago.

Despite its legal losses, Eversharp's sales also skyrocketed with the newfound popularity of the ballpoint pen. Furthermore, Eversharp's pen was of higher quality than Reynolds's quick copy. Consumers soon discovered that Reynolds's pen leaked, skipped, and often failed to write altogether.

Eversharp's pen may have been better than Reynolds's, but it too was an inefficient writing device that did not live up to the hype surrounding it. It soon became apparent that ballpoint pen technology had not really been perfected. Both products had been brought to market too quickly. As a result of poor product quality and overly generous guarantees, returns of defective pens soared at both Eversharp and Reynolds.

In the long run, the competitive battle between Eversharp and Reynolds hurt both parties badly. The frequent price wars, unrealistic guarantees, and heavy spending to expand production capacity in response to exploding demand exacerbated quality problems and sapped both firms.

At the same time, consumers lost interest in the poor-quality product. The ballpoint pen turned out to be the classic short-lived fad. Sales of ballpoints surpassed those of fountain pens in 1946, their first year on the market, then climbed again in 1947. But sales started downward in 1948, then collapsed. By 1951 it was all over. The ballpoint pen was all but dead, and the fountain pen once again reigned supreme.

Table 3.3 illustrates the share of market for fountain pens versus ballpoints during the first faddish years of the ballpoint.

The decline hit Reynolds hardest. His firm quickly disappeared with the

TABLE 3.3
MARKET SHARES FOR FOUNTAIN PENS VERSUS BALLPOINTS, 1945–51

Year	Fountain Pens Share of Market	Ballpoint Pens Share of Market	Comments
pre-1945	100%	0%	
1945	64	36	
1946	46	54	ballpoints surpass fountain pens for the first time
1947	41	59	ballpoints peak
1948	43	57	the decline begins
1949	62	38	sales collapse
1950	67	33	
1951	77	23	the low point

Source: Adapted from industry data compiled by Cliff Lawrence and Judy Lawrence, *An Illustrated Fountain Pen History, 1875 to 1960* (Dunedin, Fla.: Pen Fancier's Club, 1986.)

precipitous decline of sales. Eversharp, an old-line fountain pen seller, was hit almost as hard. Its weak position in the industry had prompted its bold move into ballpoints, but that bold move backfired. By 1948 Eversharp was in deep financial trouble and tried to switch back to fountain pens. By then it was too late. Eversharp's chairman observed that Eversharp had "expended so great a portion of its time and attention in solving the problems of the ballpoint pen that certain developments in its conventional pen and mechanical [pencil] business, were perhaps underemphasized."[21] The firm hung on, barely, until 1957, when its pen division was sold to Parker Pen. Parker repositioned Eversharp's products as low-end entries with mediocre results. Eversharp's assets were liquidated in the 1960s.

The actual takeoff of the ballpoint pen came in the mid-1950s, almost a decade after the demise of the innovators. In January 1954, more than eight years after the first failed ballpoints had made their market debut, Parker introduced its first ballpoint, the Jotter. Parker was a major fountain pen player that entered the market for ballpoints later than the innovators but with a clearly superior product and a brand name that signified excellence to consumers. The Jotter wrote five times longer than the Eversharp or Reynolds entries. With the introduction of the Jotter, ballpoint sales took off again. Once again, ballpoints were a raging success. In its first (less than a full) year on the market Parker sold 3.5 million Jotters at prices ranging from $2.95 to $8.75.

It was not until three years later, in 1957, that Parker introduced its next technological advance—the T-ball Jotter, which was also a resounding success. Ballpoints had finally arrived. Parker, the later entrant, was an innovative company in its own right, but it had learned plenty from its predecessors' mistakes. The other fountain pen sellers followed Parker's lead, each introducing its own line of ballpoints. Table 3.4 illustrates the growth in sales for ballpoints vis-à-vis fountain pens. This time ballpoints surpassed fountain pens for good. By the early 1960s the fountain pen was all but obsolete.

Although all the major fountain pen sellers—Waterman, Sheaffer, and to a lesser extent Parker—had introduced ballpoint pens, they were basically committed to fountain pens. That had been their historic mission. Furthermore, the initial experience of the innovators with ballpoints—Eversharp and Reynolds—suggested the possibility that ballpoints would once again be a short-lived fad. Throughout the 1950s and 1960s many of the major fountain pen sellers introduced gimmicky fountain pens to compete with ballpoints. What they did not do was foresee and foreclose entry by the next group of later entrants.

Ballpoints became so successful that the product eventually became a commodity. The newest competitors flooded the market with a never-ending series of cheap and highly reliable disposable ballpoints that consumers bought by the dozens. There was no more talk of refilling. Pens were either lost or disposed of long before they ever ran out of ink. The low-priced pens forever changed the pen industry. They reconfigured the product from an expensive, almost jewelry-like, purchase to an incidental disposable. None of the ballpoint innovators, nor the fountain pen giants, led the way into this latest market turn.

TABLE 3.4
MARKET SHARES FOR FOUNTAIN PENS VERSUS BALLPOINTS, 1952–60

Year	Fountain Pens Share of Market	Ballpoint Pens Share of Market	Comments
1952	70%	30%	start of the second rise
1953	52	48	
1954	46	54	ballpoints surpass fountain pens forever
1955	44	56	
post-1960	25	75	fountain pens begin to become obsolete

Source: Adapted from industry data compiled by Lawrence and Lawrence, *Fountain Pen History.*

It was a French firm, Bic, that led the way. In 1958 Société Bic acquired 60 percent of the venerable New York-based Waterman Company. By 1960 it owned 100 percent. Bic started selling inexpensive, highly reliable ballpoint pens in France in 1950. It then blitzed Europe with hard-hitting ads that dramatized the pen's durability. By the late 1950s Bic held an astonishing 70 percent of the European ballpoint market. Its success in Europe persuaded Marcel Bich, the firm's founder, to repeat those moves overseas. In 1960 Bic entered the American market with pens priced at an incredibly low 29 cents to 69 cents and more hard-hitting ads. In one ad the Bic pen was fired from a crossbow into wallboard. In another it was used as a drill bit to drill through hardened wallboard. In each instance, the tag line was "writes first time—every time."

Bic was more than successful. In fact, its entry relegated the industry giants—Parker, Sheaffer, and especially Waterman—to the now much smaller high end of the market. Fountain pens were made obsolete, and expensive ballpoints were transformed largely into gift and graduation presents.

Fountain pens made somewhat of a comeback in the 1980s as status symbols, but they never again challenged ballpoints. The brand names Parker, Sheaffer, and Waterman still hold an upscale allure. Parker and Waterman are now owned by Gillette, which intends to capitalize on them.

The history of market entries in ballpoint pens illustrates clearly that all is not lost if a firm is not "first to market." In fact, in ballpoints, moving quickly to market proved detrimental to the earliest innovators. The earliest entrants disappeared entirely, while the latest ended up virtually owning a much changed market. It is a powerful lesson of the benefits of later entry, and the risks of pioneering, in a rapidly changing market.

4. CAFFEINE-FREE SOFT DRINKS

What happened in caffeine-free soft drinks was a veritable replay of what had happened earlier in diet soft drinks (see case 9). Once again, the innovation was first brought to market by an unlikely player. Royal Crown then popularized the product by introducing a mainstream version. The soft drink giants then proceeded to steal the market away from both the innovators and the early entrants.

The very first caffeine-free soft drink was introduced by Canada Dry, a company with a respected brand name and a particularly strong position in ginger ale. Canada Dry had no cola. Since colas made up two-thirds of all soft drink sales, Canada Dry felt that it could not be a major player if it had no cola. Furthermore, the company reasoned, even a small share of that huge market would greatly increase Canada Dry's sales.

In 1967 Canada Dry introduced Sport, a caffeine-free cola, into selected test markets. Sport played off the emerging trend for health and fitness products that offered a glint of consumer interest in the late 1960s but did not really take off until the 1970s. Sport was promoted with hard-hitting ads that argued that giving a Coke to your kids was like giving them a few cups of coffee. Canada Dry waited for Coke and Pepsi to retaliate with parity products.

Instead, the industry giants attacked from an unexpected direction. According to David Mahoney, the former chairman and CEO of Norton Simon who was, previous to that, the Canada Dry executive responsible for the Sport product introduction, the politically powerful Coke persuaded the FDA to kill Sport before it reached national distribution. It did so on the grounds that the product was "illegally labeled." Coke argued that colas come from cacao beans, which by definition contain caffeine. Consequently, a cola without caffeine was not a cola at all and should not be labeled as such. It was legal hairsplitting at its finest. Canada Dry was devastated by what it perceived to be unfair tactics. Mahoney concluded in his memoirs:

> One of the lessons that was driven home to me by this experience is the penalty you sometimes have to pay for being first. . . . The biggest risk-takers, the pioneers, the inventors, the proponents of new concepts—in other words, the people who are out there on the frontier of thoughts and actions—are often the ones who pay the highest price for their imagination, their beliefs, and their actions. It is those who come later, following in the footsteps of the pioneer, who tend to harvest the biggest rewards.[22]

Ten years after Canada Dry's innovative product was deemed by the FDA to be "illegally labeled," Royal Crown toyed with the idea of introducing a healthful soft drink. By that time the "health and fitness" craze was in full swing, and many consumers felt that caffeine was an undesirable ingredient in soft drinks. In 1978 Royal Crown considered the possibilities of a soft drink with the caffeine taken out and Vitamin C added.[23] But the FDA nixed the idea of adding Vitamin C to soft drinks.

By the late 1970s it was impossible for the FDA to stop the introduction of a caffeine-free soft drink. In 1979 the FDA issued a series of reports advising pregnant women and heart disease patients to avoid caffeine. That advice accelerated interest in avoiding caffeine among the general public. The FDA could not easily rule that colas *had to* have caffeine added at the same time that it was advising consumers to avoid the additive. Once again, Royal Crown's timing was perfect.

On April 21, 1980, Royal Crown entered with RC100, a caffeine-free and

sugar-free soft drink. Thirteen years had passed since Canada Dry's truncated test market. RC100 was first tested in Chicago, then Los Angeles, then New York. By 1982 it was sold nationwide. At first, no one seemed to follow.

Royal Crown's idea to remove the sugar along with caffeine was a brilliant strategic move made for an unrelated reason. Sugar prices had skyrocketed in the late 1970s, and Royal Crown was looking for a way to save money. Happily, it discovered that the very same consumers who liked caffeine-free soft drinks also liked diet soft drinks.

Royal Crown promoted RC100 with an upbeat campaign that focused on the superior taste of the product. At first the majors did not seem worried by Royal Crown's entry. They sensed no urgency to move into the market. The industry giants expected a repeat of experiences in diet soft drinks—when the market showed its true potential they would enter and quickly move to the forefront using their vast experience and market power.

In 1982 Royal Crown expanded its line to include RC100 Regular, a decaffeinated version of its regular cola. Royal Crown had two products in its caffeine-free product line before Coke and Pepsi had even publicly announced their own entries.

Seven-Up, the third caffeine-free entrant, took a different tack. Actually, it took two tacks. First, it began a hard-hitting advertising campaign for its flagship brand that crowed: "No Caffeine. Never Had It. Never Will." Second, and potentially more threatening to the majors, Seven-Up introduced Like, a caffeine-free cola that competed directly with Coke and Pepsi in 1982.

Seven-Up was a perennial weak performer in soft drinks that, in the past, had offered no real threat to the majors. But Seven-Up was now owned by Philip Morris. Philip Morris had shown its marketing muscle a few years earlier with Lite beer, a new product entry made by its Miller Brewing subsidiary. Pepsi may have feared that Seven-Up's caffeine-free soft drinks would do to it what Lite beer had done to the major beer brewers—catch them off guard and move quickly into the number two spot in the industry, the spot Pepsi held.

Pepsi reacted quickly to thwart Seven-Up's threat. It introduced Pepsi Free in July 1982, more than two years after Royal Crown's RC100, but just after Seven-Up's Like cola. Pepsi had no time to waste testing unproven brand names. It immediately used the Pepsi name on the caffeine-free product (rather than use a lesser brand name, as it had initially done in diet soft drinks with the Patio Diet Cola line). Pepsi quickly moved to the front of the pack after spending heavily on advertising. By 1983 it held 50 percent of the fast-growing market for caffeine-free soft drinks, which at the time accounted for 7 percent of all soft drink sales.

By 1983 Pepsi had expanded its line to two caffeine-free soft drinks. In

addition to its caffeine-free version of "regular" Pepsi, it introduced caffeine-free Diet Pepsi.

Coke was last to enter. It was preoccupied with the entry of Diet Coke and did not wish to disrupt that product introduction with a simultaneous entry of a competing line of caffeine-free soft drinks. It felt consumers would be confused by the onslaught of new products.

At the beginning of 1983, nearly three years after Royal Crown had introduced RC100, Coke still questioned whether caffeine-free soft drinks represented a real opportunity. Coke's president was not worried, however. He stated confidently that "while it is nice to be first, in a nascent market like this I would want to be absolutely certain I'm right."[24] Coke knew there was no need to rush.

On April 28, 1983, almost three years to the day after Royal Crown had introduced RC100, Coke entered across a broad front. It introduced three new products: caffeine-free Coke, caffeine-free Diet Coke, and caffeine-free Tab. According to Business Week, "Coke claims it deliberately delayed moving into the area," but the magazine quotes Coke's president as saying that "we fully plan to have 50% of this market by the end of 1984."[25]

The results of the competitive battle became clear as the years ticked on. Once again, first entry seemed to count for little. As Table 3.5 illustrates, consumption of caffeine-free Coke and Pepsi exploded, while sales of caffeine-free Royal Crown stagnated.

TABLE 3.5
CONSUMPTION OF CAFFEINE-FREE SOFT DRINKS, 1982–90
(in millions of cases)

Year	Caffeine-free Royal Crown	Caffeine-free Pepsi	Caffeine-free Coke
1982	37	20	0
1983	34	160	69
1984	32	163	110
1985	34	155	118
1986	39	134	110
1987	45	130	139
1988	48	145	165
1989	51	163	202
1990	54	180	248

Source: Data compiled from John Maxwell, The Soft Drink Industry in 1990 (Wheat First Butcher & Singer, January 23, 1991)

By 1990 there was a perfect negative correlation between order of entry and market share. Canada Dry, the unsuccessful innovator, had a zero share. Royal Crown, the first successful innovator, had the lowest share of the "big three." Coke, the very last entrant, had a share of the market that exceeded the combined shares of the earlier two.

As in diet soft drinks, the reasons for the dominance of the later entrants in caffeine-free soft drinks were that distribution and advertising advantages held by the majors overwhelmed any first-mover advantages held by the pioneers.

5. CAT SCANNERS

The invention of CAT scanners—an acronym for computed axial tomography—was the most important development in x-ray technology since the discovery of x-rays themselves in 1895. CAT scanners did not emerge from the research labs of the medical equipment industry's giants. They were pioneered by a most unlikely entrant: the record company that promoted the early Beatles.

In 1967 Godfrey Hounsfield, a researcher at Britain's EMI, was working in the area of electronic pattern recognition. He stumbled across a brilliant idea: Whereas x-rays took a simple snapshot of the patient's brain, scanning the brain from multiple angles and collecting those images in a computer's memory rather than on photographic film would provide a more detailed and three-dimensional picture. Like many inventions, his discovery had ample precedent. An American researcher, Allan McLeod Cormick, had theorized about just such a procedure in a 1963 paper, but the technology to turn that theory into practice did not exist at that time. It was not until the development of the minicomputer and the integrated circuit that CAT scanners could be built. As one analysis of the product's history concludes, "Hounsfield's timing was perfect."[26] He recognized that computer technology could be used to build the first practical CAT scanner. EMI applied for patents in 1969.

In the early 1970s EMI developed a crude prototype of the first CAT scanner. The device was tested at a London neurological hospital between late 1971 and the spring of 1972. The tests confirmed what Hounsfield already knew—that the CAT scanner was a stunning diagnostic breakthrough. It allowed doctors to examine the brain without putting patients through painful and risky exploratory surgery.

EMI seemed to have stumbled upon a tremendous business opportunity. But there was a problem. EMI had no experience in the medical equipment

industry. It was a leader in music and entertainment, as well as electronics (it owned Capitol records). It was unclear whether EMI's skills in promoting rock groups could be successfully transferred to the medical equipment business.

It was not a question of wealth. EMI was a large company with a source of profits that could not be sapped by competitive counterattacks. It faced a classic battle of innovation versus experience. Could a company with a stunning technological innovation and a tremendous head start on the competition succeed in a specialized industry dominated by entrenched leaders, such as Germany's Siemen's, GE, and the Netherlands' Philips, who had considerable experience selling to the medical community?

EMI decided to go for it. It knew from the start that pioneering the new market would be expensive, and it would take years before profits were realized. It also knew that fierce competitive counterattacks would be forthcoming. Nonetheless, in mid-1972, EMI decided to manufacture and market the world's first CAT scanner.

The American market was especially important to EMI, because health care dollars in the United States were spent far more lavishly than in Britain. In 1973 EMI tested its CAT scanner at two prestigious U.S. locations, the Mayo Clinic and Massachusetts General Hospital. Once again, the tests were a stunning success. The American medical community fell in love with the new machines. They provided a better diagnosis than traditional x-rays and quickly gained the cachet of "modern" medicine. Soon, it seemed, every hospital in the United States had to have one. It was the start of an epidemic known as "CAT scan fever."

At first, there were questions about the machine's reliability and maintenance. Like any brand-new complicated technological product, it required substantial customer support and service. To spur demand, EMI agreed to service newly purchased CAT scanners at no cost to the customer for twelve months after installation. That was an expensive but necessary sales requirement. EMI was pouring money into the nascent market in the hope of a huge future payback.

Demand for EMI's CAT scanner exploded in 1973. Even though the company had started from scratch, it managed to expand production from zero units in mid-1972 to nearly one hundred in 1974. Orders poured into the company.

As the only seller of a highly popular product, EMI essentially controlled prices. Although unit volume was small in comparison with consumer products, the price of CAT scanners was high. The least expensive model cost nearly $400,000, and many popular configurations cost nearly double that

amount. Profit margins were tremendous. In addition, EMI adopted a controversial pricing practice that required customers to put down 30 percent of the purchase price when placing an order. That helped boost cash flow and lessen EMI's financial risk. Hospitals happily paid the front money to get their names on the list for a new CAT scanner. By 1975 EMI had orders for 230 high-priced CAT scanners.

EMI granted its first license to Japan's Toshiba in 1974. According to one source, Toshiba was "willing to learn about the new technology," but in 1976, after EMI transferred its manufacturing know-how to Toshiba, the Japanese electronics firm quickly developed its own version of the product and became a copycat rival.[27]

For nearly three years, EMI had the brain scanner market virtually to itself. Then competitors started to enter in droves, attracted by high profit margins like patients to a miracle cure. But rather than enter with parity products, competitors attempted a technological leapfrog. Whereas EMI's scanner focused only on the brain, the later entrants introduced "full-body" scanners, which they sold as the next type of scanner a hospital should buy. It was really the only plausible option. The later entrants knew that the limited number of hospitals in the United States with existing CAT scanners would not throw them out to buy a similar one, or even one that was slightly improved. The market and the product had to be expanded.

One of the first and most successful later entrants was the Technicare Corporation, whose Ohio Nuclear division entered in early 1975. Its "Delta-Scan" CAT scanner allowed doctors to view cross-sections of the patient's entire body.

Pfizer Medical Systems entered about the same time. In late 1974 it acquired the rights to sell a full-body scanner developed at Georgetown University. A few years later it gained the right to manufacture and market the system itself.

Another entrant was Syntex, which entered in 1976 with a rather undistinguished product. Syntex left the market after two years of crushing competition.

The earliest full-body scanners were essentially rerigged brain scanners. The technical goal was to shorten the time it took to complete the scan—from about four minutes in the earliest models. Four minutes was acceptable for brain scans—patients could easily hold their heads still for that long—but presented problems for full-body scans. Patients could not be expected to remain completely still for that long while the scanner took the picture.

Once again, EMI proved to be the innovator. By late 1975 it was ready to deliver orders from sixteen medical institutions for the first *fast* full-body

scanner with a scan-time of less than one minute. At the same time, Pfizer announced that it had "quadrupled" the resolution of its body-scan pictures.[28]

GE was a much later entrant. It sauntered into the market in 1976, nearly four years after the pioneer. GE may have been slower than its rivals, but it possessed several advantages over them. GE was a powerhouse supplier of traditional x-ray equipment with tremendous experience in the market. The move to CAT scanners was both a threat and a complement to its current product lines. For GE, it was a small jump from traditional x-ray equipment to the new CAT scanners. The innovative machines were sold to the same customers through the same channels of distribution. GE had the reputation, a long history in the industry, and the money to make it all happen, even though it entered long after the pioneer and other early entrants.

GE's entry signaled the start of legal and regulatory shenanigans that attempted to shift the competitive advantage from one seller to another. It started in mid-1976, when EMI attempted to slow down the onslaught of rivals, or at least extract profits from their sales, by suing them for patent infringement. In July 1976 EMI sued Technicare for building a machine that was too similar to the one it invented. A year later, in August 1977, EMI sued Pfizer for essentially the same thing. Then a year after that, in September 1978, EMI sued GE on the same grounds. The lawyers had a field day. The defendants uniformly claimed that the suits were without merit. In March 1978 Technicare countersued, charging that EMI was guilty of "unfair competition" and in violation of "U.S. antitrust laws." EMI was accused by the later entrants of unfairly dominating the market. In each instance, EMI attempted to thwart that claim by agreeing to license its CAT scanner technology to the later entrants—at a price, of course.

Meanwhile EMI was hurt by a regulatory action that must have delighted its American rivals. In November 1976 the FDA ruled that EMI's imported scanners had "excessive radiation emissions" and ordered a recall for corrective action. The danger to the patient was minimal to nonexistent. As the Wall Street Journal reported, the particular regulatory action taken against EMI was one typically invoked when a product "may cause temporary or medically reversible adverse health consequences or where the probability of serious adverse health consequences is remote."[29] It seemed that the harm to EMI's reputation was greater than to its patients.

It is debatable whether the recall had a significant effect on EMI's sales, but it is clear that EMI had less success with full-body scanners than with the earlier brain scanners. In fact, whereas EMI had a solid 50 percent market share before 1977, after 1977 Technicare's Ohio Nuclear—and then GE—

surpassed EMI to become the market leaders. By 1978, an EMI executive admitted that his firm's market share was "a lot less" then it had been.[30]

By 1978 GE was the clear market leader. Technicare and Pfizer fought it out for the number two spot. EMI was fading fast. By 1978 there were one thousand CAT scanners of all kinds installed in U.S. hospitals.

One of the last entrants into the CAT scanner market was Johnson & Johnson. It entered by acquiring Technicare on October 5, 1978. J&J attempted to move ahead of its competitors by extricating Technicare from the legal wrangling over EMI's patents. J&J paid EMI $15 million and the promise of royalties if sales stayed high. In return, J&J received clear title to EMI's scanner technology and the right to future scanner inventions.

By 1980 GE was still the clear market leader, and Technicare was firmly entrenched in the number two spot. EMI, in contrast, had become a shadow of its former self.

In the late 1970s EMI's parent company was experiencing financial problems. In 1979 the parent company—along with the CAT scanner subsidiary—was acquired by Thorn Electrical Industries Ltd., which renamed the entire operation Thorn EMI Ltd.

By that time EMI's CAT scanner business was on the critical list. The end came on April 29, 1980, when the pioneer announced it was leaving the market forever. According to the *Wall Street Journal*, "EMI was overwhelmed by rising research and development costs and competition from machines patterned after its scanner."[31] The copycats had crushed the pioneer.

The pioneer was forced to withdraw from the market it had created a mere eight years earlier, and it was forced to suffer one additional indignity. GE, which had entered long after EMI, announced its intent to acquire all of EMI's CAT scanner assets. EMI agreed to accept a one-time payment of $37.5 million for the assets and the promise to drop all legal action regarding its patent infringement charges. Not only was the pioneer destroyed by the later entrant, but it was forced to relinquish its charges of product copying. At the same time, the later entrant was now destined to be the overwhelming market leader.

The U.S. Justice Department was dismayed by the extent of GE's victory. In June 1980 it announced publicly that it would seek to block GE's acquisition on the grounds that it was a violation of the Clayton Antitrust Act, which forbids actions that restrict competition. The irony of the situation was lost on no one. The later entrant was now being charged with the very same claim the later entrants had used against the pioneer when it first claimed patent infringement. How the tables had turned. Whereas only a few years earlier the pioneer was accused of antitrust violations, a later entrant was now accused of the same wrongdoing.

Rather than risk losing the entire agreement, GE modified its acquisition plan to exclude EMI's U.S. operations. It was a small price to pay. GE was already the overwhelming leader in the United States and mostly wanted to gain power overseas. The Justice Department relented, and in July 1980 GE completed its acquisition of EMI's overseas scanner operation for $32 million.

The innovator had a short life span. Eight years after it had created the CAT scanner, the innovator was dead and the imitator was dominant. How was GE able to surpass and destroy the pioneer so thoroughly? One GE spokesman admitted: "There's no question that our access to the market through our x-ray sales and service capability gave us a leg up on the competition."[32]

The lessons of CAT scanners are many. The most important lesson this case illustrates is that innovation is often no match for the marketing, distribution, and financial advantages of likely later entrants. It was clear to almost everyone involved with this product at the very start—including EMI—that when the market proved enticing, the industry giants with closely related products would step in, would ignore the pioneer's patents, and would enter the market with copycat (or copyCAT) products. In CAT scanners, first-mover advantages ended up counting for very little. In fact, reputation, positioning, and other advantages often claimed for pioneering fell squarely to the imitators, who had long histories in the industry. The imitators were easily able to transfer their experience in x-rays to the new product. In the end, the prizes fell unevenly and without regard to entry sequence. Godfrey Hounsfield, the EMI scientist who invented the first practical CAT scanner, shared the 1979 Nobel prize for medicine with Allan McLeod Cormick, the theoretician who first conceived of the idea. EMI ended up enshrined as the innovator and pioneer of the new technology. But GE, and a few of the later entrants, ended up with the most coveted prize of all: the largest share of the CAT scanner market.

6. COMMERCIAL JET AIRCRAFT

The jet engine was invented simultaneously in both England and Germany in the 1930s. After the war British efforts led directly to the development of the first commercial jet airliner by deHavilland, a British firm. It was a quantum leap in air travel. Almost overnight the speed of commercial aircraft doubled, from the standard 250 mph for prop planes to 500 mph for jets.

DeHavilland was clearly the pioneer of commercial jet air travel. Its move into commercial jet service was bold, daring, and fraught with risks. It sought

to parlay its lead in jet fighter technology gained during the war into a tremendous lead in commercial jet aviation. By getting to market first, deHavilland thought it could secure for Britain a dominant role in future aircraft production before the Americans had a chance to catch up. As one analysis noted, deHavilland "staked its reputation on a daring attempt to leap-frog every other competitor in the civil markets and take a major share of the lucrative trade which had by 1945 become almost exclusively American."[33]

A working prototype of deHavilland's Comet 1 made its first public test flight on July 27, 1949. Boeing, the second entrant, would not get off the ground for another five years.

The risks to deHavilland were as high as the potential rewards. It may have been possible to build a jet fighter, but it was unclear whether the technology was commercially feasible. Air travel itself remained unproven. Although prop planes were gaining ground, most people in the 1950s still traveled by ship or train. The jet represented a giant step into uncharted territory. Furthermore, the economics of commercial jet aircraft did not make sense. Early jets used roughly three times as much fuel as prop planes, and their reliability was untested. To be successful, deHavilland had to hit every button right. Most important, it had to persuade the airlines to purchase its jets. It was a tough sell. DeHavilland argued that the greater speed of the Comet meant that each aircraft could fly farther in the same amount of time, offsetting some of those greater fuel costs.

DeHavilland was aided by the British government's involvement in industry coordination. Britain's Ministry of Supply guaranteed that the British Overseas Airways Corporation (BOAC), the nationalized British flag carrier, would order a total of fourteen Comets.

Douglas and Lockheed, the two leading American commercial aircraft manufacturers, were concentrating on prop planes. The Douglas DC-6 and DC-7 and the Lockheed Constellation were the standard-bearers of air travel in the 1950s. Both firms may have been reluctant to cannibalize those successful products. Jets were unwanted and unproven. The airlines fed this perception. They pushed Douglas and Lockheed to improve their prop planes rather than focus on a radically new technology. As a result, in the early days of commercial jet aircraft development, Douglas and Lockheed did not to respond to deHavilland's first move.

Test flights of the Comet 1 broke numerous existing speed records, which created favorable publicity for the soon-to-be-available passenger aircraft. On October 25, 1949, a test flight flew round-trip from London to Tripoli in about six and a half hours, smashing speed records set by commercial prop aircraft. On July 17, 1951, a test flight from London to Johannesburg, South Africa, broke another existing air speed record, covering the 6,212-mile dis-

tance in 7 hours, 33 minutes. The Comet's basic appeal was that it was fast and modern.

DeHavilland's Comet 1 entered commercial service on May 2, 1952, when BOAC made the first commercial jet flight between London and Johannesburg. It was not exactly a direct flight. The flight stopped in Rome, Cairo, Khartoum, Entebbe, and Livingstone. The Comet 1 jetliner carried 36 passengers at 465 mph, had a range of 1,500 miles and carried a payload of 11,800 pounds. The entire trip took slightly less than twenty-four hours, a little over half the time the trip took in a prop plane.

Comet was a resounding success. The innovative British company had taken a courageous gamble that pioneered the modern jet age. Customers clamored to fly on the new jets, and airlines lined up to purchase them. DeHavilland had beat all comers to market. At the time, it seemed the firm would dominate the market it had helped create.

Boeing was considered an outsider in commercial aircraft. Although it had produced a few unsuccessful prop planes, it was basically a defense contractor. Boeing made large bombers for the military, which it sometimes reworked into commercial aircraft. In the 1950s it produced the six-engine B-47 jet bomber followed by the eight-engine B-52. Boeing saw an opportunity to leapfrog Douglas and Lockheed if it could transfer its experience in producing jet-powered military bombers to commercial purposes. It had no current product line to cannibalize and considerable experience in producing a similar product.

On April 22, 1952, just ten days before deHavilland's Comet 1 entered commercial service, Boeing committed $15 million, a whopping 25 percent of the company's net worth, to the development of a commercial jet prototype. Boeing was betting heavily on the future of jet travel.

While Boeing planned for a prototype, deHavilland made plans for a second jetliner, the Comet 2, which had more power, a bigger payload capacity (13,800 pounds), carried more passengers (40), and had a longer range (2,535 miles).

Orders for deHavilland jets poured in from around the world. France's independent airline Union Aeromaritime de Transport (UAT) was the second airline to fly jets. On February 19, 1953, it opened Comet 1 service from Paris to cities along the West African coast. Air France followed on August 26, 1953, with once-a-week jet flights from Paris to Rome and Beirut.

Buoyed by its continuing success, deHavilland announced plans for the Comet 3, which would be larger and more powerful yet. The Comet 3 would pave the way for trans-Atlantic jet travel and an entry into the lucrative American market.

DeHavilland's future looked brightest on October 20, 1952, when it snagged a key customer. Pan American agreed to buy three Comet 3s for trans-Atlantic service. Success now seemed assured for the British jetliner. If the Comet 3 performed as promised, the British firm would almost certainly get much larger orders from the prominent American airline and was likely to earn orders from the other American carriers. At the time, the American airlines were forced to buy British; there were no American suppliers with jets even close to ready. Speeding its product to market before its competitors seemed to be paying off in spades for deHavilland. By 1953 it had cracked the American market before Boeing had even flown its entry for the first time.

Then came the crashes. During its first year of service the Comet 1 proved to be a safe and reliable means of air transport. It had flown nearly 10,000 hours and carried nearly 30,000 passengers with an enviable on-time record. During the first ten months of service there had been only one minor accident. On October 26, 1952, a BOAC Comet had sped down the runway at Rome's airport but failed to take off. There were no injuries.

A more serious accident occurred on March 2, 1953, in Karachi, Pakistan, when a Comet, which was being delivered to Canadian Pacific Airlines, sped down the runway but had problems getting airborne. The crash killed eleven crew members and deHavilland employees.

By themselves, the two accidents meant little. But events took a turn for the worse. On May 2, 1953, exactly one year after its inaugural commercial flight, a BOAC Comet crashed on takeoff from Calcutta on a return flight to London in a severe thunderstorm. Forty-three people were killed. At the time, the accident was judged to be the result of an act of god. Subsequently, however, it was suggested that structural failure might have played a role.

Orders for Comets still continued to come into deHavilland headquarters. The three crashes had not killed the Comet. They were attributed to isolated bugs that inevitably crop up when a new technology is brought to market. By the end of 1953 deHavilland had firm standing orders for roughly fifty Comets with the likelihood that one hundred more would soon be forthcoming. The Comet was tarnished but not badly wounded.

Then disaster struck once again. On January 10, 1954, another BOAC Comet crashed off the island of Elba after taking off from Rome. This time there was no act of god to absorb the blame. The plane was rocked by three explosions and seemed to break up in midair, killing twenty-nine passengers and six crew members.

As a result of the accidents, BOAC grounded all its Comets. The crashed airliner was fished from the bottom of the Mediterranean and pieced back

together in Britain. Modifications were made to the plane in order to strengthen the airframe. Some suspected, but could not prove, that sabotage was the cause of the Elba crash.

Engineers, experts, and the public at large still had confidence in the Comet's basic sturdiness and the future of air travel. The accidents were still viewed as no more than a collection of freak occurrences. BOAC jetliner service therefore resumed on March 23, 1954, less than three months after being grounded.

Two weeks later another Comet crashed. On April 8, 1954, a BOAC Comet leased to South African Airways crashed in calm weather after taking off from the Rome airport into the Mediterranean near the island of Stromboli just off the coast of Sicily. Once again, structural failure seemed to be the cause.

The closeness of the crashes and the similarity in causes hurt the Comet irreparably. Within four days the British government yanked the jet's certification to fly. Extensive tests were conducted to determine the cause of the accidents and to save deHavilland's reputation. Tests revealed that repeatedly pressurizing the cabin had weakened the metal of which it was made. The Comet had a tendency to split apart after a few thousand hours of flight. It was a problem deemed unforeseeable. Although the Comet exceeded every regulation regarding cabin pressure standards, the jet aircraft was walking in virgin forest. Jet technology had surpassed regulatory standards. Simply put, the early Comets were ahead of their time.

The crashes of the Comets and their subsequent grounding meant that deHavilland lost a key customer. PanAm was once again looking for a jetliner.

Boeing's timing was perfect. Its 707 was ready just after the devastation of the Comet crashes. Its "367-80," also known as the Dash eighty, made its first flight on July 15, 1954, five years after Comet 1 made its first flight. It flew for about an hour and a half.

The 707 was greatly influenced by Boeing's military jets. For one thing, it featured jet engine pods hung from the wings rather than engines built into the wings. One aviation expert noted: "Without the B47 bomber there would almost certainly have been no B707."[34]

Boeing's sales appeal took advantage of deHavilland's problems. Industry promotions stressed the strength and thickness of the 707's fuselage. In addition, the plane was longer, heavier, and more economical than deHavilland's Comet. Still, there were no commercial customers. The military placed the first orders.

With Boeing's entry, Douglas could no longer ignore the trend toward jet travel. In June 1955 Douglas announced that it too would produce a com-

mercial jet airline. Its later entry—the DC-8—sought to trade on the good name of Douglas's dominant prop planes.

Douglas's strategy was simple. It would leapfrog Boeing's 707 just as Boeing had leapfrogged deHavilland. Basically, Douglas intended to improve the economics of jet travel. It designed the cabin of the DC-8 to be wider than Boeing's 707. That allowed airlines to sit six passengers across rather than five. The airlines loved the idea.

On October 13, 1955, PanAm ordered twenty-five DC-8s from Douglas. Boeing was crushed. It received an order for only twenty 707s. The Comet, of course, received none. At the same time, United Airlines ordered thirty Douglas DC-8s, even though it had to wait at least a year for delivery. Economics seemed to win out over innovation. The 707 offered only one advantage—early delivery—whereas the larger Douglas planes offered superior economics. One analysis concluded: "The airlines appeared to be stampeding to Douglas, and Boeing could discern ghosts of failure past returning to haunt it."[35] It seemed, once again, that the very latest entrant would walk away with the greatest economic reward.

But Boeing reacted quickly to counteract Douglas's advantage. Boeing quickly introduced a larger, wider, more powerful version of the 707 known as the "intercontinental." The intercontinental was tailored for nonstop trans-Atlantic travel and took away the advantages claimed by Douglas. Boeing now had two entries. On the basis of the new design PanAm upped its order.

The other airlines also favored the new Boeing jet. While Douglas initially led in orders, Boeing caught up and surpassed it. By 1959 Boeing had delivered more than three times as many jet planes as Douglas. Boeing surpassed Douglas by agreeing to tailor its planes specifically for individual customers.

DeHavilland, meanwhile, was down but not out. It decided to reenter the jet aircraft market with the Comet 4, which would be twice the jet of the Comet 1. It would be twice as powerful and would carry twice the load.

This time deHavilland took the time to get it right. Not until October 4, 1958—more than six years after the first commercial Comet flight and more than four years after the last crash—did the Comet 4 enter commercial service on the New York–London route. By that time it was a structurally sound plane of impeccable design. Like its pioneering predecessors, it too set commercial speed records, flying from Hong Kong to London in just over eighteen hours.

Once again, deHavilland beat Boeing to market. While orders flew fast and furious for Boeing jets, the PanAm 707 did not make its first scheduled flight across the Atlantic until October 26, 1958, three weeks *after* the new Comet 4.

But customers stuck with the later entrants, Boeing and Douglas. Only

BOAC stood firm in its order of nineteen Comet 4s for future delivery. Even though deHavilland had dragged down BOAC's image with its accident-prone aircraft, the captive British airline was forced to come back for more.

The Comet 4 may have been soundly engineered, but its past followed it. When jet technology had finally been perfected, few potential passengers or airline buyers could forget the steady stream of early Comet crashes. No one wanted a loser. Buyers bought Boeing.

Economics also played a role. The American jets were larger and more powerful. The Comet 4 carried only about half as many passengers as the 707. DeHavilland was stuck with an old design, as well as a sullied image.

The American firms may have entered the market later than Britain's de-Havilland, but they were not saddled with a history of catastrophic crashes. DeHavilland fell victim to the "Hindenburg" syndrome. After the fiery crash of that German airship in 1936, all work on hydrogen airships ceased. The Comet suffered a similar fate. No matter how high its current reliability, consumers would forever connect the Comet with crashes. DeHavilland paid a heavy and indelible penalty for pioneering a radically new technological product where *no* failures are acceptable.

DeHavilland chose a bad market to pioneer. The product was technologically complex, and the market allowed no room for errors. The product had to be perfect. It was unreasonable to expect deHavilland to be able to plan everything perfectly on the first try. In hindsight, early design errors led to perceptual problems from which the firm could not recover.

Could deHavilland have done anything different to recover its lead? One possibility would have been to change the name of the Comet 4 to something else, which may have removed the stigma of earlier crashes and distanced deHavilland from its deadly past. There is ample marketing precedent for such actions. But that was not done, and the outcome may have been no different in any case. According to a historian of the deHavilland company, "the feeling was that a new name would suggest an avoidance of the issue, a lack of confidence, not only to the outside world but also to thousands of people in the airline and the factories who were working with spirit to re-establish the good name of the first jet airliner."[36] It was a proud move that allowed deHavilland to keep its self-respect, even though Boeing kept its customers.

What became of deHavilland's innovative jetliner? It ended up in the British military. After its failure to sustain sales in the commercial airliner business it was bought by the military, where it eventually evolved into the Nimrod, a submarine chaser that is still in use today. Ironically, the British government's attempt to broker industry collaboration in pursuit of commercial markets ended up as a defense project.

7. COMPUTERIZED TICKETING SERVICES

Fifteen years ago, if you wanted to buy a ticket to a concert or a sporting event without going directly to the arena or the stadium, you almost certainly would have done business with Ticketron. No longer. Now you would almost certainly deal with Ticketmaster. What happened? How did a spunky upstart completely unseat a standing market leader and actually drive that market leader out of business? The answer lies in actions taken by both parties. The newcomer improved upon the leader's innovative product, and the leader failed to respond to the challenge. Ticketron seemed oblivious to the threat from the smaller firm. It also had the misfortune of being owned by a parent in deep financial trouble. As a result, the ambitious newcomer was able to squeeze through a hole left by the leader. Like a boa constrictor, once the newcomer had established itself it proceeded to squeeze the life out of its former rival.

Ticketron pioneered computerized ticketing services in 1968. Its innovation consisted in using its parent company's computers to sell tickets for the Los Angeles Forum, its first fully computerized account. Ticketron was a subsidiary of the Control Data Corporation. Throughout the 1970s Ticketron expanded rapidly, first in Los Angeles, then in New York. Early on, the company virtually monopolized the sale of Broadway theater tickets. By the end of the decade it completely dominated the entire market for computerized ticketing services.

Ticketron seemed invincible. Although it faced a steady stream of regional rivals, none could match its national scope of operations or access to its parent's timesharing mainframes. By 1980 Ticketron was the only national seller of any consequence. As a result of its early moves into the market, it enjoyed a twelve-year unchallenged reign as the market leader. But, unbeknownst to its managers, the firm had reached its zenith. It would be a downhill run from there.

Ticketmaster did not start off with the intent to replace Ticketron. In fact, its inauspicious 1976 start in Scottsdale, Arizona, made it indistinguishable from other regional rivals. Actually, its founders, Peter Gadwa and Albert Lesser, were not even interested in selling tickets to the public. As computer scientists they were interested in improving the software used by commercial ticketing systems. During the second half of the 1970s Ticketmaster was struggling to survive.

Then came Fred Rosen. In 1982 Mr. Rosen, a New York corporate lawyer hired to perform some short-term legal work for Ticketmaster, recognized the potential for repositioning Ticketmaster from a software firm to a full-fledged ticket seller. Although Mr. Rosen had no experience in either the

entertainment business or computer programming, he thought he had spotted an opportunity for growth.

But growth required money, so Mr. Rosen set out to find investors. He persuaded Jay Pritzker of Chicago to pony up $1 million to finance that growth. In 1983 Ticketmaster moved to Chicago. Mr. Rosen's talent was to attract investment and to promote the service.

Then the unexpected happened. Mr. Rosen had been pestering the Los Angeles Forum to consider his improved ticketing system. He saw little chance of actually landing the account. It had been, after all, Ticketron's first account back in 1968. But the Forum wanted a ticketing system that could be integrated with its accounting function. Ticketron did not offer that feature and was not about to change its ways. Ticketron was a virtual monopoly and acted the part. The Forum had it backward: Customers did not recommend changes to Ticketron, Ticketron told customers what they would get. The Forum was miffed and made a bold move—it gave the account to Ticketmaster. Ticketron then set out to punish the renegade customer. In spite of a sixty-day cancellation clause, Ticketron pulled its system out of the Forum in ten days. Ticketmaster worked round-the-clock to install its system in a mere seven days. The industry was impressed by both Ticketmaster's hustle and Ticketron's punitive actions. Mr. Rosen later reflected: "I thought, They just gave me the marketplace, it was a signal that they thought they could muscle people."[37]

In 1984 Ticketmaster moved to Los Angeles to be closer to the promoters and entertainment industry, which served as its primary customers. Just as Ticketron had done before, Ticketmaster expanded eastward from its West Coast base.

Ticketmaster took off. Two factors propelled it skyward. First, it paid attention to the needs of its customers—helping to promote shows, offering customer service, and gauging demand for promoters. Ticketmaster understood that its success depended directly on the volume of its customers' businesses. Second, Ticketron did not respond. It was both unwilling and unable to counter Ticketmaster's moves.

Like an arrogant monopolist, Ticketron seemed unwilling to bow to the petty demands of pestering customers. Besides, Ticketron was a strong market leader with a broad customer base fighting a small competitor with few customers. There seemed no need to pick on a kid.

But, equally important, Ticketron could not really fight back because its parent company—Control Data—was in severe financial trouble. In 1985, soon after the Forum fiasco, Control Data defaulted on $383 million in short-term debt. Its losses exceeded $500 million in 1985. Control Data's problems were not with Ticketron but with its mainframe computer business. Still, Ticketron felt the effects. While Ticketmaster was moving aggressively

forward, Control Data was preparing to restructure. It was more concerned with corporate survival than with the expensive market share battles of a small subsidiary.

By the end of 1985 the results were apparent. Ticketmaster had over 50 percent of the Los Angeles market and offices in New York, Detroit, Seattle, and Indianapolis.

More important, the money invested by the Pritzkers allowed Ticketmaster to gain market share through the acquisition of regional ticket-selling services throughout the United States. Ticketmaster would purchase a local agency and expand it. In New York, for example, an office that was losing $400,000 a month on sales of $30 million in the mid-1980s produced $2 million in profits only a few years later, when telephone operations were expanded to three times their original size. Ticketmaster was investing in the future, while Ticketron struggled to survive the week ahead.

A few years later, in January 1987, Ticketmaster joined forces with Goudchaux/Maison Blanche to buy a large group of ticket-sellers in Louisiana, Mississippi, Alabama, and Florida.

In the spring of 1986, Allen & Company, a New York investment banking firm, agreed to purchase Ticketron from Control Data for an estimated price of $150 million to $200 million. It was hoped that the purchase would give Ticketron the funds it needed to invest. Later in the year, however, the agreement was canceled when the financial picture at Control Data improved somewhat.

The trajectories of Ticketron and Ticketmaster crossed for good in 1987, when Ticketmaster produced revenues of $500 million as against Ticketron's $415 million.

Ticketmaster continued to emphasize customer service. It would discover what a customer wanted and then delivered more quickly, more conveniently, and, if necessary, less expensively than Ticketron.

Ticketmaster also stressed continual product improvements. Its computers and software ran more quickly than Ticketron's and provided a seemingly ever-expanding array of desirable services, such as language translation to serve foreign markets. Ticketron could not keep up.

The competitive mismatch between Ticketmaster and Ticketron is best illustrated by the case of the Los Angeles Philharmonic. Ticketmaster agreed to provide unique and complicated reports to management, as its new customer had requested, even though Ticketmaster did not yet have the commercial technology to do so. Only an extra effort during the first year resulted in the requested reports. Such service, and steadily advancing technology, earned Ticketmaster a loyal following among customers. Ticketron, meanwhile, continued to face problems.

Until 1988 New York City remained a Ticketron stronghold. But that stronghold crumbled when Madison Square Garden left Ticketron and signed with Ticketmaster. Ticketmaster planned to do exactly what it had previously done in Los Angeles: offer better service and a better product. Ticketmaster then set out to expand steadily in New York.

Then Ticketmaster made an especially bold move. In early 1989 it offered to buy Ticketron for $20 million, an amount estimated by industry analysts to be more than its current worth. How times had changed. Only three years earlier Ticketron had been valued at more than $100 million, but Ticketron reportedly lost $2.5 million in 1989. Pride was involved, however. Ticketron rejected the offer and pledged to keep up the fight.

Ticketron's final chance at victory came in November 1989, when it accepted a competing offer to be acquired by the Carlyle Group, a privately held, Washington-based investment firm with powerful political connections. It was hoped that a fresh infusion of capital would turn Ticketron to its former glory. The competing offer was reportedly for $4 million less than the earlier Ticketmaster offer.

The Carlyle Group is a small but deep-pocketed investment partnership. Much of its capital comes from the Richard King Mellon family. Other partners include high-level executives from major firms. The Ticketron deal was unusual for Carlyle in that it usually purchased big companies with borrowed money. Nevertheless, the firm sensed opportunity.

The man behind the Ticketron purchase plan was a Washington businessman, Abe Pollin. Mr. Pollin approached his friend David Rubenstein, the Carlyle managing director, for help in putting together a group to buy Ticketron. The group pledged to provide substantial investment capital. Mr. Pollin also sought out other investors, such as the Ogden Company, the food services and arena management giant, to invest in the plan. Ogden's interests in related businesses and its connections in the industry meant that Ogden might benefit from the tie-in.

Mr. Pollin had his own connections. At the time he owned Ticket Center, a regional computerized ticketing firm that controlled 85 percent of D.C. ticket sales. He also owned the Capital Center Arena, as well as the Washington Bullets, the local pro basketball team, and the Washington Capitals, the local pro hockey team. Ticketron could surely count on those captive accounts.

The purchase of Ticketron would drastically consolidate ticket-selling services in Washington, D.C., since Ticketron was Ticket Center's chief competition in Washington.

Mr. Pollin was also eager to do battle with his nemesis Mr. Rosen, Ticketmaster's chief. Mr. Pollin was formerly a Ticketmaster franchisee, but, ac-

cording to published reports, in 1988 he and Mr. Rosen split in a bitter battle over fees, which was played out in the press. There was bad blood between the two ticketing tycoons. Mr. Pollin even sued Mr. Rosen over the dispute, an action he had never taken before.

With a fresh infusion of Carlyle's cash, Ticketron planned for its comeback. First, Ticketron announced the appointment of Peter Jablow, who formerly ran Capital Center Arena for Mr. Pollin, as the new CEO of Ticketron Limited Partnership. Second, Ticketron announced that it would launch a major upgrade of systems and hardware costing millions.

Ticketron recognized that it would be an uphill battle. By the end of the 1980s Ticketron operated in only eighteen states and Canada, while Ticketmaster operated in forty states and 120 cities. But Pollin was in for the long haul. As Mr. Jablow stated: "It may be several years before Ticketmaster feels Ticketron breathing down its neck. We are getting our house in order now. This is a very long-term effort."[38]

Ticketron's strategy was simple. Its managers and investors would use their industry connections to induce arena owners to switch from Ticketmaster to Ticketron. The plan was not far-fetched. Mr. Pollin was himself an owner. He announced publicly that he would try to talk his fellow owners into signing up with Ticketron. Cross-ownership of arenas, sports teams, and ticketing services is commonplace. One result is that the selection of a ticketing vendor does not always fall to the seller who offers the lowest price. Relationships are important in computerized ticket selling services, and Ticketron hoped to exploit that advantage.

Furthermore, some arena and sports team owners might prefer to do business with Ticketron because they were alienated by Mr. Rosen's aggressive business style. They might prefer to deal with one of their own.

Ticketron faced a formidable barrier to entry in that arena owners in most major markets had signed long-term contracts with Ticketmaster, which prevented them from switching vendors for three or four years. Ticketron's Pollin announced that he had found a way to break his long-term contract with Ticketmaster and felt others could do likewise. But would they?

Further complicating Ticketron's comeback was the competitive fact of life that most markets in U.S. cities are too small to support more than a single ticket-seller. A small fee is earned on each ticket sold, which means that a huge market share is required to make the business worthwhile. Since Ticketmaster was three times Ticketron's size and was determined to protect its turf, a shift of the market shares back to what they had been a decade before was extremely unlikely. Ticketmaster was determined not to repeat the mistakes of Ticketron under Control Data. It would and could fight vigorously.

Finally, Ticketron's system was not superior to Ticketmaster's. Owners would be switching on *claims* of future superiority, which might or might not be realized.

Ticketmaster, meanwhile, continued to expand its operations. In March 1990 it formed a joint venture with Atlanta's SEATS called Ticketmaster Southeast. That move locked up another region of the country against Ticketron's inroads.

Ticketmaster also continued to introduce product innovators. To promote events better, for example, it began to sell music videos along with some concert tickets. Such promotional tie-ins as pre-event dinner specials were also introduced. Finally, Ticketmaster built a demographic database on its customers by encouraging credit card orders. Those data were then used to target ads to likely customers.

The outcome of the battle between Ticketron and Ticketmaster was decided quickly. In February 1991, less than two years after its purchase, the Carlyle Group announced its intent to sell out. The defeat of Ticketron was complete and unequivocal. The new buyer was none other than Ticketmaster!

June 14, 1991, was Ticketron's last day of operation. Ticketmaster quickly folded Ticketron's operations into its own. It now operates 2,050 outlets in forty states and sells more than 30 million tickets a year. Few customers even noticed the innovator's demise.

The success of the later entrant over the innovator was so complete that Ticketmaster now faces accusations that it operates a monopoly, which will soon raise prices and will demand more favorable terms from its customers, such as fee-sharing arrangements. Such concerns are countered by those who point out that niche players, like Nashville-based TicketPro, which was formed in the summer of 1991 and handles all events in the middle Tennessee area, will always exist. Besides, in recent years ticket-selling software and hardware have come way down in price.

Competition may even come from unexpected sources. There has been some discussion of forming a consortium of independent ticket agents to compete with Ticketmaster. There is even a remote chance that legislation will restrict Ticketmaster's potential to gouge profits, especially if Ticketmaster tries to take advantage of lessened industry competition. Finally, home computer networks may someday move into Ticketmaster's turf.

Whatever the outcome, the battle between Ticketron and Ticketmaster is over. In reality, Ticketron had not really been a competitor for years. It was mismanaged and was outmaneuvered by a smaller but more aggressive competitor. Ticketmaster may have entered the market later, but it entered with a better product. The smaller, later entrant was helped greatly by an inno-

vator that would not and could not fight back. Ticketron's parent did not have the cash to invest in its subsidiary. But Ticketron also failed to recognize the seriousness of the threat. For those reasons the innovator paid the ultimate price, while the later entrant won the entire prize.

8. CREDIT/CHARGE CARDS

Diners Club was the first multipurpose third-party charge card of the kind with which consumers are familiar today. Tales of its origins have reached epic status. According to one legend passed down from one author to another over the years, and even repeated in a recent Diners Club publicity brochure, the idea for Diners Club was born in 1950 when Frank McNamara, a New York City businessman, was entertaining important clients at a crowded New York luxury restaurant. At the end of the meal, when the check was presented, he reached for his wallet and was shocked to discover that he had no cash. In those days there was no such thing as a charge card. It was cash or nothing. Fortunately, the restaurant agreed to let the embarrassed Mr. McNamara pay later. Frank McNamara swore it would never happen again. So he invented Diners Club.

Legend refers to McNamara's fateful meal as the "first supper." Like many legends, the story is colorful and indicative of the simple origins of profound ideas, but it is untrue. Matt Simmons, an early Diners Club executive, admitted recently that as a young publicist he made up the entire tale to attract the attention of newspaper reporters, who took the bait and unwittingly helped promote McNamara's innovative product.[39]

The genesis of Diners Club was more prosaic than the story suggests, but the innovation's impact on society was no less profound. The multipurpose charge card spawned by Diners Club was judged by *Consumer Reports* to be one of the fifty most influential innovations of the past fifty years.[40] McNamara started a multibillion-dollar international industry that by 1990 had a worldwide charge volume in excess of $200 billion. More impressive, he started a trend that ultimately altered the economic and social fabric of the industrialized world and forever changed the consumption habits of most consumers. The charge card was more than a new product; it ushered in an entirely new way of life.

Diners Club was not actually the first charge card. For more than a century, charge and credit privileges were extended by sellers to their best customers. By the 1930s hotels, department stores, and gasoline retailers allowed consumers to charge purchases and pay a single bill at the end of every month. The limitation of those card plates was that they could be used only at a single seller.

The first multifirm charge card was the Universal Air Travel Plan. Started in 1936 as a cooperative venture joined by almost every airline, it allowed companies to pay a single $425 deposit, at which time its employees received the card that they could use to charge an unlimited number of flights from any member carrier. At the end of the month the company received a single bill, which it was expected to pay promptly. The Air Travel Plan (now named the Air Travel Card) puttered along for decades and is still in business today. But it is no match for such charge card giants as American Expess. Few consumers, or for that matter reporters, are even aware of its existence. In fact, an October 9, 1989, *Business Week* article that told of the wonders of the American Express card noted: The "Universal Travelcard is only a memory."[41] An Air Travel executive was forced to write to the magazine letting it know that the card is still going strong.[42]

About the same time that the Air Travel Card was stringing together multiple sellers, department stores began experimenting with true credit cards. In the late 1930s Wanamakers, the upscale Philadelphia department store, was the first to offer revolving credit when it gave customers the option of paying off their balances in full at the end of the month or paying a minimum amount.

Diners Club took the next giant step forward. Its critical innovation was that it placed itself between the merchant and the customer, charging each a fee for the service. Its interest in the transaction was purely financial. It was thus the first firm to offer a third-party, multipurpose charge card.

Diners Club was founded in the spring of 1950 by Francis McNamara and his lawyer, Robert Schneider, with a small amount of seed money. At the outset they positioned the card as a prestige service targeted at traveling salesmen who patronized New York City restaurants.

Diners Club initially succeeded in signing up twenty-seven restaurants in New York. The restaurants were charged a 7 percent fee. That is, if a customer charged a $100 meal, the merchant received only $93 from Diners Club. The merchant discount was pioneered by Diners Club and is still one of the key ways in which both charge and credit card companies make a profit, although the discount is now much lower.

The origin of the 7 percent discount is also the subject of business myths and legends. The story is that McNamara asked a restaurant proprietor how much he would be willing to pay for business he would not otherwise get. The proprietor said 7 percent, which was less than the amount a travel agent would charge.

Originally the Diners Club card was offered to potential customers free. But McNamara quickly added a $3.00 annual fee for the privilege of carrying the card. The fee also remains an industry standard to this day, although it is now much higher.

A third partner, Alfred Bloomingdale, joined McNamara and Schneider during the early days of Diners Club. Bloomingdale balked when asked to increase his investment without acquiring a larger ownership share of the business. That disagreement led to a split with Diners Club. Bloomingdale took the idea to California, where he succeeded in signing up twenty-five Los Angeles-area restaurants under his "Dine and Sign" label. Within three months, however, Bloomingdale was back. His West Coast operations were merged with Diners Club's New York operations, and a one-third ownership of Diners Club was awarded to Bloomingdale. Diners Club was now owned by McNamara, Schneider, and Bloomingdale. The firm then moved aggressively into Boston, making Diners Club the first national charge card.

Growth followed a rocky first few years. Diners Club started with two hundred charter cardholders in 1950. By 1960, ten years later, it had 1.25 million cardholders. By the end of 1951, its first full year of operation, cardholders had racked up $6 million in charges. At first the firm lost money, but it turned a small profit shortly thereafter. The pioneer smelled success.

McNamara attracted considerable media attention, which helped promote his innovative service to both merchants and the public. A radio interview by Johnny Carson and favorable reviews by such prestigious publications as *The New Yorker*'s "Talk of the Town" column helped push the product forward.

Diners Club's success with restaurants encouraged it to expand into hotels, airlines, and a broad range of other prestigious retail establishments. Like most pioneers, it encountered stiff resistance to its innovative service with each new round of customers. Some industries were hard to crack, but once one firm signed the rest followed quickly. In the airline industry, for example, McNamara was unable to get even an opportunity to pitch his service. Then, when one airline signed on, the other airlines became instantly receptive.

Still, three key problems plagued Diners Club during its early years of pioneering the emerging market for charge cards.

- First, Diners Club had to convince more and more merchants that accepting the card would give them business that they would not otherwise get. It also argued that cardholders would purchase more than customers who paid cash, an argument American Express uses today.
- Second, and simultaneously, Diners Club had to prospect for an ever larger pool of cardholders. It solicited early members by direct mail and even sent complimentary cards to a list of Cadillac owners. But, more important, Diners Club had to change consumer attitudes and overcome the deep suspicion toward credit that was prevalent in the 1950s. To live on credit went against the social mores of those times. Diners Club was ahead of its

time. Consumers became more receptive to credit by the end of the 1950s, but Diners Club still had nearly a decade to wait.

- The third, and most pressing, problem facing Diners Club was inadequate cash flow. The firm was perpetually short of cash in a business where cash was the primary resource. During its first year and a half in business, Diners Club was forced to factor its receivables. Not until its third year would banks lend money to the fledgling firm.

The credit shortage was eased by two additional charge card innovations pioneered by Diners Club. First, it "played the float," paying California restaurants with checks drawn on New York banks and vice versa. That slowed payment and improved cash flow. Second, Diners Club engineered another "float" by paying restaurants thirty days after a customer charged a meal, while that customer was required to pay his bill at the end of the month, even if he had purchased the meal three days earlier.

McNamara never really recognized the magnitude of the innovation he had created. He cashed out in 1952, before the idea of charge cards really took off, selling his share of the business to his partner Ralph Schneider for $200,000, after only three years of operation. McNamara died in 1957 at the age of forty.

Competitors jumped on the bandwagon within a few years of Diners Club's success. By 1955 competitors included Trip-Charge, Golden Key, and Carte Blanche. Most of the later entrants offered nearly identical travel and entertainment services targeted to the same business executives as Diners Club. On paper, some of the later entries looked golden, likely to benefit from synergistic effects. Gourmet Guest Club, for example, which was fielded by *Gourmet* magazine, and the Esquire Club Card, offered by *Esquire* magazine, had subscriber mailing lists of upscale patrons ready and waiting to be culled. But to no avail. None of the later entrants had any significant success in challenging Diners Club's pioneering lead. Some entries never had a chance. Duncan Hines, the cake mix maker, entered the fray with its Signet Club, which signed off soon after entry.

One of the last major entrants in the charge card business was American Express, which did not enter until October 1, 1958, more than eight years after Diners Club was first founded. American Express, however, had a truly coveted competitive advantage: It did not face the cash flow problems that hobbled its less well-endowed competitors, especially Diners Club. American Express had a steady flow of cash from the float it earned on traveler's checks. AMEX was awash in cash in a field of competitors parched by financial drought.

AMEX was also able to make extensive use of its consumer mailing lists and had a well-respected brand name in a closely related financial product. In addition, by entering the charge card business American Express was able to protect itself against any potential decline in its traveler's check business, which it had dominated for decades.

American Express's timing was perfect. It entered just as the receptiveness of consumers to credit had improved. Its advantages became almost immediately apparent. American Express grew quickly. By the end of 1959, its first year of service, nearly 500,000 cardholders had signed up, and the card was accepted at more than 32,000 locations. In fact, the card was so successful that American Express was forced to computerize its operations in order to keep up with burgeoning demand.

During the 1960s American Express roared ahead, while Diners Club experienced significant changes in ownership. Diners Club's cofounder Ralph Schneider died in 1964. That left Bloomingdale as the sole surviving member of the original trio. But Bloomingdale did not, or could not, raise the cash to buy out Schneider's heirs. Instead, he arranged a deal for the Continental Insurance Company to buy those shares. Bloomingdale remained in charge but had to contend with the pressures of an outside investor. By 1966 there were frequent disagreements between Bloomingdale and Continental. Still, the firm did well during those years. In 1968 Diners Club earned $2.4 million in profit. In 1970 Continental Insurance bought the remaining two-thirds of Diners Club, giving it full control over the company. Bloomingdale signed a lifetime personal services contract that prevented him from working for the competition.

"The [Diners Club] card's luster faded through the 1970s."[43] Starting in 1970 it lost $31.1 million and was losing members at a rate of 5,000 per week. Continental was dissatisfied with its underperforming purchase and tried to sell out. There were no buyers. An attempt to control costs and increase efficiency stemmed the dramatic decline. But the card continued to lose ground to American Express. In fact, Diners Club survived more and more on its international operations. It grew overseas as it lost share at home.

American Express blitzed the market with a bewildering array of new products that cemented its lead over its innovative rival. In 1966 it introduced a "corporate card," which made employers responsible for their employees' purchases and saved AMEX the trouble and expense of having to check the creditworthiness of each employee. In essence, the corporate card was a variation of the Air Travel Card conceived in the mid-1930s.

Diners Club also faced competition from the bank credit cards, of which Visa and MasterCard emerged as the two dominant entries. Those cards took

a different path to market success. In the late 1950s, about the same time that American Express had entered, banks around the United States started to offer "bank cards." Many such cards were ill-conceived services that carried no annual fee and offered no credit. Most important, all were regional in scope and could not compete with national charge card operations.

Then, in 1966, the Bank of America put it all together. Basically, the bank borrowed the idea of providing consumers with a line of revolving credit from the department store charge plates, as had been done since the late 1930s, and combined it with McNamara's innovative idea of a third-party multipurpose charge card. It was a perfect mix. Banks made money by making loans, and credit cards were simply an extension of that age-old service.

With a department store-style credit card featuring revolving credit, the Bank of America first spread throughout California and then licensed its "BankAmericard" across the entire United States by forming alliances with regional banks, many of which already ran bank card operations in their respective regions. The market for BankAmericard exploded, and the card was renamed Visa in 1976. Visa eventually surpassed Diners Club in both the number of cardholders and the amount of charge volume.

At the same time, Wells Fargo, another California bank, moved to form a similar national credit card operation. In 1966 it formed a bank cartel consisting of almost eighty independent banks. Its card was called Master Charge. The Wells Fargo–led association joined with New York bank card associations. In 1980 the brand was renamed MasterCard. It, too, surpassed Diners Club in terms of cardholders and charge volume.

Citibank bought Diners Club in December 1980. That move followed its purchase of Carte Blanche in 1978, another early entrant that had been eclipsed by later entrants. More than a decade later each card remains no more than a minor player in a major market. To illustrate the extent to which the later entrants eclipsed the innovator, consider the following statistics:

- In 1960 Diners Club had slightly more than 1.25 million subscribers and was clearly the market leader, while American Express had only 500,000 subscribers. Visa and MasterCard did not yet exist.
- By 1993 Diners Club had only about 2 million domestic cardholders (and a 1.3 percent share)[44] while American Express had grown to roughly 25 million domestic subscribers (and a nearly 20 percent share).[45] Visa had an overwhelming total of 136 million U.S. subscribers, of which Citibank, the largest issuer, had about as many as American Express. MasterCard had 90 million subscribers.[46]
- Of the roughly 2 million domestic Diners Club cardholders, 860,000 come from a single account: captive U.S. Government employees.

Clearly, dominance in charge and credit cards came not to the innovator or the early followers but to much later entrants—American Express, Visa, and MasterCard. Diners Club has managed to survive, but it is a fraction of the size of the later entrants in the important U.S. market. After a glorious start in the 1950s, its pioneering efforts seemed to count for little when it came to leading the market it had created. That honor went to the later entrants.

Frank McNamara was a legend who was ahead of his time. Through either insight or good luck he foresaw an emerging trend and acted upon it before competitors. His innovation may have been pioneering, but his firm was financially weak in a business where money is the most important asset.

The historical importance of Diners Club still endures. As a final, ironic twist of fate, an early Diners Club card was recently valued as a rare collector's item from a bygone era. In 1991, a 1959 Diners Club card was sold for $505.[47] McNamara's pioneering innovation has been immortalized as a rare collectible. At the same time, American Express, Visa, and MasterCard have been immortalized as the market leaders. I wonder which outcome Frank McNamara would have preferred?

9. DIET SOFT DRINKS

Royal Crown Cola has been responsible for most of the major soft drink innovations of the past three decades. It was Royal Crown, not Coke or Pepsi, that introduced the first diet cola and decaffeinated colas. Unfortunately, Royal Crown has been unable to profit fully from its innovations. The historical pattern in the soft drink industry has been that Royal Crown comes up with, and then popularizes, a new product idea only to have it snatched away by larger rivals. While its innovations have benefited both the industry and the consuming public, the innovator itself has been unable to retain more than a tiny share of the diet soft drink market it created. The later entrants, meanwhile, have steadfastly maintained their market leadership.

Actually, Royal Crown did not invent diet soft drinks. It followed smaller regional rivals to market. It is difficult to state with certainty which firm was the very first to sell "diet" soft drinks. The sellers of Orange Crush claim that they began marketing sugar-free soft drinks in the early 1940s. Their entry was way ahead of its time, however, and was not specifically targeted at the calorie-conscious consumer. In 1947 Cott Beverage introduced a line of sugar-free soft drinks, but it too met with only limited success.

In 1952 Kirsch Beverage, a Brooklyn-based bottler, introduced its No-Cal line, which was aimed primarily at diabetics who could not consume sugar

and teenagers afflicted with acne. But something unexpected happened. Kirsch discovered that more than half of those who bought No-Cal were not diabetics at all, but calorie-conscious consumers trying to lose weight. As a result, Kirsch repositioned the brand to target dieters and increased promotional expenditures to pioneer the market in dietetic soft drinks. Sales took off, and Kirsch became the number one seller of dietetic soft drinks. In 1957, the industry sold 7.5 million cases of sugar-free soft drinks, a record amount for what had previously been considered only a small market segment based on consumers with a chronic illness.

Kirsch was in the right place at the right time. Its success was due largely to the emergence of a trend toward calorie-consciousness among (mostly female) consumers. In the 1950s thin began to be in, creating a growing market for dietetic products. That trend accelerated throughout the 1960s and 1970s. It made the market attractive to firms with a keen eye for changes in consumer behavior and the resources to exploit those changes.

Royal Crown Cola pounced on that opportunity in early 1962, when it introduced Diet Rite Cola. Diet Rite was not Royal Crown's first sugar-free soft drink entry. The company claims to have first entered the market in 1954, just after Kirsch, with a product backed by little promotional support that was also targeted at diabetics. Diet Rite was more a marketing innovation than a technologically superior product. Unlike previous sugar-free entries, Diet Rite Cola was clearly positioned and promoted at consumers with a newfound interest in losing unwanted weight. Basically, Diet Rite brought diet soft drinks into the mainstream. It did so in the following way:

- First, Royal Crown reduced the price of Diet Rite to match that of regular soft drinks. That made the dietetic product a readily accessible alternative to regular cola soft drinks.
- Second, it placed Diet Rite in returnable bottles, as were regular soft drinks. Previously, sugar-free soft drinks came in nonreturnable bottles, because they were not considered a mainstream product.
- Third, and probably most important, Diet Rite was the first sugar-free cola to be featured on the same supermarket shelves as regular soft drinks. That removed the stigma attached to consuming a product meant for the medically afflicted. Previously, sugar-free soft drinks were sold in the dietetic section of the supermarket, a special category distant from the regular soft drink aisle.
- Fourth, Royal Crown boosted promotion to push the trend toward calorie-consciousness by spending $11 million on advertising Diet Rite Cola in 1964, up from $7.5 million in 1963.

Basically, Royal Crown Cola figured out how to sell diet soft drinks to the mass market. Following closely in Kirsch's footsteps, it successfully educated consumers as to the merits of diet soft drinks with heavy promotion, by putting the product in the right form, and by making it widely available. As a result of Royal Crown's efforts, sugar-free soft drinks became less an oddity and more a mainstream consumer product.

Royal Crown pushed a growing trend further upward. Sales exploded in the years directly following its entry. In 1961, before Royal Crown entered, diet soft drinks made up 1.5 percent of total soft drink sales. By 1962 sales of diet soft drinks doubled to 50 million cases, and their share of all soft drinks rocketed to 4 percent. By 1963, 7 percent of all soft drinks sold were dietetic. Forecasts called for their share to climb to 15 to 20 percent, and maybe even 30 percent, of the entire market.

Competitors jumped into the market with abandon for fear of being left out. Canada Dry and Dr. Pepper quickly introduced parity cola products, as did regional sellers, but Royal Crown ruled supreme. First-mover advantages seemed to ensure its successful hold on the newly created market.

According to published reports at the time Diet Rite was introduced, Royal Crown Cola's strategy aimed squarely at Coke and Pepsi drinkers. Diet Rite tried to get regular cola drinkers to switch to diet colas. Since Royal Crown held only a minuscule share of the regular cola business, it had little to lose if consumers switched. Coke and Pepsi had plenty to fear, however, since most of their sales came from regular colas. They had little to gain by introducing a diet soft drink, and a lot to lose. The market leaders seemed to be trapped in a lose-lose situation. If diet soft drinks turned out to be a fad, then spending heavily on new product development would be wasteful and unwarranted. If diet soft drinks succeeded, however, Coke and Pepsi would spend heavily only to switch their loyal regular cola drinkers to their new, and unproved, "diet" versions. It was a classic case of fear of cannibalizing sales of existing products.

Coke and Pepsi were *forced* to follow Royal Crown's lead in order to thrwart Diet Rite's impressive gains. *Business Week* noted at the time: "Coca-Cola and its biggest rival, Pepsi-Cola Co., were slow to notice how Royal Crown was carving out a new market."[48] By February 1963 both Coke and Pepsi had just entered limited test markets. Both firms were reluctant to put their flagship brand names on the new unproved products. Coke entered with Tab, which was introduced by its Fanta division. Tab was test-marketed in Springfield, Massachusetts. Pepsi entered with Patio Diet Cola, which was introduced in Greenville, South Carolina.

Pepsi entered faster than Coke. By June 1963, about a year and a half after

Diet Rite's entry, Pepsi was selling in sixty key markets, while Coke was selling in only twenty-five, with no estimate as to when it would achieve national distribution.

In the beginning, Coke's Tab and Pepsi's Patio Diet Cola were defensive entries. They sought to protect their regular soft drink business from the disruptive actions of a reckless renegade. One Pepsi official remarked that "we don't want Royal Crown taking our market."[49] Instead, both firms tried to attract "new consumers—those people who because of health or weight problems never have consumed soft drinks."[50] But the trend toward diet soft drinks was bigger than either of the industry giants. They had no choice but to compete for customers that preferred a sugar-free product.

Royal Crown Cola dominated the fast-growing market for diet soft drinks through the mid-1960s. Although it was only one-twentieth the size of Coca-Cola, it owned a 50 percent share of the fast-growing diet soft drink market. Until the late 1960s Royal Crown held roughly double the share of either Coke or Pepsi in the growing diet soft drink segment.

Sales of Pepsi's Patio Diet Cola were disappointing, so it was quickly replaced with Diet Pepsi, a risky decision that entailed using the company's coveted flagship brand name on an unproven product. Like most sellers, Pepsi targeted calorie-conscious women. Its early ads featured "Debbie Drake," a well-known exercise maven with a stunning figure.

Coke's Tab sold well from the start, mostly among women, and was not supplemented until 1982, fully twenty years after Royal Crown's entry, when the firm introduced Diet Coke. Diet Coke represented only the second time in its nearly hundred-year history that Coca-Cola used its flagship brand name on a soft drink. The stakes were deemed high enough to warrant that action. Diet Coke initially appealed to a growing market for men wishing to limit caloric intake.

Royal Crown's dominance started to erode once Coke and Pepsi entered. It was not a question of clear product superiority. Diet Rite Cola was as tasty as Tab or Diet Pepsi. Basically, Coke and Pepsi entered with parity products that had no overwhelming sensory advantages. Their success was due to other factors:

1. Coke and Pepsi dominated soft drink distribution channels, and it is no secret that distribution advantages often decide the outcome of marketing battles in this industry. One expert, quoted in *Forbes* magazine, explained: "This is a distribution business. The bottler decides what goes on the shelf, and all the rest is just conversation."[51] Royal Crown was at a disadvantage when it came to distribution. In 1964, Coca-Cola had 1,120 franchised bottlers, Pepsi was a distant second with only 530 bottlers, and Royal Crown's total was a pitiful 370. A similar imbalance existed when it came to the power

to command supermarket shelf space. Coke and Pepsi used their superior distribution to win market share in diet soft drinks.

2. Both Coke and Pepsi had the financial resources to run massive promotional programs that Royal Crown could not match. Throughout the second half of the 1960s, while Royal Crown held double the market share of Coke or Pepsi, the two soft drink giants spent three to four times as much as Royal Crown on advertising. Innovation gave Royal Crown an early lead, but in the long run first-mover advantages proved relatively unimportant in deciding the competitive outcome.

The eventual outcome of the battle for diet soft drinks was probably assured from the start. By 1991 Diet Coke and Diet Pepsi were the number three and number four best-selling soft drinks in the United States, just behind "regular" Coke and Pepsi. In addition, caffeine-free versions of each diet product ranked nine and ten, respectively. Royal Crown's Diet Rite did not even make the top ten. The total industry share held and gallonage produced by each brand is shown in Table 3.6.

Some analysts contend that Royal Crown Cola's mistake was in the way it defined itself. From the earliest days of the diet soft drink competition Royal Crown Cola was never more than a fraction the size of Coke and Pepsi. One recent marketing analysis described the firm and its flagship brands as "Dinosaurs," concluding that "Royal Crown's biggest failure was its inability to accept a subordinate role to the Big Two colas."[52] In that same analysis, a former Royal Crown marketer admits that Royal Crown believed it was an equal of Coke and Pepsi. It was not, and that misperception led the firm into uneven battles, which it always lost.

Royal Crown Cola spent the 1980s in turmoil. It went through four chief operating officers between 1984 and 1991, which left many of its bottlers uncertain as to the firm's future direction. One bottler noted: "I sometimes think it's amazing RC has survived as well as it has over the years despite all the corporate games."[53]

TABLE 3.6
1991 DIET SOFT DRINK STATISTICS

Brand	1991 Industry Share	1991 Gallonage (in millions)
Diet Coke	10.0%	1,221
Diet Pepsi	6.5	794
Diet Rite	0.6	75

Source: Data adapted from "That Was the Year That Was," *Beverage World*, March 1992, pp. 66–72.

In sum, first-mover advantages seemed to count for little in diet soft drinks. Royal Crown picked a fight with much stronger opponents and got beaten up pretty badly. Those advantages provided no more than a temporary benefit. Furthermore, they instilled in managers a false sense of the product's ultimate potential. In the end, it was distribution and marketing strengths that determined the outcome of diet soft drinks leadership, not order of market entry. There seemed to be no need for Coke and Pepsi to hurry up and rush to market. They knew they could displace the weak innovator with heavy promotional spending and distribution advantages.

The history of the soft drink industry is filled with instances in which order of entry counted for little, even in competition between the two largest players. Pepsi's Teem, for example, had preceded Coke's Sprite to market, but Coke ended up in the lead position. One Coke manager reflected on the nature of competition in soft drinks: "The high ground says that we should be leading the way, but that is not our style. We like to let others come out, stand back and see what it takes to take the category over."[54] Those are not the words of a worried man. They also smack of well-founded confidence. There was no need to be worried. The evolution of diet soft drinks is a classic case of a well-heeled firm entering a market after the pioneer and then being able to buy what it was unable to obtain first. The meager resources of the pioneer proved no match for the marketing clout of larger, later entrants. When the market blossomed there was no other firm that could match the marketing prowess of Coke and Pepsi, not by a mile.

10. DRY BEER

For decades, foreign firms have been accused of reaping the fruits of American innovation. Critics claim that foreigners copy, then quickly commercialize, basic developments made here. Sometimes, but not often, the process works in reverse. Consider the case of dry beer, a product pioneered in Japan by a Japanese company, which after successfully penetrating the Japanese market, was exported to the United States with hopes of repeating its success overseas. It never happened. Major domestic breweries, in particular Anheuser-Busch, introduced their own dry beer entries, which went on to dominate the product category. Dry beer is a rare but instructive example of how American firms copy Japanese innovations.

The story starts in Japan with Asahi Breweries Limited, a minor player in the Japanese beer industry. Asahi was established in 1906. Its near monopoly of the business caused it to be broken up into three separate firms. One retained the name Asahi, and the others were called Kirin and Nippon. Asa-

hi's sales had been declining for forty years.[55] Kirin, its one-time offspring, went on to become the established market leader.

The beer business in Japan comprises four firms of unequal size. Until the late 1980s, Kirin controlled nearly 60 percent of the Japanese market and was the fourth largest brewer in the world as measured by sales. Sapporo was second with a 20 percent share. Asahi and Suntory were distant followers, each holding about 10 percent of the market.

All four competitors sold similar-tasting beers. What differed was the packaging and the amount of promotional spending. Kirin, the market leader, lavishly outspent its smaller rivals.

Asahi was looking for a way to reverse its poor fortunes. In taste tests, one of its experimental beer formulas drew rave reviews from consumers for its superior taste. Consumers especially liked the product's lack of an aftertaste. They also felt the effects of its higher (10 percent) alcohol content more quickly. Asahi called its concoction "dry beer."

What exactly is dry beer? Basically, it is an old idea in new garb, a modern reincarnation of an age-old brew. One expert called it "a classic style of stout that goes back 200 years."[56] For that reason some analysts call it more hype than true innovation. Still, its unique taste distinguished it from regular brews. Dry beer is brewed longer than traditional beers and uses a different kind of yeast. It also has fewer calories, but that point is downplayed by sellers for fear of cutting into light beer sales. Some dry beers—especially those sold in Japan—have a higher alcohol content than traditional brews; others do not. There really is no such thing as a single dry beer formulation.

Asahi launched Asahi Super Dry in the Japanese market in March 1987. The innovative brew was an instant success that quickly captured 20 percent of the entire market. No new beer had ever rocketed to such heights so quickly. The effect on Asahi's position in the industry was astounding. Its market share soared from 9.6 percent in 1985 to 25 percent in 1989. In less than three years, Asahi jumped from third or fourth place among the "big 4" to second. It easily replaced Sapporo, the number two firm, which dropped from 20 to 18 percent. But most of Asahi's gains came at the expense of Kirin, the long-time industry leader, whose market share dropped from 60 to 49 percent. By 1988 dry beer accounted for a whopping 40 percent of all beer sales in the Japanese market.

Asahi succeeded in Japan with dry beer in much the same way that Miller had succeeded in America with light beer. It was a rapid rise to second place. Unlike Miller, however, Asahi's success was almost totally dependent on its new product. Dry beer represented fully 95 percent of its sales. Asahi's fortunes were closely tied to the continued success of dry beer.

Dry beer was such a resounding success that Asahi could not satisfy de-

mand. To stretch its capacity, Asahi employees were forbidden to purchase the product, and Asahi factories dedicated to producing other beers—such as Coors in Japan under license—were diverted to dry beer production. Asahi spent heavily to increase capacity quickly.

The Japanese competitors were caught completely off guard by the instant success of dry beer but moved quickly to counter Asahi's early entry. In February 1988 Kirin, Sapporo, and Suntory introduced imitative copies of Asahi's innovative brand. Kirin parried with Kirin Dry but also introduced Ichiban, a unique product that sold 35 million cases its first year on the market. For the most part, the copies failed to gain much share against Asahi's Super Dry.

The action soon moved to American markets. Asahi sought to replicate its success in Japan in the U.S. market. It would be an uphill battle—the combined market shares of all Japanese brands were less than 2 percent—but Asahi felt it had a killer product.

Asahi, the innovator, along with its copycat rivals, entered the U.S. market with little press attention. Most of the Japanese brands entered first through the limited distribution channels already in place, mostly selling to Japanese restaurants. But as the popularity of their dry beers increased, so did their distribution alternatives.

By the late 1980s dry beer was a "hot" product in an otherwise declining American beer industry. For that reason, competitors fought vigorously for the attention of America's 129 million beer drinkers. Stateside brewers reacted quickly to stem the threat of Japanese imports.

Anheuser-Busch made the boldest moves. It was not about to be broadsided as Kirin had been in its home market. Nor was it about to allow a replay of the import penetration that had so devastated the auto and consumer electronics industries. In September 1988 Anheuser-Busch tested Michelob Dry in five selected markets. As had happened previously in Japan, the response to Michelob Dry was so encouraging that the product was rolled out nationally only a few months later, in November 1988. Michelob Dry made Anheuser-Busch the first domestic seller. Sales skyrocketed. In January 1989 Anheuser-Busch had to apologize to customers for running out of the product.

Once again, critics claimed that the product was not new at all. Some industry experts recalled that as early as the 1950s regional beers such as New York's Rheingold and St. Louis's Stag had called themselves "dry."

Kirin—the brand that had followed Asahi into the dry beer market in Japan—now claimed to be the innovator. An executive at Kirin's Canadian-based had the audacity to claim that "we're the original formulation, there seems to be an inherent value in that. We think people want an authentic dry

beer that's from Japan. We invented it."[57] An "authentic," "original" imitation was ready to do battle with Michelob Dry, a later entrant.

Competition was heating up in the American market. By 1989 more than twenty dry beers were competing for consumers' attention.

In March 1989 Anheuser-Busch made a bold move that it had made only once before in its 113-year history. It decided to use the name Budweiser on another beer entry (the first had been with Bud Light). Bud Dry was tested in California, Texas, and Wisconsin. One again, the response was overwhelming. By April 1990 the brand was being sold nationally at a rate comparable to Bud Light's record rates of 1982. Accompanying the new product was the ad campaign that asked: "Why ask why?"

Anheuser-Busch's early response to the Japanese invasion of its home markets proved successful. Bud Dry and Michelob Dry moved quickly to the front of the pack, annihilating the Japanese attackers. Although dozens of other dry brands continue to compete with one another, Bud Dry and Michelob Dry dominate. The reasons why Anheuser-Busch prevailed are clear:

- First, Anheuser-Busch moved quickly to respond to the innovator's threat. That denied the Japanese innovator and its copycat cousins a chance to establish a foothold.
- Second, the American products had a clear price advantage. Although both Michelob and Bud Dry were sold as "super-premium" products, they were priced at $3.29 per sixpack, nearly $2.00 less than their Japanese rivals.
- Third, and most important, Anheuser-Busch had a vastly superior distribution system that was already in place and could be used to quickly get a competitive product on the shelf. Anheuser-Busch's advantages in distribution more than made up for its failure to be the first to market.
- Fourth, and almost as important, Anheuser-Busch had unmatchable marketing advantages: (1) the resources to promote its product to a wide audience, and (2) the established brand names to hang on the products. The Japanese brands were less recognizable. They were niche brands that appealed to a smaller audience in search of imports.

Dry beer will probably never reach the heights of its light beer predecessor. In fact, it is debatable whether dry beer even qualifies as a successful innovation. It may simply be a quick-passing fad that will soon disappear. An initial burst in sales was followed by a sales decline. One point is clear, however: Dry beer is a case in which domestic competitors quickly countered the Japanese innovators and maintained their dominant role. Beer, unlike autos and consumer electronics, is unlikely to be a product category dominated by the Japanese, no matter how innovative their products.

11. FOOD PROCESSORS

The very name of Cuisinart is a testament to its incredible success. The brand name is nearly synonymous with the entire product category of home food processors that it singlehandedly created. Oddly, although the brand name remains instantly recognizable to millions of consumers, the firm itself has fallen on hard times. Cuisinarts may have pioneered the market for food processors, but once demand for the product was established, lower-priced copies flooded the market and swamped the innovator, driving it into bankruptcy.

The modern food processor was invented in 1963 by Pierre Verdun and was produced by Robot-Coupe, a leading French manufacturer of restaurant equipment. Its machine was sold to professional chefs in restaurants, not to individual consumers for home cooking.

In 1971 Carl Sontheimer, a retired physicist with a passion for gourmet cooking, stumbled across the product at a cooking show. Sontheimer persuaded Robot-Coupe to let him sell a scaled-down version of the industrial product for home use. The Cuisinart food processor was thus born in 1972.

Sontheimer presented his innovative food processor to the trade at a January 1973 housewares show in Chicago. Sales were slow, because prices were high. There seemed to be only a very small market for a nearly $200 kitchen counter appliance.

Luck struck in 1975, when *Gourmet* magazine ran a favorable story on the product. In addition, influential chefs and cookbook authors wrote about the wonders of the new device. The imprimatur of respected professionals caused sales to soar. The Cuisinart food processor became the cooking gadget of the decade.

Consumer trends were also moving in its direction. Skills at gourmet cooking became valued by Yuppie consumers, and the product saved time in chopping, dicing, and otherwise cutting recipe ingredients.

Exploding demand attracted myriad copycats. Early followers included the full range of small-appliance makers: General Electric (which later sold its small appliance business to Black & Decker), Hamilton Beach, Waring, Faberware, and Moulinex, another French seller. Those entrants mostly followed the same strategy: They sold their machines at about half the price of Cuisinart's Cadillac model.

The market grew rapidly throughout the 1970s. By 1977 sales reached 500,000, and Cuisinart held a 50 percent share. Cuisinart had created and held on to the dominant share of a fast-growing market for an entirely new kind of kitchen utensil.

Problems emerged. Sontheimer and Robot-Coupe, the French maker of

Cuisinart's food processors, had a falling out over problems both real and imagined. Sontheimer decided to cut costs and boost quality by switching production from France to Japan. By 1980 all Cuisinarts were made in Japan.

Robot-Coupe retaliated by selling the same machines that were previously sold under the Cuisinart brand name under its own (Robot-Coupe) label. The brand sold well in France, where its reputation was well known, but stagnated elsewhere. Cuisinart was not seriously threatened by Robot-Coupe's counterattack.

Cuisinart's reputation for selling the highest-quality food processors induced Sontheimer to move further upscale. His firm continued to introduce more and more deluxe versions. By the end of the 1970s Cuisinart's top-of-the-line model carried a whopping price tag of $275. Its strategy could be stated simply: Cuisinart sold high-quality, premium-priced products through department stores and prestigious retailers. But the market began to move in the opposite direction.

As the 1980s progressed, Cuisinart's strategy diverged more and more radically from that of the copycats. While Cuisinart focused on the high end of the market—selling only super-deluxe machines that carried a premium price tag—the copycats battled it out at the low end. Cuisinart seemed to face no strong challengers at its high end of the market. It ceded the low end to the others.

But the concept of a food processor was changing. By the mid-1980s the food processor had become so popular that all of the gourmet chefs who wanted one already had one. Whatever growth remained in the market was clustered at the low end. As had happened with so many other very successful consumer innovations, the food processor was becoming a low-priced generic product.

The trend culminated in 1984, when Sunbeam introduced the Oskar, a simple $60 (often discounted) gumball-shaped device that was used to grind up a few vegetables. Cuisinart, in contrast, sold a massive food processor with a multitude of attachments. The market spoke clearly. By 1985 Sunbeam had sold nearly 750,000 of the no-frills low-end machines. Then, in 1986 alone, Sunbeam sold 1.4 million more Oskars.

Cuisinart's response? It did what had worked so well for the firm in the past: it moved farther upscale, introducing the veritable Rolls Royce of food processors, which was a technological kitchen wonder priced at a stunning $600. A few gourmets loved it, but most of the market had no need for such an elaborate device.

By 1986 the market for food processors had peaked at six million units a year. Sales had grown rapidly for about a decade, but the market was now saturated. By the end of the decade nearly 45 percent of all homes in the

United States had a food processor. The market declined during the second half of the 1980s.

Cuisinart was unaccustomed to a declining market. Its problems were compounded by two key mistakes from which it never really recovered.

First, the firm failed to use the prestigious and respected Cuisinart name to expand into related products. There was a tremendous opportunity to put the respected Cuisinart name on a host of related kitchen appliances. It could have brought out Cuisinart mixers, coffeemakers, can openers, and other related products. One analyst noted: "It is the sort of fabled brand name that marketers usually only dream about."[58]

Second, the potential of bringing out a slew of related products led to a leveraged buyout, which ultimately sapped the firm of cash. In January 1988 Sontheimer sold Cuisinart to a group of investors led by George Barnes and Robert Fomon for $42 million. The deal was financed largely by the goodwill of the brand name, since the company had only meager tangible assets. The firm expected to pay off its debt burden by expanding on the valued Cuisinart brand name.

Like so many other ill-conceived deals of the mid-1980s, the Cuisinart deal was doomed from the start. Because the firm had so few assets to sell off, it was forced to boost sales by any means possible to pay down debt. That created more problems. Up until that time Cuisinart food processors were sold only in department stores and upscale retailers where consumers were willing to pay the high prices charged. Cuisinart decided to boost sales by selling its prestigious food processors to mass market discounters. That move created ill will among existing retailers. The discounters never sold the huge numbers of machines they were expected to, and its previous base of customers deemphasized the product. Sales dropped further, sapping more cash from already bare coffers.

In addition, because the firm lacked cash it could not pursue what had been perceived as its main opportunity for growth: expanding the product line using the Cuisinart brand name. Cuisinart was getting hit with a double whammy. Not only were sales of the overall product category declining, but Cuisinart's market share was also eroding as consumers turned to the low-end copycats. Cuisinart's market share dropped from 20 percent in 1984 to 12 percent in 1989.

The end came less than two years after the leveraged buyout. Cuisinart declared bankruptcy toward the end of 1989. But it was too late. The firm was auctioned off in December 1989. Cuisinart was acquired by the Conair Corporation for $17 million, less than half the $42 million it had sold for less than two years earlier.

Sontheimer retired a wealthy man, thanks to the buyout, but the firm he

started got caught in the crossfire of its own mistakes and the actions of competitors. Cuisinart failed to respond to the attack of low-price copycats, who ended up reaping the economic rewards of Cuisinart's—or was it Verdun's?—innovation. Cuisinart may have understood consumer demand in the beginning, when it pioneered the market, but as the years ticked on it failed to serve a larger, more price-sensitive, market. *Forbes* noted in an analysis of the case: "Cuisinart may have been the first, but it was not the best for long."[59]

12. LIGHT BEER

Low-calorie beers have been around for decades, but like many new products with a unique appeal, they took a long time to catch on. There were many false starts and a few dead ends encountered along the way to full-fledged market acceptance.

Light beers have fewer calories because they contain fewer carbohydrates than regular brews. That fact turned out to be a pitfall for the pioneers but an opportunity for later entrants.

The U.S. marketing arm of Germany's Holsten Brewery claims that Holsten developed the first "low-carbohydrate" beer before World War II. But its imported Dia-Beer was an oddball product targeted at diabetics that never served more than a minuscule share of the total market.[60]

The first direct attempt to produce a low-calorie beer was Trommer's Red Letter, which was brewed by Piels Brothers in the early 1960s. It was an innovative but unsuccessful product that failed to attract much consumer interest. There seemed little need for a "diet beer" in the early 1960s.

The real story of light beer starts in Brooklyn, New York, with Liebmann Breweries. For more than one hundred years, the Northeast regional brewer sold the popular Rheingold brand. The firm itself was renamed for its leading brand in 1964, when it was acquired by Pepsi Cola United Bottlers. Liebmann Brewers bought Trommer's Orange, New Jersey, brewery.

Throughout 1966 the industry was abuzz with talk that Rheingold was working on Gablinger's, a low-calorie beer. On October 25, 1966, Rheingold went public, announcing that it would soon introduce Gablinger's, which would be brewed by its Forest Brewing subsidiary. In December 1966 Gablinger's was introduced in upstate New York and Connecticut.

Gablinger's was promoted as a "no-carbohydrate" beer, which implied that it was a weight-control product. By eliminating the carbohydrates, Rheingold was able to reduce the calories in a 12-ounce bottle of Gablinger's from an average of 165 to 99, about the same number found in today's "light"

beers. In June 1967 distribution was expanded to the entire New York City metropolitan area, Massachusetts, southern Vermont, and New Hampshire. It was expected that as production capacity expanded, distribution would expand slowly to the rest of Rheingold's twelve-state selling region. Rheingold intended to expand nationally by licensing its product to brewers in other parts of the country. By mid-1967 Gablinger's was clearly the first popular low-calorie beer.

During its first year of operation, Gablinger's was promoted with a $6 million advertising budget that featured the slogan, "It doesn't fill you up."[61] In hindsight, the advertising slogan proved to have a longer shelf life than the beer. A dozen years later, Miller Lite used a similar slogan in its long-running ad campaign that crowed "Tastes Great; Less Filling," which ran until 1991.

Gablinger's was quickly followed to market by another small entrant. On May 22, 1967, Meister Brau, a regional Chicago brewer (which had just changed its name from the Peter Hand Brewery), introduced a brand called Lite in eight Midwestern states—Illinois, Indiana, Iowa, Michigan, Minnesota, Nebraska, Ohio, and Wisconsin. Meister Brau expanded eastward by licensing its product to P. Ballantine & Sons, a Newark-based regional brewer. Ballantine would market Meister Brau Lite from Florida to Maine. Lite beer was introduced on the East Coast in mid-September 1967.

Meister Brau's promotional strategy also stressed the product's lack of carbohydrates and, by implication, its lower calorie content. But Meister Brau used blatant sex appeal to sell its product. It hired one Dierdre Daniels, a curvaceous twenty-one-year-old blonde whose blue-and-white leotard matched the colors on the beer can's label, to act as spokesperson in the firm's Lite beer ads. It was unclear whether that appeal would attract men in search of Ms. Daniels look-alikes or women beer drinkers in search of her stunning figure. Whatever the appeal, it was lower calories that counted. Ms. Daniels noted in a press conference at the time: "We've reduced the calorie content by one-third from about 150 a bottle to 100."[62]

Meister Brau sought to piggyback on Gablinger's pioneering efforts. Its Ballantine licensee noted in 1967: "The competition has spent a lot of money and has done a good job of warming up the field. We don't have to dig—its been done for us."[63]

Gablinger's innovative efforts encountered the strong arm of the law. In December 1967, about a year after it first entered the market, the United States Attorney acting on behalf of the FDA charged Gablinger's beer with false and misleading labeling. The suit focused on two charges:

- Gablinger's claimed it had "no available carbohydrates," which erroneously implied that it was a "diet" beer. In the words of the suit, Gablinger's

was claiming it "is of significant value for use for reducing and weight control."[64]

• The product's label did not indicate the number of calories, as required by FDA regulations regarding food products sold for "special dietary uses."

The pioneer was sailing in uncharted waters. In December 1967 the government confiscated shipments of Gablinger's. The bad press was damaging to Rheingold's innovative efforts.

Rheingold claimed that it had done nothing wrong. In fact, it argued, its label had previously been approved by the Alcohol and Tobacco unit of the IRS when the product was first introduced. Rheingold seemed to be caught in a jurisdictional battle between two government bureaucracies. Rather than fight a long and painful legal case, Rheingold agreed to alter its controversial label.

Starting in mid-December 1967 Gablinger's removed the statement "no fat and 0.25 percent protein" from its labels and dropped claims of "no available carbohydrates." The new labels clearly stated that Gablinger's was not a weight-reducing product.

At the same time, on December 8, 1967, another suit was brought against Rheingold for false advertising. That suit was initiated by Holsten Imports, the firm that imported the decades-old Dia-Beer from Hamburg, Germany. Holsten also claimed that Gablinger's was not really a diet beer.

Rheingold struck back. It filed a countersuit against Holsten on December 28, 1967, claiming "false representation" and asking for $5 million in damages.

The timing of the government suit and the fact that it was extremely unusual—if not unprecedented—for the government to take such action suggest that someone was purposely trying to sabotage Rheingold's pioneering entry. If so, the campaign worked beautifully. The negative publicity helped destroy Gablinger's reputation before the product could be firmly positioned in the minds of consumers.

Gablinger's regulatory problems were compounded by financial and product shortcomings that sent the company spiraling downward. For one, its low-calorie beer tasted bad and produced little head upon pouring, a disappointment for avid consumers. As a result, sales were disappointing, estimated to be only 100,000 to 300,000 barrels a year.

Gablinger's also had the misfortune of being introduced at a time when overall profits were declining at Rheingold. The reputation of top management, which had received great press early in 1967, had cooled considerably by the end of the year. That led to disruptive shakeups and management ousters during the last quarter of 1967.

Finally, some critics even likened Gablinger's entry to that of the Edsel, a wrong product targeted at the wrong market. Experts were pessimistic about the potential of a low-calorie beer. One of them concluded that light beer would be "an important but not exceedingly large market."[65] As the future would show, nothing could have been farther from the truth. Gablinger's was merely too early. Rheingold was too far ahead of its time. Within a few years the idea of a low-calorie beer would create the fastest-growing market in the history of the brewing industry.

The future looked brighter for Rheingold when, in April 1968, Gablinger's was granted a patent for its pioneering product. Meister Brau was warned that it was proceeding on shaky legal ground in its attempt to sell a competing low-calorie beer. Not unexpectedly, Meister Brau took issue with that view. Then the tables turned again. In March 1970 the courts ruled that Gablinger's patents were invalid.

Gablinger's distribution continued to expand. By the spring of 1970 it was sold in nineteen Eastern states. But financial troubles finally crippled the struggling brewer. The firm was forced to shrink to only two breweries, in Brooklyn and in Orange, New Jersey. In 1974 Chock Full O' Nuts bought Rheingold and closed the Brooklyn brewery. Even that downsizing, however, failed to slow the firm's fall. In October 1977 C. Schmidt & Sons of Philadelphia bought the Rheingold label, and for all practical purposes Rheingold ceased to exist as an independent company.

Meister Brau faced equally horrendous financial problems. In fact, it fell at an even faster rate than Rheingold. The firm lost $2 million in 1970 and $1.2 million more in 1971. By July 1972 the competition between Gablinger's and Meister Brau effectively ended when Meister Brau filed for Chapter 11 bankruptcy protection. Seven months later, in February 1973, Meister Brau, Chicago's last brewery, was liquidated.

In 1966, meanwhile, W. R. Grace Company purchased 53 percent of Miller Brewing's stock. Three years later, in 1969, Philip Morris acquired the same 53 percent share from Grace for $130 million. Miller beat out Pepsi, which sought to buy the shares for $120 million and apply its soft drink marketing expertise to the firm's products. Philip Morris, a superb marketer in its own right, sought to apply its expertise in selling cigarettes. In mid-1970 Philip Morris bought the remaining 47 percent of Miller Brewing from the DeRance Foundation of Milwaukee.

As Meister Brau approached bankruptcy, it was forced to sell assets to raise cash. In June 1972, Miller acquired the trade names Lite, Meister Brau, and Buckeye from Meister Brau.

Less than three years later, in February 1975, Miller introduced its stunningly successful Lite beer, accompanied by a $10 million advertising blitz,

the most ever spent on a new beer entry. Lite beer was promoted using the now familiar tag line, "Everything you always wanted in a beer and less." It was a brilliant later entry strategy. The brand name was not new (that came from Meister Brau), the idea was old-hat (it had been around for decades), and the advertising slogan was similar to Rheingold's "doesn't fill you up." Miller's creativity lay elsewhere.

Miller learned much from Rheingold's and Meister Brau's mistakes. It realized that 80 percent of beer was consumed by men aged 18 to 44. More important, Miller understood the fragility of the male ego and the onerous implications ordering a diet beer in a bar with fellow workers held for those consumers. A Miller marketing manager noted in 1977 in regard to the pioneering entrants: "The appeal was mainly to dieters, and the ads showed things like bathing beauties playing with beach balls."[66] Miller set out to hire burly former athletes to announce the product's macho image. The same manager continued: "Using the ex-jocks was a way to make the product socially acceptable to our biggest customers."

Miller also entered with a superior product. Its Lite beer tasted better than the previous entries.

Miller's timing and positioning were perfect. Sales of lite beer began to skyrocket shortly after Lite's introduction. "Me-too" brands proliferated. Genesee introduced "Fife and Drum Extra Lyte. Schlitz introduced Schlitz Light into a twelve-state test market. Miller responded by suing both Schlitz and Genesee for using the name "light," which Miller claimed as its trademark.

Anheuser-Busch was among the last large firms to enter the light beer segment. It introduced Natural Light nationally in June 1977, after a brief test market.

Earlier that year, Anheuser-Busch had turned the tables on Miller by suing in federal court for a confirmation of the right to use the word "light" on its label. The suit was filed in St. Louis. The court ruled that Natural Light did not infringe on Miller's trademark.

Miller's legal battle with Schlitz eventually reached the Supreme Court, which also ruled against Miller. The "light" label was now generic.

The market for low-calorie beers was now growing quickly. In the late 1970s low-calorie beers accounted for 8 percent of all beer sales. Miller Lite held the largest share by far. Natural Light held the number two spot.

Miller's lawyers counterattacked in February 1979. They complained to the FTC that Anheuser-Busch was engaged in false and misleading advertising by calling its product "Natural." Miller charged that it was anything but. It was a highly processed product that contained a host of nasty chemicals, including sulfuric acid.[67]

In February 1978 Anheuser-Busch introduced a second low-calorie beer,

Michelob Light. The product started in a five-state test market but was quickly taken national. Michelob Light had 134 calories, high for a low-calorie beer, but 20 percent less than regular Michelob.

Miller's lawyer pounced once again. In March 1979 Miller complained to the Bureau of Alcohol, Tobacco, and Firearms that—at 134 calories a can—Michelob was not light at all. In fact, they argued, it was merely a watered-down version of the regular product.[68] The intent may have been to discredit the product, a strategy that had proved successful against Rheingold.

Anheuser-Busch countered in advertising. Hoping to chip away at Miller Lite's stable 60 percent market share, it hired away two of Lite's most popular ad spokespersons, Joe Frazier and Nick Buoniconti. It then used ads that were remarkably similar to Miller's humorous, sports-oriented ads built around the tag line: "Taste is why you'll switch." Natural Light had entered the market after Miller Lite and now employed a copycat ad campaign. The *Wall Street Journal* concluded: "Imitation is certainly there."[69]

By 1980 Miller Lite's 60 percent share seemed immutable, but Natural Light and Michelob Light weighed in at numbers two and three respectively. Coors Light, which had entered in 1978, held the number four spot.

Miller's lack of success in protecting the "light" name emboldened its competitors. Falstaff Brewing of San Francisco tested the waters when it introduced a Lite beer. Miller lawyers struck again, this time in federal court in Providence, Rhode Island, and this time they won. The court issued a restraining order against Falstaff.[70] To this day Miller retains the rights to the "Lite" (if not the "light") name.

Bud Light—the last major light beer entry—was introduced to the national market in the summer of 1982, after a one-year test market that had begun on April 30, 1981. The brand sought to capitalize on the powerful Budweiser name. Backed by a whopping $35 million ad budget, the intent was clearly to take the number one spot from Miller. Natural Light was deemphasized (but resurrected years later). First year sales of Bud Light exceeded expectations, but Miller's 60 percent share of the light beer market held firm.

Throughout the 1980s and into the 1990s, the light beer market continued to grow rapidly, while the rest of the industry experienced stagnant sales. By 1981 light beer sales made up 18 percent of all beer sales. By 1986 the category took 22 percent. By 1991, light beers represented 31 percent of the overall beer market, and they continue to gain share. In recent years premium beers, such as Budweiser, have declined slightly, while light beers have gained share. From humble beginnings, light beer has moved close to becoming the nation's favorite brew.

In recent years Anheuser-Busch's relentless attack has started to chip away at Miller's market share. Miller Lite still holds the number one spot, with

10.3 percent of the total beer market in 1991, but Bud Light and Coors Light are closing fast. Ominously, in 1991 Miller Lite experienced its first outright decline in sales. Bud Light and Coors Light, meanwhile, are in a virtual dead heat for the number two spot. Table 3.7 illustrates the changing trends in market share for the top three light beer brands.

Three lessons can be learned from the light beer case.

First, it illustrates that the power of first-mover advantages pales in comparison with the power of marketing and distribution advantages held by larger, later entrants. The earliest entrants were weak firms that were easily pushed aside once the giants decided to enter.

Second, it illustrates a two-step leadership replacement pattern. The very earliest entrants were replaced by Miller, which in turn is now challenged by Bud and Coors.

Finally, the tenacity of Bud Light illustrates the power of market signaling. Anheuser-Busch may have initially misgauged the true potential of the light beer market, but its expensive and long-running ad campaign, which seems to spare no expense and sets no time limit for taking over the market, signals competitors as to the futility of entering that firm's key markets. Those are the true lessons of the light beer market.

TABLE 3.7
TOP THREE LIGHT BEER BRANDS: SHARE OF TOTAL BEER MARKET

Year	Miller Lite	Bud Light	Coors Light
1981	9.0		1.7
1982	9.4	1.8	1.7
1983	9.8	2.0	2.1
1984	9.9	2.2	2.6
1985	10.1	3.1	3.2
1986	10.1	3.6	3.8
1987	10.3	4.4	4.2
1988	10.4	5.1	4.7
1989	10.6	5.6	5.6
1990	10.5	6.1	6.1
1991	10.3	6.4	6.4

Source: Data adapted from Eric Sfiligoj, "Top 10 Beers: Rank and Market Share," *Beverage Industry*, January 1992, pp. 14–17.

13. MAINFRAME COMPUTERS

It is ironic that an industry characterized by lightning-fast innovation actually took decades, if not centuries, to develop. Mechanical calculating machines date back to the mid-nineteenth century when they operated with

gears and shafts. Prototypes of electromechanical computers appeared just before World War II. The first all-electronic, digital, general-purpose mainframe computer was completed in November 1945. It was called ENIAC (an acronym for the Electronic Numerical Integrator and Computer) and was announced to the public on February 14, 1946. Modern computing was born with ENIAC.

ENIAC was the creation of J. Presper Eckert and John Mauchly. They started working on the project in 1943 at the University of Pennsylvania, when the U.S. Army wanted a better way to calculate cannon trajectories for the war effort. It was slow going. The machine was not completed in time for the war effort.

Typical of many other radically new technologies, ENIAC was beset by myriad technical and economic problems. It was a cumbersome and inefficient device that relied on nearly 18,000 unreliable vacuum tubes. Unlike today's laptops, ENIAC stood 8 feet tall, was 80 feet long, and consumed a whopping 174,000 watts of electricity. The price of each machine was astronomical. But what really held back its commercial potential was programming. ENIAC was a programmer's nightmare. Hundreds of hours of work were required to get ENIAC to perform even the simplest operations.

ENIAC was created with a considerable dose of imitation. John Mauchly, one of ENIAC's creators, borrowed heavily from the pioneering efforts of John Atanasoff, an Iowa State University professor. Many experts contend that it was Atanasoff, not Mauchly and Eckert, who built the world's first electronic digital computer. In late 1939 Atanasoff and his student, Clifford Berry, crafted a crude prototype of a computer that contained many of the pioneering ideas found in ENIAC. It was nicknamed the ABC computer, standing for its creators' surnames and the word "computer."

John Mauchly took an immediate interest in Atanasoff's ABC computer. In 1940, less than a year after it had been developed, Mauchly met Atanasoff at an academic conference and discussed the device briefly. The next year Mauchly wrangled an invitation to visit Iowa to view the innovative machine firsthand. Later in 1941, after he had moved to the University of Pennsylvania, he set out to develop an electronic computer of his own. He wrote to Atanasoff asking if the inventor had any objections "to my building some sort of computer which incorporates some of the features of your machine?"[71] Atanasoff did not fully understand Mauchly's true intentions, and neither man realized the magnitude of the invention at hand. One fact is clear, however: "Mauchly apparently borrowed several technical ideas from Atanasoff."[72] The most important idea he copied was the use of vacuum tubes to calculate.

How influential was Atanasoff? Before meeting him, Mauchly's attempts

to build a computer were judged by one in-depth analysis to be "scant, amateurish, and completely ineffectual."[73] Only after the meetings with Atanasoff did Mauchly's machines take form. The analysis concludes: "The mistaken view is that ENIAC, built at the University of Pennsylvania between 1943 and 1946, was the first electronic computer."[74] To many experts, Atanasoff is the true inventor.

Mauchly and Eckert had one clear advantage over Atanasoff: financial backing. A few years of waiting and a more favorable location made all the difference in the world. World War II and the war-related programs to develop a computer at the University of Pennsylvania made a success of the invention that had started in Atanasoff's lab. Whereas Atanasoff had struggled alone with almost no financial or emotional support, ENIAC had backers who believed in the project.

Iowa State University did not even bother to patent the ABC computer, even though Atanasoff claims he begged it to do so. ENIAC's creators were more fortunate. They applied for a patent on June 7, 1947, claiming they had developed "the" (not "a") first electronic digital computer. A patent battle ensued—not between Atanasoff and Mauchly, but between Mauchly and the University of Pennsylvania. The university claimed ownership because the computer had been developed on its property. But the university botched its paperwork, so Mauchly and Eckert ended up with the rights to "the" first computer, which were formally granted in 1964. With rights firmly in hand, Eckert and Mauchly parted company with the University of Pennsylvania with ill will and went into the computer business.

J. Presper Eckert and John Mauchly were clearly the first to commercialize the mainframe computer. In that sense, they are the true pioneers. In 1946 they launched the first commercial computer company, aptly named the Eckert-Mauchly Electronic Control Company of Philadelphia. They also changed the name of their pioneering computer to UNIVAC (Universal Automatic Computer). At the start they had no competitors, but they had no customers either. The pioneers were prepared to engage in the extensive market development efforts required to commercialize a radically new technology.

Financing was nearly impossible to obtain. Banks refused to lend money to the fledgling firm. A $25,000 loan co-signed by Eckert's father made up the seed money for the entire computer industry.

In the early years, most experts believed that the market for mainframes would be small. It was thought to consist of no more than a handful of customers—the military, the census bureau, and high-level scientists, all of which have unusually complex computing needs. Computers were viewed as more akin to fusion reactors than widely used business machines.

Not surprisingly, Eckert-Mauchly sold its first computer to the Census Bureau, which was being overwhelmed by punch cards. As the 1950 census approached, the Census Bureau was seeking a new data storage device that would make its task more manageable. UNIVAC offered magnetic tape drives. Wary of the patent implications of a cost-plus government contract, Eckert-Mauchly signed a fixed-fee contract with the Census Bureau for $350,000. Although that figure was lower than expected costs, Eckert-Mauchly expected to make up the difference on subsequent orders. That strategy turned out to be penetration pricing at its most destructive.

Pioneering a radically new technology proved much more costly and took much more time than Eckert and Mauchly had anticipated. The innovators were required to invent a whole host of related technologies, such as magnetic tape drives. As a result, the pioneers were perpetually behind schedule and well over budget on the Census Bureau UNIVAC. By 1947, slightly more than a year after they started, their firm was barely solvent. And still, no major financiers were interested in investing in the upstart computer industry. No one who mattered saw its potential.

Eckert and Mauchly tried to recoup the losses they incurred with the Census Bureau through sales of UNIVAC computers to business customers. Their computer sought to replace the punch card machines, sorters, mechanical tabulators, and printers being used by large businesses to perform repetitive clerical tasks. That business was dominated by IBM.

During the early years of ENIAC and UNIVAC, IBM appeared remarkably uninterested in the emerging computer industry. It was content to stay with its punch card tabulators, which had been the mainstay of its business since the start of the twentieth century. Thomas Watson, Jr., IBM's chairman, frankly admitted in his autobiography: "ENIAC was an interesting experiment way off on the sidelines that could not possibly affect us. I never stopped to think what would happen if the speed of electronics circuits could be harnessed for commercial use."[75] Like many market leaders, IBM was focusing on the past. It was a typical reaction.

IBM's inertia was also surprising because it had funded research on computers throughout the 1940s. In 1939 IBM supported the development of the electromechanical Mark I at Harvard. In 1945 it agreed to support the Selective Sequence Electronic Calculator (SSEC), another electromechanical hybrid computer. Although neither machine turned out to be the technology of the future, IBM gained considerable experience in a closely related endeavor. IBM was never too far behind.

There seemed little reason for IBM to rush its entry to market. Time was certainly not of the essence, and Eckert-Mauchly was surely no threat. Tom Watson instantly homed in on ENIAC's shortcomings. He said, "It's a great

idea you have, but you're going to run out of money."[76] He was right. Almost from the start, the fledgling upstart was perpetually short of funds. When IBM did decide to enter, it quickly made up for lost ground.

Eckert-Mauchly, meanwhile, sought new business customers. It signed a $100,000 contract with Northrop, the defense contractor, to produce a computer for guided missiles.

By the summer of 1948 Eckert-Mauchly had five contracts worth $1 million, some of which were business accounts that cut into IBM's base. Prudential Insurance ordered a computer to perform routine clerical and calculating tasks quickly. A. C. Neilsen, the market research firm, ordered two computers. But money was still tight.

In 1948 Eckert and Mauchly were forced to sell part of their firm to attract investors. In August of that year the American Totalisator Company, which made the machines used at racetracks to calculate odds and display payoffs, bought 40 percent of Eckert-Mauchly because it feared the new computers might make its mechanical devices obsolete. It was a visionary purchase that pumped much-needed funds into the growing concern.

But bad luck struck a little more than a year later when, in October 1949, Harry Straus, American Totalisator's chairman, was killed in a plane crash. His successors did not share his vision. They pulled out of Eckert-Mauchly, killing the small firm's chances before they were realized.

Eckert and Mauchly were forced to sell out altogether. On February 1, 1950, they sold their firm to Remington Rand, the typewriter and electric shaver giant. In June 1951 the first Census Bureau computer was delivered—behind schedule and grossly over budget. UNIVAC now had a stable source of funds, even though the innovators had largely lost control of the product they had developed.

Sales of computers took off in the early 1950s, spurred by a public relations coup. During the 1952 presidential election Remington Rand managed to have its computer featured on CBS-TV. With only 7 percent of the vote counted, UNIVAC predicted that Eisenhower would beat Stevenson in a landslide. The machine projected that Eisenhower would carry forty-three states while Stevenson would take only five. The experts, however, expected a close race, so UNIVAC's projection was not televised. Only when the computer proved right was the public belatedly informed of its predictive powers. Computers caught the public's imagination shortly afterward. That public included many business customers, who now became interested in purchasing the machine in large numbers.

Until 1953 UNIVAC faced virtually no competition. But with business customers now interested, IBM decided to enter. Actually, IBM had been watching and waiting since the Census Bureau first ordered a UNIVAC.

In 1951 IBM produced its first computer prototypes, fully five years after Eckert-Mauchly. IBM introduced its first business computers in 1953. Many of the computers in its line were technologically inferior to the UNIVAC, for the most part slower and less powerful. IBM's strengths lay not with its technological innovations but with its sales force. IBM's chairman Watson candidly admits that although "some of those companies had better technology than we had, and certainly a better knowledge of how to use that technology, we were able to zip right by them with that sales and service force."[77]

The case of mainframe computers is another example of later entrants who surpassed the pioneer with marketing and distribution advantages. When IBM entered, the power of UNIVAC's first-mover advantages proved weak in comparison with IBM's marketing advantages. Consider how the market shifted after IBM's entry. In late 1954 UNIVAC had an installed base of thirty large computers, as against IBM's four. Less than two years later, in 1956, the computer business was a much different place. IBM had installed seventy-six large computers, while UNIVAC had a total base of forty-six. From that point on IBM's growth accelerated, while UNIVAC's fortunes declined.

UNIVAC lost $250 million in the years that followed. In 1955, Remington Rand, UNIVAC's parent, merged with the Sperry Corporation to form Sperry Rand. But nothing seemed to stop, or even slow, the IBM onslaught. By 1960 IBM had 75 percent of the computer market. UNIVAC was a distant second with 10 percent. The remainder was split among Burroughs, Control Data (which was formed by UNIVAC defectors), Honeywell, and NCR. There were more than 10,000 computers installed by 1960, mostly in business establishments.

How did IBM do it? Three forces appear most important.

First was the sales force. IBM was a marketing powerhouse that easily made the switch from tabulating machines to electronic computers.

Second was the issue of pricing. IBM was a financial powerhouse up against much weaker rivals. IBM lowered the prices of computers where it was trying to gain share. But it kept prices high on punch card equipment, a business that IBM virtually owned. Consumers had few other suppliers to turn to. Competitors had no opportunity to cross-parry.

It was penetration pricing at its purest. IBM's first few computers produced expected negative profits. Eight years later, in 1960, profit margins were still tiny, only 11 percent. Punch cards, in contrast, carried a hefty 40 percent margin. Not until IBM completely dominated the computer market did it raise its margins on mainframes.

An IBM critic sums it up as follows:

Suddenly, after two years of having the computer market to itself, Remington faced a pair of IBM systems that were priced not to make a profit but actually to lose money for their manufacturer. Lacking IBM's deep pockets to subsidize comparable pricing of its own, Remington saw its share of the expanding market plunge irretrievably during the next few years as customers flocked to the IBM 701 and 702.[78]

Eckert-Mauchly had tried the same strategy but did not have the money or the industry experience to make it work.

The third advantage IBM offered customers was continuity. IBM tied its early computers directly to its punch card machines, with which business customers were already familiar (and which it controlled). Punch card technology may have been slower than magnetic tapes—a point that annoyed scientists and engineers—but it eased consumer adoption of the new technology. IBM traded state-of-the-art technology for customer continuity. That simple decision helped the market grow quickly as business buyers recognized that they could easily integrate IBM mainframes into their operations without disrupting business.

Demand for computers soared throughout the 1960s as computers found new applications. In the end, mainframes in particular and computers in general turned out to be one of the longest-lived growth markets in economic history. It is a market almost without equal.

The patent on computers was formally granted to Eckert and Mauchly on February 4, 1964, at a time when their firm was owned by Sperry Rand (which is now part of Unisys). Sperry then set out to extract profits from the later entrants by suing them for patent infringement. On May 26, 1967, a Sperry Rand subsidiary sued Honeywell. On the very same day, Honeywell countersued Sperry Rand, claiming antitrust violations. It was Honeywell's lawyers who discovered the Mauchly–Atanasoff connection. On October 19, 1973, ENIAC's patent was ruled invalid. The decision attracted little attention at the time, because the press was preoccupied with Vice President Agnew's resignation in the face of charges of corruption when he had been Governor of Maryland. But the judge's ruling was devastating. He ruled that "Eckert and Mauchly did not themselves first invent the automatic electronic digital computer, but instead derived that subject matter from one Dr. John Vincent Atanasoff."[79] The pioneer was found to be part imitator. In the end, there was a near perfect negative correlation between order of entry and economic success. Atanasoff received virtually nothing for his innovative efforts, not even recognition. Clive Berry, his student aide, committed suicide. Eckert and Mauchly received a measly $300,000 each over a ten-year

period for their pioneering work. IBM ended up with the bulk of the treasures. Although it had entered long after the pioneer, it emerged as (until recently) one of the largest and most profitable corporations in the world. It did not invent, nor did it pioneer, the new technology for digital mainframe computers, but when the market proved promising, it dominated the industry for decades. That is the true economic lesson on mainframe computers.

14. MICROWAVE OVENS

The microwave oven is arguably one of the most influential innovations of the postwar period. Over the course of a generation, it worked its way slowly from an obscure invention into the very fabric of American life. Unfortunately for the pioneers who parented the technology, as it slowly gained acceptance this innovation turned out to be an ungrateful child. When the product finally found sufficient numbers of customers, the Japanese moved in and took over. They then lost share to lower-cost producers from Korea, who were able to sell at even lower prices. What follows is the story of that torturous journey.

Microwave ovens grew out of wartime radar research. According to industry legend, the product was first conceived during the depths of World War II, in 1942, when Percy Spencer, an engineer at Raytheon, discovered that a chocolate bar in his pocket had melted while he had been working on a radar system to detect Nazi planes. Spencer instantly recognized the potential of his discovery. He cut a hole in a kitchen kettle, placed a radar-producing tube (called a magnetron) inside, and created Raytheon's first crude Radarange, which was patented by the defense contractor in 1949.

Raytheon introduced its first commercial microwave oven to the public at the Waldorf-Astoria Hotel in New York City in 1946. The oven was leased to restaurants in ten U.S. cities, but it failed badly as a commercial venture. Only one hundred ovens were ever built. Prices were too high, the ovens cooked unevenly, service costs were astronomical, and commercial chefs did not know how to perform, nor did they appreciate the joy of, microwave cooking. The product was a fiasco.

None of those results surprised Raytheon, which was in the market for the long haul. *Business Week* reported in 1954 that "its problem is the problem of any company that probes the frontiers of science."[80] It took time to pioneer radically new products. What Raytheon did not know was how long the market would actually take to develop.

Raytheon tested the market again in 1948 with six new microwave mod-

els, which were placed in restaurants and on ocean liners. It learned that microwave ovens were better suited to reheating precooked frozen foods than for cooking itself. When commercial customers used the product for that purpose they were happy; when they used it for cooking they were not.

The earliest microwaves possessed severe technical and economic problems. They were cumbersome devices that stood 6 feet high, weighed 750 pounds, and sold for up to $3,000 in the late 1940s. Even commercial customers were put off by those disadvantages.

Product and market development continued into the early 1950s. In 1950 Raytheon—following on an analogy from the television industry—introduced a countertop model priced at $1,875 and a console model priced at $2,975. In 1952 the console models could be found in restaurants, hotels, railroad dining cars, and prestigious oceangoing ships like the *S.S. United States*. None of those applications produced appreciable profits, however. The pioneer was still investing current funds in hopes of a future payoff.

In the early years of market development, microwave ovens were targeted exclusively to commercial customers. But most advocates of the technology believed that the ovens would one day make their way into household kitchens. When that would occur, however, was open to serious debate.

In 1952 Raytheon decided against entering the consumer market. It believed that the technology was not well enough developed for that step. Tappan thought otherwise and rushed to be the first entrant. In October 1955 the Tappan Stove Company released a prototype of a "miniature" 170-pound, air-cooled, $1,195 microwave oven. Tappan decided to capture the consumer market while Raytheon was pioneering commercial applications.

Tappan failed badly in the consumer market for the same reasons Raytheon had trouble finding customers in the commercial sector: Prices were too high, reliability problems resulted in ridiculously high repair costs, and consumers were discouraged by meat cooked to a putrid gray by the new cooking wonder.

For the next ten years Raytheon toiled on the lightning-fast cooker. By 1963 competitors included Tappan, which was still in the market, and General Electric (GE), which had just entered on a small scale but seemed to lack commitment.

Various experiments to find viable consumer applications were tried. Some ideas were nutty. Tad's Steak House in Manhattan, for example, allowed customers to select frozen foods from freezer chests and to bring them back to their tables for reheating in a tabletop microwave oven. Other applications had more staying power. PanAm installed microwaves on its airplanes to reheat passenger meals, a common practice today (even though the innovative PanAm stopped using them). Armour, a meat processor, sold

microwavable frozen "gourmet" meals to restaurants. It was an idea more than slightly ahead of its time.

In the early 1960s, technological advances in magnetrons, the key component of microwave ovens, led to much lower prices, which moved the consumer market closer to reality. In 1964 a company named Amperex used an improved design to cut the price of magnetrons in half. That helped reduce the price of the low-end microwaves to below $1,000.

At the same time the pioneer Raytheon made two crucial moves that pushed the market forward. First, in 1961 Raytheon bought a one-third interest in the New Japan Radio Company, with which it shared its microwave technology. A few years later, in 1964, Keishi Ogura, a Japanese scientist at New Japan Radio, designed a smaller, simpler, and more efficient magnetron. Then, in its second move, Raytheon acquired the Amana Refrigeration Company of Iowa in 1965.

As a result of those two actions, in February 1968 Raytheon "became the first firm to offer a portable microwave unit priced at least within the imagination of the average consumer: $475."[81] Raytheon's entry created much fanfare. It now seemed certain that after nearly fifteen years of development the microwave oven was about to take off. As early as 1965 it seemed that "microwaves . . . are beginning to make their long-awaited jump into the nation's kitchens and factories as the heat element in instant-heating ovens."[82] That forecast proved premature, however. More pioneering was needed.

By 1965, roughly ten thousand microwave ovens were in use, almost solely in commercial establishments. At the time, Raytheon was the overwhelming market leader.

Litton, another defense contractor with extensive experience in radar technology, entered in late 1964 with a microwave oven targeted at the vending machine industry. In those days, that was an important application. College students and the like would purchase frozen food from a vending machine and heat it in a nearby microwave. Production started small but increased rapidly. Although Litton was a much later entrant than Raytheon, it had gained considerable experience producing magnetrons for military applications and believed that it too could easily (just as easily as Raytheon) make the switch to commercial applications.

In 1969 Litton countered Amana's move into the home market with its own countertop model, sold under a private label. In 1971 Litton introduced its own Minutemaster brand, which was a direct competitor to Raytheon's Radarange.

At the start of the 1970s Raytheon was the clear market leader with about a 60 percent share. Litton was a strong number two.

In the early years, Raytheon, Litton, and Tappan lamented the length of time it was taking for the consumer market to grow. The microwave oven seemed to be stuck in a long, useless stage, with the payback lying perpetually in the future. One Litton executive noted: "We are creating a market where none exists."[83]

Demand started to soar soon after that. At the start of the 1970s sales reached 55,000 units a year. High volume allowed for lower costs. Retail prices fell to about $600 a unit. Raytheon's Amana and Litton, the two American leaders, essentially carved up the small but fast-growing market between themselves. Finally, after nearly twenty years in the wilderness, microwave ovens seemed to be making it big.

In the late 1960s and again in the early 1970s, criticisms arose that almost stopped the market dead in its tracks. Critics argued that microwave ovens might be unsafe. The ovens might leak "radiation" into consumers' homes. The most virulent vote of no confidence came in the April 1973 issue of *Consumer Reports*, which concluded that "we are not convinced that they are completely safe to use. We've therefore designated them all Not Recommended."[84]

But market growth took on a life of its own. The bad press may have slowed, but it did not reverse, the strong upward trend in growth. In 1972 sales of microwave ovens climbed to 314,000 units.

By 1973 there were five major entrants: Amana, Litton, Tappan, GE, and Panasonic (a new entrant).

The two American market leaders adopted a marketing strategy ideally suited to allay fears of a radiation scare. Both Amana and Litton sold quality. They positioned themselves as premium products for which the consumer would pay extra. Neither firm was much interested in competing on price. There was an investment to be paid back. Both firms offered consumers a growing variety of product features. Amana Radaranges, for example, featured "Touchmatic controls," temperature probes, and a high level of customer service. Both Amana and Litton had a few low-end models, but both were mostly interested in the high end of the market, where margins were higher and quality counted for more.

Amana reveled in its role as the pioneer. Its pre-Raytheon founder crowed: "We don't just try to pattern ourselves after anyone else."[85] With such a long history in the market, his company could afford to sound aristocratic.

Then the Japanese entered. By the mid-1970s it was apparent that microwave ovens were a growing market. The Japanese electronics giants entered with two key advantages: (1) a willingness to accept lower profit margins and (2) considerable experience producing ovens for the Japanese market, which gave them a cost structure that was lower than that of the American pioneers. Their entry changed the face of competition.

It is important to note that the Japanese did not simply copy a successful American product and enter with lower prices. They had developed their own microwaves—based on American technology—which they sold in Japan. Microwaves were successful in Japan before they were successful in the United States. The product was more ideally suited to small Japanese homes and a style of cooking that stressed reheating. The Japanese electronics giants "seized the technology, began perfecting it, and soon went beyond their backyard."[86]

Sharp quickly became the leading import soon after it entered. It sold under its own name and as a private label for Sears. Matsushita's Panasonic and Sanyo were the other key Japanese entrants.

The Japanese strategy was essentially the same as it had been in countless other product categories: They sold smaller microwave ovens at lower prices in very large numbers. The Japanese ovens were at least as good as the premium products offered by the American sellers, with one difference—they were priced much lower.

Litton replaced Amana as the market leader during the second half of the 1970s. Amana was a strong number two. But the American pioneers were starting to lose share to the lower-priced later entrants. By the late 1970s Sharp, the other Japanese entrants, and GE were on the way up, while Amana and Litton were on the way down. And real growth in the market had yet to occur.

Once the market started to grow rapidly, GE became interested in obtaining a significant share. GE followed quickly, but only after the market showed it true potential, long after the pioneers opened business. In 1978 GE committed itself to microwaves.

In 1980 the market moved sharply in favor of the Japanese sellers. Price became the most important feature. Before 1980 microwave ovens carried higher profit margins than other kitchen appliances. As the market expanded, however, consumers favored the low-priced, no-frills ovens offered by the Japanese sellers. The Americans found themselves burdened with a premium product that few consumers wanted.

Pushed by relentless price-cutting, Sharp's share of the market rose rapidly in the early 1980s. Both Amana and Litton reacted by introducing low-end models of their own, but they were at a competitive disadvantage against the low-cost Asian producers.

Sales of microwave ovens soared through the first half of the 1980s. By the middle of the decade, imports accounted for more than 40 percent of the market, up sharply from about 25 percent only a few years earlier.

Sales skyrocketed to 10.9 million units a year in 1985. At the same time prices fell to $150 for the smallest units. By the mid-1980s microwave ovens

were sold as low-priced commodities, a strategy that favored low-cost producers and punished the premium products sold by the pioneers. All ovens were deemed to be of acceptable quality, and price became the deciding factor.

The Koreans entered the market in the early 1980s with even lower prices than the Japanese. Just as the Japanese had stolen share from the American sellers with lower prices, so too did the Koreans now steal share from the Japanese. The entry of Korea's Samsung is detailed in a 1989 *Harvard Business Review* article.[87] It is a case history of reverse engineering at its finest. Samsung examined ovens from the world's top producers, selected the best features from each, then applied its talent at low-cost manufacturing to win private label business from price-conscious sellers in the United States.

Samsung started with a small order from J. C. Penney, then produced low-end models for GE. Goldstar, another Korean low-cost producer, produced low-end models for KMart, J. C. Penney, and Magic Chef.

The American producers were doomed. By 1986 Litton, the former market leader, was down to a 10 percent share. The *Wall Street Journal* remarked: "American companies are retreating quickly in the face of tough competition, principally from Japan but increasingly from South Korea. Asian producers are clearly winning the battle."[88] By the mid-1980s, imports held a 75 percent share of the market.

In 1985 GE ceased U.S. production and sold microwaves manufactured by Korea's Samsung. In 1987 sales reached a record 12.6 million units.

By 1990 the war was all but over. Litton was down to a 3.9 percent share while Amana held a measly 4.5 percent of microwave sales. Sharp, in contrast, held 13.5 percent, while GE held 11.2 percent of the market selling Korean-made ovens.

The case of microwave ovens illustrates two common components of copycat strategies. First, the microwave market took decades to develop, at great expense to the pioneers but not to the later entrants. Second, once the market started to grow, Asian producers moved in with lower prices, which consumers, of course, prefer to higher prices. Even though the pioneers enjoyed better than a twenty-five-year head start, they ended up with no real advantage over the Japanese electronics giants or, even more surprising, the Koreans, who started from scratch with no experience and no advantage whatsoever other than low-cost production. Free-rider effects seemed to be far more powerful than first-mover advantages.

I disagree with the conclusion of Ira Magaziner and Mark Patinkin: "If GE or other U.S. appliance companies had acted earlier, not at the height of market demand but ahead of it, they could have built enough scale to afford more product research and factory investment when competition got in-

tense."[89] That is not what happened, nor is that what hurt the Americans. The American pioneers acted first, fast, and with incredible diligence. They pursued the market for decades. They were simply outdone by later entrants who reaped the fruits of American basic research and sold it back to us at lower prices.

15. MONEY-MARKET MUTUAL FUNDS

Investing in short-term, low-risk financial obligations was not a new idea in the late 1960s, when the concept of money-market mutual funds was conceived. For years, corporate financial managers had invested in short-term, high-denomination government securities with staggered maturities in order to obtain the highest yield with the greatest liquidity. At the time, corporations were not allowed to open savings accounts, but financial managers made sure that their firms' money was always working.

In those days investing in the money market was restricted to those with (1) access to financial expertise and (2) large amounts of investment capital. That meant that such investments were effectively limited to large firms. Small and medium-size firms, as well as individual investors, typically did not qualify. They could not afford the high denominations. Nor could they rely on large staffs of in-house financial experts to make the system work to their advantage. Furthermore, the prestigious investment banking firms that serviced blue-chip corporations were not interested in the low end of the business.

That smelled like an opportunity for a mutual fund to Henry B. R. Brown and Bruce R. Bent, two New York investment managers from Teacher's Insurance and Annuity Association (TIAA), the giant professors' pension fund. They started the Reserve Fund of New York—a no-load money-market mutual fund that allowed small investors to invest in short-term government securities, government agency obligations, bank certificates of deposit, banker's acceptances, and othr money market vehicles. Their innovation was to apply the mutual fund concept to money-market investments. In that way, small firms and individual investors could achieve the high-yield, low-risk, highly liquid investments that had previously been available only to large corporations.

The idea itself was conceived in 1968. The Reserve Fund duo then spent three years working out the details. In 1971 they test-marketed the fund on private clients. Their prospectus was cleared by the SEC in September 1972, and in January 1973 Brown and Bent began selling their Reserve Fund of New York to the public. It was the first money-market mutual fund.

The fund specifically focused on the low end of the market, which had been shunned by the investment banks. Customers included investment advisers, bank trust departments, stockbrokers, and lawyers controlling escrow funds. Even individuals were invited to invest. In a sense, the innovative fund served as an alternative to parking cash in an interest-free checking account.

Hopes were high for stunning success. Although it started with a paltry total of $400,000 in assets in early 1973, Brown and Bent confidently projected that their Reserve Fund would be a "$1 billion fund by 1977."[90] They were also confident that they could hold competitors at bay.

Brown and Bent hoped to steal most of their customers from banks, which could not possibly match the low costs of a mutual fund. Banks had structural impediments that thwarted their ability to react. For one thing, banks do not pool customers' money. For another, banks are required to provide more individual attention (whereas mutual funds rely heavily on the telephone). Banks were simply not set up to compete in a cost-effective way with a money-market mutual fund.

As is often the case with successful innovations, the Reserve Fund's timing was perfect. Its entry coincided almost exactly with a rapid rise in interest rates that ocurred in 1973. In the second half of 1973, the fund paid—net of fees and expenses—a whopping 9.25 percent annual rate. At the time passbook savings accounts were constrained by law to a maximum interest rate of 5.25 percent. Investors rushed for a piece of the action.

Competitors also rushed for a piece of the action. It was not the banks who attacked but the giant mutual fund sellers. First, a few smaller mutual funds entered. Then, in January 1974, almost exactly a year after the Reserve Fund had started, the Dreyfus Corporation entered with a similarly structured fund labeled Dreyfus Liquid Assets. It, along with the other late entrants, was so similar to the pioneer's fund that one analyst concluded: "The funds are practically identical."[91] Early money-market funds had similar features:

- Most were open-ended mutual funds that charged "no load" (no entry or redemption fee).
- Many charged a one-half of 1 percent management fee and an expense fee.
- Many funds required a minimum investment, typically $5,000 ($1,000 if the order came from a broker).
- Many funds allowed for subsequent additions and redemptions of at least $1,000.
- Most funds invested exclusively in some combination of certificates of deposit, treasury bills, bank acceptances, government agency securities, and bank letters of credit.

The third major entrant into money-market funds was Fidelity Investments, the Boston-based mutual fund giant, which entered in June 1974, a year and a half after the pioneer, with a fund called Daily Income Trust. Fidelity pioneered the check-writing feature that allowed investors instant access to their money, but in almost every other important respect its fund was a clone of those already on the market. Fidelity's fund quickly became a contender. Its innovative check-writing feature was widely copied by competitors.

By the summer of 1974 the growth of money-market mutual funds was soaring, spurred by massive direct mail campaigns, favorable publicity in the business press, and positive word-of-mouth advertising. There were eight major look-alike funds, which, in total, managed $500 million in assets.[92]

A year and a half after it entered, the pioneering Reserve Fund was still the overwhelming market leader with $220 million in assets under management by June 1974. Dreyfus Liquid Assets was a distant second with $110 million in assets, exactly half of the amount managed by the pioneer.

In 1974 the Reserve Fund paid the highest yield. It did so by investing heavily in bank letters of credit, which had short maturities but were considered by some experts to be less liquid than other types of money-market instruments. The Reserve Fund of New York was the largest and highest-yielding money market mutual fund.

Growth accelerated into 1975. By March 1975 the funds collectively managed $3.2 billion. Almost every fund was growing larger. But a shift in market share was starting to occur. The later entrants were now growing at a much faster rate than the pioneer. Size effects now started to count for more than first-mover advantages.

In September 1974 Dreyfus Liquid Assets surpassed the Reserve Fund as the largest money-market mutual fund. In December Fidelity rushed past the Reserve Fund to capture the number two spot. The pioneer was now in the show position and fading fast relative to its larger competitors.

By April 1975 Brown and Bent's prediction that their fund would reach the $1 billion mark was realized, but with a sardonic twist: It was Dreyfus Liquid Assets, not the Reserve Fund, that neared the $1 billion mark with an astounding $997 million in assets under management. Most impressive, Dreyfus achieved that goal after only fifteen months in the business. The pioneers had correctly predicted the rate of market growth but had erred in predicting who would benefit most. It was the later entrants, not the pioneer, who reaped the largest rewards. The New York Times noted at the time that Dreyfus Liquid Assets was "by far the biggest of the funds."[93] Fidelity was also growing more quickly than the Reserve Fund. It was second largest with $835 million under management.

Within two and one-third years of its pioneering entry, the Reserve Fund was now a distant third, with $513 million in assets, a bit more than half of the amount managed by Dreyfus.

Growth peaked in mid-April 1975. After that time, investors shifted money into a rising stock market. Some experts concluded that money-market mutual funds were a fad, fueled by a freakish combination of high short-term interest rates and a bear market brought on by the first energy crisis. Throughout 1975 many of the money funds lost assets as the stock market moved ahead.

The funds faced another tough year as they entered 1976. Just as rapid growth had been unevenly distributed, so was decline. Between January 1976 and March 1976, the Reserve Fund of New York lost 12 percent of its assets to stand at $325 million. Fidelity was hit less hard, falling 5 percent to $662 million. Dreyfus Liquid Assets, the largest fund, bucked the trend. By advertising aggressively to individual investors it gained 8 percent in assets to $922 million as the others declined. The later entrant was now nearly *triple* the size of the innovator.

Marketing clout seemed more important than ever, as the *New York Times* noted in an article at the time: "The rate of attrition has been particularly hard on funds that do not have the advantage of belonging to big management companies with well-established sales outlets."[94] The later entrants excelled at those skills.

The money-market mutual funds started to grow once again in the third quarter of 1977, as short-term interest rates shot up. When interest rates surpassed 5.25 percent, money once again flowed out of passbook savings accounts into money-market mutual funds. By January 1978 sales were soaring. The forty-four funds then in the market held a total of $4 billion in assets.

But that was only an inkling of the explosive growth that followed. Sales boomed in 1980 as inflation and interest rates soared in response to the second energy crisis. Total assets of the seventy-eight funds now competing in the market rocketed to $53.1 billion in January 1980. After seven years in the minor leagues, money-market mutual funds were now big-league investments. By March 1980, eight years after they started, total assets stood at $60 billion.

Explosive growth attracted a second wave of even larger later entrants, the major stock brokerage houses. The large brokerage houses had been active in the money market for a number of years, but the stunning growth of the late 1970s forced them to embrace the consumer market fully. In February 1975 Merrill Lynch had begun offering its own customers a Ready Assets Trust on a small scale. By March 1978 Ready Assets had accumulated $600 million in

assets. Paine, Webber filed a prospectus to start a money fund in early 1978. Shearson entered in June 1979. By the end of 1979, most of the large brokerage houses offered their own versions of the now old idea of a money-market mutual fund. Their entry truly legitimized the investment vehicle. With the brokerage funds on board, investors poured money into money-market funds.

The brokerage houses also possessed a potent competitive advantage. They sold the funds through their extensive national broker networks—Merrill Lynch alone has 12,000 brokers. That meant that, in addition to prospecting for new customers, which in time could be switched to more profitable investments, the major brokerage firms could serve an installed base of existing customers who were demanding the product.

The rapid success of the largest brokerage firms was nothing less than astounding. By January 1979 Merrill Lynch Ready Assets vaulted to the number one position with more than $2 billion under management. But that was only the beginning. By March 1980 a little more than a year later, Ready Assets controlled nearly $11 billion in assets and was firmly entrenched as the number one money-market mutual fund.

In 1977 Merrill Lynch took the concept a step further when it created its Cash Management Account (CMA), which automatically invested idle funds for investors with at least $20,000. That innovation was widely copied in subsequent years by other brokerage houses and then the mutual fund giants. By 1992 CMA accounted for $255 billion of the $475 billion managed by Merrill Lynch. Cash management accounts are built around money-market funds.

In sum, like many new product ideas, money-market mutual funds started with a simple observation of an unmet need: There was no way for small players to invest in money-market instruments. The pioneer adapted an existing product—mutual funds—to fill that need. Then luck entered in. Rising interest rates attracted large numbers of consumers to the new product. The pioneer was in the right place at the right time with the right product.

But the requirements for staying on top changed as the market grew larger. Reputation and marketing clout replaced innovation as the key ingredients for success. It was the major mutual fund sellers, followed by the major brokerage houses, that excelled on those dimensions. The tiny Reserve Fund was finely managed but could not match those skills. By the time the market matured, the pioneer was only a fraction of the size of the larger later entrants.

Size seemed to count for everything in money-market mutual funds. In fact, there is a near-perfect negative, three-way correlation among order of entry, size, and market success. The results show clearly that (1) the largest

entrants entered last, (2) the largest entrants were the most successful, and (3) the later entrants were the most successful.

Table 3.8 illustrates the ultimate outcome of the competitive battle. As of 1993 the pioneering Reserve Fund managed $1.4 billion. Dreyfus Liquid Assets held $5.5 billion, while Fidelity managed $2.5 billion in its Daily Income Trust. Merrill Lynch ended up as the largest fund with $7.5 billion in its Ready Assets.

But those statistics understate the true magnitude of the later entrants' dominance of the industry. The larger funds also swamped the pioneer with product variety. By 1993 there were 871 money markets being sold to the public. It was the larger later entrants who proliferated their product lines the most. New products included municipal funds, tax-exempts, funds targeted specifically to investors in states with high tax rates, funds that specialized solely in U.S. securities, "worldwide" funds, and literally dozens of other specialized investment vehicles. The tiny pioneer, in contrast, could muster only six funds, and one of them—its original pioneering fund— accounted for nearly 50 percent of the firm's total assets. When comparisons are based on the *aggregate amounts* managed by each seller's *entire portfolio* of funds, the imitators overwhelm the pioneer. Not only do they manage larger funds, they manage more of them.

Throughout the 1970s and 1980s Bruce Bent, founder of the Reserve Fund, was widely sought out by the business press for his opinions on money-market investments. His comments were carried in almost every important article on the topic over a two-decade period. He helped the entire industry grow larger. Like the explorers of old, he had made a great discovery. But economically, many of the benefits went to the settlers who followed his innovative ideas.

TABLE 3.8
THE SIZE OF MONEY-MARKET FUNDS AS OF 1993

Sponsor	Name of First Fund	Assets in First Fund	Total Number of Funds	Total Assets in All Funds
Reserve Fund	Reserve Fund/Primary Port	$1.4 billion	6	$ 2.8 billion
Dreyfus	Liquid Assets	5.5	17	$19.4
Fidelity	Daily Income Trust	2.4	21	$33.6
Merrill Lynch	Ready Assets	7.5	8	$47.7

Source: Data adapted from *Donoghue's Fund Directory*, 1993.

16. MAGNETIC RESONANCE IMAGING (MRI)

In the early 1970s Raymond Damadian, a research professor at the State University of New York's Downstate Medical Center in Brooklyn, was experimenting with a machine that used magnetic fields and radio waves to look inside the human body. He received almost no support for his pioneering research. The government refused to grant him funds, and the top academic journals would not publish his results. Even his employer became dismayed at the path his research was taking. Damadian noted years later: "Fortunately I was tenured, or I would have been out the door."[95] He nicknamed his machine the "Indomitable" to convey its superiority over traditional x-rays and to express the tenacity required to pursue the new technology.

Magnetic resonance was not a new idea. It had been used since the 1950s in chemistry to study molecular structure. Damadian's innovation was to apply that concept to medicine and to build a working diagnostic device. Patents were awarded to Damadian for his innovative creation in the late 1970s. In 1978 he founded the Fonar Corporation to make and market his invention.

In the late 1970s MRIs went from an obscure, backwater device to the darling of the American medical community. Seemingly overnight, nearly every researcher and every medical equipment company wanted a hand in the new technology. They now realized what Damadian knew all along: that MRIs were superior to CAT scanners in at least three key ways.

1. They could more readily see through bones, which meant they provided more detailed pictures of the brain.
2. They allowed doctors to view functioning organs from outside the body.
3. They could spot much smaller cancerous tumors.

Still, there were competing technologies that clouded the picture. In the early 1980s some scientists believed that a competing technology—PET (positron emission tomography)—would emerge as the successor to CAT scanners. At the time, in fact, the market for PET scanners was somewhat more developed than that for MRIs. There were about forty PET scanners in clinical testing, as against only a handful of MRIs. Hitachi, Toshiba, and Philips were among the firms betting on PET in 1981. Other experts, however, believed that MRI would command the bigger market. A GE executive predicted in *Business Week* in 1981 that "the annual market for [MRIs would be] $100 million to $1 billion in 5 to 10 years," or by 1986 or 1987. He continued: "I think [MRI] is going to be as big as CAT."[96]

Damadian claims that later entrants infringed upon his patents. In the late 1970s an article appeared in *Popular Science* describing the potential of magnetic resonance as a diagnostic tool. Damadian says that shortly after that article appeared he was visited by Johnson & Johnson executives who were interested in purchasing the rights to the new technology. According to Damadian, J&J promised to make him an offer he "couldn't refuse," but he was unhappy with the price they ultimately offered.[97] Damadian refused to grant them a license for his technology. J&J owned Technicare Corporation, a leader in the related field of CAT scanners, and was interested in gaining a foothold in the new technology.

How did Johnson & Johnson enter the MRI market without access to Damadian's technology? Damadian claims it ignored his patent. To him, it was another case of a big firm pushing a small entrepreneur to the sidelines. In September 1982 Fonar sued Johnson & Johnson's Technicare subsidiary for patent infringement and unfair competition. J&J responded as follows: "We believe that Damadian's patent is invalid and have so informed him years ago."[98]

In 1982 the market for MRI machines was still more promise than presence. Only a handful of the innovative machines had actually been placed in hospitals. By October 1981 Johnson & Johnson was testing an MRI at the prestigious Massachusetts General Hospital and expected to test another at University Hospitals of Cleveland. GE, the world's leading supplier of diagnostic equipment, had not yet entered the market but was expecting to deliver its first unit to the University of Pennsylvania shortly. By mid-1982 Fonar was testing two MRIs, one in Cleveland, the other in New Mexico.

By 1982 J&J and GE joined Fonar as the top three sellers. As the first half of the 1980s ticked on, Johnson & Johnson emerged as the clear market leader. By 1985 about 250 MRIs had been installed in the United States. Of that number, one hundred were J&J machines, while only twenty-two were made by Fonar. The larger, later entrant had quickly surpassed the small pioneer.

Then the roof caved in on Johnson & Johnson. In November 1985 a federal court jury found that J&J had infringed upon Damadian's MRI patents.[99] Following the verdict, J&J's stock fell, while Fonar's rose sharply.

Fonar's victory was short-lived, however. Two months later, in January 1986, a federal judge reversed the jury's verdict. He commented that the jury would have seen it his way had he instructed it differently. The judge recognized that Damadian's discovery was "perceptive and pioneering" but covered only the imaging of bodily tissue, not the imaging of internal organs.[100] On that fine point of law, Fonar's stock instantaneously plunged nearly 25

percent. Investors instantly grasped the implications of the judge's verdict: The tiny pioneer faced an empowered pack of larger competitors who were now less fearful of legal retaliation. The pioneer's longbow had been broken. The larger later entrants were now free to compete on sheer market power, where they held the overwhelming advantage.

Damadian's only option was to appeal the judge's ruling. He did so, and in June 1987 the courts upheld the previous decision. Fonar lost. The MRI market was now open to all comers.

Back in 1985, meanwhile, a regulatory decision had been made that caused the MRI market to skyrocket. The federal government's Medicare program ruled that it would start reimbursing doctors and hospitals for MRI scans. As a result, the market exploded to $500 million in that year alone.

Earlier still, in 1982, Damadian's Fonar Corporation had decided to differentiate its product from competitors. It announced a radically new 200,000-pound MRI that used less electricity than competing models but, obviously, weighed much more. Fonar claimed a tremendous technological breakthrough and lower operating costs. Competitors focused on the new machine's shortcomings, in particular its obesity and its poor picture quality.

By 1990 GE, which was the leading supplier of traditional x-ray equipment and CAT scanners, was the leading supplier of MRIs. Market power had paid off once again.

But an ominous trend was forming. By 1990 there was a growing sense that health care costs were out of control. MRIs were part of the problem. Although the machines were expensive—between $1 million and $2 million apiece—there were more than 2,000 MRIs in the United States. MRIs were not only more powerful than CAT scanners, they were also much more expensive. To pay for their costly purchases, doctors and hospitals ordered a plethora of MRI scans—a total of 5 million in 1990 alone, at a price between $600 and $1,000 each. Armed with statistics like those, critics argued that MRI scans were being oversubscribed. Legislation was sought to rein in the growth of installed MRI machines and lower the cost of MRI scans.

That trend shifted the market to lower costs at the start of the 1990s. Gone were the days when elaborate engineering marvels could be sold without regard to price. Price was now the key selling point for MRIs. That created an advantage for Japanese sellers, whose costs were estimated to be 20 percent below those of GE, the market leader.[101] Toshiba, for example, sold an MRI for $250,000 less than GE's comparable model.

The Japanese gained advantage from another aspect of the trend toward lower prices. While the American innovations stressed top-of-the-line, state-of-the-art models, which made an engineer stand tall, the Japanese focused

on middle- to low-end models that performed simple tasks—like scanning a knee—reliably and at a lower cost. It was a repeat of the pattern observed in televisions, automobiles, and countless other product categories. The Japanese sellers excelled at the lower end of the market, while the American sellers became "trapped at the top."

The American sellers rushed to lower costs, a trend that continues to this day. GE was learning to lower prices by reverse engineering. The *Wall Street Journal* noted in 1990: "General Electric Co. engineers have been taking apart competitors' medical imaging machines, looking for ways to produce their own systems more economically."[102]

Many of the dominant sellers formed relationships with lower-cost Japanese manufacturers. Philips teamed up with Hitachi. Siemens joined with Asahi. Even GE began to work with Yokogama Medical Systems.

The Japanese sellers were also making moves in the American market. In 1989 Toshiba acquired Diasonics, a small San Francisco-based medical equipment supplier with a respected line of MRIs. Diasonics had introduced its first MRI in 1981, when it bought the rights to the technology from Pfizer. Toshiba's intent was to gain additional share of the MRI market. Toshiba was one of the few firms to increase its share during the late 1980s.

By 1992 MRI was a $2 billion business, most of which went to the larger medical equipment suppliers who had entered after Damadian's Fonar. In September 1992 Damadian made one last-gasp effort to extract profits from his larger competitors. He sued GE and Hitachi for patent infringement. It was a long shot. Not only did the negative outcome of the Johnson & Johnson decision diminish his chances, but GE was in a strong defensive position. Over the years it had accumulated 250 patents of its own on MRI technology, which, it would argue, showed it to be an innovator, not merely an imitator of Damadian's pioneering device.

GE ended up battling it out with the Europeans (Siemens of Germany and Philips of the Netherlands) and the Japanese (Toshiba) for market dominance. Damadian is still in the market but is not a contender for the top spot. He ended up with other rewards. His original MRI machine is now housed in the Smithsonian, where it stands in recognition of his pioneering contribution. But his competitors' products are more likely to be found housed in hospitals and clinics where the profits are made. MRIs followed a time-honored pattern. The *New York Times* commented not too long ago that "while Dr. Damadian has been honored repeatedly for his invention . . . he has not succeeded in efforts to get others in the M.R.I. industry to pay him royalties."[103] Once again, the pioneer served a specific purpose—he blazed a trail for the settlers who followed. The pioneer made history while the settlers made most of the money.

17. NONALCOHOLIC BEER

The evolution of nonalcoholic beers followed a common pattern in imitation strategy. The product was pioneered by small firms that served small market segments. Then events created an opportunity for growth. Larger entrants then moved in to dominate the product category.

In the case of nonalcoholic beer, the pioneers entered the market many years before the product category proved attractive to the major brewers. By the mid-1980s two products, one domestic and one imported, dominated the minuscule market for nonalcoholic brews.

Sales of nonalcoholic beer started to grow rapidly in 1985, when 549,000 barrels a year were sold, up 25 percent from the year before. Still, sales amounted to less than one-half of 1 percent of total beer sales.

G. Heileman's Brewing Company's Kingsbury was one of the first domestically produced pioneers. Kingsbury had been on the market for decades. By 1985 it was far and away the number one brand, with a 34 percent share of a tiny market. Sales of Kingsbury totaled only 185,000 barrels.

Moussy, an import from Switzerland's Cardinal Brewery, was another pioneer. It entered the U.S. market in 1983. By 1985 it was the number two brand with a 16 percent share and sales of 90,000 barrels a year.

Many other firms were also early entrants into the nascent market niche. By 1985 Wartek and Birell, two other Swiss imports; Schmidt's Break Special Lager; and Texas Light, a European formulation brewed domestically under license, had all entered the U.S. market.

In 1986 sales rose again to a respecable but still small 590,000 barrels per year. High growth rates began to attract an increasing number of competitors. Ireland's Guiness, which sold stout, introduced its nonalcoholic Kaliber in New York in 1985. By 1986 Kaliber was sold in thirty states. In March 1986 the Stroh Brewing Company began importing Barbican from Britain's Bass Ale brewery.

In order to maintain its leading position among imports and to expand the market further, Cardinal Brewery increased advertising expenditures for Moussy by 25 percent to $2 million in 1986. That increase allowed it to maintain its strong number two position.

Over the next few years a flood of new entrants introduced nonalcoholic beers into the U.S. market. Heineken introduced Buckler, and Germany exported its top-selling Clausthaler, hoping it would sell well in the American market. By the end of the decade it seemed that the only firms missing from the market were the major American brewers.

By 1989 sales of nonalcoholic beer reached 700,000 barrels. Kingsbury solidified its position as the number one brand by increasing is market share

to 39 percent by 1989. Kingsbury virtually owned the market for nonalcoholic beers through 1989. By the end of the 1980s nonalcoholic beer was a small and still only marginally attractive market to the major brewers, but it was becoming a market they could no longer ignore.

No one was sure how large the market for nonalcoholic beers would grow. There were reasons for both optimistic and pessimistic estimates. On the downside, Anheuser-Busch had test-marketed Chelsea, a nonalcoholic beverage made from lemon, lime, and apple, in 1978 with disastrous results. Chelsea was a "near-beer" that contained 0.4 percent alcohol (whereas nonalcoholic beers contain only 0.1 percent alcohol). Anheuser-Busch had been forced to withdraw the product when conservative protesters complained that a powerful company was trying to entice children into the beer-drinking habit at an early age. As a result of that imbroglio Anheuser-Busch moved away from nonalcoholic beers. Instead, starting in 1984, it spent $25 million introducing its 2.4 percent low-alcohol L.A. Beer, a near-beer with more kick. But L.A. met with only limited success in the marketplace. In its best year, the L.A. "near-beer" sold 400,000 barrels, which was more than the leading nonalcoholic beer had sold but not enough to satisfy Anheuser-Busch, which killed the product in view of poor sales. Given its previous experience with "no" and "low" alcohol beers, Anheuser-Busch may have seen little reason to become excited about what some saw as the growth prospects in the nonalcoholic beer market. Up until that time its experience had shown otherwise.

On the other hand, the major brewers were afraid that nonalcoholic beer might be another light beer in the making. Light beer, which had experienced a similar pattern of false starts, ended up as one the most successful new product categories of all time. With the possibility of a repeat performance in mind, none of the major brewers wanted to be left behind.

There was also the issue of social responsibility. The major brewers were being subjected to a constant barrage of criticism that they were peddling an unhealthy life-style to millions of consumers. A negative reaction to drunk driving accidents threatened the industry further. Nonalcoholic beer represented an opportunity to sell a brewed product without the accompanying intoxicating effects and, at the same time, to squelch critics.

There was also a potential for extraordinary profits. Since nonalcoholic beer contains less than one-half of 1 percent alcohol, it is not subject to the stiff federal excise tax that regular brews are. With nonalcoholic beer selling for the same price as regular brews, the difference drops directly to bottom line.

With those issues in mind, both Anheuser-Busch and Miller jumped into the market in 1989, at least six years after the pioneer. Anheuser-Busch be-

gan test marketing O'Doul's in March 1989. By December, O'Doul's was sold in most major U.S. markets. Miller Brewing entered about the same time with Sharp's, which went national in December 1989 after only a minimal amount of test marketing.

The two major competitors offered very different products. Anheuser-Busch brewed its beer in the regular way, then removed the alcohol. Miller brewed its nonalcoholic beer at low temperatures, which prevented the formation of alcohol in the first place.

Coors was the last major entrant. In April 1991 it agreed to handle all the sales, distribution, and marketing for Switzerland's Moussy, one of the leading brands. Coors also considered brewing a domestic version of the Swiss brew at its Memphis brewery. Then Coors rushed its own Coors Cutter into national distribution in October 1991, after skipping test-marketing for the product. It was eight years behind the pioneers but felt it could catch up quickly, given its other advantages.

The major brewing giants quickly eclipsed the small pioneers. The marketing and distribution advantages held by the largest brewers almost immediately overwhelmed the elusive first-mover advantages of the smaller pioneers. It was really no contest. The battle for nonalcoholic beer was a competitive battle that pitted extreme strength against extreme weakness.

Not only did G. Heileman's Kingsbury, the clear market leader through 1989, face stronger opponents, it faced them as a severely hobbled competitor. By the late 1980s G. Heileman had fallen on hard times. The old-line brewer had declared bankruptcy and could not afford to fight back for the market it had helped pioneer. One executive for the firm noted in a statement clearly meant to put the best face on what was obviously a terrible situation, Heileman had "chosen not to investment spend in the category at this time."[104] Heileman was fighting to survive as a company, not to gain market share in a small-niche market.

The majors moved quickly to the head of the pack. By 1991 Miller was the market leader with 33 percent of the 24-million-case market for nonalcoholic beer. Anheuser-Busch's O'Doul's was a close second with a 28 percent market share, and it led in some sales categories, such as supermarket sales.

Heileman's fortunes went down faster than a six-pack in the Sahara. Kingsbury's market share collapsed from a peak of 39 percent in 1989 to a mere 11 percent in 1991, just two years later. The imports were hurt even worse. Their combined market share shrank from 20 percent in 1989 to only 4 percent in 1991.

In nonalcoholic beer the outcome was quick and decisive. Although the pioneers had patiently cultivated the market while the major brewers sat on the sidelines, their early move into the market provided little protection from

later entrants. The minute the majors entered, they quickly pushed the pioneers aside and moved to the top market share positions.

It is still unclear whether the sales of nonalcoholic beer will ever approach those of light beer, but one thing is certain: If they do, the pioneers will play no more than a minor role. The marketing and distribution advantages held by the later entrants has ensured their success in this product category.

18. OPERATING SYSTEMS FOR PERSONAL COMPUTERS

A microcomputer is nothing more than a worthless maze of metal and wires without an operating system to manage its basic functions. An operating system controls how the keyboard sends information to the processor, organizes the use of memory, and manages the reading and writing of data between disks, the internal memory, and the monitor. Without an inexpensive and easy-to-use operating system, it would have been impossible for personal computers to reach large numbers of ordinary users.

The birth of operating systems for personal computers occurred shortly after 1973, when Intel introduced the 8080, the first integrated circuit suitable for use in microcomputers. Gary Kildall, an engineering consultant for Intel, foresaw the potential of the 8080 processor before the microcomputer revolution occurred. He wrote CP/M, the first crude but practical operating system for microcomputers. CP/M is an acronym for Control Program for Microcomputers.

Kildall's CP/M was, in essence, an adaptation of the operating systems used on Digital Equipment Corporation (DEC) minicomputers. It closely mimicked many of the same commands. Kildall "found much to admire and emulate in Digital Equipment's operating systems," one analyst reported.[105] CP/M was nevertheless an innovation in its own right. It was the first major program to recognize that floppy disk drives were an integral part of personal computers.

Kildall tried to interest Intel in his creation, but it was not interested. So in 1976 he founded Digital Research (not to be confused with Digital Equipment, the minicomputer maker whose operating system was "admired" and "emulated" by Kildall) and sought to sell his operating system directly to personal computer makers for a licensing fee plus a royalty on each machine sold.

Kildall's first important customer for CP/M was a supplier of floppy disk drives for the original Altair computer of the mid-1970s. But CP/M's popularity did not really blossom until the late 1970s, when microcomputers flooded into the market. CP/M was not the most sophisticated operating

system, but it was perfectly matched to meet the crude standards of early 8-bit personal computers based on Intel's 8080 and the nearly identical Zilog's Z-80 microprocessors. As a result, CP/M quickly emerged as the *de facto* standard for 8-bit microcomputers. By 1981 more than two hundred computer makers included a copy of CP/M with their machines. If a consumer bought a microcomputer in the late 1970s, that computer probably came equipped with the CP/M operating system.

For strategic reasons, the leading computer makers would have preferred to maintain proprietary operating systems for their personal computers. That would have kept early buyers loyal to that seller's brand and would have forced smaller sellers to adopt an obscure operating system standard. But consumers and programmers yearned for an industry standard. Consumers wanted to avoid the compatibility problem that prevented different software from being run on many machines. Programmers wanted economies of scale. Rather than write separate software packages for each seller's system, programmers preferred to write a single package that would serve a single, dominant operating system.

CP/M overwhelmingly won the war of standards. When it did, programmers rushed to write even more applications software—word processors, spreadsheets, and the like—for the CP/M operating system. The availability of software reinforced CP/M's stranglehold on the microcomputer industry. By the beginning of the 1980s CP/M seemed invincible.

Other, more sophisticated operating systems never had a chance. One potential competitor was UNIX, which was developed by AT&T's Bell Labs in the late 1960s. Technically, UNIX was vastly superior to CP/M, but it was hobbled by two terrible disadvantages: It required microcomputers that were far more powerful than those that existed at the time, and it was too expensive for most users. As a result, UNIX never emerged as a serious rival to CP/M.

Although CP/M did not have any real competitors, it did have a partner, Microsoft. Microsoft was founded in 1975 by Bill Gates, a Harvard dropout and programming whiz. The small firm's strength was a microcomputer version of the popular programming language "Basic." According to some published reports, during the late 1970s, when programming in Basic was one of the coveted uses of a microcomputer, Microsoft teamed up with Digital Research to provide a package of programs. Digital offered the operating system, while Microsoft sold Basic. The two firms' products complemented each other, and there was even talk of a merger. But the relationship was cut short when Digital Research introduced a Basic program of its own, and Microsoft was cut out of the picture. Microsoft then sought to counter Digital's move by introducing an operating system of its own.

Its first real opportunity came in 1981, when IBM was about to introduce its phenomenally successful personal computer, which relied heavily on outside suppliers, including software providers. IBM sought three outside software houses to supply different application packages: Kildall's CP/M was designated as the best operating system; Microsoft would supply the programming languages Basic, FORTRAN, and COBOL; and Peachtree would provide spreadsheets. That was the initial plan.

Events did not unfold according to plan. When IBM approached Kildall about licensing an updated version of CP/M, it encountered a clash of corporate cultures. Kildall's wife, one of Digital's founders, refused to sign IBM's one-sided nondisclosure agreement. Absent such a signing, IBM would not reveal its intentions regarding its personal computer. Although it is difficult to assess his motivations, Gary Kildall seemed to keep IBM at arm's length, although he has denied doing so. His company seemed to be acting like a typical market leader. IBM would have to do business on Digital Research's terms or not do business at all. Microsoft was about to gain the opportunity of a lifetime.

Microsoft did not own an acceptable operating system that could be used on the new IBM-PC. It had to obtain one quickly if it hoped to leapfrog Digital Research and become IBM's key supplier. An existing 8-bit model would not do. Since IBM had entered the personal computer market after most other competitors, it was able to choose Intel's more advanced 16-bit 8088 integrated circuit instead of the older 8-bit 8080 used in most other personal computers up until that time.

Microsoft decided to buy an existing operating system and update it. A small firm named Seattle Computer Products already made a microcomputer using a similar 16-bit chip. To make that obscure computer work, Tim Patterson, a Seattle Computer programmer, had written 86-QDOS, short for the "Quick and Dirty Operating System." According to many published reports, QDOS was not an altogether original product. In essence, it mimicked many of the features found in Kildall's CP/M but was updated to run on 16-bit machines. One analyst noted: "Every function call of CP/M was faithfully duplicated" by the new DOS operating system.[106] Tim Patterson disputes the charge of product copying, but "at one point, Gary Kildall telephoned Patterson and accused him of 'ripping off' CP/M."[107]

Microsoft paid Seattle Computer Products $25,000 for a QDOS license. A short time later Gates bought outright ownership of the operating system for a less-than-whopping $50,000. At the time, Microsoft did not tell Seattle Computing about its intent to use QDOS for the IBM-PC.

Microsoft refined the Seattle system, renamed it MS-DOS, and presented it to IBM. Since negotiations with Kildall's Digital Research were going no-

where, IBM awarded the business to Bill Gates's Microsoft. MS-DOS was renamed PC-DOS for use on the IBM machine, but Microsoft retained the right to sell its newly acquired operating system to other vendors as MS-DOS. The success of IBM's personal computer pulled Microsoft skyward. By the end of the 1980s more than 100 million copies of the not-so-innovative operating system had been installed.

Both Digital Research (the purveyor of CP/M) and Seattle Computing (the creator of QDOS) screamed foul. Kildall claimed that Microsoft was selling a product that had been copied from his CP/M, that Seattle Computer Products had pirated his product. Seattle Computer Products complained that it too had been cheated—by Microsoft, which had paid far too little for its disputed product.

Seattle Computer Products sued Microsoft and reportedly came out with a settlement of about $1 million. Kildall's Digital Research threatened to sue IBM for selling a pirated copy of its product. IBM settled the matter by agreeing to supply both DOS and CP/M with its personal computer. That pacified Digital Research, which then set out to update its own CP/M operating system so that it would run on the more advanced IBM-PC. The updated CP/M was to be technically superior to PC-DOS. By that time, however, the original was playing catch-up. Unfortunately, Digital Research ran into developmental problems that slowed its entry. In the autumn of 1981, when IBM shipped its first personal computer, CP/M-86 was still not ready. PC-DOS was, and that is all that mattered. By the time the updated CP/M-86 was finally finished in the spring of 1982, so were its prospects for market success. With tens of thousands of copies of PC-DOS in circulation, there was little incentive to switch to the new—or was it back to the old?—standard. By 1984 it was all over. At that time, there were 1.2 million copies of DOS in circulation, as against only 200,000 copies of CP/M, and many of those were not being actively used. Within only a few years, Digital Research had switched positions with Microsoft. Microsoft was now the dominant force in microcomputer software.

The next significant innovation in operating systems was the graphical user interface, which made personal computers easier to use. It, too, involved a fair degree of imitation. The graphical user interface replaced the typing of arcane commands, which must be remembered and typed without errors, with selection by means of a mouse. It allowed users to interact with their personal computers by "clicking" a mouse on "icons" or symbols to execute commands.

The pioneering work on the graphical user interface started back in the 1960s with the work of Ivan Sutherland, whose innovative program Sketchpad pioneered the manipulation of objects on a computer screen, and Doug

Englebart, who pioneered the use of a mouse. Englebart assumed that once computer experts saw the benefits of the mouse over typing they would quickly make the switch. But it took decades for that substitution to take place, and the pioneer was never fully compensated for the contribution he made to the industry's development. In retrospect, Englebart concludes: "We just thought that within a year or two there will be all sorts of people joining this pursuit, and that it would become an acceptable activity, but it didn't seem to connect."[108]

The graphical user interface was perfected in the 1970s at Xerox PARC, the Palo Alto Research Center. Xerox's pioneering computers incorporated many of the software features found in today's graphical user interfaces. The Xerox Star, for example, which was introduced in 1981, featured a mouse and had users point at and select on-screen icons. But the system was too far ahead of its time to be commercially successful. It did, however, attract the attention of two very interested observers, Bill Gates of Microsoft and Steve Jobs of Apple Computer. Gates was one of the first paying customers for a Xerox Star computer, which was promptly brought back to Microsoft and studied in detail. Steve Jobs was equally impressed with Xerox. He visited PARC in the late 1970s and quickly decided that its pioneering work should be the model for the ill-fated Lisa and the tremendously successful Macintosh computers that Apple later introduced.

The extent to which Xerox PARC influenced the industry's evolution is legendary. According to one analysis, "Gates and Jobs . . . appropriated everything they could from PARC." One profile wrote metaphorically of Gates's actions—"he and Jobs lived next to a rich neighbor named Xerox and when he broke in to steal the television set, he discovered that Jobs had already taken it."[109]

Apple also accused Microsoft of copying its operating system. Apple's account goes as follows: In the early 1980s Apple wanted Microsoft to write application software—word processors, for example—for its Macintosh computer, which was still under development. In early 1982 Apple gave Microsoft a prototype of the Macintosh. Jobs was worried that Gates would turn around and introduce the same applications software for the IBM-PC, so he insisted that Gates sign a promise not to release competing applications software for the PC. Gates did so. What Jobs did not anticipate was that Gates would introduce a graphical user interface—similar to the Macintosh operating system—for the IBM-PC. Jobs assumed that Gates would not do anything to undercut the popularity of MS-DOS. But Jobs was mistaken. Microsoft set out to introduce Windows.

Microsoft Windows was a later entrant into graphical interfaces. Many other entrants preceded Windows. In 1982 VisiCorp, the seller of the Visi-

Calc spreadsheet, announced it would soon introduce VisiOn, a graphical user interface for Apple's doomed Lisa computer. Likewise, Gary Kildall's Digital Research was working on GEM—Graphics Environment Manager—which threatened to beat Microsoft to market. Even IBM, which was growing wary of Microsoft's increasing power in software, soon introduced its own version of a graphical user interface, Topview.

Microsoft tried to speed up its introduction of the Windows software, but product development was taking longer than expected. In 1983 Gates announced that Windows would "soon" be available. Soon turned out to be more than two years later. In 1985 when most competitors had already entered the market, Microsoft belatedly introduced its Windows software. It featured a mouse, icons, and a totally graphical environment. Even though it entered later, Windows was a stunning success. Patience, sheer market power, and fortunate market timing seemed to pay off in market success.

The competitive victory in graphical user interfaces was clear and decisive. Microsoft Windows quickly became the leading entry, even though it was introduced after other entries and was, at least partially, "derivative" in design. The reasons for Microsoft's victory had little to do with first-mover advantages. The pioneers were the first to fail. Microsoft muscled its way past earlier entrants by signing up the most IBM-compatible computer makers. In addition, Microsoft coupled Windows to its MS-DOS operating system and sold the package at a very low price. That reinforced its incumbent position intead of making its dominant DOS system obsolete.

In sum, the history of operating systems is replete with success through imitation and later entry. It is a case where pioneers laid the groundwork for those who followed. In many instances, the later entrants refined, then popularized, innovative developments made elsewhere, enriching themselves in the process. In the fast-moving world of personal computer operating systems, it was the pioneers who were quickly dispatched to oblivion, allowing later entrants to take over the lead forever.

19. PAPERBACK BOOKS

There is *exactly* a hundred-year lag between the appearance of the first inexpensive softcovers in the United States in 1839 and the time the first successful paperback books were introduced in 1939. Over that period, the idea of a paperback book as we now know it evolved slowly as interest in it waxed and waned and competitors fought fiercely to promote and kill the product category.

The predecessors of paperback books started in 1839 when some pub-

lishers sold serialized English novels in a newspaper format for 25 cents. Those cheap, crude, and unbound softcovers, called "extras," were printed like newspapers and sent to customers via direct mail. The problem was that they were pirated copies of popular English novels. Publishers simply obtained books in England and copied them in the United States without compensating English authors or publishers. At the time there was no international copyright law to stop the pirates from copying.

Sales of "extras" were also aided by artificially low postal rates, which allowed publishers to earn a profit on the low-priced novels by keeping costs low. In 1845 the Post Office dealt a severe blow to the emerging product category when it forced "extras" to be mailed at the regular book rate rather than the less expensive newspaper rate. Traditional hardcover publishers may have had a hand in forcing that change.

The second coming of paperback books occurred in the 1860s, during the Civil War. It was the era of the "dime novel," when low-priced books were sold by the millions as low-level reading for the masses. Some dime novels were paperback originals, that is, they never appeared in hardcover. Others were licensed reprints. But the pirates soon entered. Once again, their strategy was to steal the work of English authors in the absence of an international copyright law. The publishing industry was outraged. One researcher who has studied the early years of paperback books in detail notes: "The pirate . . . waits for the appearance of a popular book, and the moment he sees it is likely to be profitable to the regular publisher, he takes it away from him and pockets whatever it brings."[110] The pirates, on the contrary, saw themselves as monopoly fighters who put book ownership within the reach of millions who could not afford hardcovers. Then, as now, paperbacks were targeted at the mass market.

In the end, the pirates provided an important public good, but not the one they had in mind. Largely as a result of their destructive actions, an international copyright law was signed in 1891 after nearly fifty years of bickering among publishers. Before that time American publishers saw few benefits to be gained by protecting their English counterparts. Now, however, all agreed that a strong law was needed. The law effectively shut down inexpensive paperbacks for the second time in fifty years.

Paperbacks lay dormant for decades. It was not until the mid-1930s that they returned for a third and triumphant rising. At that time, however, England was the progenitor rather than the victim of paperback books.

It started in the mid-1930s, when Allen Lane was unable to persuade the English publisher he worked for to reprint hardcover titles in paperback. Lane left his employer and went out on his own. His objective was the same as those who had preceded him for nearly a hundred years: to sell inexpen-

sive books to the masses. He understood that widespread distribution was the key to profitable paperbacks. Since the product was priced low and carried slim profit margins, it had to be sold through high-volume retailers in order to succeed. Bookstores alone simply did not generate the volume required to make paperbacks viable.

Lane was not the first to conceive of the idea of the modern paperback. Throughout the 1930s, crude softcovers were common in Germany. Lane refined and improved upon that idea for the English market.

As a small player in a giant industry, Lane had trouble obtaining reprint rights from the major English publishers. Then he got lucky. After a publisher agreed to supply him with titles, he released his first ten mass market paperback reprints in July 1935. Then he got lucky again. Woolworth's—exactly the sort of mass-market retailer he needed—agreed to carry his books. They were, as one analyst noted, an "immediate success."[111] The product prospered with mass distribution. Buoyed by his prospects of success, Lane formed Penguin Books in 1936.

In 1937 Lane turned his eye toward the American market. After numerous false starts, he hired Ian Ballantine, an American who had just completed his master's thesis at the London School of Economics on the feasibility of the paperback book business. Ballantine was sent to the United States with the task of importing British paperbacks. Penguin Books of America was formed in 1939 and carried the distinctive "penguin" brand mark—which, in the years that followed, spawned a veritable barnyard of copycat brand marks.

Penguin was not the first American seller. In 1937 Modern Age Books, an American firm, had pioneered the first truly modern paperback. But, unlike Lane in England, the small firm had problems obtaining mass distribution. As a result, the venture failed and was liquidated in 1942. Modern Age Books served as a test market for later entrants and was never a potent paperback competitor.

Penguin was not even the first *successful* seller of paperbacks in the United States. That honor went to Pocket Books, an entrepreneurial startup. In June 1939, only a few weeks before Penguin's Ian Ballantine arrived in America, Pocket Books introduced reprints of ten popular hardcover titles in paperback form. Unlike Modern Age Books, Pocket Books was able to induce a national magazine distributor to carry the product. As a result, Pocket Books is universally considered the first successful pioneer of paperback books in the United States.

Pocket Books was the brainchild of Robert de Graff, who during the 1920s and 1930s had worked for publishers that sold inexpensive hardcover reprints to the masses.[112] In the late 1930s he sought to expand that idea and to sell inexpensive softcovers to the mass market. Simon & Schuster, the

publishing powerhouse, had similar intentions, so in 1938 it teamed up with de Graff to form Pocket Books.

De Graff studied previous entrants carefully. Specifically, he studied Penguin and Modern Age Books. Penguin's success in England served as a model for Pocket Books. In one historian's formulation, Penguin "showed the way to Robert de Graff and his associate founders of Pocket Books . . . he was able to follow and even improve upon the procedures mapped by Lane."[113] De Graff also learned from the failure of Modern Age Books. Another industry expert concluded that Modern Age Books "incorporated almost all of the business practices that later ensured Pocket Book's success."[114] Even Simon & Schuster learned from Penguin's experience in England. Richard Simon, one of the principals, saw firsthand how well Penguin's paperbacks were selling in Woolworth's while touring London with Allan Lane.[115] Even Penguin's "penguin" brand mark served as a model for Pocket Books' "Gertrude the kangaroo."

The success of Pocket Books and Penguin attracted a first wave of copycat entrants. Avon was the first to respond. In December 1941—a month that lives in infamy—it introduced its line of Pocket Size Books. Avon's paperbacks were clones of Pocket Books. They followed most of the standards set by Pocket Books but copied a little too closely. Avon even went as far as to dye the edges of its pages red and to use the word "pocket" on its covers, just as the innovator did. Pocket Books was not flattered by the sincerity of Avon's imitation. It sued, claiming that Avon Pocket Size Books were so similar to Pocket Books that consumers would be deceived into thinking they were buying Pocket Books when they were actually buying an Avon book. After a volley or two, Avon dropped some of the more egregious and inflammatory copycat tactics, such as using the word "pocket" on the cover, and successfully defended the suit. That opened up the floodgates for even more copycats.

Avon's problems suggest that copying too closely can invite legal action. It is almost always better to improve upon the pioneer's product or to find some unique characteristic that can be incorporated in order to avoid such problems.

In late 1942 Popular Library was the second major later entrant. It, too, was deemed a copycat by some critics. An industry expert observed that "the format used by Popular Library emulated that of the pioneering paperback publisher, Pocket Books; the Popular books were similar in appearance and had similar tinted endpapers."[116]

The entry of both Avon and Popular Library was encouraged by the same major distributor that had first worked for Pocket Books. When Pocket Books switched to other distributors, the orphan distributor was afraid of

being left out of a growing product category and sought to create competitors for Pocket Books.

Dell was the third later entrant. For decades Dell had published detective magazines, cheap mystery novels, and comics. Sales of its mysteries started to decline when Pocket Books entered. Dell readers had switched to the higher-quality Pocket Book mysteries and abandoned the existing Dell product. In reaction, Dell introduced its own line of paperback mysteries in 1943. By 1945 Dell had fought its way to number two behind (far behind) Pocket Books, largely on the strength of its mysteries.

There was thus a three-stage entry sequence in paperback books. First, the pioneers—Pocket Books and Penguin—entered in 1939. They were quickly followed by Avon in 1941, Popular Library in 1942, and Dell in 1943, which together constituted the second stage, the quick followers. Bantam Books was the last major entrant. Its entry, along with a handful of others, made up the third and final stage of market entry.

Bantam Books was born in August 1945 as the result of three forces that converged to form a paperback powerhouse.

1. The first force came in the form of Ian Ballantine, the graduate student who had been hired to run Penguin of America. He quit Penguin to start Bantam. He brought with him a respected reputation and an intimate knowledge of the industry.
2. The most important force affecting Bantam's success came in the form of rich corporate parents. Bantam was an entrepreneurial startup, but it was backed by a consortium of powerful and prestigious publishers. In other words, Bantam was "born with the silver-spoon luxury of its corporate parents."[117] Actually, Bantam was started and owned by Grosset & Dunlap, but G&D itself had five parents: Random House; Charles Scribner's; Harper; Little, Brown; and Book-of-the-Month Club. Those parents gave Bantam a potent competitive advantage. While less fortunate publishers had to fight for reprint rights, Bantam could count on easy access to big-name authors and big-name books.
3. The third force that aided Bantam's later, but very successful, entry was distribution. Bantam Books was distributed by Curtis Circulation, the distributor of the *Saturday Evening Post* and the *Ladies Home Journal*.

Following in the pioneers' footsteps, Bantam adopted a "red rooster" as its brand mark.

Bantam's rise to market prominence was unimpeded by its later entry. By 1950 Bantam Books had worked its way to a strong number two in the industry. Ian Ballantine, who at various stages of his career started Penguin

of America, Bantam, and Ballantine Books, recalled: "We came up to speed and on a par with Pocket Books in a short time."[118]

Pocket Books remained the market leader for decades. In fact, one of the definitive authors on the subject observed, by 1963 "it was numerically at least the largest publisher of books in publishing history."[119]

It was not until the 1970s that Bantam surpassed Pocket Books. Since that time, the number one spot has rotated among a handful of industry giants. Market shares are unstable, because paperback book publishing is a business that relies heavily on a steady stream of new products that quickly become obsolete. Like the movie and record industries, market share shifts occur regularly as signed authors fall in and out of favor with the reading public or change publishers.

The publishing industry went through a binge of mergers and acquisitions during the 1970s and 1980s. Bantam had four owners between the late 1960s and the late 1970s alone. Today it is owned by Germany's Bertlesmann Publishing Group. Pocket Books is once again owned by Simon & Schuster, which in turn is owned by Paramount Communications, which now owns Macmillan, which owns The Free Press. Ownership relationships in the publishing industry sometimes read like a historical romance novel gone awry.

Clearly, Pocket Books has not failed as a pioneer. It remains among the largest firms. But just as clearly Bantam, the last major entrant, has become a paperback powerhouse. In recent years Bantam has generally outperformed Pocket Books. *Consumer Reports*, for example, judges Bantam to be "the leading paperback publisher."[120] The same goes for the author of the definitive history of the publishing industry. He notes that "Bantam was still leading the paperback field in 1980."[121]

And what of Penguin? Disputes among top managers placed this innovative firm in the unenviable position of serving as an incubator for management talent for the entire industry. Ian Ballantine, Penguin's original U.S. employee, left to start Bantam. Two other Penguin executives left shortly afterward to found New American Library (NAL) in 1948, which was bought by Penguin years later.

Overall, the success of Bantam Books illustrates an important principle: Firms that enter later often enter with a competitive advantage that negates the pioneer's early move into the market. Such advantages are not rare. In the case of Bantam it was the combination of blue-blooded corporate parents, first-rate distribution, and superb management talent that propelled it past the innovator (who was really an imitator). The fact that market power can be used to offset first-mover advantages is the true lesson to be read from paperback books.

20. PERSONAL COMPUTERS

Personal computers present a paradox of pioneering. The product is often portrayed as a testament to the power of innovation, but a succession of imitators and later entrants ultimately wound up dominating the industry. Equally contradictory is the widely held view that the world's first successful personal computer was created in a flash of inspirational genius by two kids working out of a garage in California. Closer examination reveals that the first personal computer was preceded by a long history of small incremental improvements in related technologies, making it almost impossible to pinpoint who was really first. Finally, it is widely reported that the personal computer was a radically new product that created a brand-new industry. The product, however, was not all that new. The succession of competitors in personal computers was a virtual replay of what happened in mainframes and minicomputers. Personal computers is a classic case of the past repeating itself.

The development of the personal computer marks the culmination of a trend toward miniaturization. That trend started when minicomputers stole share from mainframes in the 1960s. Minis were pioneered by the Digital Equipment Corporation (DEC), a small entrepreneurial startup. In 1959, DEC introduced the PDP-1, the first commercial minicomputer, which sold for $120,000. It followed in 1963 with the PDP-8, a superior mini with an even lower price tag. How did the principal mainframe manufacturers react to the new product introduction? They ignored it. One author notes: "Although the established computer makers—IBM, Sperry Rand, Burroughs, and so on—possessed the skill and capital to get into minicomputers, they suffered from a tunnel vision that prevented them both from recognizing the existence of major new markets for their products, and, once having seen the market, moving quickly into it."[122] IBM, for example, did not introduce its first minicomputer until 1976.

Ironically, when it came time to move farther along that same trendline—from minis to microcomputers—DEC repeated the pattern set by IBM in minis. In the early 1970s David Ahl, a Digital employee, tried to convince the company that micros were worth pursuing. He developed a crude prototype of a portable personal computer that was far ahead of its time. According to published reports, in 1974 he asked DEC's top management to fund the project and commit to personal computers on a small scale. It said no. It thought the economics simply did not make sense: Why would an individual pay thousands of dollars for an underpowered, free-standing micro when they could buy a cheap, dumb terminal and connect it to a time-sharing service? That argument seemed logical at the time. DEC decided to forgo

early entry into personal computers and to concentrate on current products. When personal computers finally did arrive, smaller companies did to DEC what DEC had done to IBM fifteen years earlier.

Just as computers were becoming smaller, the way in which business offices created paperwork was also changing. First, mechanical typewriters gave way to electric typewriters. They were then replaced by dedicated word processors. The hard-wired word processors were in turn followed by software-driven word-processing packages run on personal computers. Once again, the incumbents moved slowly. Dedicated word processors were not pioneered by the typewriter manufacturers. Outsiders took the lead. Wang Laboratories and even Exxon, the oil giant, played a pivotal role in the diffusion of the dead-end technology. In the late 1970s the oil giant invested heavily in a number of high-technology firms that it thought held great promise for the future. One of those ventures was Vydec, a dedicated word processor with cumbersome 8-inch floppy disk drives. IBM entered later with its DisplayWriter system. Typewriters lost share as business offices learned the benefits of electronic word processing. Unfortunately, the machines that pioneered that use were ultimately replaced by personal computers, which were cheaper to buy and more flexible. By the mid-1980s word-processing had become commonplace, but the pioneers were stuck with an obsolete technology.

Personal computers had to be made easier to use before they could create a boom market. Software innovations had to complement hardware innovations. Until that happened, personal computers would never have served more than a small niche market of programmers and scientists with programming skills. In the mid-1960s Xerox conducted much of the pioneering work on making personal computers easy to use. At the time Xerox was interested in computers because it was widely believed that business would soon operate in a "paperless society." Xerox was also concerned about the impending expiration of its copier patents. The combined effect of those events would clearly hurt Xerox copiers. So Xerox funded PARC, the Palo Alto Research Center. It hired the best and brightest computer experts, who set out to make computers easier to use. PARC produced many pioneering innovations that are now part of personal computers. But PARC was too far ahead of its time. Its Alto office system, priced at $45,000 apiece, was too expensive to commercialize. A later entry, the Xerox Star, a $250,000 network of personal computers, bombed badly and scared the pioneer away from the personal computer market forever. Xerox killed the PARC project and decided to focus its efforts on electric typewriters.

Xerox had entered too early. The technology was not yet available to make inexpensive, powerful personal computers. Not until years later did the price

of integrated circuits drop and performance improve to the point where personal computers made economic sense. That, more than any other single factor, created the boom market for personal computers.

A final paradox lies in the fact that technology was responsible for the success of personal computers. Large market leaders, with their incomparable research and development budgets, should have held the overwhelming advantage over small entrepreneurial upstarts and pioneered the market. But that is not what happened. For the most part, the industry giants ignored the opportunity and forced hobbyists to create a product that ranks among the most influential innovations of the twentieth century.

The world's first personal computer—to use the term loosely—was the Altair 8800. It was an incredibly crude device that had to be built from a kit. It is debatable whether the Altair 8800 even qualifies as a personal computer. It certainly was not very useful. It had no keyboard, no disk drives, no monitor, and a mighty small memory. It was simply a box with rows of lights and toggle switches. To program it, users had to align the toggle switches to mimic machine language, an onerous if not impossible task. The Altair 8800 was purely for hobbyists. Unable to perform even the most rudimentary tasks, it was really more of a gadget than a useful business tool.

In the mid-1970s the market for personal computers consisted almost solely of hobbyists. In January 1975 the influential *Popular Electronics* featured the $395 Altair kit on its cover, with the tag line "Product Breakthrough! World's First Minicomputer Kit to Rival Commercial Models." As a result of that favorable publicity, hobbyists snapped up 1,500 Altairs in their first year on the market.

The Altair 8800 was introduced by Micro-Instrumentation Telemetry Systems, an unlikely pioneer, even by the arcane standards of the computer industry. MITS was a small firm from Albuquerque, New Mexico, with a reputation more as a mail order house than as a high-technology startup. For MITS, the personal computer was merely the latest in a string of oddball put-it-together-yourself kits. The firm had previously hawked build-it-yourself calculator kits and model rocket sets. Its success was short-lived, however. It was sold in 1977, only three years after its pioneering efforts. In 1979 it was bankrupt.

The first two truly successful personal computers were introduced by Radio Shack and Apple. Tandy's Radio Shack introduced its TRS-80 personal computer in 1977. It was not a technological wonder; in fact, the TRS-80 brand was disparagingly labeled the "Trash 80." Nonetheless, this solid entry sold 100,000 units in 1978, giving Radio Shack a 50 percent share of the newly born market. Radio Shack had a competitive advantage that could not be matched by other entrants: It had more than seven thousand free-standing

retail stores, making it the largest captive computer retailer in the United States. Radio Shack stores sold only Radio Shack computers. By 1979, Tandy reaped $150 million in revenues from personal computers and was the undisputed market leader. Its key competence seemed to be availability. Like a retailer with flashlights after a severe storm, Radio Shack had inventory and distribution before others even had a product.

In the mid-1970s, before Radio Shack's entry, groups of computer enthusiasts formed around the United States. At club meetings, hobbyists sold parts to one another and showed off their own computer creations. Apple Computer emerged from those humble beginnings. Steve Wozniak and Steve Jobs jury-rigged a crude "Apple I" personal computer from available parts. Their motivation had little to do with creating the world's fastest-growing company, as "the Woz" admitted years later: "I was not designing a computer with any idea we would ever start a company, ever have a product, or ever be successful. It was just to go down to the club, show off, and use it."[123]

Luck and good timing played a crucial role in Apple's success. As two kids on their own, Jobs and Wozniak never would have made it as big as they did. They simply did not have the requisite business acumen. But Mike Markkula, a former Intel executive with extensive industry experience earned as a computer pioneer, took an interest in their creative innovation. He rounded up the investment capital needed to create the Apple Corporation, and in 1977—the same year Radio Shack introduced its personal computer—helped the inventors introduce the Apple II personal computer. For $1,195 the buyer received no monitor and a measly 16K of memory.

Apple's timing was perfect. It introduced the right product at precisely the right time. Consumers clamored to purchase an Apple II computer. In 1977, its first year in operation, the fledgling firm had less than a million dollars in sales. By 1981, only five years later, sales zoomed to nearly $350 million. By the late 1970s, Apple surpassed Radio Shack as the market leader.

IBM, meanwhile, continued to sit on the sidelines waiting for the fad to die out. IBM was cognizant of small computer technology. It had experimented with small "personal" computers for at least a decade. In the late 1960s it produced an experimental model known as the Scamp, which was never commercialized. In 1975, about the time of the Altair 8800, it introduced the IBM 5100, an $8,000 personal computer with a minuscule display screen. But, like the Xerox entry, the product was too early to appeal to business customers and was out of step with the demands and image of oddball hobbyists of the day. It failed to attract many paying customers, a result that may have given IBM the impression that there was no market for small, underpowered personal computers.

Given the history of failures, IBM took its time deciding whether to reenter

the on-again-off-again market for small computers. But by the early 1980s, with demand booming and the number of competitors increasing rapidly, it was a trend that could no longer be ignored. IBM decided to enter. Once that decision was made, IBM moved quickly. It took only one year to get its product to market. In August 1981 IBM announced the IBM-PC to the world at the Warldorf-Astoria Hotel in New York. In October 1981 it shipped the first machine to eagerly waiting customers.

The IBM-PC was designed to legitimize the market for personal computers, not to pioneer new territory. One expert rightly judged it *"not a technical breakthrough."*[124] In fact, its almost prominent feature was that it offered almost nothing innovative. It used off-the-shelf components supplied by third-party vendors. It sought to coalesce the standard for personal computers.

Following a time-honored strategy, to use the words of one observer, "as had become traditional with the company, IBM left the pioneering to others and would jump in with a significant effort to grab a large share of the business only after the concept proved both valid and profitable."[125]

Demand for personal computers, which had been growing rapidly, exploded with IBM's entry. The primary beneficiary of that growth was the very latest entrant. In 1981 IBM sold only 35,000 personal computers. By 1983, however, a mere two years later, it sold 800,000.

Watchful waiting apparently did not hurt IBM's chances of success. In fact, it enhanced its reputation. By the time IBM finally decided to enter, the market had changed from primary hobbyists, who were unimpressed with IBM's button-down style, to business customers, who were too cautious to buy from the oddball sellers who dominated the market in its infancy. Much has been made of the "little tramp" advertising campaign employed by IBM to sell its personal computers. In my opinion, its impact was complementary, at best. It was IBM's reputation with business customers and its distribution that ensured its success. The prestige of those three big blue letters reduced the risk of purchase for wary business buyers who did not know the difference between a bit and a byte.

By 1982, 150 companies sold personal computers in the U.S. market. IBM, Apple, and Tandy were the top three sellers, in that order. It was clear at the time that most sellers would not survive. A shakeout was coming, and, as *Business Week* noted, "In the end, the small-computer market will be dominated by big companies."[126] Economies of scale, access to distribution, expertise in selling to large business customers, and the money to make it all happen were fast becoming more important than technological innovation in deciding who would survive and who would be forced out of the business. Fear of the future played straight into IBM's strength. Everyone knew that when the shakeout was over, IBM would still be around to support its prod-

uct. Staying power prevailed decisively over pioneering in deciding who would win the war in personal computers.

IBM's victory in personal computers was swift and indisputable. Only two years after it had entered, *Business Week* concluded: "The battle for market supremacy suddenly is all over, and IBM is the winner."[127] Repeating the pattern of mainframes, the magazine surmised that "marketing and distribution skills are becoming more important than the latest technology." By 1984 IBM had sold more than one out of every four personal computers sold in the United States.

IBM's success carried the seeds of its own destruction. Once IBM set the standard for personal computers, the clones copied its product and sold at lower prices. IBM inadvertently aided the copycats when it decided to rely on outsider suppliers. That decision may have sped its entry into personal computers, but it allowed the copycats to put together machines made of the exact same parts and to sell them at much lower prices.

IBM was cognizant of the threat posed by copycats but mistakenly believed it had two layers of protection. The first was based on experience curve analysis. IBM assumed that, as the market leader, its volume of production was so large that the cloners could not hope to match its low costs. That was the theory. In practice, events turned out differently. One analysis concludes:

> That turned out to be precisely wrong. What happened instead was that IBM put its suppliers into the high-volume business and so bore their start-up and learning curve costs. The clone-makers then rolled in behind IBM and bought suppliers' excess capacity, so their costs were usually *lower*.[128]

In addition, suppliers from Asia mass-produced interchangeable parts, made with less expensive materials, and sold them at much lower prices to the clones. In the end, the cloners held the price advantage.

IBM's second layer of defense was its patented ROM-BIOS, which sent instructions between the computer and applications software. IBM's BIOS was hard-wired into its personal computers and could not be copied directly. Or so it seemed. Software engineers at Compaq, a small startup, quickly reverse-engineered IBM's BIOS with software, placed it on a disk, and created a compatible clone of IBM's personal computer that was portable as well as less expensive. The cloner was so successful that Compaq became one of the fastest-growing companies in American history.

Copycats came from everywhere. Small shoestring operations in the United States were able to exist on incredibly slim margins. Michael Dell started selling IBM clones out of his dorm room in 1984. His move into mail

order kept selling costs low. Whereas a few years earlier business customers were unwilling to risk a mail order purchase, the market had changed. IBM had, in effect, created a generic personal computer, which buyers soon felt secure enough to buy through the mail.

Asian copycats, such as Korea's Leading Edge, assembled by Daewoo, relied on components that were reverse-engineered and produced more cheaply. It was able to sell a personal computer for $1,500 that was similar to one sold by IBM for $2,100.

IBM faced a number of poor strategic choices. It could match the lower prices charged by the copycats, but that strategy would wreak havoc with profit margins. IBM could cede the low end of the personal computer market to the clones, but at the risk of future attacks on higher-end products. IBM could rely on innovation, which it did. It introduced new models, such as the XT and the AT, but the cloners always followed quickly with much lower prices. Finally, IBM could introduce a new proprietary standard, which could not be copied. But that move would alienate current users and would render their favorite software obsolete. With that strategy, IBM faced the risk that loyal users would not follow its move to the new incompatible standard.

According to *Business Week*, the clones as a group surpassed IBM for good in 1986.[129] Since that time, they have increased their share of the personal computer market. Early cloners, such as Dell, have lost share to even later mail order entrants, such as Gateway, which was founded in 1985. Gateway's strategy?—"to continue undercutting the competition [with price] and low costs."[130]

In sum, the case of personal computers is a story of incumbent inertia and the success of imitative later entrants. Although the market was pioneered by entrepreneurial startups, which were allowed to prosper because the industry leaders did not recognize the magnitude of the opportunity, once the market became larger and more attractive, those startups were pushed out of way by IBM, which earned the greatest rewards. Then, as the market matured, price became the most important ingredient in the competitive battle. When that happened, cloners reaped the rewards of a market they neither pioneered nor entered early. Imitation and later entry proved prosperous strategies for the sellers of personal computers.

21. POCKET CALCULATORS

Pocket calculators did not burst upon the scene without precedent. They were the latest step in a long evolution of calculating machines. Devices to mechanize arithmetical calculation had been around at least as long as the

abacus, which was developed by the Babylonians nearly five thousand years ago. The slide rule, which was capable of more advanced calculations, was invented around 1630. A series of mechanical adding machines, most notably those of Pascal and Liebniz, were invented during the second half of the seventeenth century. The first commercial calculator, the "arithmometer," was introduced by Charles Xavier Thomas in Colmar, France, in 1820. Borrowing heavily from his ideas, an American named Frank Baldwin developed a hand-cranked adding machine in 1875 that eventually evolved into the electromechanical Monroe calculator, a popular brand name of the 1960s. By 1900 mechanical adding machines were commonplace fixtures of modern business offices.

In the 1960s calculators changed with the advent of semiconductors. Up to then calculators were basically mechanical devices powered by electricity. They were replaced by the electronic calculators that are so common today, which have no moving parts. Many firms tried to crack the portable calculator market. In 1962 Britain's Shamrock Corporation sold what may have been the first electronic calculator. A portable electronic calculator was introduced by the Bell Punch Corporation in 1963. In 1964 *Business Week* reported that most of the major adding machine makers—Remington Rand, Olivetti-Underwood, SCM, and Victor Comptometer, the market leader— were zeroing in on the home market. One executive said: "The consumer market for this product has hardly been scratched."[131]

None of those entries resembled pocket calculators as we know them today. As in the early days of personal computers, they were 8- to 16-pound "portable" desktops with a handle added. They seemed small in comparison to the bulky electromechanical models they replaced, but in comparison to today's tiny pocket calculators they are huge. Throughout the 1960s firms jumped in and out of the market for desktop electronic calculators aimed at the consumer mass market.

The Bowmar Instrument Corporation of Fort Wayne, Indiana, pioneered the consumer market for pocket calculators in 1971. Bowmar was an unlikely and somewhat unwilling entrant. Its basic business was making defense-related items that employed a technology similar to that used in making the light-emitting diodes (LEDs) found on early calculators. Bowmar had been in business since 1951 but had no experience selling consumer products. It turned to consumer markets only after it lost an Air Force contract and had found itself with few other options.

Bowmar was forced to pioneer the market for pocket calculators. As early as 1970 the firm tried to induce the traditional electromechanical calculator manufacturers in both the United States and Japan to enter the consumer market for small pocket calculators. Bowmar was more interested in selling

its LEDs to those firms than it was in making calculators. But no important seller saw potential in the market. Bowmar's president and CEO told reporters at the time: "We felt sure there was a market and so there was nothing to do but go into the market ourselves."[132] It was unclear at that point whether pocket electronic calculators were merely faddish gadgets or useful consumer products that would serve a large market.

Bowmar's entry would not have been possible without Texas Instruments' basic research. In 1957 a TI engineer named Jack Kilby invented the integrated circuit, a device that revolutionized consumer electronics. Patents for the integrated circuit were granted to TI in 1964. By 1967 TI engineers had created the "calculator-on-a-chip," the integrated circuit that lay at the heart of the electronic pocket calculator. Bowmar assembled calculators based on a chip supplied by TI. TI started shipping calculator chips to Bowmar in August 1971.

Bowmar introduced the first pocket calculator into consumer markets in September 1971, within three months of receiving TI's chips. Its calculator was priced at $179. Saks Fifth Avenue was the first large retailer to carry Bowmar's innovative product. It was an instant success, selling well as an expensive Christmas gift item. The pioneer's success attracted a flood of competitors into the market with similar products.

Bowmar was not the first firm to think of small calculators. A handful of firms had been selling hand-held $300 calculators for about a year before Bowmar's entry. None of them, however, had met with the stunning success that Bowmar did. Bowmar was the first firm to popularize pocket calculators. Up until its entry, pocket calculators were an outrageously expensive novelty.

The earliest followers consisted mostly of other small firms. Rapid Data Systems, for example, a Canadian company, jumped in quickly with a cheaper but less sophisticated model. Its Rapidman 800 sold for $99 by mid-1972.

Within a year of Bowmar's entry the number of competitors increased exponentially. Like Bowmar, many of the early followers were firms that simply assembled parts provided by others. Abatron, Commodore, Craig, Eldorado, Electrodata, Ragen Precision Industries, and Witco were among the firms that had entered the market by the fall of 1972. Prices ranged from $75 to $120, with Bowmar's 901B selling at the top of that range.

The semiconductor companies, which could do more than merely assemble calculators, smelled opportunity and planned to enter in droves. By the end of 1972 Rockwell International (which did not officially introduce its line of calculators until August 1974), National Semiconductor, Litton In-

dustries, Sperry Rand, Burroughs, and even Hughes Aircraft were either test-marketing pocket calculators or planning to do so shortly. They had a tremendous competitive advantage. They manufactured and controlled the chips that formed the heart of the modern pocket calculator.

Some of the Japanese consumer electronics giants had already entered by the autumn of 1972. Canon's Pocketronic, a calculator with a paper printout, was selling for $150. Sharp sold its ELSI-8M, which had a memory (an unusual and expensive feature at the time), for $200. Casio was planning to introduce a $60 bare-bones calculator. Most of the Japanese entrants were also assemblers who relied on supplies from the semiconductor industry.

Texas Instruments—the firm that had developed the chip used in Bowmar's pioneering entry—was, as one article at the time noted, "a relative latecomer."[133] By the summer of 1972 TI was still test-marketing its $149.50 calculator in Texas. There seemed to be no need for TI to rush to market. It controlled the core technology of most consumer calculators. As it turned out, it also controlled the fate of the pioneer.

TI officially entered the fray on September 20, 1972, almost exactly a year after Bowmar's pioneering entry, when it introduced the TI-2500 portable calculator, aimed directly at Bowmar's 901B. Both calculators sold at retail for $120. TI was unconcerned about the pioneer's early lead. One of its executives said that the pocket calculator market was "so new that there is no established consumer brand preference and no brand loyalty."[134]

By the summer of 1972, less than a year after Bowmar's entry, nearly 500,000 pocket calculators had been sold. Bowmar held 50 percent of a fast-growing market. American firms now dominated the emerging market for pocket calculators. There was gleeful talk in the press that American firms had displaced the Japanese firms that dominated the desktop calculator market.

Japanese firms had come to dominate the market for desktop calculators by providing lower assembly costs. The numerous, tedious, and labor-intensive connections between transistors that were required to make a calculator meant that labor costs were a substantial part of the product's price. The Japanese had an important cost advantage. The invention of the "calculator-on-a-chip" negated that advantage. Assembly costs were reduced to nearly nothing, while the role of technology became more important. American firms seemed to be gaining the upper hand.

As competitors flooded in, retail prices for pocket calculators plummeted. In 1972 quarterly price declines of 40 percent were common. At the very beginning of the emerging market, some experts crazily predicted that within a few years prices would fall to $60, a forecast that in hindsight turned out to

be too conservative. Ten-dollar calculators would have been more accurate. Price declines favored the large producers, but Bowmar's commanding share of the market made it a competitive player.

The market boomed in 1973. As expected, sales of pocket electronic calculators ate into sales of the old-fashioned desktops. As a result, Sony terminated production of desktop calculators and left the business.

Then the roof fell in on Bowmar. In June 1974 patent number 3,819,921 was awarded to TI for the "calculator-on-a-chip," which had been invented in the mid-1960s by Jack Kilby, Jerry Merryman, and James Van Tassel. Since TI and Bowmar were now competitors, there was no compelling reason for TI to supply Bowmar with scarce chips at favorable prices. Bowmar saw every reason to sue. On September 9, 1974, only three months after TI's patent had been granted, Bowmar began legal proceedings in a federal court, alleging that TI was guilty of violations of the Sherman and Clayton Antitrust acts. Bowmar also claimed that TI was engaging in discriminatory pricing practices for its "calculator-on-a-chip," which was in violation of the Robinson–Patman Act. Bowmar sought damages of $80 million, which would be trebled to $240 million if it won. Most important, Bowmar wanted a resupply of inexpensive chips. In essence, Bowmar charged that TI was cutting off its supply. Not surprisingly, TI responded that Bowmar's allegations were totally without merit.

Without inexpensive chips Bowmar was without competitive calculators. The company was caught between rising supply costs and rapidly falling retail prices. The combined effect of those two trends wrought havoc on Bowmar. One industry analyst noted at the time: "The problem with Bowmar was that they were dependent on Texas Instruments, their competition, for their chips. Every time Bowmar got comfortable, TI, with the cost advantage, would slash its prices. And that really took Bowmar's advantage away."[135] Competitive advantage had shifted clearly to the vertically integrated semiconductor companies. By mid-1974 roughly 70 percent of calculator manufacturing costs consisted of semiconductor components.

Recognizing its predicament, Bowmar rushed to create its own supply of calculator chips. In 1974 it invested $7 million in a Chandler, Arizona, manufacturing facility. Bowmar expected to be making all its own chips by mid-1975.

Bowmar never had a chance. Within a few months it was all over. On February 10, 1975, a mere eight months after TI's patent was granted, Bowmar filed for bankruptcy protection. Its president had been as prescient in predicting the firm's demise as he had been in predicting the market's emergence. A *New York Times* article reported that back in 1972 he had stated "that the pocket calculator market had a very bright future unless price cut-

ting started . . . that could be a disaster."[136] It was, for Bowmar. At the beginning of June 1975 Bowmar announced that it was suspending all production of pocket calculators. It could no longer compete. It closed a Mexican factory and an Arizona warehouse. The pioneer was out of the market it had created for good.

Bowmar did not go out alone. Many of the smaller early entrants that were assemblers of calculators were dependent on the large semiconductor companies for their chip supplies. When the semiconductor companies entered the market in force, the assemblers were forced out by lower prices and more expensive supplies. Vertical integration, not order of entry, turned out to be the crucial success factor in pocket calculators.

The market expanded in the mid-1970s, and the industry consolidated. The market had grown from a few million units in the first full year of sales to more than 25 million in 1974. At the same time, the number of competitors declined precipitously. The peak year was 1973, when about ninety competitors sold pocket calculators. A year later, about 30 percent of those firms had dropped out.

Today prices of pocket calculators are even lower, and most of the earliest entrants are gone. A few American firms—such as TI and Hewlett-Packard—have solid positions, especially at the high end of the market. The Japanese consumer electronics giants, who were deemed uncompetitive in the early days, have also done well. In pocket electronic calculators, pioneering seemed to count for little. The pioneers provided an important but short-lived economic function. Bowmar, in particular, proved that there was a viable consumer market for what had previously been an expensive business product. Bowmar was far more prescient about market trends than its larger rivals. Unfortunately, that pioneering effort went largely unrewarded. In the end, Bowmar had little to show for its market foresight or its bold and innovative efforts.

22. PROJECTION TELEVISION

The story of projection television is a classic tale of how a technology pioneered by a small, entrepreneurial upstart wound up in the hands of industry giants. It started in 1973, when the Advent Corporation introduced the VideoBeam 1000A, a front-projection system that consisted of two pieces: a 4-by-6-foot screen and a projection console that sat 8 feet to the front of it. The price was initially set at $2,495.

Advent was an unlikely innovator of projection television. The firm's history and reputation were as a seller of low-priced, high-quality stereo speakers.

Advent was the creation of Henry Kloss—one of those larger-than-life American inventors—who was determined to bring projection television to market. Kloss's experience with startups was extraordinary. In the mid-1950s he founded Acoustic Research, a company that popularized affordable audio speakers. He left AR in 1957 to start KLH, a firm that earned a respected reputation for selling reasonably priced, high-quality stereo components, especially speakers, during the 1960s. Henry Kloss was the "K" in KLH. Then, in 1967, Kloss left KLH to start Advent. Although Advent's reputation followed in the time-honored Kloss tradition of offering stereo speakers to the masses, Kloss was primarily interested in projection television. Loudspeakers were a way to produce capital. Advent's entry into projection television was heavily subsidized with profits from its loudspeaker business.

In August 1972, just before it introduced its pioneering projection television, Advent went public with an initial stock offering of 155,000 common shares. Investors were being let in on the next hot growth market.

The market for projection television started from humble beginnings. In December 1973 Kloss test-marketed the device in a single Dayton, Ohio, stereo store. The store sold twelve VideoBeams during the first six months. It could have sold more, but Advent's supply was extremely limited. Through mid-1974 Advent sold a total of only about 120 VideoBeam projection sets, mostly to what we now call sports bars, along with a few upscale individuals who just had to have one of the new video devices, even if it was priced at $2,495.

By 1974 sales and production capacity had increased considerably, but projection television was still a small business compared with traditional television sets. Kloss was optimistic, however. He predicted in 1974 that "there's going to be hundreds of millions of dollars of this product sold."[137] The TV giants were less enthralled. Although Kloss offered to license his technology to major television manufacturers for a pittance, none was interested in the impractical device. One Zenith official remarked: "You try to imagine that in somebody's house and it's hard."[138]

Advent had almost no competition in the retail market at first. The closest anyone came to a retail projection television was Sony's $3,045 three-compartment projection system, which was sold to corporations for use in training salespeople. Sony's system was priced much lower than GE's $43,000 projection television, which was also targeted to businesses, schools, and government buyers. But as the retail market showed promise, Sony moved closer to Advent's position.

At the time there was a near-consensus among industry experts that Advent's system was far superior to Sony's. One expert judged that "the Video-Beam is far in advance of Sony in just about every category: brightness,

definition, picture size and sound quality."[139] Advent seemed to be off to a stunning start.

By 1976 the market had grown significantly but was still small. Advent held a 40 percent market share of the 15,000 sets sold that year. No one else came close. According to published reports, Sony sold fewer than five hundred projection television sets in 1976. The industry nevertheless expected stunning growth to follow shortly.

Advent expanded its product line in the summer of 1976 to include a second model, the VideoBeam 750, which had a smaller 3¾-by-5-foot screen. The new model was a response to criticism that Advent's 4-by-6-foot screen was too large for most living rooms.

Matsushita's Panasonic brand entered the American market in late 1978. Although its sets would initially carry a high price, Matsushita was following a familiar strategy: It would strive to lower prices as the market expanded, which would expand the market further. By the late 1970s Advent had its eye on Matsushita.

Instead of focusing on the competition, however, Advent started to self-destruct. That process started with a series of wrenching internal shakeups. Henry Kloss had invested heavily in projection television, which had created losses at Advent. In alarm over those losses, Advent's board, with the blessing of its lenders, first demoted and then fired Henry Kloss from the firm he had founded exactly ten years earlier. By 1977, Kloss was gone. Profits had not come quickly enough to satisfy the investors.

Kloss immediately formed the Kloss Video Corporation and set out to settle a score with the firm that forced him out. He started by running down his former creation in public. "Advent's days of technological leadership are long gone," he said, and "Advent has no reason to be in business except the name Advent."[140] Right after his departure, he observed: "I think the company is badly managed."[141] Kloss introduced his competing Novabeam 100 in 1977.

Advent stumbled badly after Kloss left. Among other blunders, Advent tried to expand into videodisc players (a technology that lost upwards of $500 million for RCA, its primary proponent) and videocasette recorders (it intended to sell Sony's ill-fated Betamax under its own label). Nothing seemed to pan out for the new Advent.

Advent lingered for a few more years. In March 1981 it declared bankruptcy. Soon afterward it ceased production of projection television sets and tried to refocus its energies on loudspeakers, its core business. But even that failed. In April 1982 the brand name Advent and the firm's assets were sold to Jensen Inc. It took exactly ten years for the pioneer of projection televisions to move from creation to total destruction. Most irksome of all, Ad-

vent's demise occurred just as the market it had created was ready to explode. The pioneer was not around to harvest the fruits of its labor.

Meanwhile, in 1979, sales of projection televisions soared to 50,000 sets. The number of competitors had grown as well. Now, nearly all television sellers recognized the opportunity in projection television and belatedly introduced their own models. The market was so hot that scam artists even sold worthless devices that turned regular televisions into projection sets with the use of magnifying glasses. The press warned consumers to avoid these nonsensical devices.

Then the technology changed. Later entrants pulled a technological leap-frog on the innovator. In the early 1980s a new "rear-projection" design emerged that solved the problem of a large, obtrusive console sitting in the middle of an average-size living room. Some manufacturers of "front-projection" sets tried to disguise the console as a coffee table. But no matter what they called it, the front-projection system was simply too large for most American homes.

As is the case with many first-generation technological products, Kloss did not, and probably could not, anticipate the design that would ultimately dominate the market he created. Kloss recognized the problem with front projection systems but thought it could be solved by hanging the projector from the ceiling.[142]

Nor did Kloss embrace the new design. Most of the later entrants—including GE, North American Philips (under the Sylvania brand), Zenith, and Matsushita's Panasonic—adopted the new rear-projection design. The earliest entrants—in particular Kloss Video and, to a lesser extent, Sony—stuck with the old standard. Mitsubishi, one of the last major entrants, started with a front-projection design, then switched to rear-projection when it became clear that that design would dominate. Unlike the earlier entrants, the late-comers were not tied—emotionally, financially, or in terms of production capabilities—to the old and decreasingly popular design.

In the early 1980s, before it was liquidated, Advent tried to raise capital to build and market a rear-projection set called the VBT100, but financial problems killed the project in its early stages.

By 1981 industry sales of projection televisions exceeded 100,000, and forecasts correctly called for more rapid growth ahead. Sales soared throughout the 1980s. By 1986 sales reached 304,000 sets annually. But the benefits of that growth went almost entirely to the consumer electronics giants, most of which were later entrants.

In 1987 Kloss Video's Novabeam 100 held a colossal 50 percent share of the market for front-projection television sets, but the market for front-

projection units had declined to only 5 percent of overall sales! The pioneer had a huge share of what was now a minuscule market.

The pioneer's system quickly became obsolete. Kloss might have switched to the rear-projection design, but by the late 1980s Kloss was having financial problems. Sony, backed by a rich parent, had no such problems. It had switched completely to rear-projection televisions by the mid-1980s.

By the middle of 1987 Kloss was the only major seller of front-projection television sets. Twelve other major entrants, most of them Japanese, sold rear-projection sets.[143]

The end came quickly for Kloss Video. It could no longer compete in the market Henry Kloss had first created. Its assets were sold to AmPro, a small firm with specialized interests.

By 1989, Henry Kloss was on to something new—actually, something old. He created another new company, Cambridge SoundWorks, for the sole purpose of selling quality stereo speakers at "hundreds of dollars below the competition."[144] Kloss had returned to the strategy that had been so successful for him over the previous forty years.

Sales of projection televisions reached a record 305,400 in 1990. By that time, however, the later entrants owned the market. By 1991 Mitsubishi was the acknowledged industry leader. It claimed a 30 percent share of the over-30-inch large-screen television market, which included direct view (using a large regular picture tube) and projection televisions. Sales were so strong in the early 1990s that shortages of key components cropped up, which crimped sales.

Also during the early 1990s demand shifted to larger screens. Mitsubishi introduced to great fanfare a whopping 70-inch screen, which was hailed by the press as a stunning big-screen innovation. In fact, two decades earlier, Henry Kloss was severely criticized for producing a 4-by-6-foot screen that was too large for most American households. The market was now ready for an update of Kloss's original innovation.

In the end, the innovator of projection television provided inspiration for those who followed. One expert noted: "All projection TVs basically follow the concept pioneered by Henry Kloss."[145] Unfortunately, the pioneer's ideas also provided profits to later entrants.

In 1993 *Consumer's Guide* recommended three rear-projection televisions: Hitachi, RCA, and Mitsubishi. After Kloss's exit, Sharp was now the only major front-projection system featured.

The three leading sellers of projection televisions in 1993 were Mitsubishi, Philip's (primarily through the brand name Magnavox and the Sears private label), and RCA. Together those top three sellers accounted for 60

percent of the market. By that time the pioneers, Advent and Kloss Video, accounted for exactly zero.

RCA, now owned by France's Thomson Electronics, entered long after Henry Kloss but ended up in a far superior market position. In 1974, a year after Advent's initial entry, an RCA spokesman had said: "We've got nothing pinned down in the way of concrete experiments on large-screen television for the home because right now, it just doesn't seem very practical. It's at least five years away, as far as we're concerned."[146]

Later entry did not seem to hurt RCA, however. Along with the other later entrants, RCA moved into the market only as it showed its true potential. There seemed to be no need to rush. Once the market proved attractive, the later entrants easily displaced the weak pioneer. Once again, first-mover advantages counted for little when it came to projection television.

23. SPREADSHEETS FOR PERSONAL COMPUTERS

The ubiquitous computer spreadsheet did not come from IBM, nor did it come from Lotus, the ultimate market leader. VisiCalc, the first personal computer spreadsheet, came from two MIT students, Dan Bricklin and Bob Frankston. In the 1970s Bricklin was a graduate student and Frankston was an undergraduate working on an early version of the UNIX operating system. Both were accomplished software engineers. After working as a software designer for Digital Corporation, Bricklin returned to the Harvard Business School for an MBA. While there he got the idea of easily recalculating financial projections based on different assumptions using an electronic "blackboard." Although a Harvard finance professor warned Bricklin there was little need for such a product, he persevered.

The idea of spreadsheets—calculating numbers arrayed in rows and columns—had been around for centuries. Bricklin's innovation was that he adapted it for easy use on personal computers, which had yet to diffuse beyond a small core of hobbyists but would soon become extremely popular for business applications.

Bricklin teamed up with his former classmate Frankston and during the summer of 1978 decided to write and sell the first commercial spreadsheet. A prototype was ready by the autumn of 1978. In January 1979 the pair incorporated Software Arts, the Massachusetts company that would produce their innovative spreadsheet. VisiCalc, the pioneering spreadsheet for personal computers, was introduced on October 17, 1979. It was priced at $99.

In the late 1970s it was unclear just how a personal computer software firm should be structured. Using the model of book publishers, the two

software designers acted like authors and signed a contract with twenty-eight-year-old Dan Fylstra, a new products editor at *Byte* magazine, who had been at Harvard Business School with Bricklin. Fylstra's firm, Personal Arts, had been founded in 1978 to sell computer games out of his apartment. According to their agreement, Fylstra's firm would market the VisiCalc program. Since VisiCalc was by far its biggest product, Personal Arts was renamed VisiCorp and established its headquarters in Silicon Valley on the West Coast.

VisiCalc was purposely designed to be a very simple product. It had to be. The first spreadsheet was written so it would run on the then-popular 32K Apple II personal computer. As a result, it had severe limitations. VisiCalc could set column width, for example, but all columns had to be set to the same width. VisiCalc also had to be easy to use in order to attract business consumers familiar with calculating rows and columns but unfamiliar with the intricacies of personal computer programming. In the beginning, VisiCalc competed with paper, pencils, and calculators. Bricklin and Frankston felt that a complicated package would scare away business users.

As is often the case with radically new technological products, the authors and VisiCorp invested a great deal of effort in educating both dealers and the public as to VisiCalc's benefits. One of the program's authors recalled in a later interview: "Nobody even knew what VisiCalc was."[147] VisiCalc faced a daunting marketing task.

VisiCalc was slightly ahead of its time. It was introduced before the boom for personal computers began. The VisiCalc program was among the first truly successful application programs for the small but burgeoning computer market. In fact, VisiCalc helped create the personal computer boom that followed its entry. Business consumers bought personal computers just to run VisiCalc. Before the spreadsheet's entry, most personal computer users were hobbyists, not business users. In the beginning, the authors sold a thousand copies a month, but sales soon reached $10 million, and Software Arts found itself with more than a hundred employees.

By the early 1980s the number of personal computers on the market had proliferated greatly, and each used a different operating system. Bricklin and Frankston were busy writing different versions of VisiCalc to run on Radio Shack, Atari, Commodore, and other computers.

The original VisiCalc entered before 64K CP/M machines hit the market and became the *de facto* industry standard. Consequently, Sorcim's Super-Calc, a VisiCalc clone, was the first spreadsheet sold for use on those very popular personal computers. It was around this time that Microsoft first entered the market with Multiplan. Still, VisiCalc maintained its commanding lead.

The next important advance in personal computers came in August 1981 with the introduction of IBM's phenomenally successful PC. The VisiCalc Advanced Version was designed to meet the challenge of the more powerful 128K Apple III, which was introduced in May 1980 and was quickly adapted to serve 256K IBM-PC users.

In 1981 Context MBA, the first integrated software package, was introduced. It combined windows, graphics, word processing, and spreadsheet functions into one software package. It failed quickly, however, because it was not compatible with the IBM-PC. Still, the newest spreadsheet programs offered more features than VisiCalc's increasingly outdated program.

VisiCalc responded in 1982 with a plethora of software products under the IBM VisiSeries trademark. That series, which was marketed by VisiCorp, included VisiTrend/Plot, VisiFile, VisiSchedule, VisiDex, a Business Forecasting Model, and IBM Desktop/Plan. VisiCalc seemed to have all bases covered with a series of single products. In 1983 VisiCorp reported revenues of more than $40 million, almost 60 percent of which came from the VisiCalc program.

Buoyed by its success, in November 1982 VisiCorp introduced Visi-On, a mouse-driven spreadsheet that allowed an IBM-PC to act like Apple's newest Lisa personal computer.

Lotus 1-2-3 was among the last major entrants. It entered in 1983, just as sales of the IBM-PC began to take off. Lotus 1-2-3 borrowed heavily from VisiCalc, the spreadsheet pioneer. Early versions of 1-2-3 clearly illustrate its lineage. The command structure of Lotus—its "look-and-feel"—is close to that of VisiCalc's Advanced Version, the most current version available when Lotus was being written. One analyst noted in a review of Lotus: "Looking at VisiCalc is like looking at a grandfather and trying to figure out where this stellar grandchild came from."[148]

The similarity between VisiCalc Advanced Version and early versions of Lotus 1-2-3 was no coincidence. Mitch Kapor, Lotus's founder, had been instrumental in developing VisiCalc's VisiPlot program, part of the IBM-VisiSeries that created graphics from VisiCalc files.

But Lotus did more than merely copy VisiCalc. It incrementally improved upon VisiCalc's crude single-purpose spreadsheet. VisiCalc may have been the innovator, but Lotus was the ultimate refiner, and Lotus refined the product just as the market for spreadsheets soared with the sale of PCs for business purposes.

Lotus 1-2-3 was easier to use and more comprehensive than VisiCalc. For one, its headings used words rather than letters. Using Lotus was much less cumbersome and more versatile than its predecessor. Lotus was also more facile with graphics, a likely advantage given its designer's experience with

VisiCalc's graphical routines. Finally, like Context MBA before it, Lotus integrated a spreadsheet, graphics, and an information management capability into its 1-2-3 program. VisiCalc seemed to be standing still, while Lotus rushed past it with technological enhancements.

VisiCalc, meanwhile, was caught in the crossfire of a legal battle between Software Arts and VisiCorp, the companies set up to make and market the programs. While Lotus became more and more identified with the IBM-PC for which it was designed, VisiCalc's parents set out to destroy each other in a bitter internal battle. VisiCorp sued Software Arts for not moving fast enough to update the program. Software Arts countered that VisiCorp was not doing a good job marketing the program. In September 1984 the suit was settled; VisiCorp agreed to return the marketing rights for VisiCalc to Software Arts. Software Arts had won the legal battle but it lost the competitive war. By that time there was little left to take back: VisiCalc was hopelessly behind the new technological leaders and irreparably damaged by the legal battle.

The end came in May 1985, when Lotus bought the assets of Software Arts and ceased sales of VisiCalc. Between October 1979, when it was first introduced, and May 1985, when it was killed, VisiCalc sold more than 800,000 copies. It was an innovative product that died for a greater good of technological advancement. In 1989 *Inc.* magazine interviewed Dan Bricklin, VisiCalc's creator. The first question asked was: "It must be pretty hard to help launch an industry and then watch your company get swallowed up by it." Bricklin's response: "Yes, I'd say it was hard at times."[149] His experience spoke volumes as to the merits of pioneering new and unproved products.

The West Coast VisiCorp fared little better. By November 1984 it had agreed to be taken over by a small software startup. Its Visi-On program had failed miserably, as had the Apple Lisa computer. To raise cash, VisiCorp sold Visi-On to Control Data.

The most ironic twist to the tale of computer spreadsheets involves Lotus's reaction to subsequent copycats. The success of Lotus 1-2-3 spawned a slew of imitations eager to imitate Lotus. Its response? Lotus has led the fight in computer software to protect the "look-and-feel" of its program from subsequent imitators. Lotus has successfully stopped others from copying the command structure of its program, with which many PC users are now intimately familiar. It is part of a larger move to restrict incremental innovation in software development. Dan Bricklin, VisiCalc's founder, argues that "those little changes are the genetic mutations that cause evolution in our industry."[150]

Could VisiCalc have done anything different to affect the ultimate outcome? Of course, its creators could have avoided the fight that destroyed the

program. But, more important, they could have set up a different organizational structure in the beginning, not the one that mixed authors and friends and used separate companies to make and market the program. They could also have taken the time to patent their program, something they did not do, but that would have slowed development, and neither Bricklin nor Frankston knew that their product would be as successful as it ultimately became. Anyway, all this wise counsel has the benefit of being offered after the fact. It is easy to say in hindsight what should have been done, but pioneering radically new technological markets is fraught with risks. Unexpected outcomes are simply part of the pioneering process, often a part that aids later entrants and punishes those who are first to market.

24. TELEPHONE ANSWERING MACHINES

The telephone answering machine did not burst upon the scene unexpectedly. As early as the 1940s, Bell Labs technicians predicted that a "telephone that will answer itself and talk back to you when you come home" would soon be available.[151] Like many technological innovations, however, "soon" turned out to be later than expected. It took more than thirty-five years for the telephone answering machine to work its way from the lab to business and then, eventually, to residential customers.

Like other pioneering innovations, the first telephone answering machine was not pioneered by the telecommunications giants. It was first introduced by Code-A-Phone, a small Portland, Oregon, firm that specialized in niche communications products. One of its better-known products, for example, introduced years after the first telephone answering machine, was the intercom system for Boeing 747 commercial aircraft, which pilots use to make passenger announcements.

Code-A-Phone was incorporated on September 25, 1958. In 1962 it signed a contract with Western Electric to supply telephone answering machines for the Bell system, which then sold them to business customers. The early Code-A-Phone devices were cumbersome machines that had to be hard-wired into phone lines. In those days AT&T had federal and state authority to monopolize the phone system. It was argued that non-Bell equipment might cause irreparable harm to the national phone grid if outside firms were allowed to connect their equipment to it without AT&T oversight. That practice served to keep outsiders away. In those early days Code-A-Phone operated at the fringes of a highly regulated industry.

In 1965 Code-A-Phone started a commercial division that sold telephone answering machines to business customers through independent dealers.

The word "independent" is deceiving, however. Code-A-Phone's machines were still closely controlled by AT&T, being required to work in conjunction with an AT&T "interface," which had to be installed by AT&T technicians. Business customers were also charged a monthly rental fee by AT&T. AT&T generated a steady flow of income with the sale of each Code-A-Phone system.

Early answering machines were targeted at businesses, doctors, and other professionals who would be hurt financially if they missed incoming calls. For the first two decades of their existence they served as mechanical substitutes for telephone answering services, which used live people to answer phones when business customers were unavailable.

Early attempts to replace people with machines occurred throughout the 1960s and 1970s. In 1971, for example, Safeco Insurance decided to automate some of its dealings with agents in the sparsely populated Northwestern United States. The company installed a Code-A-Phone answering machine that featured—just as many do today—two tape recorders, one to play the prerecorded announcement, the other to receive the caller's message. Safeco would record messages, then respond in writing at a later date.

In the 1970s Code-A-Phone started to attract competitors. Phonemate went public in 1972 in order to raise funds to compete on a more equal footing. More important, in 1975 Phonemate brought legal suit against AT&T to end its requirement that an AT&T "interface" be installed with every answering machine. Its settlement opened the doors for other competitors. It also planted the seeds for a much larger market.

Code-A-Phone entered the retail market in 1976. Although it once had the entire market to itself, competitors now entered in droves. Major domestic sellers included Phonemate, Record-a-Call, and Tandy Radio Shack, while imports included Panasonic and Sanyo.

The residential market for telephone answering machines boomed in the mid-1980s. Three trends converged to expand the market greatly.

The first trend was toward less government regulation. AT&T had been broken up and deregulated. Arcane, anticompetitive rules that adversely affected telephone answering machines were reduced or eliminated. The Reagan Administration was pushing for more competition.

The second trend was largely demographic. Growing numbers of single professional and dual-income households discovered that the device could be used to answer personal calls while the occupants were out working. Those were the same upscale customers who at the same time were acquiring microwave ovens and fax machines. As the decade ticked on, the telephone answering machine moved from a high-end luxury item to an indispensable household appliance. Sales shot upward. After the telephone answering ma-

chine had languished in limbo for a long time, *Business Week* in 1986 labeled it "a product whose time has arrived."[152]

The third trend had to do with lower prices, which were both the cause and the result of a rapidly growing market and the lessened regulatory environment. As had happened with countless other technological consumer products, falling prices drew more and more consumers into the market. At the same time, more customers led to higher sales volume, which allowed for production efficiencies and lower per-unit costs. Costs were further reduced by less regulation.

Prices fell fast. In 1981, for example, a clunky, bare-bones Code-A-Phone model 1000 telephone answering machine sold for $140. By 1986 the average price had fallen to $90, then it fell again to $50 in 1987. Sales doubled from less than 1 million units in 1982 to 2.1 million units only a year later in 1983. They doubled again to 4.4 million units in 1986.

It was Japanese sellers, in particular Matusuhita's Panasonic, who led the change to lower prices. As had happened in microwave ovens, VCRs, fax machines, and a host of other popular consumer electronics products, the telephone answering machine moved from a commercial to a household product as prices declined.

The Japanese also worked hard to improve quality. In the first half of the 1980s a telephone answering machine was basically two tape recorders and a loudspeaker. By the middle of the decade, however, the number of features available was staggering. A master's degree was almost needed to operate all of the features on top-end models.

According to some reports, the Japanese offered superior value. *Consumer Reports* rated telephone answering machines in its May 1983 issue. It designated Panasonic's model KXT-1505 a "best buy," ranking it first among fifteen inexpensive machines.[153] Code-A-Phone's 1075 model, in contrast, was ranked twelfth (although it did significantly better in later years).

By mid-1983 GTE, Sony, and a host of other entrants, both large and small, were selling telephone answering machines. Each seller offered a bewildering array of models.

Consumer demand for telephone answering machines grew so rapidly in 1983 that shortages appeared among some of the leading suppliers. Nonetheless, prices continued to fall precipitously. At the same time, retailers demanded respectable profit margins—between 30 and 40 percent. That meant costs had to be lowered in order to remain competitive.

By the mid-1980s the essential competitive ingredient in telephone answering machines was low-cost production. Innovation was still important, but the market was more and more driven by lower costs and lower prices. Sellers who could not drive down costs were about to be shaken out of the

market. The *New York Times* noted after the trend had played itself out: "Answering machines have become low-profit commodities, as humdrum as potatoes."[154] That trend should have favored the pioneer, assuming that advocates of first-mover advantages are correct in their contention that experience effects accrue primarily to the pioneer. But that never happened. In fact, the exact opposite occurred. Later entrants, in particular the Japanese, used their advantages in low-cost overseas production to nullify the pioneer's early lead. It proved an easy fight to win.

Code-A-Phone may have been the first seller of telephone answering machines, but it was the last firm to move production overseas. Not until 1985 did Code-A-Phone close its U.S. assembly operations and switch to lower-cost Asian factories, becoming, as *Business Week* noted, "the last large U.S. manufacturer [to stop] domestic assembly work."[155] Instead of leading in lower costs, the pioneer was *forced* to move offshore in order to survive. In that important respect, it did not lead, it followed.

In the mid-1980s Phonemate, a major domestic seller of telephone answering machines, took the ultimate step in moving its production overseas. It sold 43 percent of its stock to the Japanese firm Asahi, which was its key supplier. In July 1991 Casio bought a majority interest in Asahi.

By 1986 Phonemate had surpassed Code-A-Phone as the market leader with a 16 percent share. Panasonic, a perennial low-cost producer, was second with a 15 percent share. Code-A-Phone came in a close third with 14 percent. Just behind it were Tandy Radio Shack and Record-A-Call. Low-cost Asian producers now led in another industry pioneered by domestic producers. Sharp and Toshiba were among the last entrants.

Code-A-Phone responded with the introduction of an innovative new product: the all-digital, tapeless telephone answering machine. In 1985 it demonstrated a prototype of the new machine, then in late 1988 it introduced the new model into the market. Unfortunately for Code-A-Phone, Sharp made it to market first. Its FP-M62 was introduced directly into the market in early 1988.

Overall, Code-A-Phone set a stellar record on innovation but a terrible record of keeping its developments proprietary. Among the innovations it claims to have pioneered:

- In 1962, the first variable announcement, which allowed the owner to record an outgoing message of any length
- In 1963, the first voice-controlled message length, which allowed the caller to leave a message of any length
- In 1963, the first replaceable tape cartridges (which preceded the invention of the cassette tape)

- In 1972, the first integrated telephone/telephone answering machine all in one unit
- In 1978, the first one-touch control, which allowed the user to rewind, play back, stop, and rest by pressing a single button
- In 1978, the first telephone answering controlled by a microprocessor
- In 1983, the first beeperless remote
- In 1984, the first commercially successful machine to use a microcassette
- In 1986, the first to offer decorator colors
- In 1987, the first to introduce power failure memory protection

In short, Code-A-Phone claims to have pioneered just about every major technological development in telephone answering machines. But in the end the firm seemed to serve as a test market for the rest of the industry. Others always seemed to sell its developments at lower prices.

In order to buy share, Code-A-Phone acquired the GTE line of telephone answering machines in 1988.

One of the last entrants into telephone answering machines was AT&T, which did not enter until 1983. Later entry apparently did not hinder this telecommunications giant fresh from deregulation. By 1985 AT&T had earned a 9 percent share of the telephone answering machine market against a crowded field of competitors.

At the time of AT&T's entry, Code-A-Phone was still the number one seller. AT&T's later entry was supported by a massive national print ad campaign. By 1984 most of the other sellers had also started advertising campaigns. Code-A-Phone parried with a belated ad campaign of its own. But its efforts were too little, too late. A marketing manager at Code-A-Phone noted: "We got complacent. But we learned our lesson."[156] But Code-A-Phone could not hope to match the vast resources of competitors as well endowed as AT&T and Panasonic.

At the end of 1990, just in time for Christmas, AT&T introduced its 1337 all-digital answering system, which sold for $139 and looked like a vertical tower. Its unique design, along with the seller's close identification with telephone technology, made the product stand out. AT&T also decided to make the machines outside the United States (e.g., in Mexico) to keep costs low. AT&T may not have been the first to market, but when it decided to enter it ultimately moved quickly to the head of the pack.

By the early 1990s AT&T was the clear market leader with at least a 25 percent share. Panasonic was second with about 18 percent. Phonemate and General Electric (which sells a French-made phone under its own brand name) made up the second-tier players with 15 percent shares. Code-A-

Phone came in far down the list with roughly 6 percent.[157] One Code-A-Phone executive admitted that the pioneer now considers itself a niche player and is out of contention for the top spot.

Record-a-Call, another early entrant, has also fared poorly. By 1991 it had been sold to Planned Technologies Inc., which kept the brand name alive but bought the answering machines from someone else. Record-a-Call was able to maintain only an infinitesimal share.

Not only was Code-A-Phone hurt by others, but it also hurt itself. Starting in 1963, Code-A-Phone was owned by Roseburg Lumber, which saw a bright future for the firm's innovative products. Code-A-Phone was purchased in 1982 by the Conrac Corporation, which also saw a bright future for the hi-tech firm. Then, in 1987, Code-A-Phone got caught up in the kind of financial manipulations that plagued other firms in the 1980s. In June 1987 Mark IV industries purchased the Conrac Corporation. In October Code-A-Phone went through a leveraged buyout, which created disruptive internal problems at the very time the firm should have been focusing on competitive threats. During those crucial years, a veritable revolving door for management was operating at Code-A-Phone. The firm went through three presidents and three marketing directors within a four-year period. There seemed to be no strategic focus. Then Code-A-Phone became a unit of Technology Applications Ltd., of Bankok, Thailand, in 1989. Code-A-Phone is now pursuing fax forwarding, another technological innovation.

Telephone answering machines now face a threat from newer technologies. Just as dual-deck machines substituted for people-based telephone answering services, voice mail now threatens to make telephone answering machines obsolete. Critics contend it will never happen. They argue that voice mail is simply too expensive. It is like buying a telephone answering machine over and over again, or like renting rather than buying. But voice mail advocates gained strength in 1990 when sales of telephone answering machines dropped 19 percent and voice mail revenues rose 28 percent.

Whatever the outcome of this most recent technological battle, one point is clear: It is unlikely that Code-A-Phone will ever again regain preeminence in the market it helped create. When the market grew larger and more attractive, Code-A-Phone was pushed aside first by the Japanese consumer electronics giants who used a familiar strategy—lower prices gained from production efficiencies—and second by AT&T, the telecommunications giant with unlimited resources, a coveted brand name, and south-of-the-border production. In telephone answering machines, as in like product categories, pioneering offered only a chimera of protection against copycats and later entrants.

25. VIDEOCASSETTE RECORDERS (VCRs)

Just as television replaced radio, so too did videotape recorders replace audio tape recorders. It all started with the Germans. In the 1930s Allgemeine Elektricitaets Gesellschaft (AEG), the German electrical giant, developed the first practical sound tape recorder, called the Magnetophon. It used magnetic tape rather than wire, a dead-end technology pursued in the United States. Tape had numerous advantages over wire as a recording medium, making the quality of the Magnetophon recordings vastly superior to that of the crude American models.

The Germans lost the war, and with it their innovative Magnetophons. An American GI named John Mullin stumbled upon the Magnetophons in war-torn Germany and pirated a few of them back to the United States in pieces. After the war he reassembled the machines and attempted to bring them to market. He demonstrated his tape recorder to a San Francisco meeting of the Institute of Radio Engineers in May 1946. The pirated German Magnetophons attracted the attention of numerous engineers in the audience.

One of those engineers subsequently went to work for the Ampex Corporation, a small defense contractor in search of civilian work now that the war had ended. He convinced Alexander M. Poniatoff, the firm's founder (who named Ampex using his three initials, then adding an "ex" for excellence) that magnetic tape recorders were the way to go. Poniatoff signed on. Ampex engineers then set out to copy the German design directly. As John Diebold notes in his book on innovators, however:

> The tape recorder that Lindsay and his associate Myron Stolaroff set out to create was based on the German magnetophon but could not be an exact copy because Jack Mullin never permitted them to see the electronics of his machine.[158]

That may have slowed the copycats down, but it did not stop them. By 1947 Ampex had created a tape recorder of its own design that actually improved upon the original German model.

Mullin, meanwhile, unsuccessful in his own business venture, nevertheless was instrumental in getting Ampex audio tape recorders installed at major radio stations. Starting in 1948, radio programs shifted from live performances to taped playbacks. From that point on, Ampex specialized in selling professional audio tape equipment to commercial broadcasters.

Just as Ampex started to reap the fruits of its labors, radio started to give way to television. It was obvious to nearly everyone involved that sound recorders could be transformed into video recorders. Ampex funded re-

search and development into the possibility but gave the project low priority. Competitors moved more quickly. They jury-rigged crude video recorders from existing sound recorders, but the quality of the crude reworks was poor, and the very first entries quickly disappeared. Ampex moved more slowly. Through the first half of the 1950s it developed a number of experimental models. Then, on April 15, 1956, exactly ten years after Mullin had introduced the German sound recorder to the American public, Ampex demonstrated its videotape recorder at the convention of the National Association of Radio and Television Broadcasters in Chicago. Nayak and Ketteringham concluded in their book *Breakthroughs!*: "The Ampex machine was a spectacular breakthrough, and the impact on the broadcast industry was epochal."[159] Orders poured in for the pioneer's product. Within four days of the convention's opening, Ampex had booked orders for seventy-three recorders worth nearly $4 million from customers who before the convention had not even known of the device's existence.[160] Thus was born the first commercially successful videotape recorder.

The first Ampex videotape recorders were far from "home" models. They made black-and-white recordings, were gigantic in size (resembling a refrigerator lying on its side), and had a price tag to match ($75,000). They were strictly for commercial broadcasters. Ampex targeted its video recorders in exactly the same way it had targeted its sound recorders, offering exactly the same benefit: The Ampex video recorder was to be used by broadcasters to time shift programming and edit out errors. The first videotape recorder entered service on November 30, 1956, when it was used by CBS to rebroadcast a popular news show three hours later on the West Coast.

Videotape recorders represented a tremendous improvement over existing technology. Kinescopes, derived from a process whereby shows were filmed right off a television monitor, provided woefully poor picture quality. Between 1956 and 1960 Ampex virtually monopolized the broadcast market for commercial videotape recorders.

Emboldened by its success and eager to penetrate new broadcast markets, Ampex tried to patent and sell its product in Japan but was unsuccessful at both endeavors. The Japanese National Broadcasting Corporation bought an Ampex videotape recorder in 1958 and promptly turned it over to the Japanese electronics giants for the purpose of reverse-engineering. With the help of government subsidies, Sony quickly knocked off the American design. According to one analysis, "the Sony VTR was a virtual copy of Ampex's."[161] The other Japanese companies followed soon after. Ampex cried foul.

Inexplicably, Ampex signed an agreement with Sony in July 1960 that granted Sony the right to make and sell a videotape recorder using Ampex

technology to "nonbroadcast customers" in return for Sony's providing Ampex with transistorized circuits. The deal quickly turned sour. Within a short time the other Japanese electronic companies began selling video recorders that were nearly identical to the Ampex machine to the same broadcast customers. Sony may have held to the agreement, but its brethren did not. Adding insult to injury, Ampex then entered into partnerships with some of its Japanese competitors and even granted licenses that legitimized the imitative technology they had created. Sony emerged as a major competitor and a long-term legal combatant.

Both Sony and Ampex introduced a series of new models throughout the 1960s, but the paths taken by the two firms diverged. Ampex focused on the high end of the market, specifically broadcast customers, while Sony was committed to the long-term goal of making a home VCR feasible. In 1966 Sony introduced what it claimed was the first home video recorder. *Consumer Reports* judged the product to be too far ahead of its time. Picture quality was poor, and prices were still too high. Customers stayed away in droves.

The emergence of color television in the second half of the 1960s compounded the problems of VCR makers. Just as engineers had started to improve the quality and lower the prices of black-and-white recorders to within reach of the home customer, consumers adopted color television and proved unwilling to take a step backward. The market was put off a little longer, while researchers perfected the color VCR.

By the late 1960s the U.S. press was abuzz with talk of the impending boom in home VCRs. If it was possible to land a man on the moon in 1969, the pundits thought, then it was reasonable to expect that we would all soon have video recorders in our homes.

Recognizing the error of its ways, Ampex hurriedly changed course and introduced a prototype of Instavideo, its version of the home VCR. It was a grand gesture in contrast to Sony's incremental improvements. The Instavideo machine was a competent device scheduled for a January 1971 introduction. It was lightweight, was priced competitively with Sony's products, and would have a camcorder as an available option. The product seemed destined for instant success. But it carried two heavy burdens that ultimately killed its chances.

1. In order to price Instavideo competitively with Sony's machines, Ampex would have to keep production costs low. Toshiba agreed to produce the device for Ampex, but when cost estimates were tallied, the economics simply did not make sense. Instavideo would never make a profit. As a result, Toshiba never manufactured a single machine for the market.

2. Compounding the problem, Ampex ran into financial difficulties that sapped the firm's strength. Ampex did not have the resources to incubate the emerging market. The pioneer was hobbled by its own shortcomings.

In October 1971 Ampex announced publicly that it was discontinuing work on the project.[162] The pioneer of video tape technology was now out of the home market before it even started to grow.

By the late 1960s, a flood of new entrants sensed an opportunity and introduced competing technologies with the intent of leapfrogging the pioneer and stealing the home market before it had formed. Many of those entrants thought that the key to commercial success was coordinating the sale of hardware and software. It was an attempt to solve the chicken-and-egg problem. Consumers were reluctant to buy expensive video systems until movies were available in large numbers, and the movie people were reluctant to blanket the country with rental inventory before there was a large base of installed units.

One of the more unusual entries was by CBS. CBS introduced in 1970 the Electronic Video Recorder (EVR), an "oddball" device that used miniaturized film packaged in small cassettes rather than magnetic tape, as did the Sony and Ampex models. Motorola was to make 100,000 of the $795 playback units annually, and CBS would supply cassettes containing prerecorded movies from its huge film library. Twentieth Century Fox agreed to provide 15,000 more titles from its film library. At first EVR would target schools and insurance sales-training applications. But in mid-1972 CBS expected to have a $350 home version ready for market.

In November 1970 CBS delivered the first EVR to the Equitable Life Assurance Society with great fanfare and claimed it had orders from more than fifty other government, educational, and business institutions. The press was kind to the fledgling venture. *Time* magazine thought that the film-based standard might have a chance over magnetic tape: "It is too early to discern which technology is leading the cartridge race."[163] *Forbes* concluded: "At the moment, CBS has the lead [but] its competitors are coming up fast."[164] It seemed CBS might walk away with the home market.

EVR's unique design was protected by numerous patents, but it was not protected from a hostile, unsupportive parent, which held the purse strings. When sales fell below expectation, costs exploded, and cash flow proved nonexistent, CBS head William Paley, who had been adamantly opposed to the project from the beginning, pulled the plug on EVR. CBS was not committed to the project. EVR ceased to exist in 1971 after only a year on the market.

The next unique design that sought to conquer the market by coordinat-

ing hardware and software sales appeared in July 1971 when Cartridge Television Inc., a subsidiary of the Avco Corporation, another defense contractor, went public with the goal of finally bringing VCRs into homes. Cartrivision, as its system was known, would be sold through mainstream retailers and would coordinate the rental of feature-length films for home use. It was the first truly home VCR brought to market.

Cartridge Television arranged for Sears to sell a Cartrivision VCR housed inside a Sear's 25-inch color television console for $1,600. By 1972 the sets, which were produced by Admiral, were on the market. In the same year Cartridge Television formed a joint venture with Columbia Pictures called the Cartridge Rental Network, which would rent full-length feature films to consumers. It was predicted that within a year, 100,000 cartridges would be available in retail stores. The cartridges were different from those available today. Cartridge Television was able to scotch the deal with Columbia only because it agreed to ensure that prerecorded cassettes could be viewed only once. They then had to be returned to the rental shop for rewinding. Shops were charged for each rewind (viewing), a practice adapted from movie houses.

Cartrivision was quickly hobbled by the chicken-and-egg problem that had plagued previous entries: Consumers would not buy its consoles until movies were available, and movies were scarce because there were few rental customers. Cartrivision also erred in packaging its VCR inside a console television. Most upscale customers already had a color TV.

In the end Cartrivision was a grand vision, but an equally grand failure. Sales lagged badly behind expectations, quality problems cropped up everywhere, and costs went through the ceiling. Pioneering the market for home VCRs proved to be tougher than anyone expected. By 1973 the firm was liquidated after delivering only about 6,000 units. Buyers were burdened with an "orphan" format for which there were no tapes. Investors were also orphaned. In February 1974 they filed a class action suit charging that the firm's exuberance had really been an attempt to mislead investors. Among the many charges made was one alleging "bugs making the system unsalable."[165] Like Sony and CBS before it, Cartrivision was too far ahead of its time. The product was not ready for the home market, and the home market was not ready for Cartrivision. Cartrivision also ran afoul of Ampex's patents. Ampex sued and then settled with Cartrivision over the machine's mechanisms.

Sony, meanwhile, continued to make incremental improvements to the videotape recorder it introduced in the mid-1960s. Unlike its American competitors, Sony was in for the long haul. Its U-matic recorder hit the magical $1,000 price point in 1971, which put it within reach of the home customer.

The U-matic was the first sales success. By the mid-1970s nearly 200,000 units had been sold in the United States. But, like previous entrants, it too gained acceptance mostly in schools, government agencies, and as a sales training tool. In hindsight, the U-matic was a bridge between the commercial and home markets.

By 1974 Sony had driven down prices and improved performance to the point where a home VCR was feasible. It's entry was Betamax. Before going to market, Sony tried to get the other Japanese sellers, in particular JVC and its parent Matsushita, to adopt the Beta tape format. Sony knew that a standard tape format would allay consumer fears and make the market grow faster and to greater height, which would benefit all sellers. Sony also wanted to co-opt Matsushita, a firm more than three times its size. But JVC and Matsushita had no intentions of making a captain out of a seaman. There was also the issue of recording time. Betamax could record for only one hour, which was too short a time to record movies, a key use of machines in the home market. JVC and Matsushita decided to spurn Sony's offer and plow ahead with a home VCR of their own design.

In April 1975 Sony introduced the Betamax in Japan for somewhat more than half the price of the U-matic from which it had descended. The Betamax was smaller, cost less, and came with a few more features, but essentially it was a derivative of the original U-matic design.

In November Sony entered the American market with a $2,295 Betamax recorder housed inside a 19-inch Trinitron color television console. It was a monstrous affair that possessed the same disadvantage as the Cartrivision system that had failed five years earlier. Most affluent consumers in the target market already had a color TV and were not interested in buying another.

Sony quickly stripped the Betamax deck from the console television and in February 1976 started selling it in the United States as an independent unit for $1,295. Betamax benefited immensely from the experience of earlier entrants who had softened up the market. Consumers were now more familiar with recording devices. Favorable press reviews and media attention made the product seem more mainstream than "oddball." As a result, sales soared. Ads for the Betamax sidestepped the necessity of prerecorded tapes. The Betamax was sold strictly as a time-shifting device. Consumers could record programs while not at home or record one show while watching another. Even with the unpleasant one-hour recording limit, sales of Betamax made it the first truly *successful* home VCR. After a long and difficult delivery, a new market was now born.

But Sony's Betamax really just softened up the market for JVC and its parent Matsushita, which entered last with a different format. JVC's Video Home System was first introduced in Japan in September 1976, a little more

than a year after Sony's initial entry. VHS had one key advantage: It recorded for two hours, twice as long as Betamax. Sony was surprised by JVC's fast second entry. Akio Morita, Sony's chief, accusingly stated: "It's a copy of Betamax."[166]

RCA introduced its "SelectraVision" VHS VCR in the United States in August 1977. RCA selected the JVC machine, made for it by Matsushita, for three key reasons: (1) It recorded for two hours; (2) it was designed for low-cost production and would survive the price wars that were certain to start; and (3) Zenith, its U.S. rival, had selected Sony's Betamax format. The RCA VCR was priced at about $1,000, which Sony was forced to match.

The results of the competitive battle were quick and decisive. By early 1978, within six months of its entry, RCA pulled equal in market share to Sony's Betamax. After the first full year of competition RCA held double the market share of pioneer Sony. From that point on, it was all downhill for Sony and the adopters of its format.

Almost every seller—except Sanyo and Zenith—went with the VHS format. Consumers also preferred it. They overwhelmingly favored the two-hour recording time. When Sony lengthened its recording time, VHS lengthened its also, keeping the advantage constant.

Sony could do nothing to reverse the downward spiral. Early buyers found themselves stuck with an obsolete standard as video rental stores stocked up on VHS tapes and eschewed Beta-format tapes. Sony was unable to stop, or even slow, the later entrants, even though it had sold more than 100,000 of its Betamax VCRs before they entered. Advocates of first-mover advantages would argue that Sony should have been able to install its format as the world's standard. But that did not happen. Instead, the very last entrants, who had been working on the technology for years, took advantage of their size and the fact that their system recorded for twice as long to move into the lead position. Sony's success was short-lived. After nearly twenty-five years in development, what happened last seemed to matter most in VCRs. Konosuke Matsushita commented that "it is natural that the product coming out later is better."[167] A sage observation.

26. VIDEOGAMES

The development of videogames largely parallels the diffusion of computers. Throughout the 1960s mainframe programmers played videogames written by other programmers in their spare time, or at least when the boss was not looking. As early as 1962 a game written by an MIT student entitled "Spacewar" was making its way around college computer labs. None of those

pioneering efforts, however, was a commercial success. Most were never meant to be.

The business of videogames started in 1972, and it started on two fronts. Magnavox pioneered the market for home videogames, and at the same time Atari pioneered coin-operated electronic arcade games.

In September 1972 Magnavox introduced Odyssey, the first home videogame system. Like today's systems, Odyssey consisted of a control unit, which hooked to a television and two player controls. Unlike today's videogames, however, Odyssey was an "oddball" innovation that came bundled with twelve game program "cards" and required users to attach a transparent plastic sheet to their television screens in order to simulate the playing field of a particular sport. Games included table tennis, football, target shooting, and roulette. For $100 the buyer got crude graphics and mediocre action. It was a modest first start for a radically new technology.

Magnavox ended up pioneering videogames as the result of an odd sequence of events. The invention did not come from their R&D labs. Instead, it was the latest version of a 1960s device made by an independent inventor, who then tried to sell his idea to the major television manufacturers. None saw much potential. RCA seemed interested at first but ultimately turned the project down. When an RCA employee joined Magnavox, he got that company interested. In 1970 Magnavox agreed to license the inventor's videogame.

Magnavox's Odyssey sold well. More than 100,000 of the home videogames were sold during the first year. By 1975 sales reached $22 million.

While Magnavox was moving into the home market, Atari introduced the first coin-operated electronic arcade game. Pong, its first successful entry, was introduced in mid-1972. The game featured a less than stunning black-and-white video version of table tennis. Still, according to *Business Week*, the game was an "overnight success."[168] Pong created the consumer excitement that propelled the market skyward for the next two decades.

Pong was the brainchild of Nolan Bushnell, a stereotypical computer whiz, who combined an interest in computer games gained as an engineering student at the University of Utah in the 1960s with the "management experience" he earned while working his way through college at the arcade of a Salt Lake City amusement park. By early 1971 Bushnell had developed Computer Space, an electronic alternative to the mechanical pinball machine, which one analyst deemed "a knockoff of Spacewar," the game he had played in college.[169] Bushnell licensed the game to a small-time arcade game manufacturer. It bombed big time. The problem was that it required users to read the instructions before they played the game, a task far too daunting for the bar patrons who made up the target market. Bushnell then went out on his

own. In June 1972 he teamed up with a pal, each put up $250, and Atari was born. Pong, his second game, was so simple that no instructions were necessary.

Copycats came out of the woodwork to meet the surge in demand. Atari, being small and poor, was forced to license its creation to Midway Manufacturing, the pinball powerhouse, which sold more than nine thousand in the first six months. Atari itself was able to make only six thousand Pong games during the first year of sales. Most other sellers never bothered licensing. By 1974 more than 100,000 Pong arcade games had been sold. Clones accounted for 90 percent of sales, while Atari sold only 10 percent.

The economics of video arcade games were as enticing as the soaring demand for them. The games themselves were cheaper to produce than mechanical pinball games and much more reliable. They consisted of far fewer parts, so almost nothing could break. Surging demand led to higher prices, while lower labor and maintenance requirements led to lower costs. Margins were obscene. Consumers poured quarters into Pong in the mid-1970s.

Atari's fortunes soared with the success of its innovative product. Sales went from nearly nothing in early 1972 to $15 million in 1973, the first full year of operation.

Still, some of the old-line pinball manufacturers saw video arcade games as a fad that would soon fade away. One pinball company executive predicted: "The small companies will be in trouble when the crunch arrives."[170] Atari's Bushnell had a different vision. He viewed early sales as "the tip of the iceberg," a view that proved more accurate as demand soared over the next decade.

In the fall of 1975, just in time for the Christmas season, Atari challenged Magnavox with a home version of Pong. Sears helped. It formed an alliance with Atari in which Sears paid the bills in return for the exclusive right to purchase the entire production run of 100,000 units. Sears was the only retailer to carry Atari's Pong home game in a market where shortages were chronic.

Other threats loomed as the market expanded. Atari was basically an assembler. It purchased integrated circuits from the semiconductor industry and put them into videogames, which meant that someone else controlled the essential component of its product. That smelled like an opportunity to the major semiconductor companies, who glimpsed a repeat performance of the competitive battles in calculators and digital watches. In both of those cases, the pioneers were pushed out of business by chip suppliers who cut off their supply and entered themselves. The semiconductor industry was watching and waiting. An executive at National Semiconductor noted omi-

nously: "Next year [1976] people like us will really go to work on this market."[171]

Once again, Atari's Bushnell saw a different vision. He believed there were fundamental differences between calculators and videogames. Whereas calculators and digital watches were stand-alone products that could be mass-produced at low cost, videogame systems were only as good as the games that could be played on them. Since the games changed constantly with the whims of a fickle public, the benefits of low-cost mass production were less important than advantages in software design. That skill did not favor the semiconductor sellers. Indeed, the semiconductor manufacturers never became a force in videogames. National Semiconductor entered in 1977 and sold 200,000 units of its Adversary system, but it withdrew a few years later.

Demand started to soar in late 1975. By year's end 300,000 to 400,000 games were sold at a retail value of $75 million. Demand continued to exceed supply throughout 1975 and 1976, as a shortage of integrated circuits held back production.

Until the mid-1970s home videogames were "dedicated" to playing a single game. Atari's Pong played Pong and Pong alone. In August 1976 Fairchild Camera & Instruments took the technology a step further when it introduced Channel F, the first "programmable" videogame system to play multiple game cartridges.

Atari needed money to compete in the fast-growing and increasingly competitive market. The small firm seemed to be perpetually short of cash. Atari had two choices: It could either go public or sell out to a larger company. Bushnell decided on the latter. MCA and Disney were interested but decided to pass. In 1976 Warner Communications acquired Atari for $28 million in cash and debentures, of which Bushnell got to keep $15 million. For the next eight years the two companies were intimately entwined. By 1978 Warner had pumped $120 million into Atari to finance growth. In return, Atari contributed about one-third of Warner's operating income by 1980.

Atari introduced its most successful new product ever, the "video computer system" (VCS), in 1977. The $150 "programmable" system worked with game cartridges priced at about $30 each. About the same time RCA introduced its unsuccessful Studio 2 system.

By the late 1970s Atari was the undisputed leader of the home videogame market. One analyst called Atari "the fastest-growing major company in the history of American business."[172] Atari easily roared passed Magnavox. By 1978 industry sales had soared to 500,000 units, of which 400,000 went to Atari. Through 1982 Atari consistently maintained a 70 to 80 percent share of the home videogame market.

The technology took another jump forward in 1980, when Mattel introduced Intellivision, based on a second-generation technology that offered users better graphics. Mattel quickly moved into second place with a 10 percent share. Odyssey, the home videogame pioneer, withdrew from the market after failing to bring out a technologically advanced product.

Sales of home videogames exploded between 1980 and 1982, largely on the popularity of Space Invaders, a home version of the popular arcade game Atari had licensed from a Japanese firm. The home version was a stunning success that broke every existing sales record. Atari's system sales also benefited, growing from 2.2 to 8.2 million units between 1980 and 1982. Sales of game cartridges grew from 9 to 60 million units. A total of 350 new game cartridges were released in 1982.

Atari followed up with Pac-Man, which was released as a home game in 1982. Pac-Man was yet another example of a successful arcade game recycled into the home market.

The number of competitors also exploded. By 1982 more than twenty companies competed for share in the fast-growing market. Coleco, which had first entered in the mid-1970s and then dropped out in 1979, reentered with Colecovision, another second-generation technology, which it hoped would ride to success on the backs of Zaxxon and Donkey-Kong, two popular arcade games licensed for home use. Other entrants included Milton Bradley, whose Vectrex system went nowhere, and a host of such unlikely entrants as Quaker Oats and General Mills.

Atari was caught in a strategic quandary. Later entrants like Mattel offered consumers more sophisticated systems with better graphics. Atari had to choose between two tough alternatives: It could stick with its older, technologically inferior system, which had a large base of existing users, or it could introduce a new system, which would be more technologically advanced but would be incompatible with the existing system, a move that might alienate current users and negate the firm's advantage. Clouding its decision was the fact that Atari could not even meet current demand for the old-fashioned system.

In late 1982 Atari belatedly introduced the 5200, a second-generation videogame system that offered more power and superior graphics. The only problem was that it was incompatible with Atari's existing system.

At the same time Atari had its hands full fighting off copycats. Since its VCS system was the most popular videogame system, a handful of software firms tried to hitch a free ride on Atari's success. Activision, for example, which was started in 1979 by a group of former Atari game designers, sold cartridges that played on the Atari system. In the early 1980s Activision held about 20 percent of the software market.

Imagic, a hot concept stock of the early 1980s, tried to do the same thing. It made game cartridges that played on both the Atari and the Mattel systems. In 1982 Atari tried to sue Imagic for copyright infringement, claiming Imagic's Demon Attack game was nothing more than a copy of Centuri's Phoenix, which Atari had the exclusive right to produce for the home market.

Coleco tried a different tactic. It introduced a module that allowed users of its systems to play Atari cartridges. Atari sued for $350 million. At the time the Atari chief executive announced: "We regard the Coleco adapter as merely a thinly disguised copy of Atari's VCS unit."[173] Coleco judged otherwise. It countersued for $500 million, claiming antitrust violations.

Even the innovator of home games was acting like a copycat. In 1982 Atari forced North American Phillips, Magnavox's parent, to stop producing KC Munchkin, an obvious knockoff of Atari's popular Pac-Man game.

In late 1982 some observers were seeing signs that the fad was finally dying out. Prices were falling, and advertising expenditures were rising in order to stimulate demand. Kids seemed to be getting tired of the games they once loved to play. An article in *Fortune* noted: "Some observers even talk of a collapse similar to that suffered by CB radios, digital watches, and pocket calculators."[174] Maybe there was an analogy between videogames and those other ephemeral growth markets after all. As a result of those pessimistic expectations, stock prices for Warner and Mattel, the two leaders, fell fast. Videogames were contributing heavily to each company's bottom line at that time.

Pessimism was also driven by the emergence of home computers, a technology that cast a potential death pall over videogames. There was a widespread belief in the early 1980s that home computers would replace, or at the very least merge with, game players. An article in *Fortune* pointed out in 1983: "Home computers are so inexpensive now that consumers are buying them as substitutes for game players. Some observers think that will spell the end of the market for separate video game players."[175]

There was ample precedent for that belief. There had been an obvious trend in videogames toward more flexible machines. Whereas the earliest systems were "dedicated" systems that played only one game, later "programmable" systems allowed users to play an unlimited number of game cartridges.[176] It seemed reasonable to expect that trend to continue. This time, however, home computers could be used to accomplish other tasks as well as play games.

That view was bolstered by skyrocketing sales of personal computers in 1982. Personal computers were following a pattern similar to that experienced by videogames a few years earlier. The *Wall Street Journal* noted at the time that "it seems people want more for their money than just games."[177]

Atari and the other videogame sellers bought into the view that computers were the technology of the future and stand-alone game players were the technology of the past. By 1983 Atari had all the bases covered. It competed in home videogames, coin-operated arcade games, and home computers. It was difficult, however, to get the game division to cooperate with the home computer division. One analysis concluded that "at a time when those very categories were meshing in the marketplace and minds of consumers, Atari chose to isolate them totally from each other."[178] In June 1983, in what turned out to be a never-ending string of management shakeups, Warner Communications chose sides. It combined the two groups into a single unit and appointed the head of the computer group as president of Atari Products. One expert called the appointment a "tacit admission that the market for stand-alone video games is dead."[179]

Atari's sales peaked in 1982 at $2 billion. The bottom fell out of the market in 1983. Atari plummeted from $323 million in profits in 1982 to a loss of $539 million a year later! It was a nightmare. Not only had home videogames fallen out of favor, but arcade games were down also. At the same time, falling prices for home computers sapped corporate profits.

Atari contributed to its own demise. In an attempt to earn quick profits from a dying market, it rushed to market with high-profile, poor-quality game cartridges. The low point came in 1982, when Atari introduced E.T., a videogame based on the phenomenally successful movie. The game was a quick hit that captured Christmas season sales but created long-term customer dissatisfaction. E.T. sold an astonishing 3 million copies, making it one of the most successful videogames of all time, but basically the game was a derivative of Pac-Man. Consumers felt deceived and lost interest in the entire product category even faster than they would have otherwise.

The entire videogame industry seemed to be going to hell in a hand basket. Demand was down, supply was up, and cutthroat price competition in home computers forced the industry to become obsessed with one issue: low costs. Atari sent production overseas. The videogame industry did indeed seem to be going the way of calculators and digital watches. The industry had degenerated into pure price competition among low-priced commodities.

Mattel dropped out in 1983. Atari continued to hemorrhage money so severely that Warner was willing to dump the company at nearly any price. In July 1984 Warner turned control of Atari over to Jack Tramiel, whom *Fortune* described as "a feared and relentless master of low-cost production."[180] Tramiel paid no cash for the company but assumed a $240 million debt and promised to invest $75 million of his own money in the business. Tramiel's focus was fixed squarely on home computers. He shelved a new videogame system proposed by his predecessor and intended to sell clones,

such as the Jackintosh, a clone of the Apple Macintosh (ultimately labeled the ST), at a fraction of the price of the real thing. In 1985 Atari turned a small profit and went public.

The age of videogames had passed, or so it seemed.

Nintendo proved that impression wrong with the introduction of its Nintendo Entertainment System (NES) in 1985. Nintendo, a hundred-year-old Japanese company with a history in the playing cards business, experienced tremendous success in Japan with its Fami-Com game system about the same time that Atari had finished its boom-to-bust roller coaster ride in the United States. Whereas the U.S. market went into the tank, videogames quickly found their way into 25 percent of Japanese households. Buoyed by its success in the Japanese market and unaffected by the downward spiral that beset American sellers, Nintendo first started selling its system in New York in the fall of 1985. It went national in 1986 with a confidence unmatched by traumatized domestic competitors.

In 1986, its first year of sales, Nintendo sold 1.1 million NES units, largely on the strength of Super Mario Brothers, a game that eventually sold 40 million copies. The firm followed up in 1987 with Mike Tyson's Punch Out. In total, Nintendo sold an astounding 3 billion game systems and 15 billion game cartridges in 1987. Nintendo held 70 to 80 percent of the $2.3 billion U.S. videogame market. Growth had returned with a vengeance. By 1988 industry sales had surpassed the 1982 peak from which they had previously crashed.

Domestic observers were skeptical of the market's staying power, and the American sellers were reluctant to commit heavily for fear of being burned again. *Business Week* echoed the timidity of the industry in 1988: The "current video game revival may already be past its prime."[181] An Atari executive acknowledged that "we're not overextending ourselves on a category that might go south again."[182] Nintendo, some seemed to think, was repeating past mistakes. It simply did not know the risks inherent in the American market.

But Nintendo had learned an important lesson from Atari's failure. It surmised that the unbridled competition of the early 1980s destroyed the industry. The helter-skelter entry of hundreds of games by dozens of software producers resulted in quantity at the expense of quality. In search of quick hits, supply overwhelmed demand, and the industry degenerated into fierce price competition. Nintendo was determined not to repeat those mistakes and set out to impose "managed" competition on the industry.

Nintendo exercised tight control over the games produced for its machine. It was able to do so because its games required a patented microchip, which it controlled. Outside software designers were limited to a half-dozen

games per year. Once written, the code had to be submitted to Nintendo, which manufactured the games, then shipped them back to the software firms in shrink-wrap for sale to retailers. In that way Nintendo ensured that the games were challenging and of high quality, and not in gross oversupply. It also allowed Nintendo to make sure that each game was truly unique, not merely a slight variation on the same repetitive theme. Tight control of supply also kept prices high.

Nintendo also controlled the price of its game players. For years, the system sold at retail for $99 and was almost never found on sale, a point challenged by consumer advocates.

Nintendo also stressed quality. It system was more advanced than Atari's and, as a result, produced much better graphics.

In short, Nintendo was managing the market for the long term. At the end of 1988 a Nintendo executive summarized the firm's strategy as follows: "We have to deliver more sophisticated software, to create a category of entertainment as opposed to just an individual, short-term product.[183]

Nintendo was also unencumbered by the mistaken world view that home computers were about to absorb videogame players. Luckily for Nintendo, or as a result of its tenacity, the two technologies stayed separate. IBM went on to dominate personal computers, while Nintendo ruled videogames.

Nintendo's control over the industry was so complete that Atari cried foul and sued Nintendo, claiming, in effect, that it was a monopoly. In particular, Atari took issue with Nintendo's practice of not allowing independent software designers to sell to the competition. If they did so, they would lose their largest buyer. Atari argued that the practice monopolized the best designers and stifled competition. The case went to trial in February 1992. Atari lost. Nintendo was cleared of being a monopoly and promptly continued to do business the way it always had.

By the late 1980s the videogame business was dominated by the Japanese. Nintendo was clearly number one, and Sega, another Japanese competitor, which had entered in 1986 with a system that offered superior graphics, was number two.

In 1989 two Japanese competitors—Sega and NEC—pulled a technological leapfrog on Nintendo. Just as Mattel and Coleco had challenged Atari in the late 1970s with technologically superior systems, both firms introduced 16-bit game players with outstanding graphics capabilities. Not only were the sets better, they were also priced lower.

Nintendo's response was the same as Atari's had been. Its 8-bit NES system was still selling well, its market share was overwhelming, and there was an installed base of more than 30 million sets in 25 percent of American households. A radical new product introduction seemed unnecessary.

Nintendo finally responded with its 16-bit Super NES in September 1991, two years after Sega's Genesis and NEC's TurboGrafx. Its entry into the American market followed its successful introduction in Japan in November 1990.

Sega and NEC responded to Nintendo by lowering prices. By the end of 1991 Nintendo's Super NES sold for $200, Sega's Genesis for $150, and NEC's TurboGrafx for a mere $100. Prices fell again in 1992.

Sega offered the greatest challenge to Nintendo, thanks largely to the popularity of a game called Sonic the Hedgehog and the fact that it had more games available by the time Nintendo entered. By the early 1990s Sega's Genesis held a competitive, if not commanding, market share for 16-bit systems, a small but growing segment of the overall market.

Nintendo remains the videogame leader. It currently holds about 80 percent of overall sales, the same dominant share that Atari held a decade ago. Atari, meanwhile, holds a minuscule share of the market it helped pioneer. Atari may have been first in home videogames (actually it was second), but it ended up last in a four-way race against much later entrants.

27. WAREHOUSE CLUBS

In 1976 Sol Price pioneered a radically new retailing concept: He sold giant-size portions of popular consumer goods at rock-bottom prices in stark, bare-boned warehouses to a select clientele of small business owners who signed up as "members" of his club. Sol's first store was located on the outskirts of San Diego. It was named the Price Club in honor of both his name and the store's key selling feature.

Actually, the Price Club concept was only partially new. There have always been discounters. E. J. Korvette, for example, succeeded by undercutting department stores in the 1950s. Sol Price himself had a history in that end of the business. In the 1950s he had founded FedMart, a West Coast discounter, which began as a membership-only retailer but later went mainstream. FedMart was acquired by a German investor in the mid-1970s and eventually went out of business.

The concept of huge, warehouse-like retailers was popular in Europe before it caught on in the United States. In Europe, small food and drug retailers would often purchase supplies in bulk at huge wholesale supermarkets.

Still, the Price Club was unique in many respects. Its stores carried a smaller selection than the traditional supermarket (3,000 as against 25,000 items) and were much larger (100,000 sq. ft.). The decor was spartan, and the location was often inconvenient. The Price Club, like most of its imitators, picked out-of-the-way sites, often in industrial parks, where real estate

costs were low. The warehouses had concrete floors and unadorned display racks. Services were few. No credit cards were accepted, and no delivery was available; it was a strictly cash-and-carry operation. Even the number of customers was restricted, as membership fees were required. The intent was to focus on the small business customer, who bought often and bought in bulk. Individuals, if they were let in at all, had to be government employees or members of a union in order to join.

The overall focus of the Price Club was to keep costs low, which allowed the stores to feature very low prices. From its inception the Price Club concept was based on high-volume, low-profit margins (about 10 percent, versus 30 percent at more traditional retailers), and high inventory turnover. The belief was that consumers would put up with the inconveniences of warehouse shopping to obtain rock-bottom prices.

Through the late 1970s and the early 1980s the Price Club expanded slowly but steadily. By 1983, eight years after the first store had been opened, the Price Club had expanded to only twelve stores, most of which were located in its home base of Southern California. The Price Club was intent on maintaining control over the operation it had created. It knew that fast growth had been the downfall of other startups and sought to avoid those hazards. The Price Club was a financially conservative operation that stressed stability over rapid sales growth.

For nearly seven years the Price Club faced no large competitors. None of the large retailing giants counterattacked, because, as with most radically new ideas, pundits perceived the Price Club to be a fringe operation with few opportunities for big-time growth. One expert remarked back in 1983: "There aren't enough small businesses to support warehouses, and consumers won't tolerate the inconvenience."[184] But by the early 1980s that view had changed. The Price Club had gone public to raise funds for expansion, and the rest of the industry recognized that warehouse retailing was a market on the rise. Competitors entered in droves in 1983. Amazingly, after seven years of total inaction all of the copycats entered at exactly the same time.

The Price Club's conservatism created opportunities for the later entrants. While the pioneer focused on the Southern California market, competitors found it easy to copy the Price Club concept and apply it in territories where the pioneer had no presence. Four major later entrants moved quickly to the forefront.

The most potent competitor to enter in 1983 was Sam's Club, a creation of Wal-Mart, the discounting powerhouse from Bentonville, Arkansas. Sam's Club quickly established a beachhead in Texas with little competition from the Price Club.

Another competitor was Costco, based in Seattle, Washington. Costco's

principal markets were in the Pacific Northwest and Florida. Costco was initially funded by Carrefour S.A., France's largest retailer. Costco went public in 1985 to raise funds for expansion.

Pace Membership Warehouse Inc., from the Denver suburbs, opened its first 100,000-square-foot store in the summer of 1983. It started in the Rocky Mountain region but then expanded to the Atlantic coast. Like the Price Club, Pace started as an independent. It was created in July 1983 by Henry Haimsohn, then went public in 1985 to finance expansion. By the mid-1980s, however, its O-T-C stock was being heavily "shorted." Many investors were betting that Pace, as an independent, would be unable to compete in a market soon to be dominated by the retailing giants. That turned out to be a misplaced concern. By the late 1980s Pace Membership Warehouse was a division of Kmart, one of the retailing giants investors feared.

The final, and smallest, later entrant was BJ's Wholesale Club, which began in 1984 with three clubs. BJ's was started by Zayre's, the Northeast discount chain. By 1986 BJ's had expanded to only eight clubs but was nicely positioned in the coveted Northeast.

Most of the later entrants were blatant imitators of the Price Club concept. *Business Week* observed in the mid-1980s: "Most owners unabashedly admit to copying the formula developed by Price Club."[185] Still, each of the copycats managed to gain a significant share of the market even though the pioneer had a seven-year head start. By the end of 1984, only a year after the later entrants had entered, there were four top players—Price Club, Sam's Club, Costco, and Pace—which together accounted for about 80% of total industry sales.

The Price Club held its market leadership through the mid-1980s. In fact, it had grown so large that in 1985 Standard & Poor's dropped Nabisco and added the Price Club to its 500 stock index. The Price Club had reached its peak.

But the market soon started to change. By the mid-1980s the warehouse club concept had really caught on. Demand soared as consumers clamored for a club in their area. Money to grow now became the key ingredient for success. Access to expansion capital became the best indicator of who would win and who would lose. Size started to matter most. The clubs that could grow fastest would realize the greatest economies of scale and would be able to build dominant positions in unserved geographic areas. Ten years after the Price Club had pioneered the first club, there was a mad dash to blanket the country with warehouse retail stores.

The fast-growth, capital-intensive character of the market favored large firms with deep pockets. It especially favored Sam's Club, whose parent supplied it with a virtually unlimited amount of investment capital and a

reputation for market dominance. The market now discriminated against the independents, especially the Price Club, which had grown slowly and cautiously. The Price Club was further hampered by it focus on real estate. It typically built its own stores and often built entire shopping centers in which its stores were located. Most of its money and a substantial amount of its management time were tied up in the real estate business instead of the warehouse club business it had pioneered. The Price Club had traded security for opportunity.

By the late 1980s warehouse retailing had become a big-time business that required big-time investment capital to compete. Whereas sales at warehouse clubs had been only $1 billion in 1983 when the imitators first entered, sales soared to nearly $30 billion by 1991. Independents were on the way out.

The better-financed imitators then went on an acquisition spree. In 1987 Wal-Mart acquired the Super Saver Warehouse Club. In 1990 it purchased the Wholesale Club of Indiana. The industry was starting to consolidate.

By 1987, only three years after they had entered, the imitators had expanded faster than the pioneer. Sam's Club operated forty-nine warehouse stores, Costco had thirty-nine, and the pioneering Price Club trailed with thirty-five. In September 1987 *Chain Store Age* proclaimed Sam's Club the number one warehouse club operator.[186]

Sam's Club consolidated its hold on the industry in the 1990s. As Table 3.9 illustrates, by the end of 1992 Sam's Club swamped its competitors in terms of the number of clubs it operated and overall retail sales.

The knockout blow to Price Club was delivered in June 1993, when the pioneer announced that it was forced to merge with Costco, a move that *Business Week* described as "a stunning reversal of fortune." In the end, the

TABLE 3.9
COMPETITIVE RANKINGS OF WAREHOUSE CLUBS (AT THE END OF 1992)

Warehouse Club	Number of Stores	Overall Sales (in billions)
Sam's Club	256	$12.3
Kmart's Pace	116	4.7
Costco	101	6.5
Price Club	81	7.3
BJ's Wholesale Club	39	1.8
Totals	**593**	**32.6**

Source: Data adapted from Stephanie Strom, "A Shuffle of Warehouse Clubs," *New York Times*, May 22, 1993, p. L33.

Price Club found that it could no longer compete on its own. Sol Price, the founder, lamented: "We were up against such mammoth companies that we're better off together than apart."[187]

Costco seemed to hold the upper hand in the merger. James Sinegal, Costco's CEO, was slated to take the helm of the newly formed Price/Costco Inc. He had truly learned much from the master. Ironically, before joining Costco, Sinegal had spent twenty-three years working for Sol Price. Now he headed the company Price had founded.

The Price Club–Costco merger was completed in October 1993, catapulting it into a challenging, if not leading, role in the industry. But Sam's Club further consolidated the industry in May 1993, when it acquired fourteen of Kmart's Pace warehouse stores. It acquired the remaining ninety-one Pace stores in November of that year, when Kmart decided to leave the industry and concentrate on its traditional discount operations. The *de facto* merger of the number one and number two warehouse chains further strengthened Wal-Mart's grip on the industry.

The case of warehouse clubs illustrates two important lessons regarding the merits of imitation. First, spending money later can often be substituted for spending money on pioneering brand-new markets. In the case of Price Club, the pioneer had a seven-year head start on the imitators, but when the market showed its true potential and the industry giants decided to enter, the imitators easily caught up by spending heavily. They entered later but with greater power. Second, later entry must precede the most substantial market growth. Had imitators entered in the late 1980s, after most of the growth had occurred, they would never have had a chance. But the imitators entered before the most substantial growth had materialized. That meant they missed very little, even though many years had past. It is not being first that necessarily matters, but being in before the bulk of the growth occurs, which may be years or decades after the pioneer's entry.

28. WORD PROCESSING PACKAGES FOR PERSONAL COMPUTERS

Word processors revolutionized the practice of writing. They represented a quantum leap in the ability to edit over IBM's correcting Selectric typewriter, which when introduced in 1974 allowed users to backspace, "white-out," and then type characters one at a time.

The first word processors were "hard-wired" into machines that were dedicated to that single purpose. But dedicated word processors were ultimately supplanted by word processing software packages for personal computers.

WordStar was the first high-grade word processor that produced polished, professional-looking documents in the hands of users unfamiliar with the intricacies of arcane computer code. As such, it was truly a pioneering product.

WordStar 1.0 was released in 1979 by MicroPro International. MicroPro was a firm founded in 1978 by Seymour Rubenstein to market the WordStar program, which had been written by the programmer Rob Barnaby. Mr. Rubenstein was MicroPro's President and CEO.

WordStar was originally designed to run on personal computers that used the CP/M operating system, the dominant standard before 1981. It had two key innovative features. First, it used the "cursor diamond," whereby touch-typists moved around the display screen by pressing keys that formed a diamond on the keyboard (the keys E-S-X-D). The top key moved the cursor up, the bottom key moved it down, and so on. This feature was important in the days before keyboards had arrow keys. It was helpful for touch typists, who valued the placement of keys more than their mnemonic worth. That was WordStar's second important feature. Its commands matched the placement of fingers on the keyboard. That design proved unique. Subsequent word processors relied on mnemonic commands, where keystrokes were easier to remember even if they were harder to reach. Since many commands had to be memorized, and mnemonics were not used, WordStar developed a reputation for being difficult to learn but easy to use, once learned.

As Table 3.10 illustrates, MicroPro's fortunes soared with the success of early personal computers, such as the popular Kaypro computer. It even came bundled with some of the early machines. Sales soared during the first half of the 1980s.

WordStar was easily the most popular word processor in the United States during the first half of the 1980s. By 1984 Multimate held the number two market share position, while WordPerfect held the number three spot.

TABLE 3.10
WORDSTAR'S RISE: 1980 TO 1984

Year	Revenues
1980	$ 1.5 million
1981	4.4
1982	22.3
1983	43.8
1984	66.9

Source: Compiled from numerous articles over the five-year period.

Multimate was a clone of Wang's dedicated word processor. The keys it used even matched those on the Wang machine. It was basically a system for secretaries.

WordPerfect 1.0 was introduced in 1980 by Satellite Software International of Orem, Utah, but did not run directly on personal computers. It was originally designed for the more powerful Data General minicomputers. In the beginning it did not compete directly with WordStar, because the two sellers served separate markets. Not until nearly three years later—fully four years after WordStar's innovative entry—did a version of WordPerfect designed specifically for personal computers enter the market. WordPerfect got off to a tardy start.

WordPerfect 2.0 was introduced in December 1982 and had two key advantages over WordStar:

- WordPerfect commands were executed using IBM's function keys, which made for fewer keystrokes.
- It contained a 30,000-word dictionary, a mail merge program, and a print spooler. It also had the ability to add footnotes, format newspaper columns, and execute proportional spacing. WordStar offered a dictionary and mail merge as expensive independent add-ons and was unable to perform any of the other functions.

Still, the odds argued against WordPerfect's success purely on the basis of product superiority. Changing word processors entails considerable switching costs. The user has to learn a new system, much as a native of one country has to learn a new language when switching countries. In both instances, there is a strong incentive to stay with the mother tongue. With word processors, the tendency is to favor the first system with which the user has become fluent.

But WordPerfect's timing was perfect. While WordStar had entered the market early and had captured a smaller group of dedicated computer hobbyists and early users of word processing, WordPerfect overwhelmingly captured the larger group of PC owners who entered the market when IBM introduced its phenomenally successful PC. By simply waiting, WordPerfect's entry coincided almost exactly with the explosive growth of the PC.

The new computer inadvertently aided the new word processor. The PC used the MS-DOS operating system rather than the soon-to-be obsolete CP/M. As a result, WordPerfect was designed specifically for the new standard while WordStar had been designed for the obsolete standard.

A version of WordStar that was compatible with the IBM-PC was introduced in 1982, about the same time as WordPerfect 2.0 was introduced. But

the program was a Band-Aid remedy. Unfortunately for MicroPro, the original WordStar had been written in such a way that the computer code could not easily be updated. The update turned out to be the software equivalent of putting jet engines on a prop aircraft or a diesel engine in an old sailing ship. WordStar was shackled with a program designed for an obsolete standard.

Oddly, WordStar's DOS version also kept the multikeystroke commands it had used in CP/M instead of giving users the option of using the function keys that were an integral part of PC technology.

Given the problems encountered with adapting the old WordStar to the new standard, MicroPro decided to start anew. It scrapped the original WordStar program and introduced an entirely new word processor, Word-Star 2000 Plus, in November 1984. The new program was based on an entirely different computer code.

At the same time, however, MicroPro made a horrific marketing blunder. It also changed the entire look and feel of the WordStar program. WordStar 2000 Plus had a new interface, a new command structure, and new file formats. The programmers must have loved it, but loyal WordStar users could not use it. It had nothing in common with the original WordStar. In one cruel stroke, MicroPro made two dreadful errors.

- First, WordStar 2000 Plus failed to attract the large number of new users its developers thought it would, because it contained few benefits over an ever-widening field of competitive entries. For one thing, it ran more slowly than competitive word processors.
- Second, and more important, it abandoned loyal WordStar users, who would gladly have upgraded to a more familiar package. The new package was so different, and so incompatible, that few original WordStar users made the switch. Instead, they either stuck with the old WordStar and suffered or, since they were forced to learn a new language anyway, switched to WordPerfect and learned that language instead.

Clearly, WordStar should have kept the familiar interface. Its disastrous move threw away its valuable franchise with consumers. In hindsight, an attempt at a quantum leap turned into a quantum fall for MicroPro.

As if that were not enough, MicroPro was beset by internal strife and perpetual restructurings, which weakened the company further at a time when it was being wounded by competitors. In 1981, in order to raise money to fund its phenomenal growth, Mr. Rubenstein sold 25 percent of the company to Fredrick Adler, a venture capitalist, for $1 million. As is often the case with fast-growing startups, Mr. Rubenstein and Mr. Adler promptly proceeded to disagree on just about everything, and a power struggle for

control of the company ensued. Mr. Rubenstein, the founder, was replaced as chief executive in September 1983 by a seasoned manager hand-picked by Mr. Adler. But Rubenstein and Adler continued to control roughly equal shares of the company's stock and stayed at each other's throats.

Mr. Adler emphasized financial matters. He focused on cost cutting, which continued through the first half of the 1980s as sales skyrocketed. Through 1985, nearly 50 percent of MicroPro's workforce was laid off, then hired back, then laid off again. That maximized revenues and controlled spiraling costs, but critics claim it was short-sighted.

Given the good sales and profit figures during the first half of the 1980s, MicroPro went public in March 1984, raising $13 million. The venture capitalists were thrilled with the quick return on their investment. The bottom line looked good. But, some critics contended, the firm was already living off its past glories.

WordPerfect, meanwhile, continued to improve its product by adding new features. In November 1984 it scored another coup by introducing WordPerfect 4.0, which signaled the beginning of the end for WordStar. WordPerfect 4.0 received great reviews from the computer critics. It was judged to be a better product for the following reasons:

• It ran faster than WordStar.
• It was priced lower.
• It took full advantage of IBM's function keys.
• It continued to integrate additional features, such as the ability to create tables of contents, indexes, outlining, lists, and word counts; it also provided numerous ways to move around the document.
• It came with better documentation.
• Unlike WordStar, there was a tremendous emphasis on customer support, especially an 800 number that allowed users easy and cost-free access to technical support. Access to the 800 number was free and forever. It was expensive, but it paid off.

Sales of WordPerfect soared just as WordStar's fortunes took a turn for the worse. In 1982 WordPerfect had sales of only $1 million (as against WordStar's $22.3 million). The companies crossed paths for good in the mid-1980s, however. In 1985, WordStar experienced its first outright decline in sales (to $42.6 million from $66.9 million a year earlier). In 1986, sales of WordPerfect reached $52.2 million, then in 1987 soared to an astonishing $100 million! WordPerfect has never lost money. In 1986, Satellite Software changed its name to the WordPerfect Corporation in recognition of its blockbuster product.

WordStar was also busy, but on other matters. The favorable sales figures that allowed MicroPro to go public in 1984 at $7 a share promptly turned downward; 1984 would turn out to have been the peak year. The stock price quickly followed suit. Shareholders were disheartened, to say the least. In 1985 they filed a class action suit against MicroPro, claiming that the initial public offering had been fraudulently misrepresented. The suit dragged on for three years. In September 1988 MicroPro refunded nearly $2 million (of the original $13 million) to investors.

Given such distractions, along with its strategic decision to go with Word-Star 2000 Plus, it took MicroPro nearly four years to introduce a new version of the original WordStar that would appeal to its now smaller, but still loyal, installed base of users. In early 1987 MicroPro introduced WordStar 4.0, a product that was good but no better, critics complained, than WordPerfect 4.0. By 1987 WordPerfect's market share was double that of the pioneer—26 percent versus 13 percent. MicroPro started to lose money and users big-time.

Bad times brought more layoffs, a parade of short-lived executives, and continued declines to the once glorious innovator. The best programmers left the firm in droves, and WordStar went through five CEOs between 1983 and the end of the decade. Throughout the second half of the 1980s the firm lost money almost every year.

WordPerfect continued to grow stronger as WordStar grew weaker. By 1991 it was no contest. WordPerfect's market share had grown to 60 percent, while WordStar's share fell to about 10 percent. The innovative former market leader was now struggling to survive. Multimate, the other early entrant, was also struggling.

Distribution advantages had also shifted radically. In 1984 WordStar was sold in almost half the nation's software retailers. By the dawn of the 1990s you had to search to find WordStar. WordPerfect, in contrast, could be bought almost anywhere. In fact, unit sales of WordPerfect's word processor represented 5.7 percent of *all* software sold at retail in 1991.[188]

WordStar failed in its competitive battle with WordPerfect for the following reasons:

- It did not react quickly enough to counter the threat from WordPerfect.
- When it did react, it made the wrong move, in essence abandoning its loyal users. It waited years before bringing out a compatible product. A former CEO of the company admitted: "MicroPro broke the implied promise to the customer: I will support you. I will keep your technology up to date."[189]
- When it did backtrack and offer a compatible product, it ended up com-

peting with itself. Consumers were confused as to whether "WordStar" meant WordStar 2000 or WordStar 4.0.

- It did not support users. As the market for personal computers changed from self-sufficient hobbyists to business users who required extensive technical support, WordStar did nothing. It never understood that shift in consumer behavior.
- It adopted a short-term orientation. It traded current profits for long-term market share. Basically, its strategy for the second half of the 1980s was to cut expenses and reduce the workforce to the lowest levels possible.

It is easy to dissect a business case after the fact. Had MicroPro's strategies worked, the firm would have been hailed as brilliant. But the important point is that WordStar was unable to hold its initial lead. In the words of one expert, Micropro "suffered a lot for being the pioneer."[190]

WordStar continued to restructure into the 1990s. It decided to return to its roots and refocus its efforts on the touch typist. WordStar Professional, the updated version of its original program, was reemphasized and continually updated. WordStar 2000 was deemphasized. Like WordPerfect, MicroPro changed its name from MicroPro to WordStar International. But it is almost certain that the firm will never regain its former glory.

Competition has now shifted to a new set of combatants. The next important change in the word processing software business came in the early 1990s, when the popular Windows gained favor among PC users. Windows is based on graphical/icon selections rather than convoluted keystroke combinations. That change created a problem for WordPerfect, because it has built its reputation on typed commands rather than mouse selections. A change to the Windows system had to be sure to keep the familiar look and feel of the old WordPerfect package, without seeming cumbersome. WordPerfect had learned a valuable lesson from WordStar's early mistakes. It did not want to alienate its loyal customers, as one of the firm's founders made clear: "Those products are intended for existing WordPerfect users, to provide them with an interface and a format that they're familiar with."[191]

The introduction of Windows created an opportunity for a new word processor to gain share against WordPerfect—Microsoft Word. Microsoft Word is designed specifically to take advantage of screen icon selection. It is also offered by the same company that makes and sells the Windows software. WordPerfect was now in the position of rewriting its software to run on a competitor's system. Microsoft tried to integrate Word and Windows as closely as possible.

Microsoft Word was one of the last major entrants. It was introduced in

March 1983 (before Windows) and has been heavily promoted in the print media. It surpassed WordStar in market share at the end of the 1980s.

By 1992 Dataquest Inc. claimed that Word had surpassed WordPerfect to become the number one selling word processing software package for personal computers.[192] Whereas in 1990 WordPerfect held 45 percent of the market versus Word's 32 percent, by 1993 the positions had reversed: Word now held 46 percent while WordPerfect had slipped to 32 percent.

The reasons for WordPerfect's slip in market share were the popularity of the Windows 3.0 environment and the fact that Word was available almost immediately for that version, while WordPerfect took more than a year to perfect its version. An executive at WordPerfect noted: "Sometimes, if you are behind, you must sprint to catch up. Other times you must simply keep up. We view ourselves in a marathon, rather than a sprint. Sprinting doesn't help anyone in this situation. It just wears you out."[193]

Pioneering did not seem to help much either. The very latest entrant—the Microsoft team of Word and Windows—seemed to be inexorably powering its way to the forefront. WordStar, the pioneer, ended with only a small share of the nearly $2 billion market it once dominated. In word processing software, technological and market changes seemed to favor the later entrants and hurt those that were there first. That is the lesson to be learned about word processing.

Patterns of Successful Imitation

Innovations exhibit many common patterns as they make their way from lab to market. The same is true for imitation. This chapter discusses some of the common patterns observed as imitators push their way to market dominance.

THE LONG, LONG USELESS STAGE

In 1935 S. C. Gilfillan concluded that innovations typically get stuck in a long, long useless stage.[1] Once a major new product idea is conceived, it typically takes years, sometimes decades, for the idea to transform itself into a commercially successful product. After more than half a century Gilfillan's findings still ring true. Many innovations still spend years incubating in laboratories and in the marketplace at great expense to a long string of pioneers. Often the pioneer spends heavily only to find that consumers prefer the wares of a later entrant.

There are really two phases to the long, long useless stage. First there is the lag between the time a product is first conceived and the time it first reaches the market. Second, there is the lag between when it is first placed on the market and when it achieves commercial success.

In both instances the problem with pioneering is that it takes enormous staying power to shepherd new products over the long, long useless stage. That provides an advantage for imitators and later entrants, who are able to enter after the pioneer has exhausted himself. The imitator starts fresh, just as the pioneer ends wasted.

Gilfillan conducted a series of studies on the subject. One of them constructed case histories of nineteen of the most important inventions to come into being in the twenty-five years before 1913.[2] The inventions he examined were selected by polling readers of *Scientific American*. Gilfillan found that, on average, fifty years had passed before the first serious work on the invention had resulted in the first important commercial use. He quotes

another researcher, H. S. Hatfield, when referring to the problems presented to pioneers by the long, long useless stage:

> [The pioneer] conceives of a fundamentally new idea, which he feels is assured of startling and immediate success. It is a notorious fact that many if not most of the pioneer inventors to whom the edifice of modern technology owes some of its chief pillars have died in poverty, or if alive, are receiving absolutely no reward at all for the incalculable benefits conferred upon industry by their labors.[3]

It is difficult to pinpoint the precise moment of conception of a new product idea; its first emergence in thought, while theoretically intriguing, can lead to results having slight practical value.[4] More relevant to the topic of pioneering versus imitation is the time lag between first entry and the time a product reaches commercial acceptance. That lag gives an indication of how long the pioneer has to wait (and the imitator has to enter) before demand for the product materializes.

Of the twenty-eight innovations listed in Table 3.1, about half spent more than five years floundering in the market before attracting much consumer interest. Those products are listed in Table 4.1

The other products, those not listed in Table 4.1, caught fire more quickly.

Consider some specific cases of products that spent time in the long useless stage. In light beer, for example, there was a nine-year gap between Rheingold's pioneering entry and the stunning commercial success of Miller's Lite beer. That allowed plenty of time for the pioneer to stumble and the later entrants to learn.

A similar pattern was observed for diet soft drinks. There was at least a ten-year gap between the first commercial entry and the first sustained commercial success. It took even longer for the latest entrants to prevail.

Microwave ovens took even longer to attract large numbers of customers. First invented in 1946, they took ten years to get to market, then twenty years more to gain commercial success. By the time the product became a commonplace fixture in American homes, it was low-cost Asian producers, who had entered last, that dominated the product category—at the expense of the pioneers.

The long, long useless stage tends to work against pioneers and in favor of later entrants. In many cases, either the product is not ready for the market or the market is not ready for the product. Either way, entry turns out to be premature and uneconomic. The pioneer ends up trapped by those products instead of enjoying sustainable competitive advantages. That disadvantage was recognized many years ago, and it still holds true today.

TABLE 4.1
PRODUCTS STUCK IN A LONG, LONG USELESS STAGE

Product	Time Between First Appearance and Commercial Acceptance	Comments
35mm cameras	40 years	The product was introduced in the 1920s, but demand stayed small until the 1960s, when the Japanese reduced prices and brought the product into the mainstream.
Ballpoint pens	8 years	The idea was patented in the late 1800s. The first commercial success occurred in the late 1940s, but not until eight years later did the product overcome its fad status.
Credit/charge cards	8 years	The first charge and credit cards appeared in the 1930s, but Diner's Club started in 1950. It was not until the late 1950s, however, that the product gained widespread acceptance.
Diet soft drinks	10 years	It was not until royal Crown promoted the product that it gained widespread acceptance.
Light beer	9 years	The pioneers spent nearly a decade trying to figure out how to position the product to consumers.
Mainframe computers	10 years	First introduced in 1946, there were only slightly more than 100 computers sold by 1956, the year IBM surpassed Univac.
Microwave ovens	20 years	Discovered in 1946, the first commerical microwave was not introduced until 10 years later. After numerous false starts, it was not until the mid-1970s that microwaves gained widespread acceptance.
Nonalcoholic beer	6 years	Imports lingered on the market for at least six years until consumers valued the benefits offered by the new product.
Paperback books	5 years	Paperbacks have really been around since the Civil War, but in their modern format they started in the 1940s. A number of pioneers failed before consumers became interested.
Personal computers	6 years	The market started with hobbyists, but demand did not explode until IBM entered.
Telephone answering machines	15 years	The market evolved slowly, starting in the late 1950s. Demand did not explode until the mid-1980s.
VCRs	20 years	The first commercial model was introduced in 1956. It was not until 1975 that the home market took off.
Videogames	13 years	Started in 1972, the market boomed, then went bust. Not until 1985, when Nintendo entered, did demand materialize for the long term.
Warehouse clubs	7 years	Sam's Club did not enter until seven years after the Price Club.

A START WITH "ODDBALL" PRODUCTS

In hindsight, many pioneering entries turn out to be "oddball" products, which means they are not fully formed when first brought to market. Often they are technically crude devices based on first-generation technologies. Being little more than first attempts to move a product from the lab to the market, they wear their weaknesses on their sleeve.

Ballpoint pens were rushed to market in the mid-1940s by the Reynolds Pen Company, a small entrepreneurial upstart, and Eversharp, a perennial second-tier player in the then dominant fountain pen industry. The first commercially successful (if short-lived) ballpoints were crude devices that leaked, skipped, smudged, and generally failed to write the way they were supposed to. At a minimum price of $12.50, they were expensive as well as inefficient writing instruments. They were the first and the worst.

The same pattern was observed with videogames. Magnavox Odyssey, the first attempt at a home entry, had extremely crude graphics and required users to hang an acetate sheet on the TV set as a background playing field. Odyssey was odd in comparison with today's games.

Early entry seemed not to help the early entrants. Weaknesses in their products conveyed an "oddball" image that hobbled their efforts instead of providing an early advantage in terms of product positioning. The pioneers paid a heavy price for being first and reaped few benefits beyond a footnote in industry history.

A start with "oddball" innovations points up the incremental nature of innovation. Rarely do inventions spring forth from the lab fully formed without close ties to what has gone before. Instead, technological progress usually takes a series of small steps forward, each step pushing the innovation a little farther ahead and a little closer to market acceptance.

Consider the case of credit and charge cards. Neither innovation burst upon the scene without precedent. Each evolved slowly from the nineteenth-century practice of informally extending credit to valued retail customers whom the merchant knew personally. Throughout the twentieth century, that basic idea evolved slowly into the third-party charge/credit card.

The idea of innovation as an incremental process contrasts with the general tendency to portray innovation as a series of astonishing breakthroughs driven by genius inventors and bold entrepreneurs who dream of radical new product ideas and shepherd them from concept to commercial success. That sometimes happens, but it is rare. The myth of the genius inventor may be part of our cultural heritage, but it is first and foremost a myth.

The business press helps reinforce the myth by portraying innovation as a series of stunning "firsts," whereby bold entrepreneurs, such as Diner's

Club's Francis McNamara, the originator of the first third-party charge card, create and then pioneer brand new markets.

The myth of the genius inventor first became popular during the early years of the twentieth century, when memories of inventors like Eli Whitney and the cotton gin, James Watt and the steam engine, and Thomas Edison and the light bulb colored the popular view of how breakthrough innovations made their way to market. But that view is misleading. It attributes to individual inventors a mythical genius they rarely deserve. Few innovations appear out of nowhere. Almost always there is a long history of small steps that precede, and then follow, the pioneer's product. Products evolve slowly. They don't burst upon the scene without precedent.

The pioneer's product, being the first to enter the market, is almost always ill-formed and flawed. It pays a price for first entry. It almost always enters with one foot still in the lab. Those flaws often allow later entrants to take the next step, leapfrogging the pioneer's "oddball" product with a more workable design.

Consider the case of diet soft drinks. Kirsch entered first with a product targeted to diabetics and teenagers with acne. Kirsch then repositioned the product for women dieters but was quickly followed by Royal Crown, which entered with a mainstream product.

In light beer the earliest entrants, Rheingold's Gablinger's and Meister Brau's Lite, adopted "odd" positions as "diet" beers, which repelled customers and called down the wrath of the FTC. Miller Lite, the first brand to see a sustained surge in sales, avoided those problems and entered with what turned out to be a mainstream product.

The very earliest entrants are often gone from the scene by the time the latest entrants prevail. Their "oddball" products quickly fail, and the firms' contributions recede quickly back into obscurity. That means the true innovators are often forgotten, giving unearned glory to subsequent entrants, who, in a revisionist view of history, are deemed the creators of something they actually copied.

Even in brand-new industries, where change is rapid and innovation is frequent, the earliest entrants are often stuck with "oddball" products that hurt rather than help. In word processors and personal computer spreadsheets, for example, the earliest entrants were stuck with crude packages designed for small-memory machines, which faded in popularity with the obsolete machines for which they were designed. In most instances the first entry is not the best entry. Rushing to market with a pioneering product does not convey the potent competitive advantage advocates say it should. Instead, the pioneer is often stuck with an "oddball" product that was ahead of the market but ultimately behind the times.

TIMING IS EVERYTHING FOR LATER ENTRANTS

Many times, the most successful entrant is not the very first firm to enter but the first to enter when demand explodes. Pioneers may simply be *too* early. They enter before demand materializes, risking what Francisco-Javier Olleros calls "burnout." He contends that "again and again we see industries emerge *over the dead bodies* of early pioneers.[5] Olleros is right. It is easy to enter a nascent market—entry barriers are low to nonexistent—but difficult to survive the long, long useless stage until demand explodes.

Successful imitators have superb timing when it comes to later entry. That timing can be affected by many factors. Some imitators wait until a change occurs in the market—a change that is sure to boost growth—before entering. In the case of nonalcoholic beers, which have been on the market for decades, sales were minuscule for years. In the late 1980s, however, when inebriation became less socially acceptable and the trend against drunk driving accelerated, sales of nonalcoholic beers spurted upward. Now there were sound reasons for consumers to demand nonalcoholic brews. At that time, the major beer sellers moved in and drank from the pioneer's mug, moving quickly to the forefront. The imitators had little to lose by waiting.

A similar pattern afflicted Diner's Club in its battle with American Express. Throughout the early 1950s social mores held that buying on credit was somehow immoral. For nearly a decade Diner's Club was forced to bear singlehandedly the entire burden of persuading consumers to use its new service product. It faced two bad choices: either to change existing attitudes or wait until they changed on their own. The change took eight years. By 1958 consumers had become comfortable with and even attracted to the idea of easy credit. That change corresponded almost perfectly with American Express's entry. Its product carried the gloss of modern sophistication, while Diner's Club was reeling from its eight-year ordeal.

Timing can also be based on changes in the underlying technology. Firms that enter first frequently do so with first-generation technologies that quickly become obsolete. That happened in early personal computers. Few of the pioneers who sold computers based on the Z-80 chip were able to make the switch to the more advanced chip used in the IBM-PC. Those pioneers performed a valuable market function—they created and promoted a new technological product—but they were stuck with the small sales and even smaller profits that come with nascent markets. Their timing was off. They were too early.

Some imitators enter very late in the game. They wait until the potential exists to create a huge market to which they can apply very low-cost production. In microwave ovens, 35mm cameras, and food processors, for ex-

ample, the imitators did not enter until market growth was well under way. They then entered with lower-priced products that drew in additional customers and expanded the market further.

That brings us to the issue of intent. It is too easy to argue that imitators hold back and deliberately wait for a market to form before entering at exactly the right time. That happens sometimes, but not always. To suggest that it does gives the later entrants credit for a talent they often do not possess. In many cases, later entrants just happen to be *in the right place at the right time with the right product.* By sheer chance, they enter just as demand explodes.

Scores of later entrants have benefited from such fortunate circumstances. Nike, for example, was formed on a shoestring in 1964 to sell running shoes to a tiny market of dedicated track athletes. Ten years later, in 1974, sales had climbed only to a paltry $4.8 million. Then the market exploded. Weekend athletes and nonathletes in search of comfortable, casual footwear entered the market in droves. The trend toward health and fitness, which had started in the 1960s, accelerated in the 1970s. Nike found itself in an enviable position: It had the right product in the right place at the right time. By 1976 sales had still reached only $14 million. By the early 1990s they had soared to an astounding $3 billion.

A similar pattern explains the rapid growth of diet soft drinks and low-calorie beer. Demand for both products accelerated when consumers exhibited a newfound interest in a lower caloric diet and the beauty of a slender figure. At that point the large sellers entered just as demand exploded. Their entry was simultaneously a reaction to an emerging trend and an action that fueled that trend.

The same trend affected sales of caffeine-free soft drinks. Sales languished for years, and early brands failed, but demand soared once caffeine was perceived to run counter to the trend toward health and fitness. Once again, the major soft drink sellers entered later but benefited economically from that innovation when the timing was right.

In every one of those cases, the imitator benefited from a rapidly growing market but also caused additional growth. They caused that growth by legitimizing the market. As industry incumbents, the later entrants allayed the fears of cautious consumers. In the case of money market funds, a small pioneer was quickly followed by Dreyfus and Fidelity, and then Merrill Lynch, the industry giants. Once they entered, growth accelerated as mainstream investors poured money into the new investment vehicle. Not only was their entry timed to coincide with a change in the economic environment that favored money market investments, but their entry attracted mainstream investors wary of placing money with small firms with which they were unfamiliar.

INCUMBENT INERTIA

Large market leaders are often the last to see the true potential of innovations that threaten their current product lines. Typically, they let upstarts enter their markets with impunity and are then forced to play catch-up once the magnitude of the opportunity becomes clear. Incumbents, in other words, exhibit inertia when it comes to pursuing products that are natural extensions of their business. Table 4.2 lists twenty cases where innovations were pioneered by minor industry players or industry outsiders but not by incumbents.

There are four reasons for incumbent inertia.

First, market leaders may not perceive the innovation as a real threat. It is often viewed as a short-lived fad that will soon fade back into obscurity. That view is often well founded. Many times there is a long history of failure preceding the latest entry. Incumbents expect the pattern to be repeated by the current pioneer. When the opposite happens, the impact is profound, if unexpected. The backwater product emerges as a major market opportunity that was not recognized by the industry leaders. In those instances, the industry experience hurts rather than helps the incumbents.

Second, incumbents may feel few pressures to move first because they do not have to. They may simply set a strategy of "not being too far behind" should the product take off and show itself to be a real rather than an imaginary opportunity. Incumbents may understand that they can often make up lost ground with advantages in marketing, distribution, and financial resources. Pioneers do not have that option. They must enter first, because their chances of unseating an entrenched market leader are slim if the market leader moves first.

Third, incumbents are slow to see new trends and opportunities because they are short-sighted, defining their markets in terms of specific products rather than broad market needs. Radically new products are not viewed as natural extensions of current product lines but as something foreign and unrelated. The tendency is for incumbents to define their markets narrowly. They exhibit "product provincialism." Critics contend that that is a mistake.

A *fourth,* and related, reason why industry incumbents do not react is that they are reluctant to cannibalize current product lines. They are unwilling to replace surefire winners with risky, unproven new products. Critics contend that such firms are reluctant to engage in "creative destruction," a term popularized by the economist Carl Schumpeter and adopted by others in subsequent decades. The idea of creative destruction is that new products and technological innovations make existing products and technologies obsolete, or at least relegate them to a minor economic role.

TABLE 4.2
EXAMPLES OF INCUMBENT INERTIA

Innovation	Status of Pioneer	Outcome
Ballpoint pens	Industry outsider and minor industry player	None of the major fountain pen sellers—Parker, Sheaffer, or Waterman—entered first. Reynolds, a small, entrepreneurial upstart, pioneered the product, followed closely by Eversharp, a minor industry player.
Caffeine-free soft drinks	Minor industry player	Caffeine-free soft drinks came first from Canada Dry, then from Royal Crown. Only later did Coke and Pepsi enter.
Commercial jet aircraft	Minor industry player	Neither Douglas, the market leader in prop planes, nor Lockheed, another industry player, seemed interested in cannibalizing their existing products. Britain's deHavilland and Boeing, with a strength in military aircraft, were willing to risk early entry.
Diet soft drinks	Minor industry player	Diet soft drinks came from Kirsch, then from Royal Crown. Only later did Coke and Pepsi enter.
Digital watches	Industry outsider	Digital watches were based on electronics technology. The leading Swiss watchmakers did not have expertise in that area and did not respond.
Dry beer	Minor industry player	Dry beer did not initially come from the major American beer brewers. It first came from Japan and was then copied by the Americans.
Food processors	Industry outsider	Food processors did not come from the major appliance sellers but from a small entrepreneurial upstart.
Frozen yogurt	Industry outsider	Frozen yogurt was not pioneered by the major ice cream sellers, even though it should have been viewed as a natural extension of their current business. It was first introduced by small entrepreneurial upstarts.
Herbal teas	Industry outsider	Herbal teas did not come from Lipton. That honor went to Celestial Seasonings, an oddball entrepreneur from the mountains of Colorado.
Inline skates	Industry outsider	Rollerblades, founded by two hockey enthusiasts, created the product. The major ice skating or sporting goods companies did not see much chance for success.
Light beer	Minor industry player	Light beer first came from small regional brewers. Only later was it copied by the industry leaders.
Mainframe computers	Minor industry player	Mainframe computers were not pioneered by IBM or the other office machine suppliers. Sperry Univac was the pioneer.
Money market funds	Minor industry player	This innovation was not pioneered by the major financial houses such as Merrill Lynch, nor was it introduced by the major mutual funds, Dreyfus and Fidelity. Instead, the tiny Reserve Fund of New York was the pioneer.
Mountain bikes	Industry outsider	Individual biking enthusiasts pioneered the product. Schwinn, Huffy, and the other industry giants reacted to the trend long after it began.

TABLE 4.2 (continued)
EXAMPLES OF INCUMBENT INERTIA

Innovation	Status of Pioneer	Outcome
Nonalcoholic beer	Minor industry player	Nonalcoholic beer was the domain of oddball imports and small regional brands. Only years later did the majors show an interest.
Paperback books	Minor industry player	Paperbacks were not introduced by the major publishing houses but were first copied from a British innovation by Pocket Books.
Personal computers	Industry outsider	Personal computers were not pioneered by the major mainframe sellers, such as IBM. Nor were they pioneered by minicomputer sellers, which had entered unchallenged in minis. Personal computers were pioneered by such upstarts as Apple and Osborne.
Pocket calculators	Industry outsider	Calculators did not come from the major sellers of "portable" electromechanicals. Monroe, Sweda, and Friden did not make the switch to the new technology. The assemblers even beat the chip designers, such as TI.
Projection TV	Industry outsider	Projection TV did not come from the major television set manufacturers. Instead, it came from Advent, a small entrepreneurial upstart.
Wine coolers	Industry outsider	Wine coolers were not introduced by the major wine sellers such as Gallo, which later reacted with Bartles & Jaymes. Instead, it was pioneered by California Coolers, a small entrepreneurial upstart.

Creative destruction is a cost of technological progress. It displaces workers in current industries and renders investments in old technology obsolete. It produces long-term economic gains at the expense of short-term costs to individual firms. Creative destruction is inevitable. If incumbents ignore it or, worse yet, try to fight it, someone else will destroy their current product lines for them.

It is easy to argue, with the benefit of hindsight, the firms *should have* engaged in creative destruction, but it is a difficult to call to make before the fact. The reluctance of incumbents to embrace creative destruction is both rational and understandable. Most new products never progress beyond the idea stage. Why should incumbents jeopardize their core products by replacing them with new and unproven ideas, most of which will never amount to anything? It is a risk with an unlikely reward. Take, for example, the oil industry, which was harshly criticized by Theodore Levitt in his landmark 1960 article "Marketing Myopia" for engaging in "product provincialism." Levitt contended that the large oil companies were unwilling to accept the basic tenets of creative destruction. He noted that by focusing solely on a single energy source, oil, the industry "let others steal marvelous opportu-

nities from it."[6] Natural gas, missile fuels, and jet engine lubricants were among the alternative products the oil giants missed. At the time, he advised the major oil companies against an overemphasis on trying to improve hydrocarbon fuels and, instead, to take a broader perspective. What did he recommend? New energy sources, such as battery-powered cars, fuel cells, and solar-powered cars, were the fuels of the future. Levitt predicted (actually he conveyed the prediction of an industry expert) that "solar-powered cars might be common by 1980."

Therein lies the dilemma of creative destruction. By focusing too intently on current products, incumbents typically miss opportunities pursued by more entrepreneurial pioneers with less to lose in the way of current product lines. But, from the market leaders' perspective, it is extremely difficult, and probably impossible, to distinguish between true opportunities and traps that sap their strength. Many incumbents have pursed opportunities that did not pan out, then found their core products weakened and under attack. The wisdom or folly of the incumbent's decision regarding a new technology is only apparent *after the fact*.

THE PIONEER SELF-DESTRUCTS

Pioneers often contribute to their own demise. In many cases, just as the imitator attacks, the pioneer engages in actions that cause it to self-destruct. A careful study of the historical record reveals that often it is the actions of *both* parties that lead to the pioneer's defeat, not solely the aggressive actions of the later entrant.

The finding that pioneers are partly responsible for their own downfall is new but not rare. Although it has seldom been mentioned in previous studies on the success of later entry, a surprisingly large number of pioneers examined in this study clearly hobbled themselves with a host of self-imposed maladies that led directly to their downfall. Those problems included internal legal battles over control of the company, ill-conceived leveraged buyouts, the misfortune of being owned by a financially weak parent, and bitter disagreements between founders who love the product and investors who crave short-term returns.

Consider the first reason why a pioneer self destructs. In some cases, the pioneer is crippled by personal animosities among founders of the pioneering firm. Such personal resentments are common. They are almost to be expected when a small-scale, almost hobbyist endeavor turns quickly into big business. Feuding founders are the dark side of a rapidly growing market. Business decisions and ownership arrangements made under a hobby-

ist's assumptions often return to haunt the principals when the stakes grow large. It is not unusual for the principals to feel cheated and to seek to right perceived wrongs in the courts. Imitators, meanwhile, enter with a different, more realistic set of expectations. They focus on the growing market and are not engaged in internal strife.

VisiCalc, the pioneering spreadsheet for personal computers, was created by a couple of former MIT students. The marketing rights to the package were given to a twenty-eight-year-old entrepreneur who, at the time, sold software out of his apartment. When the product took off and the stakes became high, the makers and seller began to criticize and blame each other for the problems that inevitably crop up in such high-growth situations. With their attention focused on destroying and discrediting each other, there was little time left to compete. Imitators, unencumbered by internal strife, sailed straight ahead, while the pioneers rowed in different directions.

Henry Kloss, the inventor of the first commercially successful projection television, also set out to destroy the company he created. In 1972 his Advent Corporation introduced its first set. By the mid-1970s the sets were selling well, but the company was hemorrhaging money. Advent's board fired the inventor, who promptly started Kloss Video, which introduced competitive products. Kloss himself spoke ill of Advent to the press. By 1981 Advent was gone, Kloss was struggling, and the Japanese owned the market he created.

The flames of personal animosity are often fanned by the founder's desire to cash in on the firm's newfound success. WordStar, the first popular word processing package for personal computers, failed partly for such reasons. After the product became successful, WordStar's creator found himself living a fairly ordinary lifestyle with ordinary trappings, even though he owned a world-class product. He cashed in on his invention by selling part ownership to a venture capitalist. The two co-owners then proceeded to bicker over just about everything at a crucial time in the company's history. WordPerfect surpassed WordStar, in part, because the principals focused on each other while WordPerfect's creator focused on its customers.

A similar fate befell Diner's Club, the first third-party charge card. After the death of its two founders, the remaining owner had control of the firm within his grasp. But he needed money—money he didn't have—to buy out the others' shares. To raise cash he was forced to sell part ownership to a rich corporate partner. The entrepreneur and the corporate giant then began to quarrel endlessly. As they fought, the product fell from grace. A decade later Diner's Club was a shadow of its former self. American Express, meanwhile, soared upward, untarnished by the tussle.

In some cases the pioneer has the misfortune of being owned by a financially crippled parent that cannot provide the funds needed for the pioneer to defend its innovative entry. Ticketron, which held a virtual monopoly in concert ticketing services until the mid-1980s, was attacked by TicketMaster, a small entrepreneurial upstart. Ticketron made a few devastating marketing mistakes that empowered the embryonic rival. When it came time to fight back, Ticketron was impotent. It was owned by Control Data, which had defaulted on its debts about the time of TicketMaster's attack. Needless to say, the financially strapped parent was more concerned with its corporate survival than with the trivial marketing problems of a small subsidiary.

Other pioneers fail because they are the victims of ill-conceived leveraged buyouts. The creator of Cuisinart, the pioneering food processor, seems to have fought with nearly everyone at one time or another. Cuisinart first fought with its French supplier just after the machine became successful. But, most damaging, the firm went through a leveraged buyout that effectively stopped new product introductions and forced the firm to sell machines at any price to raise cash. The pioneer was so busy satisfying its lenders, it had no time to fight off its attackers.

Some pioneers are forced to fight against the short-term interests of venture capitalists who provide needed funds in return for part ownership. WordStar was weakened by this problem. The venture capitalist who ran the company extracted cash to boost short-term return on his investment at the very time when competitors were investing heavily in research and development to modernize their software for the newer, more powerful computers, bolstering their chances of long-term success.

WordStar was also weakened by a shareholder suit. After selling shares to the public at what turned out to be the peak of its success to raise cash for future growth, the fledgling company faced increased competition. Competitors gained market share on WordStar, causing its stock price to fall. Shareholders sued, and the company was forced to fight with its public owners at the worst possible time, a time when it should have been concentrating on its competitors.

Legal battles also besieged the first two ballpoint pen sellers. Instead of incubating the market to sustained growth the earliest sellers—Eversharp and Reynolds—sued each other silly over who stole whose pen idea. The outcome was a draw. The market was a bust. The dickering destroyed the pioneers.

Finally, Britain's deHavilland, which pioneered the first commercial jetliner, faced the ultimate in self-destruction. Its innovative jets may have been first to market, but they were based on a flawed design. They *literally* self-destructed, typically on takeoff, taking the company down with them.

CREATING LEGAL PROBLEMS FOR THE PIONEER

Innovation creates change. Sometimes innovations are so radical that they do not fit into the current way of doing things. Industry giants—those with the most to lose from the success of a radically new innovation—have sometimes slowed or even killed the diffusion of innovations by ensuring that the system will not change to fit the new product. Lawyers and regulators can help (or hinder, depending on your perspective) in that regard.

That is what happened to the first caffeine-free soft drink. Coke felt threatened by Canada Dry's innovative entry. It may have felt that if companies started to remove the unhealthy ingredients in soft drinks there would be little left to sell. According to one assessment (Lee case), Coke persuaded the FDA to rule that Canada Dry's product was illegally labeled. It reasoned that colas are made from cacao beans, which contain caffeine. A cola without caffeine, therefore, could not be a cola at all. It was a brilliant day for regulatory wrangling. Canada Dry's cola was judged to be illegally labeled. It failed and was withdrawn—at least until a few years later, when the majors decided to introduce caffeine-free colas of their own. By that time, even the government itself was urging consumers to avoid high doses of caffeine.

Gablinger's, the first popular diet beer, met with a similar fate. Within a year of its entry the FDA charged it with false and misleading labeling. The suit took particular issue with the implied claim that Gablinger's was a "diet" beer that contained fewer calories. The government's actions were carried out in public, in full view of the eager media, just as the product was starting to attract customers. The alleged fraud, and attendant negative publicity, tainted the product and weakened its chances at market success. Oddly, the government remained silent when the major beer brewers introduced low-calorie beers of their own eight years later.

CAT scanners ran into regulatory problems as well. In the mid-1970s, just as the market was starting to take off, copycats entered in droves. The British pioneer sued its new competitors, claiming they had copied its patented diagnostic machine. Competitors countersued, using the familiar refrain that the pioneer was monopolizing the market. Then the FDA struck. At precisely the worst time, it forced the pioneer to recall its scanners for excessive radiation. The danger to patients was virtually nonexistent. The damage to the pioneer's reputation was more pronounced. From that point on, GE soared to the lead while the pioneer withered.

A more insidious legal pattern was created by Texas Instruments to stop the early gains made by Bowmar, the pioneering entry in pocket calculators. Bowmar may have been first, but TI held the patent for the underlying chip technology upon which the pocket calculator was built. TI supplied the basic

ingredient of Bowmar's products. When TI decided to enter, it merely raised Bowmar's costs while lowering the prices of its own calculators. Bowmar cried foul in the courts but was pushed to the sidelines before the outcome could have any meaningful result. TI used its legal rights to win back the market it had failed to pioneer.

LARGE FIRMS REPLACE SMALL FIRMS

One of the most prominent patterns in the battle between innovators and imitators is for large firms to replace small firms once the market becomes more attractive. That happened in nearly three-quarters of the cases examined in this study. Industry giants, whose current products are challenged by the pioneer's innovative entry, introduce imitative designs and use their market power to push the pioneer to the sidelines.

In the cases examined in this study, size clearly counted as a competitive advantage when it came to market dominance. Smaller firms may be more entrepreneurial, faster-moving, and more insightful—and they are typically the first to spot emerging trends and product opportunities—but it is the large industry leaders who possess the power to muscle their way into emerging markets, which they then quickly dominate.

That happened in both diet and caffeine-free soft drinks, where Coke and Pepsi dominated a market that was pioneered by Royal Crown, which, incidentally, had "borrowed" its innovative idea from even smaller earlier rivals. The incumbents' power ensured that outcome.

An identical pattern was observed with three innovations in the beer industry—light beer, dry beer, and nonalcoholic beer. In each case, the innovation was pioneered by a succession of weak competitors. But when the market showed it true potential the industry giants, especially Anheuser-Busch, jumped in and quickly crushed the innovative pioneers, in some cases pushing them into oblivion. Size proved crucial in beer brewing.

The only cases where that pattern did not hold up were in brand-new industries where there were really no entrenched market leaders to react to the pioneers' entry. In word processors, spreadsheets, and operating systems for personal computers, for example, small firms supplanted other small firms for reasons that had nothing to do with size-based advantages. Since all of the competitors were small entrepreneurial startups, relative market power did not appreciably affect the outcome.

But those cases are more peculiar than they are representative of most markets. A more typical pattern is for a small entrepreneurial startup to invade the turf of a powerful incumbent. The giant is then awakened to an

opportunity that it did not initially see. It counterattacks with an imitative entry and uses its vast market power to fight back. The pioneer is at a disadvantage. It is somewhat like the war with Iraq: The outcome was never in doubt, only the timing and other tactical issues were uncertain.

As Exhibit 4.1 illustrates, nineteen of the twenty-eight cases examined resulted in a large firm's replacing a small entrepreneurial startup. Not a single case was observed where a small firm entered an emerging market with an imitative product after a large pioneering industry leader. The graph shows that (1) large firms most frequently replace small firms, (2) small firms sometimes replace other small firms, (3) large firms sometimes replace other large firms, and (4) small firms rarely (or never) supplant a large market leader.

Given the tendency for larger imitators to supplant smaller startups, the next chapter considers how they do it.

EXHIBIT 4.1
Large Firms Tend to Replace Small Firms

		Imitator	
		Small Firm	Large Firm
Pioneer	*Small Firm*	5 Cases Computerized ticketing services Operating systems Paperback books Spreadsheets Word processors	19 Cases ATMs Ballpoint pens Caffeine-free soft drinks CAT scanners Credit cards Diet soft drinks Dry beer Food processors Light beer Money market funds MRIs Mainframe computers Nonalcoholic beer Personal computers Pocket calculators Projection TV Telephone answering machines Warehouse stores VCRs
	Large Firm	No Cases	4 Cases 35mm cameras Commercial jet aircraft Microwave ovens Videogames

Imitation Strategies

Imitators and later entrants succeed using one or a combination of three strategies. They (1) offer lower prices than the pioneer, (2) sell a superior product, or (3) use their market power to overwhelm the weaker pioneer. Table 5.1 summarizes the strategies used in each of the twenty-eight cases examined in Chapter 3. It shows that in ten cases lower prices played a role in successful later entry, in eleven imitators won with an imitate-and-improve strategy, and in seventeen market power was a factor. There was considerable overlap. More than one strategy was used, by either a single later entrant or a sequence of later entrants, to gain the dominant market position in eight of the cases. In one instance, projection television, the later entrants used all three strategies to surpass the pioneer.

LOWER PRICES

One of the most popular and successful imitative strategies is to sell knock-offs of a pioneer's product at bargain-basement prices. Typically, there are two ways to pursue that strategy: (1) by selling an exact duplicate of the pioneer's product at a reduced price, or (2) selling a trimmed-down, bare-bones version at a *much* lower price. What both strategies have in common is that they attempt to expand the market into the mainstream, attracting consumers who would otherwise be unwilling to pay the high prices demanded by the pioneer.

Lower Costs Equal Lower Prices

The essence of a lower-price imitation is to keep costs low, passing those savings along to consumers. As noted in Chapter 2, the imitator sometimes has an advantage when it comes to lower costs, being able to avoid the heavy up-front costs associated with research and development. The imitator merely copies a product that already exists. The innovator has had to create that product from scratch.

TABLE 5.1
HOW IMITATORS SURPASSED PIONEERS

Product	Lower Prices	Imitate-and-Improve	Market Power
1. 35mm cameras	X	X	
2. Automated teller machines (ATMs)			X
3. Ballpoint pens	X	X	
4. Caffeine-free soft drinks			X
5. CAT scanners (computed axial tomography)		X	X
6. Commercial jet aircraft		X	
7. Computerized ticketing services		X	
8 Credit/charge cards			X
9. Diet soft drinks			X
10. Dry beer			X
11. Food processors	X		
12. Light beer			X
13. Mainframe computers			
14. Microwave ovens	X		
15. Money-market mutual funds			X
16. MRI (magnetic resonance imaging)	X		X
17. Nonalcoholic beer			X
18. Operating systems for personal computers		X	X
19. Paperback books			X
20. Personal computers	X		X
21. Pocket calculators	X		
22. Projection television	X	X	X
23. Spreadsheets		X	
24. Telephone answering machines	X		X
25. VCRs	X	X	
26. Videogames		X	
27. Warehouse clubs			X
28. Word processing software		X	

Lower price-point imitators also save on promotional expenditures. In many cases they are able to catch a free ride on the pioneer's ads and positioning. The pioneer may have created interest in the product category—VCRs, microwave ovens, and food processors, for example—but when the consumer visits a retailer to make a purchase, he or she is often drawn to lower-priced imitations, which are perceived to be of acceptable if not equal quality.

Some imitators create the impression that they sell the same product or service as the innovator, but at lower prices. That practice infuriates competitors. Consider the case of Helene Curtis, whose Suave shampoo built its name in the 1970s by bootstrapping on the ads of the leading brands. At the time, Helene Curtis sought to gain market share by advertising Suave as

follows: "We do what theirs does for less than half the price." Competitors were livid. Their response: "It's parasitic to leech off the reputations and advertising of established brands."[1] That may be so, but it is often an effective entry strategy. Suave's sales rocketed skyward as a result of lower prices.

Suave's experience is not unique. Similar price-point strategies have proved successful in nearly every consumer product category. They offer consumers a less expensive alternative to the leading national brands. Their appeal is almost always the same: similar quality at lower prices. The imitator lets the leader do the bulk of the advertising, then seeks to steal sales with lower prices.

Another case of successful price-point imitation is Malt-O-Meal. An old-line, minor player in the breakfast cereal business, it cannot hope to compete with the industry giants—Kellogg, General Mills, and Quaker—on innovation. Instead, its strategy is to sell knockoffs of popular cereal brands at much lower prices.[2] How similar are Malt-O-Meal's cereals to those of its larger competitors? Its Toasty O's are nearly identical to General Mills' Cheerios, its Tootie Fruities are near exact copies of Kellogg's Froot Loops, and its Crisp 'n Crackling Rice even sounds like Rice Krispies. Sold in bags rather than more expensive boxes, the price of the imitations averages about half that of the major leading brands.

Timing Entry to Match Market Growth

Timing is an essential ingredient in the success of price-point imitations. Successful imitations have had the good fortune of entering—either by chance or by design—just as the market has grown larger and more price-sensitive. Price-point imitations often succeed because they match their less expensive wares to the needs of an expanded mass market, which is less enamored of top-of-the-line models and is unwilling to pay the high prices demanded by the pioneer.

In food processors, Cuisinart, the innovative pioneer, sold a product that for years was nearly synonymous with the entire product category. In the early years, cooking aficionados fell in love with Cuisinart's expensive, feature-laden machine. But that small market segment was soon saturated. Cuisinart, a small firm that lacked resources, ran into sales resistance when average consumers, who did not need the myriad features its product offered, were unwilling to pay the high prices charged. That created an opportunity for the traditional kitchen appliance giants to offer bare-bones devices at much lower prices. Sunbeam took Cuisinart's idea down market with its $60 "Oskar," which served the mass market. Cuisinart ended up stuck at the high end.

What happened to Cuisinart may be extreme, but the nature of the knock-offs it faced is by no means unusual. A similar pattern occurred in microwave ovens, VCRs, and a host of other product categories, where price-point imitators succeed by serving a larger group of mainstream customers who were not aficionados and were put off by high prices. In every instance, the pioneer found itself stuck at the high end of the market as a result of actions taken by an imitator who offered lower-priced, generic goods. Time played a key role. The later entrant's product both benefited and caused the emergence of a mass market.

Telephone answering machines were pioneered by Code-A-Phone in 1958. When the product caught fire in the 1980s, nearly twenty-five years after it was first created, the later entrants moved production overseas, lowered prices, and pushed their way to the forefront with imitations of equal, if not superior, quality. Code-A-Phone was the last major seller to move production overseas. By the time it reacted, it was too late. The pioneer was a shadow of its former self.

Making the Product Generic

When technological products are involved, the success of price-point imitation depends on the extent to which the product has been standardized. Product designs and the underlying technology must "stand still" before the product can be successfully copied. The reason is simple. It is difficult to knock off a new product that is quickly changing form. In such instances, the imitator is always one step behind the innovator. By the time the imitator moves in, the pioneer has moved elsewhere. Not until the technology settles down can the imitator readily copy it.

Later entrants can benefit from the passage of time, rather than be hurt by it. That is because in the early years of a new technological product there are many competing standards and formats. Competition consists mostly of product innovation, where each seller offers a proprietary design. Eventually, however, a dominant design emerges, which determines what the product will look like. Once that occurs, radical product innovation gives way to incremental product evolution. Small improvements tend to be made in existing designs, changes that can be made by imitators and innovators alike. More important, the focus of innovation shifts from product innovation to process innovation. Price competition becomes more important, as producers seek to lower costs and prices. At that point there is an opportunity for price-point imitators.

Consider what happened to IBM in personal computers. In the late 1970s

and early 1980s small, entrepreneurial, made-in-the-garage pioneers sold crude personal computers based on proprietary standards. Throughout the first half of the 1980s, Asian knockoff artists, including the Japanese electronics giants, had almost no success in selling personal computers. Some of the industry analyses of the day exuded confidence that American manufacturers of personal computers would not go the way of American consumer electronic firms. The business was just too different. Or so it seemed. In reality, the Asian knockoff artists were hindered by the lack of a technological standard. By the time they copied a popular model—such as the Z-80, CP/M machines—the technology would change, leaving them with lower-priced obsolete goods that nobody wanted.

All that changed once IBM's popular personal computer emerged as the industry standard. Price-point imitators now had a stationary target to shoot at. And shoot they did. From that point on, Asian and American copycats alike offered products nearly identical to IBM's but at much lower prices. In fact, the entire product category became a generic where price was the key factor. As a result, much later entrants ended up dominating the PC market.

A similar pattern was observed in microwave ovens. Once the product became a generic commodity, Korean producers, starting from scratch, moved in, manufactured knockoffs of the most popular ovens cheaply with lower-cost labor, and sold them at much lower prices. Even though they entered last, the Korean sellers ended up as market leaders.

That pattern has been observed in industry after industry. Time and time again, price-point imitators have been able to dominate markets even though they entered much later than the pioneer. In 35mm cameras, VCRs, pocket calculators, and many other product categories, once the product became standardized, low-cost producers turned their efficient manufacturing skills toward the newly expanded market and ended up dominating it with much lower prices.

A Two-Step Imitation Process

It is the very last round of entrants who are most likely to succeed with price-point imitations. Often a two-step imitation process, as illustrated in Exhibit 5.1, can be observed.

In the first step of the imitation process, the pioneer is challenged by either knockoff artists selling at lower prices or later entrants who follow the pioneer to market with a superior product. Either strategy can work.

The second step occurs much later, sometimes years later, when a second group of imitators enters the market with still lower-priced knockoffs, which

EXHIBIT 5.1
A Two-Step Imitation Process

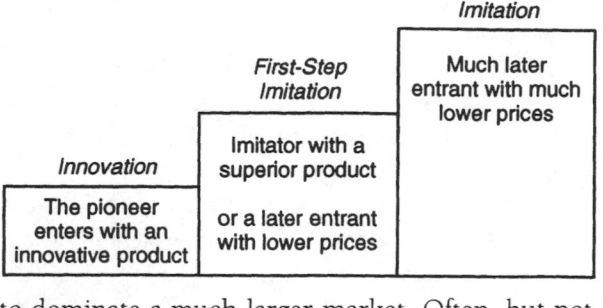

then go on to dominate a much larger market. Often, but not always, this group of later entrants comprises low-cost Asian producers with an eye toward export markets.

Many examples of the two-step imitation process can be cited. Pocket calculators were pioneered by a number of small assemblers who spotted a market opportunity before the electronics giants who made the integrated circuits used in early calculators. Second into the market were those integrated circuit manufacturers, who observed the success of the early pioneers and then quickly entered with products of their own, a move that crushed the pioneers. But as calculators moved from a specialty product used by engineering students and other small market segments willing to pay the high prices charged, low-cost Asian copycats mobilized their manufacturing muscle and sold millions of cheap, highly reliable calculators to the masses for a few dollars each.

A nearly identical two-step imitation process occurred in digital watches. The small pioneers were driven from the market by a second group of entrants. Then, as the market expanded, low-cost Asian copycats combined much later entry with much lower prices to dominate a much larger market.

The same pattern was also observed in microwave ovens, which were pioneered by American firms, then challenged by Japanese sellers using lower prices soon after the product became popular with consumers. Eventually, however, the market was dominated by even lower-cost producers from Korea, who sold strictly on the basis of lower prices.

Ballpoint pens also experienced a two-step imitation process. The two initial pioneers were an entrepreneurial startup and a weak industry incumbent. Both were replaced by the industry leaders in the related fountain pen business, particularly Parker Pen. Then, nearly fifteen years after the pioneers first entered, Bic transformed the market by once again selling low-priced generics, essentially disposable pens, which were sold by the bagful strictly on the basis of price.

Even well-heeled pioneers are vulnerable to attack by price-point imitators. A case in point is Intel, whose innovative microprocessors, the heart of personal computers, are perpetually challenged by lower-priced generics from Advanced Micro Devices (AMD) and others.

Intel's troubles began in 1982, when it granted AMD a license to clone its early microprocessors. At first that decision helped Intel overcome supply problems. But eventually the help turned to hurt. By 1991 Intel's 286 microprocessors had become generics. And, as *Business Week* noted, "the smaller company ultimately ran past Intel."[3] AMD held 52 percent of the 286 market, while Intel, the innovator, held only 33 percent.

Intel was a natural target for clones. It kept prices high and earned extraordinary margins, which attracted competitors. Even though the cloners had higher costs, they could sell for less than Intel and still make a profit. Intel's strategy was not to compete on price. It focused on innovation. When the cloners started to move in, Intel would introduce the next generation microprocessor.

That is exactly what happened in 1987, when Intel prepared to introduce its 386 microprocessor. AMD's success with the 286 made Intel question whether it really needed a designated second source. The answer was a resounding no. Intel denied AMD the legal right to clone the 386. AMD counterattacked on two fronts. First it sued Intel, claiming it had the rights to the 8086 and 80286 chips and therefore also had the rights to the 386 chip. Second, AMD hedged its bets: Just in case its legal case fell apart, AMD set out to copy and improve upon Intel's 386 chip.

AMD's copycat microprocessor—also named the 386—was first shipped in March 1991. It was cheaper and faster, and used less power, than Intel's chip, a coveted feature in laptops, the fastest-growing segment of the market.

Intel sued AMD over the use of the name 386, which it claimed was a protected trademark. Eventually, but only after many millions of dollars in legal fees, AMD won the right to use the 386 name and retained the right to clone Intel's microprocessor. AMD then set out to surpass Intel as the number one 386 seller, a goal it achieved shortly afterward. AMD's strategy was simple: It sold a superior product at a lower price.

But low prices often beget even lower prices. Not unexpectedly, AMD was soon challenged by the entry of even lower-cost producers, such as Chips & Technology and Cyrix, who had little overhead and even less invested in R&D, and, most important, took advantage of extremely low-cost Asian production. Those firms and others were able to sell at even lower prices than AMD. In fact, their entry caused a price war. AMD's colorful chairman, Jerry Sanders, was outraged by the tactics of the latest entrants. His lament: "I sell genuine copies; those guys sell fake copies."[4]

The Only Choice for Much Later Entrants

Imitators with lower prices are not necessarily restricted solely to the very last stages of entry, but other strategies seem not to succeed as well that late in the game. Advocates of pioneering are right when they claim that later entrants are at a severe competitive disadvantage when they enter that long after the pioneer. But that claim holds true only *when all other things are equal*, a condition that rarely holds with successful later entrants. Firms that sell generic products at much lower prices to a much larger market are often able to negate the pioneer's lead.

IMITATE-AND-IMPROVE

Some imitators succeed by being "second but better." Such later entrants do not seek to clone the pioneer's product. Nor do they seek to compete on the basis of lower prices. Instead, their strategy is to improve upon the pioneer's design and to hope that consumers will prefer a superior design to early entry. As Table 5.1 illustrates, in fifteen of the twenty-eight case histories later entrants succeeded by using an imitate-and-improve strategy.

Technological Leapfrog

When technological products are involved, an imitate-and-improve entry strategy typically takes the form of a "technological leapfrog." In such cases the imitator enters with a second-generation technology that eclipses the pioneer's product, rendering it obsolete.

In projection television, the innovation was created in 1973 by Henry Kloss, an American inventor and industry pioneer. In the early 1970s his front-projection systems sold well, but by the 1980s the tables had turned. Later entrants introduced rear-projection designs that eliminated the need for bulky projection units sitting in the middle of a customer's living room. By the mid-1980s rear projection units outsold front-projection units six to one. But the pioneer did not make rear-projection units. Kloss was stuck on an obsolete standard that served a shrinking market.

The case of projection televisions illustrates that the setting of early standards sometimes offers an opportunity for a technological leapfrog. The pioneer, by virtue of first entry, may have bet on an inferior standard, which proves difficult to switch away from once the technology advances. Sunk assets and experience in the first-generation technology may hold the pioneer back.

Two other cases in which later entrants leapfrogged pioneers stuck on an inferior standard are word processors and spreadsheets. Later entrants were able to surpass pioneers because they did not enter until the memory capacity of personal computers had grown large enough to support full-featured programs. In the end, the pioneers were caught with crude programs purposely designed to match the limited capacity of early computers. As a result, WordPerfect and Lotus moved ahead while Word-Star and VisiCalc were stuck on an old standard into which they had sunk considerable assets. They were forced to rejigger their products, while the imitators had a fresh start.

Aside from the purely economic reasons, a pioneer is often reluctant to adopt the latest standard because of emotional ties as well. To switch to another standard, especially a standard set by a later entrant, is implicitly to admit defeat. At the very least, it is an affront to the pioneer's pride. Pride and sheer stubbornness often keep pioneers loyal to the old design long after they should.

That happened in the case of Sony's Betamax VCR versus JVC's VHS format. After the vast majority of the world's sellers had switched to the VHS standard, Sony stayed loyal to its own offspring. Sony argued that the picture quality of the Beta was better.

Disposable diapers sold in Japan offer another example. Disposable diapers were pioneered in the United States by Procter & Gamble. Actually, the product had been around for decades, but early models like Chux, Drypers, Klienerts, and KDs were inefficient and expensive. Parents therefore used them only when there was no other option, such as when traveling.

Until the mid-1960s disposable diapers accounted for only 1 percent of total diaper sales and service. P&G changed all that in 1965 when it started selling Pampers nationally. Pampers virtually replaced commercial diaper cleaning services for a generation of parents. As a result, P&G dominated the disposable diaper market until the late 1980s, when Kimberly Clark's Huggies gained share with a superior design of its own.

P&G also pioneered the Japanese market for disposable diapers in 1977, which earned it a 90 percent share of the market. But in 1982 Japan's Uni-Charm Corporation copied the product and improved upon it by using gel rather than paper pulp absorbent. One year later, in 1983, the giant Japanese soap seller Kao Corporation followed with its own line of disposables under the Merries label. P&G stuck with the old standard until 1985, long after it should have. Its loyalty cost it dearly. By the mid 1980s market leadership had changed hands. Uni-Charm held 50 percent of the market, while Kao had 30 percent and P&G fell back to 15 percent. The pioneer became a victim of technological leapfrogging.

Is Fast Second Entry Important?

Implicit in an imitate-and-improve strategy is the belief that later entrants should react quickly to the pioneer's first move. Time is of the essence, advocates argue. Instead of trying to replace a standard set by the pioneer, a fast second entry tries to gain share before the pioneer has had a chance to impose its standard on the marketplace.

In VCRs, for example, Sony's early success with the Beta format was quickly countered by Matsushita's VHS format, which played longer and was priced lower. The fast second entry of VHS occurred before the Beta standard could be established. That is one reason why it was successful.

The case of VCRs, however, is unique. While widely touted as the essential ingredient of later market entry, only a few examples of "fast second" imitations were observed in the twenty-eight cases examined in this study. More often than not, a fast second century did not seem to be that important for the success of an imitate-and-improve strategy. Time was not of the essence.

The most important success factor seemed to be the extent to which changes in the product, its underlying technology, or the market presented an opportunity for imitators to improve. In other words, it was not how quickly the imitator followed that mattered, but whether there was *an opportunity to enter* with a better product. It also helped if the pioneer made errors.

What happened in computerized ticketing services is typical. TicketMaster, a much later entrant, took the lead from Ticketron by offering customers a superior software package providing customized reports that the pioneer was too arrogant and unwilling to provide. TicketMaster's opportunity came not from its fast second entry but from an opportunity created by the pioneer's unwillingness to give customers what they wanted.

The same pattern was observed in ballpoint pens. While the pioneers rushed to market with flawed, premature products, the later entrants waited years until they could perfect the technology and offer customers a superior product. The pioneers were long gone by the time the imitators entered—victims of a technological leapfrog.

The opportunity to imitate and improve upon the pioneer's product is frequently available to the later entrant. It is well documented that pioneers rarely get everything right on the first try. In their rush to enter first, pioneers often make what in hindsight turn out to be mistakes in product design, segments served, or promotional appeals. By definition, most nascent markets are poorly formed and not well understood. It is virtually impossible for the pioneer to foresee clearly and in detail how the market and product

technology will unfold. That suggests that imitators often have an opportunity to learn from mistakes made by the pioneer and to correct them.

In commercial jet airliners, deHavilland's Comet, the pioneering entry, was riddled with defects that jeopardized passenger safety as well as the product's long-term prospects. Boeing was able to leapfrog the pioneer with a fuselage design that was far superior to that of the Comet—one that did not break up in midair. It was inevitable that deHavilland would encounter some design problems, which would give Boeing an opportunity to leapfrog.

Previous studies have frequently found that later entrants with the opportunity to imitate and improve are easily able to gain share on the pioneer. In cigarettes, for example, one study found: "Later entry brands which were early to take advantage of growing market trend or which were significantly differentiated were often able to gain a 'toehold' within the submarket, and some were able eventually to dislodge the first entrant brand from the dominant position."[5]

Another empirical study, one that found generally in favor of pioneers, concluded: "The results indicate that when a later entrant has a major product advantage, important share gains are possible."[6] That study, however, found that the opportunity to imitate and improve was not always available to later entrants.

The Importance of Staying Technologically Current

Another important success factor in an imitate-and-improve strategy is the presence of an ongoing research and development program. Later entrants should not have to start from scratch. In personal computers, projection television, and VCRs, to name but a few of the products examined, every one of the later entrants had extensive research efforts under way at the time of the pioneer's initial entry. Their work on technology had paralleled the pioneer's efforts. They simply were not the first to enter.

MARKET POWER

In theory, pioneers erect impenetrable barriers to entry that keep copycats at bay. In practice, however, those barriers are weak to nonexistent when matched against the sheer market power held by well-heeled industry giants whose existing products are challenged by the pioneers' innovative entry. The incumbents may not have the foresight of their smaller but quicker-moving challengers, but when they decide to move into a market they do so with unparalleled strengths that many times overwhelm the pioneer.

Market power was the most frequent reason why imitators were able to supplant pioneers. In seventeen of the twenty-eight cases examined, large later entrants muscled their way past more innovative pioneers using sheer market power.

Industry leaders possess three potent strengths that they can use to fight back against the pioneer:

1. Large industry leaders have the *marketing clout* to promote their imitative products. They can also have the respected brand names, coveted reputation, and existing customers to help their products gain share.
2. Incumbents have *existing distribution channels* into which they can place their imitative products.
3. Finally, incumbents have the *financial resources* to make the business grow, an advantage smaller pioneers often cannot match.

Consumers also benefit from the incumbents' entry. When brand-new technological products are involved, customers can rest assured that industry giants are likely to survive the shakeout that will occur once the market matures. Buying early entries from unknown pioneers entails a high degree of consumer risk.

Advocates of pioneering underestimate the effect of marketing power. They mistakenly assume that first-mover advantages are on a par with marketing power. They are not. Of course, the imitator must shout louder than the pioneer. But the imitator *can* shout louder and, by doing so, can overcome the pioneer's early lead. In the majority of the cases considered in this study, large industry leaders with well-known brands had no trouble shouting louder—and then shouting down—smaller, weaker pioneers. Size, in other words, had a lot to do with who won the battle. The *Wall Street Journal* noted some years ago: "David seldom defeats Goliath on the corporate battlefield."[7]

The importance of market power has received support from previous studies. One study compared the relative potency of market power versus pioneering. Four variables were examined. Two had to do with market power: (1) advertising and (2) positioning. The other two had to do with pioneering: (3) order of entry and (4) lag between entries. The study focused on inexpensive, frequently purchased drugstore and supermarket products. It found: "The positioning variable has the greatest impact on share, followed by advertising and order of entry."[8] The "lag between entries" variable was insignificant. In other words, the two marketing variables were more important than the two pioneering variables.

The authors conclude: "The results of our analysis imply a significant

market share penalty for later entrants,"[9] but their finding assumes that pioneers and later entrants spend the same amount on advertising. The authors themselves go on to note that "the second brand will . . . earn less than three quarters of the share of the pioneering brand if its advertising and positioning *are equal.*"[10] That turns out to be a big if. It suggests that later entrants can overcome the pioneers' lead by spending more on advertising. In fact, the findings suggest that since "advertising" and "positioning" have stronger effects on market share than "order of entry" or "lag between response times," a focus on them, rather than on pioneering, may result in higher market share. The authors state this point clearly: "If the pioneer does not carefully design its product and an improved product is subsequently introduced and aggressively promoted by a competitor, the market share reward for innovation may be lost."[11]

Another study found that existing brand names helped large industry leaders gain ground on pioneers.[12] It found that large companies with well-known brands tend to enter markets later than startups, who enter with previously unknown brands. After looking at ninety-six brands in eleven product categories, the author concludes that larger later entrants can easily make up lost ground by attaching a popular brand name to an imitative new product. After a while the market share of the brand extension, which entered later, turns out to be about the same as that for the pioneering product.

Finally, the power of marketing is magnified when imitators are able to combine superior marketing capabilities with a superior product. One study, which reviewed the empirical evidence on first-mover advantages, concluded: "The combination of a superior product with superior marketing effort, finally, is *the most powerful entry strategy for a follower.*"[13]

Moving In from an Allied Area

Sales of new products almost always impinge upon sales of existing products. The problem for pioneers begins when their new product steals sales from the wares of an industry giant with expertise in marketing and the money to fight back. The industry giant may have missed the new product opportunity created by the pioneer, but once the potential of the pioneer's product becomes apparent, the incumbent will rely on its expertise in selling and distributing similar products to push the pioneer out of the way and dominate the new category. There is an advantage to "bigness" in imitative later entries. The pioneer may have made a large leap forward by creating a brand-new product, but the powerful incumbent has only to make a short leap sideways from its current products to the new related ones.

Telephone answering machines were pioneered in the late 1950s by Code-

A-Phone, anything but an industry giant. For years the small firm toiled to perfect its pioneering product. But by the 1980s, when the market had grown huge and attractive, its efforts counted for little. Its barriers to entry were virtually nonexistent against the likes of AT&T and Panasonic, which moved in and dominated the market.

Ditto for automated teller machines, money market funds, warehouse clubs, CAT scanners, MRIs, and dozens of other product categories. In every case, a small, entrepreneurial startup pioneered the market, only to lose it when the giants marched in.

Most Effective Where Advertising and Distribution Are Key

Not unexpectedly, the imitator's advantage is greatest in those product categories where advertising and distribution are most important. Small pioneers who rush to market with innovative entries face the worst odds of all in such circumstances. Two industries in particular, beer and soft drinks, have a long history of new market opportunities opened up by small producers while the biggest sellers stood by. Then, when the market proved attractive, the industry giants muscled their way in with superior advantages in promotion, distribution, and money to push the pioneers to the sidelines. The pattern has been repeated time and time again. It is a depressing picture for dedicated pioneers who enthusiastically pursue new product opportunities but have little real chance of success once the market grows larger.

The undisputed innovator in soft drinks over the past thirty years has been Royal Crown, which introduced (or at least popularized) diet cola, caffeine-free cola, and cherry cola. In every case, its success attracted Pepsi and then Coke (typically in that order), which were able to dominate those markets quickly and decisively once they decided to do so. There was never really any doubt about the outcome. Royal Crown's resources were minuscule compared with those of the industry giants. The idea that this tiny firm could erect entry barriers or concoct some conceptual competitive advantages solely on the basis of first-mover advantages is pure fantasy.

The same pattern has been followed in the beer industry. Once again, major innovations have not come from the industry giants but from the second- and third-tier players. Light beer, nonalcoholic beer, and dry beer were all pioneered by small firms. The incumbents then introduced imitations of those pioneering products and went on to dominate the industry.

A third industry—financial products—also proved receptive to later entry by industry giants with a potent combination of imitative products and market power. In both charge cards and money market funds, later entrants bullied their way past smaller pioneers.

In charge cards, a small, weak entrepreneurial startup pioneered the product. It took quite a few years, however, before the product caught on. Once it did, American Express entered with a pocketful of cash and a respected reputation, both of which were generated by its traveler's check business. Diner's Club had far more meager resources. It lacked money in a business where cash was the primary product.

Reputation played a prominent role in the emergence and ultimate dominance of money market funds by the major financial products companies. Money market funds were pioneered in the early 1970s by the tiny Reserve Fund of New York. Once the funds caught on, however, the major sellers of mutual funds, in particular Dreyfus and Fidelity, moved in and dominated the market. When the dust settled, the Reserve Fund of New York was left with a minuscule share of the market.

Beating Back Innovative Imports with Market Power

Marketing and distribution advantages have helped some American firms win back markets initially dominated by Japanese pioneers. In at least two of the cases encountered in this study—disposable cameras and dry beer—Japanese firms introduced innovations that were copied by American firms, which ended up with the dominant market share.

Dry beer was first launched in Japan by Asahi, a minor Japanese brewer, in 1987. It was an overnight success and was quickly copied by Kirin, Sapporo, and Suntory, the Japanese brewing giants. Asahi, along with its copycat compatriots, then sought to replicate its success in American markets, but Anheuser-Busch quickly countered the Japanese entry with copies of its own. In 1988 it introduced Michelob Dry, then followed with Bud Dry in 1989. It was never much of a contest. Anheuser-Busch's massive distribution system overwhelmed the pioneering foreign competitors, who were set up to serve Japanese restaurants and other low-volume specialty markets. Besides, Anheuser-Busch had the money, the promotional expertise, and well-known brand names. It was quickly apparent that the dry beer market would not go the way of the American auto or consumer electronics industries. The pioneers were shut out of the market by an aggressive and competent domestic seller who reacted quickly with an imitative entry.

A virtual replay of those circumstances occurred in disposable cameras. It started in 1986 when Fuji film introduced an inexpensive throwaway camera in the Japanese market. The camera was basically a roll of film in a cardboard case with a crude lens built in. At the time most experts thought the product had little chance of success. Most consumers, they reasoned, already owned quality cameras and for years the trend had been away from low-

priced convenience cameras, such as those that had been offered every ten years or so by Kodak (e.g., the Brownie, the Instamatic, and the failed Disc camera line). Instead, consumers had moved en masse to higher-priced, higher-quality 35mm cameras. Disposables seemed to take a giant step in the wrong direction. But when sales soared to $200 million in 1992, Kodak jumped in. Kodak's advantage in distribution seemed to matter more than Fuji's first-mover advantage. By 1992 Kodak held 65 percent of the throw-away camera market, while Fuji held only 25 percent.

In sum, the evidence shows that there is a *tendency* for pioneering to lead to market dominance. But that tendency is weak and can be negated by later entrants selling at lower prices, offering superior product designs, or possessing sheer marketing power.

Competitive Aspects of Imitation

Competition in emerging markets is often an interesting mix of innovation and imitation. The case of running shoes is instructive. For all practical purposes the market began in the late 1950s, when Germany's Adidas started selling its innovative high-quality running shoes in the United States. Adidas quickly emerged as the overwhelming market leader. Its success attracted copycats. In Oregon, Phil Knight, a former track star, prevailed upon Japan's Tiger to give him the right to sell its shoes in America. By the mid-1960s, Knight was selling Tiger's "imitation Adidas shoes. [The Tiger shoe] looked like an Adidas shoe, but it had a light cushion in the sole that Adidas didn't."[1] Tiger even mimicked the Adidas trademark, which was not legally protected. The Japanese copy used three "nonparallel" stripes on its shoes, while Adidas used three parallel stripes. But then the imitator was copied. A decade later, when Tiger threatened to revoke Knight's distribution franchise, Knight introduced a virtually identical copy of Tiger's best-selling Cortez running shoe under the brand name Nike, which he also called the Cortez. There were now two Cortez running shoes—one by Tiger and one by Nike. Tiger sued, claiming, in essence, that Nike had copied its product. A few years later Nike turned innovative. It pioneered airsole inserts in its running shoes, a technology that had been turned down by Adidas. That innovation was then widely copied by almost every other competitor, including Tiger's Asics line. Competitors tried to imitate and improve upon Nike's airsoles by introducing "gel" inserts, as Tiger did, or by adding other gizmos and gadgets to produce every conceivable variation on Nike's original design. In running shoes, as in many other markets, there has been a continual interplay between innovation and imitation.

Understanding the dynamics of competitive imitation is important to both pioneers and later entrants. Whereas imitators seek weaknesses that will allow them to enter successfully, pioneers adopt defensive actions that minimize that threat. This chapter looks at some of the ways in which competitive advantage can be gained or lost.

OPPORTUNITIES FOR IMITATION

The opportunities for imitation are greatest when one or some combination of the following factors is present.

When Small Firms Pioneer New Markets

There is an inherent mismatch in the market power held by small pioneers versus large later entrants. When that mismatch is present, it is easier for imitators to make up for later entry. Unlike the biblical tale of David and Goliath, in most cases of competitive imitation the giant prevails over the small upstart.

Small pioneers are further weakened by the fact that they must grow rapidly to meet surging demand. That growth creates a "pioneer's dilemma," which offers an opportunity to larger later entrants. In other words, the small pioneer must choose between two courses of action.

For one, they can manage internal growth in an attempt to regulate how fast the firm grows. That solves the internal control problems that have destroyed so many fast-growing firms, but it creates another problem: It allows excess demand to fall easily into the hands of later entrants. Pioneers who restrict the rate at which they grow thus provide an opportunity for competitors to enter their markets unchallenged.

That is what happened to the Price Club, which pioneered the concept of warehouse retailing. It chose to restrict the rate at which it grew so that it would avoid many of the problems encountered by failed pioneers that had grown too quickly. Price Club focused on the Southern California market. As the appeal of warehouse shopping grew, later entrants, such as WalMart's Sam's Club, easily entered geographic areas where the Price Club did not compete and then went on to dominate the industry.

The alternative option is for pioneers to grow quickly with the expanding market they seek to serve. The idea is to leave no unserved demand for later entrants. But fast growth is always traumatic and sometimes fatal. The business press is littered with examples of the wreckage of small firms that could not manage rapid growth. Those pioneers flew apart because they could not maintain internal control.

Both Reynolds and Eversharp, the pioneers of ballpoint pens, fell victim to that side of the pioneer's dilemma. They expanded quickly to meet exploding demand for their newfangled products. Quality suffered, and both companies were forced to make good on the ironclad guarantees they had hastily offered. Both firms paid with their lives. Later entrants then moved in and

took over the product category. The two pioneers were fortunate to have found a fast-growing market, but the seeds of their destruction were buried within that opportunity.

In the Absence of Patents, or When Patents Can be Circumvented

Although there has been a clear trend over the past decade to protect intellectual property rights, patents still afford much less protection than might be expected. One study found that patent protection explained little in the way of market share gains among pioneers. "Only 21% of the pioneers claim a significant benefit from either a product patent or trade secret."[2] The reason patents afford so little protection is that there are so many ways to get around them.

The first step an imitator must take is to find out whether a U.S. patent has been granted for the product in question. Some small-time pioneering products, especially those "started in a garage" by hobbyists or developments in fast-moving—soon to be obsolete—computer areas, are never patented. The pioneer is so preoccupied with getting his product to market that he neglects to protect it from copycats.

It is important to remember that specific products are patentable, not abstract ideas. Patents cannot be obtained for broad product concepts, such as money market mutual funds or food processors. That means that even if a patent has been granted, it may be possible to circumvent it. There are three ways in which imitators can enter emerging markets in the presence of patents. All three have been used successfully in the past, but each case is unique, and a good patent lawyer must advise on the chances of successful imitation in each specific case.

Show Previous Patents or Usage

In the United States patents are granted to "the first to invent." It is an unusual system. Almost every other country in the world patents on the basis of "first to file." That quirk in the U.S. system makes it possible for imitators to copy legally if they can show that someone else had previously thought of the idea. They can argue that the pioneer's product is not really new. There are various ways to prove the argument, but two are especially common.

First, the imitator can point to previously granted patents, preferably long expired, that cover the same ground. That is what happened in ballpoint pens, where the pioneer was powerless to enforce its U.S. patent once the copycat showed that the underlying rollerball mechanism had been patented

seventy-five years earlier. Airsoles in running shoes could not be protected for the same reason. The first air sole was patented in 1882, almost a century before Nike perfected it.

Second, imitators can point to previous research, sometimes in obscure technical journals, to show that there was previous knowledge of the pioneer's device. That research may not even be in the same field as the disputed patent. It can still be used to negate the pioneer's claim that it was the "first to invent" the product. The incremental nature of most scientific developments suggests that there is almost always an opportunity to find precedents for newly discovered products.

Come Up with an Alternative Design to Accomplish the Same Task

Even if the pioneer's patent cannot be negated, it is often possible to circumvent it with a modified design that avoids infringement. There are many ways to do so. Imitation in this case requires a fair amount of innovation. Different materials can be used, different configurations can be designed, or different processes employed. The goal is always to reach the same destination by a different route.

Sometimes it is possible to design an imitative product that performs a more expanded task than that first envisioned by the pioneer, who entered when the market was small and restricted to a small segment. That is what happened in MRIs. When Fonar sued Johnson & Johnson for patent infringement, the courts ultimately decided that the pioneer's patent was specific to one use and did not cover the expanded use for imaging internal organs. Fonar lost the suit, and market leadership, to the later entrant.

The Defensive Use of Patents

In recent years patents have taken on strategic importance. They are used both offensively and defensively by both imitators and pioneers. A DEC attorney recently observed: "Our patents can be a sword or a shield."[3] That is why there has been a surge of interest in patents in recent years.

Imitators who can show past patterns of innovative behavior are likely to fare better than outright knockoff artists in lawsuits brought by less prolific pioneers. Patents, in other words, can be used defensively. In MRIs, for example, Fonar sued GE for patent infringement, but GE was able to show that it had accumulated 250 imaging patents over a twenty-year period. It argued that, far from being an imitator, it was the innovator of imaging technology. As a result, it beat back Fonar's claim that royalties were due to it from the later entrant.

Imitators should use patents as both a sword and a shield. In cases of later entry, they should act aggressively and defensively. They should be ready to defend against accusations of patent infringement and be prepared to argue why a preliminary injunction should not be issued. To prepare, imitators should scour technical journals in search of evidence of previous usage. They should also search for "submarine patents"—those obscure patents that precede a pioneer's claim. In every case, imitators should defensively seek to negate the pioneer's patent and promote their own role as innovator.

When There Is an Opportunity for Shared Experience

An imitator's chances improve when it has experience in making and selling closely related products. That experience can be in manufacturing, in related product lines, in distribution, in marketing, in transferable reputation benefits, or in merely serving the same customers. Shared experience can easily negate the first-mover advantages held by the pioneer.

When the Pioneer Is Positioned at Only One End of the Market

Imitators have an opportunity when the pioneer stays stuck at one end of the market. Pioneers, especially small pioneers, usually enter an emerging market when it is small and focused on a tiny segment. The pioneer may start out with the best position in that initial segment, but as the market grows beyond those bounds, the pioneer often ends up with the best position in an increasingly inconsequential segment of the market. That creates an opportunity for imitative later entrants to preempt the most desirable position. That is what happened to Cuisinart in food processors. The pioneer stayed stuck at the high end of the market, while later entrants dominated the larger mass market for lower-end models.

IMPROVING THE ODDS OF IMITATIVE ENTRY

Imitation is not always successful. Many times the later entrant is unable to unseat the pioneer. The following actions help improve the chances of successful later entry.

Treat Unlikely Threats as Likely

Incumbents typically fail to see the importance of emerging innovations. In some instances, that is because the pioneer's idea is not new at all. There is often a long history of previous entries that met with failure. That sets up the

expectation of continued failure as new entrants try their hand at the market. It also explains why incumbents often let pioneers enter their markets unchallenged. The threat simply does not seem real, because it is often intermingled with other ideas that never go anywhere. Incumbents assume that the current pioneer will fall into the same hole as previous unsuccessful entrants. Their industry experience hurts rather than helps.

It is probably impossible to separate winning ideas from losing ideas beforehand. The way in which innovations make their way to market is too chaotic for accurate forecasting. The only sensible course for incumbents is to widen their net and hope to attend more quickly to potentially threatening innovations.

The Importance of Concurrent R&D

The call to imitate is not a call to substitute later entry for R&D. Most successful imitators have ongoing R&D projects of their own. They simply enter later; they do not start from scratch. That is especially true for technological products that require substantial startup experience. IBM, for example, entered mainframes and personal computers with extensive research experience. In mainframes, IBM had funded research on the Mark I computer before the commercial entry of Univac. Likewise in personal computers. Its 1973 Scamp prototype, created at the Palo Alto Science Center, which was later turned into the commercial 5100 model, gave it the experience to react quickly once the market showed its true potential. In neither case was IBM caught completely unprepared. The same pattern was observed with Boeing, which entered commercial jet aircraft well after deHavilland but had experience producing military jets that aided its entry.

Slowing Down the Pioneer with Legal and Regulatory Challenges

Later entrants, especially powerful industry incumbents, have the opportunity to slow down the pioneer's entry with legal, regulatory, and publicly stated challenges to the pioneer's reputation. Safety issues offer one such avenue of attack. Incumbents should study the pioneer's product, looking carefully for potential safety problems, which can be reported to authorities and the press with the intent of tarnishing the pioneer's reputation and, as a result, lessening the pioneer's grip on the market. That buys time for later entrants. In the past, other challenges have scrutinized ingredients contained in the product and advertising claims.

Safety concerns helped to hobble the pioneer of CAT scanners. In 1976, just as EMI was suing competitors for patent infringement, the FDA ordered

a recall of EMI's machines for excessive radiation leakage. The harm to the pioneer's reputation was far greater than the threat posed to consumers by radiation leakage. It was all downhill for EMI from that point onward. Incumbents then entered with higher-quality scanners and moved to the forefront of the market.

A Conditional Quick Follower Strategy

It is widely advised that later entrants quickly follow the pioneer into a newborn market. I found no support for that advice. The earliest pioneers usually entered long before the market had sufficiently formed to create demand or profits. In many cases the technology itself had not advanced to a stage that made entry practical. Those conditions set the pioneer up for early failure. A "quick follower" is likely to fall into the same trap. Instead, successful followers should *enter quickly after the market has formed, not necessarily quickly after the first pioneer has entered.* The imitator's reaction should be to market potential, not to the pioneer's first move. In other words, quick later entry is conditional upon the market showing itself to have potential. Only then should entry occur. Otherwise, it is better to keep current and keep out of the market.

It seems hard to believe, but the most successful later entrants seem to favor patience over a panicked quick response. In charge cards, microwave ovens, telephone answering machines, and myriad other examples, the most successful entries were timed to match the greatest surge in market growth. Timing entry in growth markets, it seems, can be too early as well as too late.

Avoid Copying Too Closely

Some imitators get too close for comfort. They imitate the pioneer's product too closely and get caught. Typically, it is an industry giant who enters a market pioneered by a small entrepreneurial upstart with a copy that is virtually identical to the pioneer's product. The small pioneer then plays the role of a martyr being attacked by a large bully. The courts and bad press then force the imitator to withdraw.

Some imitators compound their problems by combining identical copies with brutish competitive behavior. That reinforces the pioneer's position as a martyr. The result can be devastating for the imitator in terms of both market position and negative publicity. The lessons are clear: It is okay to imitate, but do not come too close. And be careful not to combine close copies with competitive actions that can cause cries of unfair competition. Be especially wary when those actions are arrayed against a small pioneer.

Hallmark Cards Versus Blue Mountains Arts

Hallmark's entry into "nonoccasion" greeting cards, a fast-growing segment in an otherwise stagnant market, exemplifies the dangers. Nonoccasion greeting cards contain cute, emotion-laden sentiments that are sometimes irreverently stated. They are sent at times outside the traditional holiday card-sending season.

Once again, the product category was not pioneered by the industry leader but by Blue Mountain Arts and a number of other small artistic upstarts. Blue Mountain Arts, based in Boulder, Colorado, was founded in 1970 by Susan Polis Schutz and her husband Stephen. The business began by making silk-screen posters, which the couple sold off the back of their pickup truck. That business gradually evolved into nonoccasion greeting cards, which combined poetry with artistic design. As the years ticked on, the small-scale artistic endeavor turned into a mainstream product.

Growth attracted the incumbents. In the spring of 1985, Hallmark Cards, the overwhelming industry leader, introduced its own line of nonoccasion greeting cards, which promptly failed. A year later, in April 1986, Hallmark tried to buy Blue Mountain Arts from its owners, but they would not sell. So in May 1986 Hallmark reentered the market on its own with its Personal Touch line of cards, which were virtual duplicates of those sold by Blue Mountain Arts. In fact, the copies were so close that Susan Polis Schutz mistook them for her own. She wrote to Hallmark seeking a solution. None was found. So in October 1986, Blue Mountain Arts sued Hallmark for $50 million, claiming that Hallmark had violated its trade dress and copyright.

On November 20, 1986, a federal judge in Denver slapped an injunction on most of Hallmark's nonoccasion cards, stopping the firm from selling them until the facts of the case could be sorted out at trial. Blue Mountain Arts publicized its plight as a struggle between a small—$12 million in sales—David versus a $1.5 billion Goliath. The pioneer positioned itself as a martyr. Schutz claimed she cried after first seeing the Hallmark imitations.

Particularly damaging to Hallmark was its attempt to remove the pioneer's cards from retailers' racks. A centerpiece of Hallmark's promotional strategy was an incentive program that offered discounts to retailers who refused to carry competitor's cards. The program was a stunning success. California Dreamers, another small pioneer, had placed its cards with five hundred retailers before Hallmark's entry but found that only 150 stores carried them after the promotional push. The *Wall Street Journal* reported that "the giant is copying its smaller competitors' designs and illegally using its financial muscle to push their offerings off card racks around the country."[4]

Corporate memos within Hallmark reinforced the negative image. One

internal memo declared that the "Personal Touch line was created . . . to displace Blue Mountain."[5]

Hallmark, of course, disputed the charges. It claimed its cards merely captured current design trends and its promotional actions were strictly in the spirit of competition. In fact, Hallmark claimed that it was the wronged party. Hallmark alleged: "The court has effectively granted Blue Mountain Arts a perpetual monopoly."[6] Hallmark appealed. But the higher courts continued to find for Blue Mountain Arts. Hallmark had copied too closely and had tried to crush a weaker competitor.

In October 1988 Blue Mountain Arts won its final victory. Hallmark signed a consent degree in which it did not admit guilt but agreed to cancel its Personal Touch line. The terms of the financial settlement with Blue Mountains Arts were not disclosed.

Soho Natural Soda Versus Anheuser-Busch's Zeltzer Seltzer

Anheuser-Busch experienced a similar debacle when it copied Soho Natural Soda and tried to crush the tiny pioneer. It started in 1977, when Sophia Collier teamed up with a friend, Connie Best, in that hotbed of innovation Brooklyn, New York, to make and sell a premium soft drink. Their strategy was simple and unsophisticated: They would use the highest-quality natural ingredients to produce a pure and great-tasting soft drink reminiscent of those sold in old-fashioned soda fountains. The result was Soho Soda, which had higher costs than other brands but commanded a premium price. Even the label on the bottle was the finest. The entrepreneurs gave Doug Johnson, a top-flight designer, a piece of the action in exchange for designing a catchy four-color label.

Sales grew a thousandfold for the premium product, from $20,000 during the first year of operations to $20 million by 1986. Once again, growth attracted the major players. In particular, it attracted Anheuser-Busch.

Soho did not make its own soda. It was made under contract by an independent bottler in Maryland owned by Tetley Inc. In 1986, on a visit to the plant, Collier noticed that the bottler was producing a test batch of natural soda for Anheuser-Busch. She then discovered that Anheuser-Busch was about to buy the plant. Collier immediately sought another supplier. More ominously, Collier claims, the giant beer-maker obtained her soda recipes and customer lists when it bought the bottling plant.

In early 1987 Anheuser-Busch introduced Zeltzer Seltzer, a virtually identical copy of Soho Natural Soda. Even the label was a knockoff.

Anheuser-Busch used a popular imitation strategy. It sold Zeltzer Seltzer as a lower-priced alternative to Soho Soda. With lower costs from Anheuser-

Busch's experience with large-volume production, and what Collier claimed were cheaper ingredients, Zeltzer Seltzer could easily underprice Soho's premium product while claiming to be of equal quality. Collier also charged that Anheuser-Busch pressured suppliers to choose between Soho Soda and Zeltzer Seltzer, effectively restricting the pioneer's distribution.

Collier was infuriated. She wrote to Anheuser-Busch demanding that it immediately withdraw its copycat product. The giant's high-powered law firm responded with a denial that it had copied Soho's soda. It claimed that Zeltzer Seltzer "was developed independently, with every intention and effort to establish a distinct product image."[7] Packaging similarities were called "trivial." Anheuser-Busch seemed to assume that the tiny upstart did not have the will or the resources to fight a protracted legal battle.

But Collier did not behave like most small pioneers. She reacted immediately and decisively. She hired lawyer Richard Ben-Veniste, the former Watergate prosecutor, and sued Anheuser-Busch in April 1987. She also went to the press and played the role of the martyr. She positioned her plight as two powerless women being picked on by an $8 billion (1987 sales) giant. Anheuser-Busch was infuriated with the tactic and countersued for defamation of character.

A judge sided with the pioneer and ordered Anheuser-Busch to change its label. The combination of unfavorable legal rulings and bad press caused Anheuser-Busch to cut its losses. By the end of 1987 it sold off the Zeltzer Seltzer brand and left the business. It had copied too closely to recover.

Kodak Versus Polaroid Instant Cameras

From the late 1950s to the end of the 1960s, Polaroid shared its technological secrets with Kodak so that Kodak would help it make negatives from instant prints. That decision turned out to be a dreadful error. In the fall of 1975 Kodak demonstrated an instant film of its own. Then, in April 1976, it introduced its own line of instant cameras that competed directly with Polaroid. In terms of quality, some experts judged the cameras to be equal. But Kodak held two key advantages: (1) It offered dealers higher profit margins than Polaroid, and (2) it had an advantage in distribution owing to its omnipresence in the market.

Polaroid sued six days after Kodak entered, claiming that Kodak had infringed on ten of its key patents. Kodak now had to fight a battle on two fronts. It was forced into a protracted legal contest while it was trying to build market share in a maturing market.

On May 16, 1976, Kodak countersued, arguing that Polaroid's patents had been artificially extended beyond the seventeen-year limit by making

trivial changes in the underlying technology. Polaroid's technology, it contended, was in the public domain.

Charges and countercharges dragged on for a decade. Kodak faced an uphill battle because, as *Business Week* noted, it was fighting against "Polaroid's iron ring of patent protection that had preserved its 30-year monopoly of the instant photography market."[8] Unlike many other pioneers, Polaroid was well protected. It was also willing to spend any amount to fight off challengers. The legal bill quickly topped $10 million.

As the years ticked on, the market stakes grew smaller as the legal stakes grew larger. By the mid-1980s Kodak had failed to build a dominant share of the instant photography market, and the entire instant photography market was shrinking. What had looked like an enticing market opportunity now turned into a legal quagmire.

In September 1985 a Boston federal judge ruled that Kodak had indeed illegally copied Polaroid's patents. Polaroid claimed that Kodak had reverse-engineered its products. After ten years in the business, an injunction was slapped on Kodak to stop selling its copycat cameras. Kodak ceased selling its instant cameras on January 9, 1986.

Kodak appealed the ruling with the complaint that its costs of leaving the business would be staggering. First, eight hundred jobs were at stake (and no one, not even a judge, would want to eliminate jobs). Second, 6.5 million customers would be stuck with an orphaned camera for which there would be no film. Third, an investment of $230 million would be wasted. Nonetheless, in February 1986 the courts refused to lift the injunction. Kodak was out of the instant photography business for good.

But its biggest liability still lay ahead. Polaroid claimed $4 billion in lost sales and sought treble damages totaling $12 billion from Kodak. Legal losses now swamped market losses. Kodak offered to settle for a paltry $177 million. Polaroid refused.

In October 1990 the courts announced the largest award ever in a patent infringement suit. Kodak was ordered to pay $909 million, significantly less than the $12 billion sought by Polaroid, but still a hefty sum. In July 1991 Kodak paid $925 million (interest added) to Polaroid, which ended a colossal case of copying too close that cost Kodak plenty.

Stress Continuity Rather than Radical Technological Change

With all of the talk about the rapid rate of change in today's world, the fact is that most business customers prefer continuity to radical change. That presents an opportunity for later entrants, since many pioneers are technology-driven firms intent on selling the latest advance without regard

to current practices. Incumbents are more closely tied to past practices. That difference can be turned to the incumbents' advantage in markets where radically new technologies must coexist with existing systems. Almost always, there is a strong resistance to throwing out the old and bringing in the new.

That creates an opportunity for later entrants with strong existing channels of distribution and a coveted reputation in the industry. Those firms may not have been as quick or as nimble as the pioneers they followed, but they can stress continuity to customers who are reluctant to embrace radical change. Incumbents have an opportunity to meld the new technology with the current business practices. That is what IBM did in the 1950s in mainframe computers. While the pioneers sold more efficient tape drives to store data, IBM connected its computers to the less efficient but more familiar card readers. That allowed business customers to add computers to their existing operations instead of completely replacing one system with another.

The more radical the innovation, the more important it is to tie it to existing systems and practices. Customers will be reluctant to buy radically new products and learn totally new skills. Presper Eckert, one of the two creators of ENIAC, the first mainframe, recognized the importance of continuity: "If you have a radical idea . . . for God's sake don't be radical in how you carry it out as well. Be as conservative as you can. Become a right-wing conservative in carrying out a left-wing idea."[9]

DEFENDING AGAINST IMITATIONS

Pioneers can rarely stop imitators from entering their markets entirely, but they can slow their entry, raise the costs of imitation, and lessen the chances of ultimate success. The first choice a pioneer must make is whether to sell out, share its technology with later entrants, or fight. Each alternative has its benefits and drawbacks.

Selling Out

A pioneer that has established a strong position in a small but growing market can often reap a handsome reward by selling out to a larger firm with greater resources. That transaction compensates the pioneer for his creation and attracts much-needed investment capital to the growing firm. But the pioneer pays a price: He loses control of the firm he created. In some instances pioneers are effectively forced to sell out. Ecker and Mauchly, for

example, whose ENIAC revolutionized mainframe computing, found themselves perpetually short of cash and had no choice but to sell their firm to Remington Rand.

In other cases the pioneer is forced to share ownership with outside investors brought in to provide much-needed cash. The magnitude and bitterness of disagreements between pioneers and investors are legendary. In the case of WordStar, for example, the founder's goals were at odds with those of his principal investor. The dispute contributed to the pioneer's demise. In the case of Atari, the pioneer of videogames, Nolan Bushnell sold out to a corporate giant but was then kept on as an executive, where he clashed with his corporate benefactors.

Licensing and Joint Ventures

An intermediate step between selling out entirely and fighting off copycats is to form a joint venture with a larger partner or to agree to license the technology. The benefits of either action are to attract outside capital and spread the financial risk of pioneering while still maintaining control. The risk is that partners or licensees will steal your ideas, leave the partnership, and emerge as major competitors. Ampex, for example, the American pioneer of video recorders, fell victim to a joint venture gone bad. It gave Sony access to its video technology, but the relationship soured, and Sony emerged as the strongest competitor to the pioneer.

Fighting Off the Copycats

The ultimate choice for pioneers, especially small entrepreneurial upstarts, is to go it alone and fight off the copycats as they appear. The first step a pioneer should take if it intends to fend off later imitators is to establish clearly that it was the first to develop the new product. The pioneer should carefully document the details of product conception and development. All preliminary designs and plans should be saved and witnessed. Those actions alone will not keep imitators out of the pioneer's markets, but they lay the groundwork for legal actions that may follow.

If an imitator's entry is a blatant copy of the pioneer's product, the pioneer can sue, seeking a preliminary injunction, which stops the copycat from selling the disputed product until the courts sort out the merits of the case. The popularity of preliminary injunctions grew rapidly during the 1980s.

In many cases preliminary injunctions force copycats to settle with the pioneer or to seek a license for its technology rather than risk a long and

costly trial with a potentially huge judgment. In fact, an offer to license is often coupled with the threat of a patent infringement suit and a notification of intent to seek a preliminary injunction.

Licensing can serve a defensive purpose as well. It can illustrate to the courts that the pioneer is interested not in maintaining a monopoly but in being fairly compensated. That reduces the power of countercharges made by later entrants that the pioneer is trying to monopolize the market and is guilty of unfair competition, a condition where consumers might be hurt.

Patent infringement suits and preliminary injunctions can serve as offensive weapons as well as ways of defending one's own turf. Preliminary injunctions have been used to put small competitors out of business before they have a chance to threaten the pioneer. Once the junction is granted, the growth capital for small imitators typically dries up, starving the firms for cash until the courts sort out the details. Some critics contend that the trend toward preliminary injunctions has gone too far.[10] In an attempt to protect intellectual property rights, the courts have squashed competition.

If legal remedies fail to dissuade imitators from entering the pioneer's market, four defensive strategic alternatives must be considered.

The first two choices occur when a market starts to mature. At that point imitators typically enter with generic versions of the pioneer's product, which they sell at much lower prices. The pioneer can also defend its turf by choosing between the third and fourth alternatives.

1. *Cover the low end.* The pioneer can reduce the opportunity for later entrants by introducing low-end generics of its own, thereby denying, or at least forcing the imitator to share, that part of the market. The risk of that strategy is that the pioneer will reduce overall profit margins by focusing on low-end products.
2. *Cede the low end to clones.* An alternative strategy is to let later entrants have the low end of the market and focus on the more profitable top half. That strategy secures higher profit margins but risks having the low-end entrants move upward once they have established a beachhead at the low end. Pioneers who cede the low end to later entrants may be only postponing a battle they will ultimately have to fight.
3. *Perpetually innovate.* Pioneers can also reduce the effectiveness of outright copycats by forcing them to stay one step behind in technology. Pioneers who continually update their products close off the opportunity for a technological leapfrog by later entrants. Merle Crawford, a respected new products expert, advises pioneers to "see yourself as developing not one product, but a stream of products . . . cover the ones that offer competi-

tors the most potential, thereby leaving adapters to bridge into the market on more trivial attributes."[11]

4. *Set a proprietary standard.* The final defense against imitators is not to let them copy, either as clones or as improved versions of the pioneer's product. In some cases, especially with technological products, it is possible for the pioneer, once in the lead, to switch users to a proprietary standard that cannot be copied. Some experts argue that IBM should have done this with its popular personal computer (albeit IBM was not the pioneer but the market leader). That would have stopped the clones from selling essentially the same machine at lower prices. It would also have stopped the imitate-and-improve crowd, such as Compaq, which offered a portable version of the leader's product. The risk of that strategy, especially in the case of personal computers, is that it would alienate current users by rendering their software unusable on the new machines.

AND THE LAST WILL BE FIRST

In conclusion, the argument I have tried to make in this book is that the conventional wisdom regarding order-of-entry effects is oversold but not incorrect. There are many instances where pioneering pays off in the premier market position. But at the same time there are many other cases where first entrants came in last and last entrants came in first. That is not a new argument. Nearly two thousand years ago the bible—or at least the New Testament—challenged the conventional wisdom regarding order effects in a larger context. Matthew 19:30 summed it up best: ". . . many who are first will be last, and many who are last will be first." Now that is sage advice for later entrants.

NOTES

Introduction: The Argument for Imitation

1. Theodore Levitt, "Innovative Imitation," *Harvard Business Review*, September–October 1966, p. 63.
2. "Coke's Big Marketing Blitz," *Business Week*, May 30, 1983, p. 60.
3. Laura Zinn, "Pepsi's Future Becomes Brighter," *Business Week*, February 1, 1993, p. 75.
4. Richard Gibson, "Cereal Makers Turn to Copying Rival Products," *Wall Street Journal*, July 2, 1991, p. B1.
5. "Hiram Walker: A Move into Rum Fills a Major Product Gap," *Business Week*, April 24, 1978, p. 92.
6. Amy Dunkin, "What Stirs the Spirit Makers: Vodka, Vodka, Vodka," *Business Week*, June 12, 1989, p. 54.
7. "The Behemoths Move Into Biotechnology," *Business Week*, November 5, 1984, p. 137.
8. Orrin Dunlap, "Radio Industry Sees Signs of a Brighter Future: Surveying the Future," *New York Times*, June 4, 1933, sec. 9, p. 1.
9. Patricia Ferris, "Knock-off . . . Knock-out? Brand Names vs. Generics," *Licensing Product Times*, Fall 1990, p. 3.
10. Eric Schine, "These RVs Are Doing Wheelies off Dealers' Lots," *Business Week*, May 21, 1990, p. 104.
11. Sam Walton, *Sam Walton: Made in America, My Story* (New York: Doubleday, 1992), p. 36.
12. Woody Hochswender, "How Fashion Spreads Around the World at the Speed of Light," *New York Times*, May 13, 1990, p. E3.
13. Andrew Pollack, "One Day, Junior Got Too Big," *New York Times*, August 4, 1991, sec. 3, p. 6.
14. This story is drawn partially from "Reference Chips," *Forbes*, July 20, 1992, p. 12.
15. Constance Hays, "You Could Look It Up: 2 Dictionaries Go to War," *New York Times*, October 22, 1991, pp. B1, B4.

Chapter 1. The Elements of Imitation

1. Pete Engardio, "Companies Are Knocking Off the Knockoff Outfits," *Business Week*, September 26, 1988, pp. 86–88.
2. Fleming Meeks, "So Sue Me," *Forbes*, November 28, 1988, p. 72.
3. David Woodruff, "A New Era for Auto Quality," *Business Week*, October 22, 1990, p. 86.
4. Doron Levin, "Hot Wheels," *New York Times Magazine*, September 30, 1990, pp. 32, 78ff.
5. Richard Nelson and Sidney Winter, *An Evolutionary Theory of Economic Change* (Cambridge, Mass.: Belknap Press of Harvard University Press, 1982), p. 123.
6. Rita Koselka, "A Long Way from Hell's Kitchen," *Forbes*, July 9, 1990, p. 59.
7. Nathan Rosenberg and W. Edward Steinmueller, "Why Are Americans Such Poor Imitators?" *American Economic Review*, May 1988, p. 230.
8. Edwin Mansfield, "How Rapidly Does New Industrial Technology Leak Out?" *Journal of Industrial Economics*, December 1985, pp. 217–23.
9. D. Eleanor Westney, *Imitation and Innovation* (Cambridge, Mass.: Harvard University Press, 1988).
10. Jeremy Main, "How To Steal the Best Ideas Around," *Fortune*, October 19, 1992, p. 102.
11. Gerald Nadler, "The Best Breakthroughs," *New York Times*, January 27, 1991, sec. 3, p. 13.
12. Seth Lubove, "Retail Is Detail," *Forbes*, September 30, 1991, p. 144.
13. Rita Koselka, "Give 'em What They Want," *Forbes*, September 30, 1991, p. 97.
14. Theodore Levitt, "Exploit the Product Life Cycle," *Harvard Business Review*, November–December 1965, p. 82.

Chapter 2. First-Mover Advantages Versus Free-Ride Effects

1. "Old Standbys Hold Their Own," *Advertising Age*, September 19, 1983, p. 32.
2. Richard Schmalensee, "Product Differentiation Advantages of Pioneering Brands," *American Economic Review*, Fall 1982, p. 360.
3. Celia Conrad, "The Advantage of Being First and Competition Between Firms," *International Journal of Industrial Organization*, December 1983, p. 363.
4. Theodore Levitt, "Exploit the Product Life Cycle," *Harvard Business Review*, November–December 1965, p. 82.
5. Roger Kerin, P. Rajan Varadarajan, and Robert Peterson, "First-Mover Advantage: A Synthesis, Conceptual Framework, and Research Propositions," *Journal of Marketing*, October 1992, p. 48.
6. Michael Moore, William Boulding, and Ronald Goodstein, "Pioneering and Market Share: Is Entry Time Endogenous, and Does It Matter?" *Journal of Marketing Research*, February 1991, p. 103.
7. William Robinson and Claes Fornell, "Sources of Market Pioneer Advantages: The Case of Consumer Goods Industries," *Journal of Marketing Research*, August 1985, p. 309.

8. Mary Lambkin, "Order of Entry and Performance in New Markets," *Strategic Management Journal*, Summer 1988, p. 137.

9. William Robinson, "Sources of Market Pioneer Advantages: The Case of Industrial Goods Industries," *Journal of Marketing Research*, February 1988, p. 93.

10. Gregory Carpenter and Kent Nakamoto, "Consumer Preference Foundation and Pioneering Advantage," *Journal of Marketing Research* August 1989, p. 297.

11. Ira Whitten, *Brand Performance in the Cigarette Industry and the Advantage of Early Entry*, 1913–1974 (Washington D.C.: Federal Trade Commission, Bureau of Economics, 1979), p. 47.

12. A. Glazer, "The Advantages of Being First," *American Economic Review*, June 1985, pp. 473–80.

13. Peter Golder and Gerard Tellis, *Do Pioneers Really Have Long-Term Advantages? A Historical Analysis* (Cambridge, Mass.: Marketing Science Institute, Report no. 92-124, September 1992).

14. Cyndee Miller, "Survey: New Product Failure Is Top Management's Fault," *Marketing News*, February 1, 1993, p. 2.

15. C. Merle Crawford, "New Product Failure Rates—Facts and Fallacies," *Research Management*, September 1979, p. 12.

16. Edwin Mansfield and Samuel Wagner, "Organizational and Strategic Factors Associated with Probabilities of Success in Industrial R&D," *Journal of Business*, April 1975, p. 181.

17. Glenn Urban, John Hauser, and Nikhilesh Dholakia, *Essentials of New Product Management* (Englewood Cliffs, N.J.: Prentice-Hall, 1987), p. 41.

18. C. Merle Crawford, *New Products Management* (Homewood, Ill.: Richard D. Irwin, 1987), p. 12.

19. Edwin Mansfield, "How Rapidly Does New Industrial Technology Leak Out?" *Journal of Industrial Economics*, December 1985, p. 219.

20. Edwin Mansfield, Mark Schwartz, and Samuel Wagner, "Imitation Costs and Patents: An Empirical Study," *The Economic Journal*, December 1981, pp. 907–18.

21. *Ibid.*, p. 912.

22. *Ibid.*, p. 913.

23. Ronald Bond and David Lean, *Sales, Promotion, and Product Differentiation in Two Prescription Drug Markets* (Washington, D.C.: Federal Trade Commission, Bureau of Economics, February 1977), p. 28.

24. *Ibid.*, p. 46.

25. Robert Cooper, "New Product Success in Industrial Firms," *Industrial Marketing Management*, July 1982, pp. 215–23.

26. Glen Urban, Theresa Carter, Steve Gaskin, and Zofia Mucha, "Market Share Rewards to Pioneering Brands: An Empirical Analysis and Strategic Implications," *Management Science*, June 1986, p. 655. Emphasis added.

27. *Ibid.*, p. 656.

28. William Abernathy and James Utterback, "Patterns of Industrial Innovation," *Technology Review,* June–July 1978, pp. 41–47.

29. Joe Bain, *Barriers to New Competition* (Cambridge, Mass.: Harvard University Press, 1956), p. 216.

Chapter 3. Imitators Who Surpassed Pioneers

1. John Jewkes, David Sawers, and Richard Stillerman, *The Sources of Invention* (New York: Macmillan, 1958).

2. Peter Golder and Gerard Tellis, *Do Pioneers Really Have Long-Term Advantages? A Historical Analysis* (Cambridge, Mass.: Marketing Science Institute, Report Number 92-124, September 1992).

35mm Cameras

3. Brian Coe, *Cameras: From Daguerreotypes to Instant Pictures* (New York: Crown, 1978), p. 13.

4. *Ibid.,* p. 111.

5. "Canon," *International Directory of Company Histories* (Chicago: St. James Press, 1991), 3: 120.

6. Actually, the firm's name at the time was Nippon Kogaku, but for the sake of clarity it is referred to here as Nikon. Nippon Kogaku officially changed its name to Nikon in 1988 to match the brand name of its key product.

7. "Nikon," *International Directory of Company Histories* (Chicago: St. James Press, 1991) 3: 583.

8. Michel Auer, *The Illustrated History of the Camera from 1839 to the Present* (Boston: New York Graphic Society, 1975), p. 217.

9. *Ibid.,* p. 219.

10. "Nikon Crowds into Leica's Picture," *Business Week,* December 11, 1965, p. 51.

11. *Ibid.,* p. 50.

12. Peter Fuhrman, "New Focus at Leica," *Forbes,* October 31, 1988, p. 102.

13. *Ibid.*

14. *Ibid.*

2. Automated Teller Machines (ATMs)

15. John Diebold, *The Innovators* (New York: Plume Books, 1990), p. 179.

16. Teresa Tritch and John Manners, "The Money Hall of Fame," *Money,* October 1992, p. 138.

17. Joseph D'Cruz, "Docutel Corporation," in Derek Abell and John Hammond, *Strategic Market Planning* (Englewood Cliffs, N.J.: Prentice-Hall, 1979), p. 65.

18. "24-Hour Automatic Tellers: How Big a Boom?" *Banking,* February 1973, p. 19.

19. Diebold, *Innovators,* p. 184.

20. D'Cruz, "Docutel," pp. 80–81.

3. Ballpoint Pens
21. Glen Bowen, *Collectible Fountain Pens* (Gas City, Ind.: L-W Book Sales, 1982), p. 191.

4. Caffeine-free Soft Drinks
22. David Mahoney, "How the Sparkle Turned to a Fizzle," *Advertising Age,* March 7, 1988, p. 36, is excerpted from David Mahoney, *Confessions of a Street-Smart Manager* (New York: Simon & Schuster, 1988).
23. Bob Lederer, "Creator of the No-Caffeine Market," *Beverage World,* May 1982, p. 23.
24. Paul Brown, "Beverages," *Forbes,* January 3, 1983, p. 189.
25. "Coke's Big Marketing Blitz," *Business Week,* May 30, 1983, p. 61.

5. CAT Scanners
26. Cheryll Barron, "What Scarred EMI's Scanner," *Management Today,* February 1979, p. 152.
27. *Ibid.,* p. 74.
28. "EMI Has Orders for Its Scanner," *Wall Street Journal,* October 28, 1975, p. 19.
29. "Many X-Ray Devices in Hospitals, Clinics, Are Being Corrected," *Wall Street Journal,* November 26, 1976, p. 6.
30. Jonathan Spivak, "EMI Ltd. Envisions Expanding Market for X-Ray Scanner," *Wall Street Journal,* November 11, 1978, p. 2.
31. Jonathan Spivak, "EMI Ltd. Leaves X-Ray Scanner Business, Plans Sale of Assets to GE in the U.S.," *Wall Street Journal,* April 30, 1980, p. 16.
32. Gail Bronson, "As Once-Bright Market for CAT Scanners Dims, Smaller Makers of the X-Ray Devices Fade Out," *Wall Street Journal,* May 6, 1980, p. 48.

6. Commercial Jet Aircraft
33. R. E. G. Davies, *A History of the World's Airlines* (London: Oxford University Press, 1964), p. 452.
34. *Ibid.,* p. 483.
35. Robert Serling, *The Jet Age* (Alexandria, Va: Time-Life Books, 1982), p. 69.
36. Martin Sharp, *D.H.—A History of deHavilland* (Shrewsbury, England: Airlife Publishing, Ltd., 1982), p. 327.

7. Computerized Ticketing Services
37. Jobeth McDaniel, "The Struggle to Sell Tickets," *New York Times,* November 26, 1989, sec. 3, p. 11.
38. "Ticketmaster Corp.: Selling Service Before Technology," *California Business,* October 1, 1990, p. 13.

8. Credit/Charge Cards
39. Thomas Forbes, "Looking Back: Portrait of a Young Diner's Club as a Publicist's Dream," *Adweek's Marketing Week,* April 16, 1990, p. 18.

40. *I'll Buy That: 50 Small Wonders and Big Deals That Revolutionized the Lives of Consumers* (Mount Vernon, N.Y.: Consumers Union, 1986).
41. *Business Week,* October 9, 1989.
42. "Readers Report," *Business Week,* November 27, 1989, p. 12.
43. Thomas Forbes, "Those Magnificent Men and Their Cards," *Adweek's Marketing Week,* April 16, 1990, p. 19.
44. "The American Express Card: Don't Shuffle Papers Without It," *Business Week,* September 13, 1993, p. 36.
45. *VISA Case Study,* The American Advertising Federation, 1992 (estimating that between 70 and 75 percent of worldwide cards are of U.S. issue). *Business Week,* September 13, 1993, reports 34 million American Express cards worldwide.
46. *Ibid.*
47. Cara Grenberg, "Future Worth: Before It's Hot, Grab It," *New York Times,* February 27, 1992, p. C1.

9. Diet Soft Drinks
48. "Sales Bubble For Diet Drinks," *Business Week,* June 27, 1964, p. 90.
49. *Ibid.*
50. *Ibid.,* p. 92.
51. Joshua Levine, "Affirmative Grunts," *Forbes,* March 2, 1992, p. 91.
52. Dan Koeppel, "Dinosaur Brands," *Adweek's Marketing Week,* June 17, 1991, p. 19.
53. "Bottlers Ponder Latest Shakeup at RC," *Beverage Industry,* August 1991, p. 27.
54. "Coke's Big Marketing Blitz," *Business Week,* May 30, 1983.

10. Dry Beer
55. Karen Lowry Miller, "Can Asahi Brew Another Blockbuster?" *Business Week,* March 4, 1991, p. 41.
56. Florence Fabricant, "Dry Beers That Are Flooding the Market: Wave or Mirage?" *New York Times,* August 16, 1989, p. C6.
57. Mitch Katz, "Michelob Optimistic About Success of Its Dry Beer," *Marketing News,* May 8, 1989, p. 10.

11. Food Processors
58. N. R. Kleinfield, "How Cuisinart Lost Its Edge," *New York Times Magazine,* April 15, 1990, p. 46.
59. Kerry Hannon, "Diced and Sliced," *Forbes,* October 2, 1989, p. 72.

12. Light Beer
60. "Gablinger's Beer Ads Are Labeled False by Rival Company," *New York Times,* December 9, 1967.
61. Felix Kessler, "Rheingold's Troubles with Gablinger's Beer Come to a Head with a Government Lawsuit," *Wall Street Journal,* December 11, 1967, p. 34.
62. Philip Dougherty, "Advertising: In This Corner, the New Mug," *New York Times,* September 14, 1967, p. 65.

63. *Ibid.*
64. Philip Dougherty, "Advertising: Shake Hands with N.W. Ayer," *New York Times,* December 8, 1967, p. 2.
65. Kessler, "Rheingold's Troubles," p. 34.
66. Frederick Klein, "Wherein Mickey Spillane Gets the Girl," *Wall Street Journal,* October 10, 1977, p. 14.
67. Bill Abrams, "Miller Is in Ferment at Anheuser's Claim of Natural Beers," *Wall Street Journal,* February 2, 1979, p. 18.
68. "Anheuser's Rival Takes a Dim View of Michelob Light," *Wall Street Journal,* March 23, 1979, p. 10.
69. David Garino and Gay Sands Miller, "Battle of Light Beers Is Coming to a Head and Turning Heavy," *Wall Street Journal,* March 20, 1980, p. 1.
70. "Miller Beer Wins Round over Use of Lite Name," *Wall Street Journal,* October 9, 1980, p. 21.

13. Mainframe Computers
71. David Ritche, *The Computer Pioneers* (New York: Simon & Schuster, 1986), p. 151.
72. Stan Augarten, *Bit by Bit* (New York: Ticknor & Fields, 1984), p. 121.
73. Alice Burks and Arthur Burks, *The First Electronic Computer: The Atanasoff Story* (Ann Arbor: University of Michigan Press, 1988), p. 102.
74. *Ibid.,* p. 257.
75. Thomas Watson, Jr., *Father, Son & Co: My Life at IBM and Beyond* (New York: Bantam Books, 1990), p. 136.
76. *Ibid.,* p. 135
77. Nancy Linde, "The Machine That Changed the World: Inventing the Future," WGBH public television, Boston, 1992.
78. Richard DeLamarter, *Big Blue: IBM's Use and Abuse of Power* (New York: Dodd, Mead, 1986), pp. 33–34.
79. Katherine Fishman, *The Computer Establishment* (New York: Harper & Row, 1981), p. 33.

14. Microwave Ovens
80. "Raytheon: Learning New Markets for Electronics," *Business Week,* May 15, 1954, p. 114.
81. "Home on the Radarange," *Newsweek,* March 4, 1968, p. 69.
82. "Industry Warms Up to Microwaves," *Business Week,* March 13, 1965, p. 152.
83. *Ibid.,* p. 154.
84. "Microwave Ovens: Not Recommended," *Consumer Reports,* April 1973, p. 221.
85. Kenneth Wong, "Amana Microwave Ovens," in *Strategic Marketing,* ed. John Cady and Robert Buzzell (Boston: Little, Brown, 1979), p. 367.
86. Ira Magaziner and Mark Patinkin, "Fast Heat: How Korea Won the Microwave War," *Harvard Business Review,* January–February 1989, p. 85
87. *Ibid.*

88. "Yen's Rise Isn't Likely to Significantly Trim Japan's Exports to U.S.," *Wall Street Journal,* March 21, 1986, p. 10.

89. Magaziner and Patinkin, "Fast Heat," p. 92.

15. Money-Market Mutual Funds

90. Robert D. Hershey, Jr., "Overnight Mutual Funds for Surplus Assets," *New York Times,* January 7, 1973, p. 5.

91. Deborah DeWitt Malley, "Making Your Money Work Fast," *Fortune,* April 1974, p. 84.

92. Six were no-load funds: Reserve Fund, Dreyfus Liquid Assets, Fidelity Daily Income Trust, Money Market Management, Capital Preservation, and Temporary Investment Fund—and two were load funds: Anchor Reserve and Oppenheimer Monetary Bridge.

93. Robert Cole, "Interest Rates Come Down, but Money Funds Roar Ahead," *New York Times,* March 2, 1975, p. F3.

94. Richard Phalon, "Rate Decline Turns Small Investors from Money-Market Mutual Funds," *New York Times,* September 6, 1976, p. 22.

16. Magnetic Resonance Imaging (MRI)

95. "The Inventor," *U.S. News & World Report,* January 26, 1987, p. 66.

96. "Seeing Inside the Body Without X-Rays," *Business Week,* August 24, 1981, p. 42D.

97. "Johnson & Johnson and Unit Are Charged with Infringing Patent," *Wall Street Journal,* September 22, 1982, p. 28.

98. "Johnson & Johnson Denies Patent-Infringement Charge," *Wall Street Journal,* September 23, 1982, p. 12.

99. "Johnson & Johnson Found to Infringe on Fonar Patent," *Wall Street Journal,* November 25, 1985, p. 13.

100. "Johnson & Johnson Patent Case Ruling Reversed by Judge," *Wall Street Journal,* January 4, 1968, p. 25.

101. Amal Kumar Naj, "Diagnostic Equipment Field in Squeeze," *Wall Street Journal,* September 6, 1990, p. B12.

102. *Ibid.,* p. B1.

103. Edmund Andrews, "Patents: New Lawsuit on Magnetic Resonance," *New York Times,* September 5, 1992, p. 32.

17. Nonalcoholic Beer

104. Marj Charlier, "Big Beer Makers Go After the Sober Set with Assortment of Nonalcoholic Brews," *Wall Street Journal,* March 30, 1992, pp. B1, B12.

18. Operating Systems for Personal Computers

105. Bill Machrone, "Roots: The Evolution of Innovation," *PC Magazine,* May 26, 1987, p. 166.

106. *Ibid.*

107. James Wallace and Jim Erickson, *Hard Drive: Bill Gates and the Making of the Microsoft Empire* (New York: John Wiley & Sons, 1992), p. 194.
108. Jon Palfreman and Robert Hone, "The Machine That Changed the World: The Paperback Computer," WGBH public television, Boston, 1992.
109. Wallace and Erickson, *Hard Drive*, p. 269.

19. Paperback Books
110. Charles Madison, *Book Publishing in America* (New York: McGraw-Hill, 1966), p. 53.
111. *Ibid.*, p. 548.
112. The "Blue Ribbon" label seems to bring good luck. Before starting Pocket Books de Graff was involved with Blue Ribbon Books, which, coincidentally, carried a moniker similar to Phil Knight's Blue Ribbon Sports, later renamed Nike.
113. Madison, *Book Publishing in America*, p. 548.
114. Allen Crider, *Mass Market Publishing in America* (Boston: G. K. Hall & Co., 1982), p. 219.
115. *Ibid.*
116. *Ibid.*, p. 235.
117. Kenneth Davis, *Two-Bit Culture* (Boston: Houghton-Mifflin, 1984), p. 341.
118. Robert Carter, "Pioneers! O Pioneers!" *Publishers Weekly*, May 26, 1989, p. S14.
119. John Tebbel, *A History of Book Publishing in the United States*, Volume IV: *The Great Change 1940–1980* (New York: R. R. Bowker, 1981), p. 371.
120. *I'll Buy That* (Mount Vernon, N.Y.: Consumers Union, 1986), p. 118.
121. Tebbel, *History of Book Publishing*, p. 383.

20. Personal Computers
122. Stan Augarten, *Bit by Bit* (New York: Ticknor & Fields, 1984), p. 259.
123. Jon Palfreman and Robert Hone, "The Machine That Changed the World: The Paperback Computer," WGBH public television, Boston, 1992.
124. Charles Ferguson and Charles Morris, *Computer Wars* (New York: Times Books, 1993), p. 24.
125. Robert Sobel, *IBM: Colossus in Transition* (New York: Times Books, 1981), p. 311.
126. "The Coming Shakeout on Personal Computers," *Business Week*, November 22, 1983, p. 83.
127. "Personal Computers: And the Winner Is IBM," *Business Week*, October 3, 1983, p. 76,
128. Ferguson and Morris, *Computer Wars*, p. 53.
129. Geoff Lewis, "The PC Wars: IBM vs. the Clones," *Business Week*, July 28, 1986, p. 62.
130. Lois Therien, "Why Gateway Is Racing to Answer on the First Ring," *Business Week*, September 3, 1993, p. 92.

21. Pocket Calculators

131. "Adding Machines Loom as Mama's New Helper," *Business Week*, June 6, 1964, p. 34.
132. William Smith, "Hand-Held Calculators: Tool or Toy?" *New York Times*, August 20, 1972, sec. 3, p. 7.
133. Terry Robards, "Mini-Calculator Shakeout," *New York Times*, October 8, 1972, p. 4.
134. Gene Smith, "Texas Instruments Puts 3 Calculators on Market," *New York Times*, September 21, 1972, p. 79.
135. Nathaniel Nash, "Shakeout Time for Calculators," *New York Times*, December 8, 1974, sec. 3, p. 4.
136. William Smith, "Bowmar Will Ask Reorganization," *New York Times*, February 11, 1975, p. 55.

22. Projection Television

137. David Gumpert, "Does Anybody Want a TV Set That Has a 4-by-6 Foot Screen?" *Wall Street Journal*, June 11, 1974, p. 1.
138. *Ibid.*, p. 23.
139. "A Little Guy Gets Big Attention with His Large-Screen Sets," *Broadcasting*, May 13, 1974, p. 47.
140. Thomas Baker, "Self-Inflicted Wounds," *Forbes*, August 31, 1981, p. 100.
141. "Advent Corp. Founder, Another Director Quit at Suggestion of Firm," *Wall Street Journal*, April 18, 1977, p. 24.
142. "Little Guy," p. 47.
143. GE, Goldstar, Hitachi, Magnavox, Mitsubishi, NEC, Panasonic, Pioneer, Quasar, RCA, Sony, Zenith.
144. Edward Welles, "What Becomes of a Legend," *Inc.*, June 1989, p. 21.
145. Peter Mitchell, "The Big Screen Comes Home," *High Technology*, April 1987, p. 52.
146. "Little Guy," p. 48.

23. Spreadsheets for Personal Computers

147. "Birthing the Visible Calculator," *Byte*, December 1989, p. 327.
148. Christopher Barr, "From VisiCalc to 1-2-3: How Much Did 1-2-3 Really Borrow from Its Predecessor, VisiCalc?" *PC Magazine*, May 26, 1987, p. 169.
149. Bo Burlingham and Michael Hopkins, "My Company, My Self," *Inc.*, July 1989, p. 35.
150. Barr, "From VisiCalc to 1-2-3," p. 169.

24. Telephone Answering Machines

151. Russell Maloney, "The Shape, if Such It Can Be Called, of Things to Come," *New Yorker*, April 3, 1943, p. 22.
152. Susan Gelfond, "You'll Hear a Lot of That Beep," *Business Week*, February 4, 1986, p. 108.

153. "Ratings: Telephone Answering Machines," *Consumer Reports*, May 1983, p. 250.
154. Anthony Ramirez, "All About Answering Machines: For Yuppies, Now Plain Folks, Too," *New York Times*, January 27, 1991, sec. 3, p. 5.
155. Gelfond, "That Beep," p. 109.
156. Michael Garry, "Telephone Answerer Market Up for Grabs as Plunging Prices Bring in Consumers," *Merchandising*, February 1984, p. 46.
157. Ramirez, "All About Answering Machines," p. 5.

25. Videocassette Recorders (VCRs)
158. John Diebold, *The Innovators: The Discoveries, Inventions, and Breakthroughs of Our Time* (New York, Plume Books, 1990), p. 206.
159. P. Ranganath Nayak and John Ketteringham, *Breakthroughs!* (New York: Rawson Associates, 1986), p. 25.
160. Val Adams, "Tape Recorders for TV a Big Hit," *New York Times*, April 20, 1956, p. 51.
161. James Lardner, *Fast Forward: Hollywood, the Japanese and the Onslaught of the VCR* (New York: W. W. Norton, 1987), p. 62.
162. "Ampex Discontinues Work on Instavideo Equipment," *Wall Street Journal*, October 12, 1971, p. 38.
163. "Video Cartridges: A Promise of Future Shock," *Time*, August 10, 1970, p. 40.
164. "The Greatest Thing Since the Nickelodeon?" *Forbes*, July 1, 1970, p. 14.
165. "Class Action Charges Investors Were Victims Buying Cartridge Stock," *Wall Street Journal*, February 15, 1974, p. 24.
166. Lardner, *Fast Forward*, p. 152.
167. *Ibid.*

26. Videogames
168. "A Red-Hot Market for Video Games," *Business Week*, November 10, 1973, p. 212.
169. Scott Cohen, *Zap: The Rise and Fall of Atari* (New York: McGraw-Hill, 1984), p. 17.
170. *Ibid.*, p. 212.
171. "TV's Hot New Star: The Electronic Game," *Business Week*, December 29, 1975, p. 24.
172. Bob Marich, "New Atari Unit to Escalate Videogame Market Battle," *Advertising Age*, April 12, 1982, p. 86.
173. "Coleco Asserts Sales of Video-Game Lines Continue to Grow," *Wall Street Journal*, December 10, 1982, p. 40.
174. Peter Nulty, "Why the Craze Won't Quit," *Fortune*, November 15, 1982, p. 114.
175. Gary Hector, "Atari's New Game Plan," *Fortune*, August 8, 1983, p. 48.
176. The exception was Magnavox's pioneering Odyssey system, which relied on program cards.

177. "Video-Game Rivalry Is Behind the Big Drop in Warner Stock Price," *Wall Street Journal*, December 10, 1982, p. 40.

178. John Anderson, "Atari," *Creative Computing*, March 1984, p. 52.

179. "Rewired: Changes at Atari," *Fortune*, June 27, 1983, p. 7.

180. Peter Petre, "Jack Tramiel Is Back on the Warpath," *Fortune*, March 4, 1985, p. 46.

181. Maria Shao, "Jack Tramiel Has Atari Turned Around—Halfway," *Business Week*, June 20, 1988, p. 50.

182. Stephen Williams, "Video Games Are Back; Nintendo Leads the Pack," *Newsday*, November 27, 1988, p. 74.

183. *Ibid.*, p. 75.

27. Warehouse Clubs

184. Frank James, "Big Warehouse Outlets Break Traditional Rules of Retailing," *Wall Street Journal*, December 22, 1983, p. 27.

185. "Boom Times in a Bargain-Hunter's Paradise," *Business Week*, March 11, 1985, p. 116.

186. "Sam's No. 1 in Wholesale Clubs," *Chain Store Age*, General Merchandise Trends, September 1987, p. 7.

187. Amy Barrett, "A Retailing Pacesetter Pulls Up Lame," *Business Week*, July 12, 1993, p. 122.

28. Word Processing Packages

188. *PC World*, January 1992, p. 142.

189. Kate Bertrand, "Can MicroPro Catch Its Fallen Star?" *Business Marketing*, May 1989, p. 58.

190. *Ibid.*, p. 60.

191. "What's So Special About WordPerfect?" *Personal Computing*, March 1988, p. 113.

192. Kathy Rebello, "The Glitch at WordPerfect," *Business Week*, May 17, 1993, pp. 90–91.

193. Yvonne Lee and Rachel Parker, "Leader of the Pack," *Infoworld*, May 25, 1990, p. 46.

Chapter 4. Patterns of Successful Imitation

1. S. C. Gilfillan, *The Sociology of Invention* (Chicago: Follett Publishing, 1935), p. 94.

2. Interestingly, twenty innovations were selected at first, but "calculating machines" had to be dropped from the analysis because they could not be properly defined.

3. Gilfillan, *Sociology of Invention*, p. 96.

4. Gilfillan claimed that the "idea" of jet propulsion has been made from time to time for more than 252 years. *Ibid.*, p. 98.

5. Francisco-Javier Olleros, "Emerging Industries and the Burnout of Pioneers,"

Journal of Product and Innovation Management, March 1986, p. 8. Emphasis added.

6. Theodore Levitt, "Marketing Myopia," *Harvard Business Review,* July–August 1960, p. 52.

Chapter 5. Imitation Strategies

1. Gwen Kinkead, "Me-Too Strategy That Paid Off," *Fortune,* August 7, 1979, p. 87.
2. John Harris, "Your Taste Buds Won't Know, Your Pocketbook Will," *Forbes,* September 3, 1990, pp. 88–90.
3. Richard Brandt, "Congratulations, It's a Clone," *Business Week,* April 15, 1991, p. 69.
4. Julie Pitta, "Live by the Clone, Die by the Clone," *Forbes,* October 28, 1991, p. 109.
5. Ira Whitten, *Brand Performance in the Cigarette Industry and the Advantage of Early Entry, 1913–1974* (Washington, D.C.:, Federal Trade Commission, Bureau of Economics, 1979), p. 47.
6. William Robinson, "Product Innovation and Start-up Business Market Share Performance," *Management Science,* October 1990, p. 1287.
7. Lawrence Ingrassia, "In High-Tech Battles, Goliaths Usually Win by Outlasting Davids," *Wall Street Journal,* September 13, 1982, p. 1.
8. Glen Urban, Theresa Carter, Steve Gaskin, and Zofia Mucha, "Market Share Rewards to Pioneering Brands: An Empirical Analysis and Strategic Implications," *Management Science,* June 1986, p. 654.
9. *Ibid.,* p. 655.
10. *Ibid.* Emphasis added.
11. *Ibid.,* p. 656.
12. Mary Sullivan, *Brand Extension and Order of Entry* (Cambridge, Mass.: Marketing Science Institute, Report no. 91-105, March 1991).
13. Reinhard Angelmar, "Product Innovation: A Tool for Competitive Advantage," *European Journal of Operational Research,* 1990, p. 185. Emphasis added.

Chapter 6. Competitive Aspects of Imitation

1. J. B. Strasser, *Swoosh: The Unauthorized Story of Nike and the Men Who Played There* (New York: Harcourt Brace Jovanovich, 1991), p. 55.
2. William Robinson, "Sources of Market Pioneer Advantages: The Case of Industrial Goods Industries," *Journal of Marketing Research,* February 1988, p. 93.
3. Peter Coy, "The Global Patent Race Picks Up," *Business Week,* August 9, 1993, p. 57.
4. Cynthia Thomas, "Hallmark Is in David-and-Goliath Battle," *Wall Street Journal,* July 18, 1986, p. 6.
5. Mark Ivy, "Dear Hallmark: See You in Court. Best Wishes, a Competitor," *Business Week,* December 8, 1986, p. 42.

6. "Hallmark Line Is Barred in Suit Over Copyright," *Wall Street Journal,* November 21, 1986, p. 8.
7. Gail Collins, "Welcome to the Big Leagues," *Venture,* June 1987, p. 29.
8. "Kodak vs. Polaroid in Market and Court," *Business Week,* September 9, 1976, p. 21.
9. Katherine Fishman, *The Computer Establishment* (New York: Harper & Row, 1981), p. 27.
10. James Lyons, "Smash the Competition," *Forbes,* September 3, 1990, p. 46.
11. C. Merle Crawford, "How Product Innovators Can Foreclose the Options of Adaptive Followers," *Journal of Consumer Marketing,* Fall 1988, p. 18.

CASE BIBLIOGRAPHY _____

1. 35mm Cameras

Auer, Michel. *The Illustrated History of the Camera from 1839 to the Present.* Boston: New York Graphic Society, 1975.
"Bargains in Photography." *Business Week,* June 2, 1975, pp. 69–73.
"Can Canon Copy Its Camera Coup?" *Business Week,* January 28, 1990, pp. 41–42.
Coe, Brian. *Cameras: From Daguerreotypes to Instant Pictures.* New York: Crown Publishers, 1978.
Dolphin, Ric. "Photography's March of Time." *Maclean's,* April 24, 1987, pp. 51–52.
Dreyfuss, Joel. "How Japan Picks America's Brains." *Fortune,* December 21, 1987, pp. 79–80.
Fuhrman, Peter. "New Focus at Leica." *Forbes,* October 31, 1988, pp. 100, 102.
Helm, Leslie, and Rebecca Aikman. "Canon: A Dream of Rivaling Big Blue." *Business Week,* May 13, 1985, pp. 98–99.
International Directory of Company History. Vol. 3. Chicago: St. James Press, 1991.
"Nikon Crowds into Leica's Picture." *Business Week,* December 11, 1965, pp. 49–52.
"West Germany: A Leica That Is Made in Japan." *Business Week,* September 29, 1973, pp. 47–48.

2. ATMs

Asinof, Lynn. "Teller Machines See Record Growth as New Locations Abound." *Wall Street Journal,* January 25, 1990, p. A1.
D'Cruz, Joseph. "Docutel Corporation." In Derek Abell and John Hammond, eds., *Strategic Market Planning.* Englewood Cliffs, N.J.: Prentice-Hall, 1979, p. 65.
Diebold, John. *The Innovators.* New York: Plume Books, 1990.
"IBM, Diebold Form Venture to Develop, Sell Bank Machines." *Wall Street Journal,* July 13, 1990, p. B4.
Mallory, Maria. "Will This ATM Team Be a Money Machine?" *Business Week,* September 17, 1990, pp. 142ff.
Searle, Gregg. "ABMs: Short History, Long Future." *Canadian Banker,* November–December 1992, pp. 20–23.

Tritch, Teresa, and John Manners. "The Money Hall of Fame." *Money,* October 1992, p. 138.

"24-Hour Automatic Tellers: How Big a Boom?" *Banking,* February 1973, pp. 17–19, 78.

Zimmer, Linda. "ATMs: An Industry Status Report." *Bank Administration,* May 1987, pp. 30–37.

———. "Rethinking ATMs." *Bank Administration,* June 1989, pp. 50–59.

3. Ballpoint Pens

"Bic Ballpoints Get Saturation Spot TV Drive." *Advertising Age,* January 9, 1961, p. 2.

Bowen, Glen. *Collectible Fountain Pens.* Gas City, Ind.: L-W Book Sales, 1982.

Lawrence, Cliff, and Judy Lawrence. *An Illustrated Fountain Pen History, 1875 to 1960.* Dunedin, Fla.: The Pen Fancier's Club, 1986.

"Waterman-Bic Sets Eastern Test for Bic Dart Pen." *Advertising Age,* August 15, 1960, pp. 2, 118.

4. Caffeine-free Soft Drinks

Brown, Paul. "Beverages." *Forbes,* January 3, 1983, pp. 188–89.

"Coke's Big Marketing Blitz." *Business Week,* May 30, 1983, pp. 58–63.

Davis, T. "Put the Principal on Detention." *Beverage World,* October 1991, pp. 44, 46.

Koeppel, Dan. "Dinosaur Brands." *Adweek's Marketing Week,* June 17, 1991, pp. 17–19.

Lederer, Bob. "Creator of the No-Caffeine Market." *Beverage World,* May 1982, pp. 23–26.

Mahoney, David. "How the Sparkle Turned to a Fizzle." *Advertising Age,* March 7, 1988, pp. 36, 39.

———. *Confessions of a Street-Smart Manager.* New York: Simon & Schuster, 1988.

Maxwell, John. *The Soft Drink Industry in 1990.* Wheat First Butcher & Singer, January 23, 1991.

5. CAT Scanners

"American, Briton Share Nobel Prize for Medicine." *Wall Street Journal,* October 12, 1979, p. 40.

Barron, Cheryll. "What Scarred EMI's Scanner." *Management Today,* February 1979, p. 152.

Bishop, Jerry. "Maker of Computerized X-Ray Scanners Says They Sharply Cut Diagnostic Costs." *Wall Street Journal,* July 26, 1977, p. 26.

———. "New X-Ray Method for Brain Disorders to Have Wider Use." *Wall Street Journal,* March 14, 1975, p. 18.

Bronson, Gail. "As Once-Bright Market for CAT Scanners Dims, Smaller Makers of the X-Ray Devices Fade Out." *Wall Street Journal,* May 6, 1980, p. 48.

Ella, Charles. "Wall Street Is Zeroing In on Latest Advances in Computerized X-Ray Scanning Technique." *Wall Street Journal,* November 21, 1975, p. 47.

"EMI Faces Countersuit by Unit of Technicare in Fight Over Patents," *Wall Street Journal*, March 28, 1978, p. 19.

"EMI Has Orders for Its Scanner." *Wall Street Journal*, October 28, 1975, p. 19.

"EMI Ltd. Sues Technicare Unit." *Wall Street Journal*, July 13, 1976, p. 2.

"EMI Ltd. Will Boost Capacity in U.S., U.K. for X-Ray Scanners." *Wall Street Journal*, December 12, 1975, p. 6.

"EMI Sues GE on Use of 8 Patents Related to X-Ray Scanning." *Wall Street Journal*, September 26, 1978, p. 34.

"EMI Sues Pfizer, Unit over Patent for Scanner." *Wall Street Journal*, August 9, 1977, p. 37.

"EMI Unit Says Action by U.S. Stalls Delivery of Only One Scanner." *Wall Street Journal*, September 30, 1976, p. 19.

"EMI Unveils Series of X-Ray Scanners." *Wall Street Journal*, September 27, 1978, p. 21.

"GE Completes Purchase of Some Thorn EMI Assets." *Wall Street Journal*, July 24, 1980, p. 20.

"GE Plan to Purchase CAT Scanner Assets Faces Antitrust Suit," *Wall Street Journal*, June 24, 1980, p. 7.

"GE to Modify Plan to Buy CAT Assets of Thorn EMI Ltd." *Wall Street Journal*, June 25, 1980, p. 27.

"Johnson & Johnson Granted EMI License for Medical Scanners." *Wall Street Journal*, February 23, 1979, p. 37.

"Justice Unit Allows GE's Revised Plan For Thorn/EMI Purchase." *Wall Street Journal*, June 30, 1980, p. 18.

"Many X-Ray Devices In Hospitals, Clinics, Are Being Corrected." *Wall Street Journal*, November 26, 1976, p. 6.

Spivak, Jonathan. "EMI Ltd. Envisions Expanding Market for X-Ray Scanner." *Wall Street Journal*, November 11, 1978, p. 2.

———. "EMI Ltd. Leaves X-Ray Scanner Business, Plans Sale of Assets to GE in the U.S." *Wall Street Journal*, April 30, 1980, p. 16.

"Technicare Denies EMI Charges." *Wall Street Journal*, July 14, 1976, p. 34.

"U.S. Assets Excluded from GE Bid to Buy Scanning Business." *Wall Street Journal*, June 27, 1980, p. 28.

6. Commercial Jet Aircraft

Davies, R. E. G. *A History of the World's Airlines.* London: Oxford University Press, 1964.

Serling, Robert. *The Jet Age.* Alexandria, Va.: Time-Life Books, 1982.

Sharp, Martin. *D.H.: A History of deHavilland.* Shewsbury, U.K.: Airlife Publishing, 1982.

7. Computerized Ticketing Services

Evans, Heidi. "Ticketmaster Emerging as Force in L.A." *Los Angeles Times*, January 31, 1985, Business sec., pp. 1, 13.

Fahri, Paul. "Carlyle Group to Buy Ticketron Division." *Washington Post,"* November 10, 1989, p. 8.
————. "Competitor to Acquire Ticketron." *Washington Post,"* February 28, 1991, sec. B, p. 1.
Gold, Howard. "No Quick Tix Fix." *Forbes,* March 10, 1986, p. 150.
McDaniel, Jobeth. "The Struggle to Sell Tickets." *New York Times,* November 26, 1989, sec. 3, p. 8.
Reilly, Patrick. "2 Bitter Rivals Heat Up New York Ticket Battle." *Crain's New York Business,* March 17, 1986, p. 3.
Shiver, Jube. "Rosen's Key to Show Biz: He Has All the Hot Tickets." *Los Angeles Times,* March 26, 1990, pp. D1, D12.
"Ticketmaster's Dominance Sparks Fears." *Wall Street Journal,* June 19, 1991, sec. B, p. 1.
"Ticketmaster Deal to Get Ticketron." *New York Times,* February 28, 1991, p. D4.
"Ticketmaster Is Buying Its Bitter Rival." *Billboard,* March 9, 1991, p. 92.
"Ticketmaster to Buy Significant Assets of Main Competitor." *Wall Street Journal,* February 26, 1991, sec. C, p. 11.
"Ticketron Struggles for a Profit." *Business Week,* June 17, 1972, p. 106.
"Ticketron Unit to Be Sold to Group in Washington." *Wall Street Journal,* November 10, 1989.
Vise, David. "Bitter Bout for the Box Office." *Washington Post,* February 25, 1990, pp. H1, H4.

8. Credit/Charge Cards

Forbes, Thomas. "Looking Back: Portrait of a Young Diner's Club as a Publicist's Dream." *Adweek's Marketing Week,* April 16, 1990, p. 18.
————. "Those Magnificent Men and Their Cards." *Adweek's Marketing Week,* April 16, 1990, p. 19.
Greenberg, Cara. "Future Worth: Before It's Hot, Grab It." *New York Times,* February 27, 1992, p. C1.
I'll Buy That: 50 Small Wonders and Big Deals That Revolutionized the Lives of Consumers. Mount Vernon, N.Y.: Consumers Union, 1986, pp. 39–42.
Mandell, Lewis. *The Credit Card Industry: A History.* Boston: Twayne Publishers, 1990.
Meehan, John. "All That Plastic Is Still Fantastic." *Business Week,* May 28, 1990, pp. 90–92.
"Readers Report" *Business Week,* November 27, 1989, p. 12.
Shepherdson, Nancy. "Credit Card America." *American Heritage,* November 1991, pp. 125–32.
Siler, Charles. "Easy to Leave Home Without It." *Forbes,* September 4, 1989, p. 140.
Spiro, Leah Nathans. "The American Express Card: Don't Shuffle Papers Without It." *Business Week,* September 13, 1993, p. 36.

9. Diet Soft Drinks

"Bottlers Ponder Latest Shakeup at RC." *Beverage Industry,* August 1991, p. 27.

Chadwick, Kyle. "Coke Gives Tab a Second Chance," *Adweek's Advertising Week,* July 17, 1989, p. 17.

"Coke's Big Marketing Blitz." *Business Week,* May 30, 1983, pp. 58–63.

Curtin, E. M. "RC: Forgets Lunch Money." *Beverage World,* August 1988, pp. 64–66.

"Diet Cola Makers Fatten Up Ad Budgets for Head-On Fight," *Printers' Ink,* May 31, 1963, pp. 8, 11.

"Diet Drinks Outpace Field; No-Caf Segment for Real." *Beverage World,* March 1983, pp. 30–31.

Koeppel, Dan. "Dinosaur Brands." *Adweek's Marketing Week,* June 17, 1991, pp. 17–19.

Levin, Gary. "Cola War Turns to Battle Royal." *Advertising Age,* June 2, 1986, pp. 4, 70.

Levine, Joshua. "Affirmative Grunts." *Forbes,* March 2, 1992, pp. 90–91.

"Little David." *Forbes,* December 15, 1965, pp. 14–15.

"New Coke–Pepsi War." *Printers' Ink,* February 22, 1963, p. 61.

Nolan, Martha. "Taste Is It." *Madison Avenue,* July 1984, pp. 76–82.

"Royal Crown to Spend $23,000,000 in '64 Promotion." *Advertising Age,* April 13, 1964, p. 3.

"Sales Bubble for Diet Soft Drinks." *Business Week,* June 27, 1964, pp. 88–90.

"That Was the Year That Was." *Beverage World,* March 1992, pp. 66–79.

Worthy, Ford. "Coke and Pepsi Stomp the Little Guys," *Fortune,* January 7, 1985, pp. 67–68.

10. Dry Beer

"Asahi's Plan to Export Dry Beer May Spill Over." *Tokyo Business Today,* March 1990, pp. 11–12.

Borrus, Amy. "Will U.S. Guzzlers Go for This Japanese Brew?" *Business Week,* July 4, 1988, p. 48.

Bryant, Adam. "An Epistemological Approach to That Elusive Phenomenon Known as Dry Beer." *New York Times,* March 4, 1993, p. D20.

Fabricant, Florence. "Dry Beers That Are Flooding the Market: Wave or Mirage?" *New York Times,* August 16, 1989, p. C6.

Katz, Mitch. "Michelob Optimistic About Success of Its Dry Beer." *Marketing News,* May 8, 1989, p. 10.

Miller, Karen Lowry. "Can Asahi Brew Another Blockbuster?" *Business Week,* March 4, 1991, p. 41.

Smith, Charles. "Satisfying a Thirst." *Far Eastern Economic Review,* September 1, 1988, p. 50.

Teinowitz, Ira. "A-B Goes to the Well and Comes Up Dry." *Advertising Age,* March 20, 1989, pp. S2, S4.

————. "New Dry Beer Gets Bud Name." *Advertising Age,* March 27, 1989, p. 3.

————. "Zeal Brewing for New Beers." *Advertising Age,* March 11, 1991, p. 16.

11. Food Processors

"Cuisinart's Bonanza Brings Lawsuits, Brutal Competition," *New England Business*, May 4, 1981, pp. 22–24.

Hannon, Kerry. "Diced and Sliced." *Forbes*, October 2, 1989, p. 72.

Howard, Niles, and Henriette Sender. "Robot-Coupe vs. Cuisinart." *Dun's Business Month*, March 1982, pp. 93, 96.

Kleinfield, N. R. "How Cuisinart Lost Its Edge." *New York Times Magazine*, April 15, 1990, p. 46.

12. Light Beer

Abrams, Bill. "Miller Is in Ferment at Anheuser's Claim of Natural Beers." *Wall Street Journal*, February 2, 1979, p. 18.

"Anheuser-Busch Files Suit to Call Its New Beer Light," *Wall Street Journal*, February 1, 1977, p. 5.

"Anheuser-Busch Has Another Entry in Light Beer Field." *Wall Street Journal*, February 13, 1978, p. 10.

"Anheuser-Busch Is Upheld on Light-Beer Description." *Wall Street Journal*, August 18, 1978, p. 10.

"Anheuser-Busch New Light Beer." *Wall Street Journal*, May 9, 1977, p. 5.

"Anheuser's Rival Takes a Dim View of Michelob Light." *Wall Street Journal*, March 23, 1979, p. 10.

"Budweiser Light Beer Hits a Sales Snag." *Wall Street Journal*, October 6, 1983, p. 33.

Byrne, Harlan. "Brewers Tap Light Beers to Spark Sales." *Wall Street Journal*, September 9, 1980, p. 29.

Dougherty, Philip. "Advertising: Big Day for Skin and Spirits." *New York Times*, December 11, 1967.

———. "Advertising: In This Corner, The New Mug." *New York Times*, September 14, 1967, p. 65.

———. "Advertising: New Borden Look but Old Moo." *New York Times*, December 29, 1967, p. 44.

———. "Advertising: Shake Hands with N.W. Ayer." *New York Times*, December 8, 1967, p. 2.

———. "Advertising: Woman of the Year Somehow Stays Busy." *New York Times*, August 2, 1967, p. 16.

Flaste, Richard. "All About Low-Calorie Beer," *New York Times*, December 10, 1975, p. 67.

"Gablinger's Beer Ads Are Labeled False by Rival Company." *New York Times*, December 9, 1967.

Garino, David. "Anheuser-Busch Will Let Bud Light Flow Coast-to-Coast." *Wall Street Journal*, March 1, 1982, p. 16.

———. "Battle of Light Beers Is Coming to a Head and Turning Heavy." *Wall Street Journal*, March 20, 1980, p. 1.

Kessler, Felix. "Rheingold's Troubles with Gablinger's Beer Come to a Head with a Government Lawsuit." *Wall Street Journal*, December 11, 1967, p. 34.

Klein, Frederick. "Wherein Mickey Spillane Gets the Girl." *Wall Street Journal,* October 10, 1977, p. 14.

"Meister Brau Files Chapter 11 Petition for Reorganization." *Wall Street Journal,* July 12, 1972, p. 22.

"Meister Brau Inc. to Sell Low-Calorie Beer in 8 States." *Wall Street Journal,* May 9, 1967, p. 8.

"Meister Brau Is Bankrupt as Reorganization Fails." *Wall Street Journal,* February 20, 1973, p. 28.

"Meister Brau Sues Rheingold on Patent for Gablinger's Beer." *Wall Street Journal,* May 27, 1968, p. 15.

"Miller Beer Wins Round over Use of Lite Name." *Wall Street Journal,* October 9, 1980, p. 21.

Nagle, James. "Personality: Putting Gold into Rheingold." *New York Times,* June 18, 1967, sec. 3, p. 3.

"Philip Morris's Miller Is Suing Jos. Schlitz over Beer Brand Name." *Wall Street Journal,* November 3, 1975, p. 19.

Reckert, Clare. "USLIFE Corp. Offering Stock for Old Line Life Insurance Co. (Miller Brewing Deal)." *New York Times,* June 30, 1972, pp. 47, 52.

"Rheingold Corp. Set to Sell Beer Free of Carbohydrates." *Wall Street Journal,* October 27, 1966, p. 12.

"Rheingold Low-Calorie Beer." *Wall Street Journal,* June 6, 1967, p. 27.

"Rheingold Says Drive for Gablinger's Beer Succeeding in Southeast." *Wall Street Journal,* April 12, 1968, p. 14.

"U.S. Court Nullifies Gablinger's Beer Patent: Meister Brau Upheld." *Wall Street Journal,* March 12, 1970, p. 6.

13. Mainframe Computers

Augarten, Stan. *Bit by Bit.* New York: Ticknor & Fields, 1984.

Burks, Alice, and Arthur Burks. *The First Electronic Computer: The Atanasoff Story.* Ann Arbor: University of Michigan Press, 1988.

DeLamarter, Richard. *Big Blue: IBM's Use and Abuse of Power.* New York: Dodd, Mead & Company, 1986.

Fishman, Katherine. *The Computer Establishment.* New York: Harper & Row, 1981.

Linde, Nancy. *The Machine That Changed the World: Inventing the Future.* WGBH public television, Boston, 1992.

Ritche, David. *The Computer Pioneers.* New York: Simon & Schuster, 1986.

Watson, Thomas, Jr. *Father, Son & Co.: My Life at IBM and Beyond.* New York: Bantam Books, 1990.

14. Microwave Ovens

"Amana Puts the Heat on the Oven Critics." *Business Week,* July 16, 1973, p. 30.

"Amana Radarange: What Price Speed?" *Consumer Reports,* November 1968, pp. 573–74.

"Electronic Cookstove." *Business Week,* April 3, 1954.

"A Four-Minute Cake." *Business Week,* September 12, 1964, pp. 94–96.

"Home on the Radarange." *Newsweek,* March 4, 1968, pp. 69–70.

"Industry Warms Up to Microwaves." *Business Week,* March 13, 1965, pp. 152–56.

Kanner, Bernice, "Microwave Oven Market Is Really Hot," *New York,* July 15, 1985, pp. 22–27.

Magaziner, Ira, and Mark Patinkin. "Fast Heat: How Korea Won the Microwave War." *Harvard Business Review,* January–February 1989, pp. 83–92.

"A Microwave of the Future." *Wall Street Journal,* September 14, 1989, sec. B, p. 1.

"Microwave Ovens Really Blast Off." *Business Week,* July 16, 1984, pp. 30–31.

"Microwave Ovens" (market share data). *Weekly Home Furnishings,* March 19, 1990, p. 104.

"Microwave Ovens: Not Recommended." *Consumer Reports,* April 1973, pp. 221–30.

"Raytheon: Learning New Markets for Electronics." *Business Week,* May 15, 1954, pp. 114–18.

"The Two-Minute Oven." *Business Week,* October 25, 1963, pp. 95–96.

Wiersema, Fred. "General Electric Microwave Ovens." In *Strategic Marketing,* ed. John Cady and Robert Buzzell. Boston: Little, Brown, 1979, pp. 344–49.

———. "Litton Microwave Ovens." In *Strategic Marketing,* ed. John Cady and Robert Buzzell. Boston: Little, Brown, 1979, pp. 354–58.

———. "Microwave Ovens: The Japanese Manufacturers." In *Strategic Marketing,* ed. John Cady and Robert Buzzell. Boston: Little, Brown, 1979, pp. 389–94.

Wong, Kenneth. "Amana Microwave Ovens." In *Strategic Marketing,* ed. John Cady and Robert Buzzell. Boston: Little, Brown, 1979, pp. 364–75.

"Yen's Rise Isn't Likely to Significantly Trim Japan's Exports to U.S." *Wall Street Journal,* March 21, 1986, p. 10.

15. Money-Market Mutual Funds

"Cash Floods the Money Funds." *Business Week,* March 27, 1978, p. 120.

CDA/Wiesenberger. *Investment Companies Service.* Investment Companies, 1992.

Cole, Robert. "Interest Rates Come Down, but Money Funds Roar Ahead." *New York Times,* March 2, 1975, p. F3.

———. "Personal Finance: Cash-Managing Fund," *New York Times,* June 20, 1974, pp. 57, 61.

DeWitt Malley, Deborah. "Making Your Money Work Fast." *Fortune,* April 1974, pp. 81–86.

Donoghue's Money Fund Directory, 1993.

Hershey, Robert D., Jr. "Overnight Mutual Funds for Surplus Assets." *New York Times,* January 7, 1973, p. 5.

"Inflow Sets Record for Money Funds." *New York Times,* January 11, 1980, p. D9.

Lohr, Steve. "Money Funds: Here's How They're Run." *New York Times,* March 9, 1980, pp. F1, F15.

Metz, Robert. "Marketplace: Money Funds Weather Stock Surge." *New York Times,* March 12, 1976, p. 6.

————. "The Money Funds Face Maturity." *New York Times,* July 13, 1975, p. F7.
"Money Market Funds Are Still Riding High." *Business Week,* February 17, 1975, p. 26.
"Money-Market Funds: A Place to Park Cash." *Business Week,* December 27, 1976, p. 130.
"More Magnetism in Money Funds." *Business Week,* February 12, 1979, pp. 96–97.
"A No-Load Fund for Cash Managers." *Business Week,* October 14, 1972, p. 70.
Phalon, Richard. "Personal Investing: Big Days for the Money-Market Funds." *New York Times,* January 14, 1978, p. 31.
————. "Rate Decline Turns Small Investors from Money-Market Mutual Funds." *New York Times,* September 6, 1976, pp. 22–23.

16. MRIs

Andrews, Edmund. "Patents: New Lawsuit on Magnetic Resonance." *New York Times,* September 5, 1992, p. 32.
"Fonar Order Backlog Running 41% Ahead of Year-Ago Level." *Wall Street Journal,* August 28, 1987, p. 12.
"The Inventor." *U.S. News & World Report,* January 26, 1987, p. 66.
"Johnson & Johnson and Unit Are Charged with Infringing Patent." *Wall Street Journal,* September 22, 1982, p. 28.
"Johnson & Johnson Denies Patent-Infringement Charge." *Wall Street Journal,* September 23, 1982, p. 12.
"Johnson & Johnson Found to Infringe on Fonar Patent." *Wall Street Journal,* November 25, 1985, p. 13.
"Johnson & Johnson Patent Case Ruling Reversed by Judge." *Wall Street Journal,* January 4, 1986, p. 25.
Naj, Amal Kumar. "Diagnostic Equipment Field in Squeeze." *Wall Street Journal,* September 6, 1990, p. B12.
"A New Image for Fonar." *Business Week,* March 10, 1986, p. 102.
Pollack, Andrew. "Medical Technology Arms Race Adds Billions to the Nation's Bills." *New York Times,* April 29, 1991, pp. 1, B8.
"Seeing Inside the Body Without X-Rays." *Business Week,* August 24, 1981, pp. 42B–42D.
"Superfast Scans of the Whole Body." *Business Week,* December 15, 1986, p. 100.
Waldholz, Michael. "Doctors Excited About Device That Could Replace CT Scans." *Wall Street Journal,* October 23, 1981, p. 29.
————. "Fonar Corp. Reports Big Advance in Work on Diagnostic Gear." *Wall Street Journal,* November 30, 1982, p. 17.
————. "Fonar, After Long Struggle, Expects Medical Imaging Device to Yield Profits." *Wall Street Journal,* January 20, 1986, p. 4.

17. Nonalcoholic Beer

Blumenthal, Karen. "Coors Sets Rollout of New Dry Beer, No-Alcohol Brew." *Wall Street Journal,* July 29, 1991, p. B3.

"Boozeless Bonanza." *Time,* October 7, 1991, p. 65.

Charlier, Marj. "Big Beer Makers Go After the Sober Set with Assortment of Nonalcoholic Brews." *Wall Street Journal,* March 30, 1992, pp. B1, B12.

"Coors to Distribute Nonalcoholic Beer." *New York Times,* April 4, 1991, p. D4.

Fisher, Lawrence. "Brewers Offer Non-Alcoholic Beers." *New York Times,* December 25, 1989, pp. 37, 40.

Leerhsen, Charles." A Beer by Any Other Name: So Long Shirley Temple." *Newsweek,* October 13, 1986, p. 64.

McMath, Robert. "Low-Alcohol Beers." *Ad Forum,* August 1984, p. 41.

Miller, Annetta, and Karen Springen. "This Safe Suds Is for You." *Newsweek,* March 6, 1990, p. 42.

18. Operating Systems for Personal Computers

"Battle of the DOSes." *Byte,* February 1983, pp. 431–32.

"Battle of the Operating Systems." *Byte,* February 1982, p. 330.

"CP/M Background and History." *Mini-Micro Systems,* February 1981, p. 168.

Dahmke, Mark. "CP/M Plus." *Byte,* July 1983, pp. 360–84.

Ferguson, Charles, and Charles Morris. *Computer Wars.* New York: Times Books, 1993.

Fierman, Jaclyn. "A Fallen Software Star Tries a Comeback." *Fortune,* January 21, 1985, p. 55.

Machrone, Bill. "Roots: The Evolution of Innovation." *PC Magazine,* May 26, 1987, pp. 166–74.

"MS-DOS Versus CP/M." *Byte,* June 1982, pp. 442–43.

Palfreman, Jon, and Robert Hone. *The Machine That Changed the World: The Paperback Computer.* WGBH public television, Boston, 1992.

Wallace, James, and Jim Erickson. *Hard Drive: Bill Gates and the Making of the Microsoft Empire.* New York: John Wiley & Sons, 1992.

Weizer, Norman. "A History of Operating Systems." *Datamation,* January 1981, pp. 118–26.

19. Paperback Books

Carter, Robert. "Pioneers! O Pioneers!" *Publishers Weekly,* May 26, 1989, pp. S10, S14.

———. "How It All Began." *Publishers Weekly,* May 26, 1989, pp. S4–S38.

Crider, Allen. *Mass Market Publishing in America.* Boston: G. K. Hall & Co., 1982.

Davis, Joann, and William Goldstein. "Realizing the Potential at Pocket Books." *Publishers Weekly,* January 23, 1987, pp. 45–48.

Davis, Kenneth, *Two-Bit Culture.* Boston: Houghton-Mifflin, 1984.

I'll Buy That. Mount Vernon, N.Y.: Consumers Union, 1986.

"Leon Shimkin: Betting on the Stork." *Forbes,* February 5, 1966, pp. 34–35.

Madison, Charles. *Book Publishing in America.* New York: McGraw-Hill, 1966.

Tebbel, John. *A History of Book Publishing in the United States,* Vol. IV: *The Great Change 1940–1980.* New York: R. R. Bowker, 1981.

20. Personal Computers

Augarten, Stan. *Bit by Bit.* New York: Ticknor & Fields, 1984.

"The Coming Shakeout on Personal Computers," *Business Week,* November 22, 1983, p. 83.

Ferguson, Charles, and Charles Morris. *Computer Wars.* New York: Times Books, 1993.

Lewis, Geoff. "The PC Wars: IBM vs. the Clones." *Business Week,* July 28, 1986, p. 62.

Palfreman, Jon, and Robert Hone. *The Machine That Changed the World: The Paperback Computer.* WGBH public television, Boston, 1992.

"Personal Computers: And the Winner Is IBM." *Business Week,* October 3, 1983, p. 76.

"A Pioneer Goes Bankrupt." *Time,* September 26, 1983, p. 52.

Sobel, Robert. *IBM: Colossus in Transition.* New York: Times Books, 1981.

Therien, Lois. "Why Gateway Is Racing to Answer on the First Ring." *Business Week,* September 3, 1993, p. 92.

21. Pocket Calculators

"Adding Machines Loom as Mama's New Helper." *Business Week,* June 6, 1964, p. 34.

"Alas, Poor Mastodon of Mathematics." *New York Times,* July 11, 1976, sec. 3, p. 13.

"Bowmar Drops Some Products." *New York Times,* June 3, 1975.

Lichtenstein, Grace. "New Calculators Catch Public's Fancy." *New York Times,* October 28, 1972, p. 33.

Metz, Robert. "Marketplace: Keeping Your Figures in Your Pocket." *New York Times,* May 27, 1972, p. 36.

Nash, Nathaniel. "Shakeout Time for Calculators." *New York Times,* December 8, 1974, sec. 3, pp. 1, 4.

Rehr, Darryl. "Calculators: You Can Count on Them." *Office,* July 1991, pp. 56–57.

Robards, Terry. "Mini-Calculator Shakeout." *New York Times,* October 8, 1972, sec. 3, p. 4.

"The Semiconductor Becomes a New Marketing Force." *Business Week,* August 24, 1974, pp. 34–39.

Smith, Gene. "Texas Instruments Puts 3 Calculators on Market." *New York Times,* September 21, 1972, pp. 67, 79.

Smith, William. "Bowmar Will Ask Reorganization." *New York Times,* February 11, 1975.

———. "Hand-held Calculators: Tool or Toy?" *New York Times,* August 20, 1972, sec. 3, p. 7.

"Texas Instruments, Inc. Is Sued by Bowmar." *New York Times,* September 10, 1974.

22. Projection Television

"Advent Corp. Big-Screen TV." *Wall Street Journal,* September 30, 1980, p. 16.

"Advent Corp. Founder, Another Director Quit at Suggestion of Firm." *Wall Street Journal,* April 18, 1977, p. 24.

"Advent Says Its Plan for Reorganization Rejected by Court." *Wall Street Journal,* January 21, 1982, p. 39.

"Advent Sells Some Assets and Pays Some Secured Debt." *Wall Street Journal,* April 26, 1982, p. 37.

"Advent's Founder Quits Research Post, Plans to Remain a Director." *Wall Street Journal,* October 18, 1976, p. 22.

"Advent's New Big-Screen TV." *Wall Street Journal,* June 16, 1976, p. 14.

"Anderson Pins Advent's Hopes on Big Screen." *New York Times,* May 11, 1979, p. D2.

Angus, Robert. "Large-Screen TV Basics." *High Fidelity,* July 1986, pp. 50–53.

Baker, Thomas. "Self-Inflicted Wounds." *Forbes,* August 31, 1981, pp. 100–102.

"Big Screens That Don't Vex Viewers." *Business Week,* October 21, 1991, p. 142.

"A Fine-Tuning for Big Screen TV." *Business Week,* June 8, 1981, p. 94.

"400,000 Projection TV Sales Forecast for 1991." *Television Digest,* February 4, 1991, p. 11.

"Here Comes Projection Television." *Economist,* October 8, 1977, p. 102.

Gumpert, David. "Does Anybody Want a TV Set That Has a 4-by-6 Foot Screen?" *Wall Street Journal,* June 11, 1974, pp. 1, 23.

"Kloss-Novabeam 100 Front-Projection Monitor." *High Fidelity,* July 1986, pp. 28–32.

Levine, Martin. "Tall Troubles For Big-Screen Pioneer," *Newsday,* June 22, 1987, part 3, p. 5.

"A Little Guy Gets Big Attention with His Home Large-Screen Sets." *Broadcasting,* May 13, 1974, pp. 47–48.

Mitchell, Peter. "The Big Screen Comes Home." *High Technology,* April 1987, pp. 52–54.

"Superscreen TV: Learn Before You Leap." *Business Week,* June 8, 1981, pp. 115–16.

Vizard, Frank, Frank Barr, and Stephen Booth. "Giant TV." *Popular Mechanics,* September 1991, pp. 47–103.

Welles, Edward. "What Becomes a Legend." *Inc.,* June 1989, p. 21.

23. Spreadsheets

Barr, Christopher. "From VisiCalc to 1-2-3: How Much Did 1-2-3 Really Borrow From its Predecessor, VisiCalc?" *PC Magazine,* May 26, 1987, p. 169.

"Beyond VisiCalc." *Personal Computing,* July 1982, p. 13.

Burlingham, Bo, and Michael Hopkins. "My Company, My Self." *Inc.,* July 1989, p. 35.

Licklider, Tracy. "Birthing the Visible Calculator." *Byte,* December 1989, pp. 326–28.

———. "Ten Years of Rows and Columns." *Byte,* December 1989, pp. 324–31.

Mueller, Robert. "Business Planning Software." *Personal Computing,* November 1982, pp. 115–92.

Pollack, Andrew. "Visicorp Is Merging into Paladin. *New York Times,* November 3, 1984, pp. 29, 37.

24. Telephone Answering Machines

"Automated Telephone Improves Service." *Best's Review,* July 1971, pp. 66–68.

Coy, Peter. "AT&T Is Strutting Its Stuff in Consumer Goods." *Business Week,* July 6, 1992, p. 70.

"Hello, You've Reached . . ." *Popular Science,* August 1989, pp. 76–78.

Farmanfaraian, Roxane. "Answering Machines with New Talents." *Working Woman,* June 1987, p. 114.

Garry, Michael. "Telephone Answering Market Up for Grabs as Plunging Prices Bring in Consumers." *Merchandising,* February 1984, p. 46.

Gelfond, Susan. "You'll Hear a Lot of That Beep." *Business Week,* February 4, 1986, p. 108.

Jacobs, Sanford. "Lonely Phone Mates Will Be Pining Away in the Warehouse." *Wall Street Journal,* March 6, 1975, p. 22.

Maloney, Russell. "The Shape, if Such It Can Be Called, of Things to Come." *New Yorker,* April 3, 1943, p. 22.

Miller, Deborah. "Take a Close Look at Telephone Answerer Mix." *Merchandising,* January 1983, pp. 62–118.

"New Developments: Answering Machines Abandon Cassettes." *High Technology Business,* April 1988, p. 8.

"Phone-Answering Machines." *Consumer Reports,* May 1986, pp. 295–301.

"Phone-Mate's Rise and Fall." *Consumer Reports,* January 1989, p. 48.

Ramirez, Anthony. "All About Answering Machines: For Yuppies, Now Plain Folks, Too." *New York Times,* January 27, 1991, p. F5.

"Ratings: Telephone Answering Machines." *Consumer Reports,* May 1983, p. 250.

Schneider, Jim. "Retailers, Suppliers Cite Both Ends of Price Range for Booming Sales." *Merchandising,* November 1979, p. 81.

Trunzo, Candace. "Answering Machines Worth Listening To." *Money,* April 1984, pp. 141–44.

25. VCRs

Adams. Val. "Tape Recorders for TV a Big Hit," *New York Times,* April 20, 1956, p. 51.

———. TV Is Put on Tape By New Recorder." *New York Times,* April 15, 1965, p. 1.

"Ampex Discontinues Work on Instavideo Equipment." *Wall Street Journal,* October 12, 1971, p. 38.

"Cartridge TV Forms a Videotape Venture with Columbia Pictures." *Wall Street Journal,* April 26, 1972, p. 10.

"CBS' Fast Draw on Home TV Tapes." *Business Week,* March 28, 1970, pp. 50–52.

"Class Action Charges Investors Were Victims Buying Cartridge Stock." *Wall Street Journal,* February 15, 1974, p. 24.

Diebold, John. *The Innovators: The Discoveries, Inventions, and Breakthroughs of Our Time.* New York: Plume Books, 1990.

"Goldmark's Variation on a Video Theme." *Fortune,* May 1970, p. 70.

"The Greatest Thing Since the Nickelodeon?" *Forbes,* July 1, 1970, pp. 13–15.

"Industry Takes to TV Cassettes." *Business Week,* August 12, 1972, pp. 124–28.

Lardner, James, *Fast Forward: Hollywood, the Japanese and the Onslaught of the VCR.* New York: W. W. Norton & Co., 1987, p. 62.

Marcial, Gene. "Sony Gets Renewed Attention on Wall Street Due to Soaring Profit, Video Tape Recorders." *Wall Street Journal,* July 7, 1976, p. 21.

Nayak, P. Ranganath, and John Ketteringham. *Breakthroughs!* New York: Rawson Associates, 1986, pp. 23–49.

Rosenbloom, Richard, and Michael Cusumano. "Technological Pioneering and Competitive Advantage: The Birth of the VCR Industry." *California Management Review,* Summer 1987, pp. 51–76.

"Sears Roebuck to Sell Home Videotape Unit." *Wall Street Journal,* January 21, 1972, p. 8.

"Sony to Begin Offering Video-Tape Recorder in the U.S. for $2,295." *Wall Street Journal,* October 30, 1975, p. 18.

"Spinning Head Tapes TV at Home," *Popular Science,* January 1965, p. 86.

Synder, R. "Ampex's New Video Tape Recorder." *Tele-Tech & Electronic Industries,* April 1956, pp. 72–110.

"A TV Recording System Begins to Catch On with Consumers." *Wall Street Journal,* July 8, 1976, p. 1.

"A Video Cartridge Bows—to Muffled Applause." *Business Week,* November 14, 1970, pp. 100–102.

"Video Cartridges: A Promise of Future Shock," *Time,* August 10, 1970, pp. 40–41.

26. Videogames

"All-Electronic Game Hooked to TV Set by Magnavox." *Wall Street Journal,* May 11, 1972, p. 15.

Anderson, John. "Atari." *Creative Computing,* March 1984, p. 52.

"Atari Sells Itself to Survive." *Business Week,* November 15, 1976, p. 120.

"Atari Sues Imagic on Copyright Issue." *New York Times,* November 30, 1982, p. D4.

Bernstein, Peter. "Atari and the Video-Game Explosion." *Fortune,* July 27, 1981, pp. 40–46.

Cohen, Scott. *Zap: The Rise and Fall of Atari.* New York: McGraw-Hill, 1984.

"Coleco Asserts Sales of Video-Game Lines Continue to Grow." *Wall Street Journal,* December 10, 1982, p. 40.

Cuneo, Alice. "At $200 a Pop, Will Super Nintendo Have Legs?" *Business Week,* September 16, 1991, p. 30.

"Demand Overwhelms Video Game Makers." *Business Week,* November 29, 1976, p. 31.

Hector, Gary. "Atari's New Game Plan." *Fortune,* August 8, 1983, pp. 46–51.

———. "The Big Shrink Is On at Atari." *Fortune,* July 9, 1984, pp. 23–36.

"How Jack Tramiel Hopes to Turn Atari Around." *Business Week,* July 16, 1984, p. 30.

Marich, Bob. "New Atari Unit to Escalate Videogame Market Battle." *Advertising Age,* April 12, 1982, p. 86.

McGill, Douglas. "A Nintendo Labyrinth Filled with Lawyers, Not Dragons." *New York Times,* March 9, 1989, pp. A1, D23.

Moffat, Susan. "Can Nintendo Keep Winning?" *Fortune,* November 5, 1990, pp. 130–36.

Nulty, Peter. "Why the Craze Won't Quit." *Fortune,* November 15, 1982, pp. 114–24.

Petre, Peter. "Jack Tramiel Is Back on the Warpath." *Fortune,* March 4, 1985, pp. 46–50.

"A Red-Hot Market for Video Games." *Business Week,* November 10, 1973, p. 212.

"Rewired: Changes at Atari." *Fortune,* June 27, 1983, p. 7.

Schmitt, Richard. "Atari Corp. Fails to Prove Losses in Antitrust Suit." *Wall Street Journal,* May 4, 1992, pp. A1, A4

———. "Nintendo Suit Filed by Atari Is Going to Trial." *Wall Street Journal,* February 13, 1992, pp. B1, B8.

Shao, Maria. "Jack Tramiel Has Atari Turned Around—Halfway," *Business Week,* June 20, 1988, p. 50.

———. "There's a Rumble in the Video Arcade." *Business Week,* February 20, 1989, p. 37.

"TV's Hot New Star: The Electronic Game." *Business Week,* December 29, 1975, pp. 24–25.

"Video-Game Rivalry Is Behind the Big Drop in Warner Stock Price." *Wall Street Journal,* December 10, 1982, p. 40.

Williams, Stephen. "Video Games Are Back; Nintendo Leads the Pack." *Newsday,* November 27, 1988, pp. 74–75.

Wolpin, Stewart. "How Nintendo Revived a Dying Industry." *Marketing Communications,* May 1989, pp. 36–40.

27. Warehouse Clubs

Barrett, Amy. "A Retailing Pacesetter Pulls Up Lame." *Business Week,* July 12, 1993, pp. 122–23.

Blumenthal, Karen. "Shopping Clubs Ready for Battle in Texas Market." *Wall Street Journal,* October 21, 1991, pp. B1, B11.

"Boom Times in a Bargain-Hunter's Paradise." *Business Week,* March 11, 1985, p. 116.

Helliker, Kevin. "Consolidation of Warehouse Clubs Increases," *Wall Street Journal,* November 7, 1990, pp. B1, B6.

James, Frank. "Big Warehouse Outlets Break Traditional Rules of Retailing." *Wall Street Journal,* December 22, 1983, p. 27.

Petit, Dave. "Big Retailers' Moves to Acquire Stakes in Wholesale Clubs Add Life to Market." *Wall Street Journal,* November 7, 1990, p. C8.

"Sam's No. 1 in Wholesale Clubs." *Chain Store Age,* General Merchandise Trends, September 1987, p. 7.

Soporito, Bill. "The Mad Rush to Join the Warehouse Club." *Fortune,* January 6, 1986, pp. 59, 61.

Strom, Stephanie. "A Shuffle of Warehouse Clubs." *New York Times,* May 22, 1993, p. L33.

"Wal-Mart Completes Purchase." *Wall Street Journal,* June 30, 1987, p. 7.

Zellner, Wendy. "Warehouse Clubs Butt Heads—And Reach for the Ice Pack." *Business Week,* April 19, 1993, p. 30.

28. Word Processing Software

Ahrens, Kristine. "Word Processing: 50 Years in Retrospect." *Office,* June 1982, p. 101.

Atchison, Sandra. "A Perfectly Good World for WordPerfect: Gutsy." *Business Week,* October 2, 1989, pp. 99, 102.

Bertrand, Kate. "Can MicroPro Catch Its Fallen Star?" *Business Marketing,* May 1989, pp. 55–65.

"The Businessware Top 20." *PC World,* January 1992, p. 142.

Churbuck, David. "Calling Dr. Posner." *Forbes,* April 29, 1991, p. 142.

Kulkosky, Edward. "The Word Processing War Is On." *Financial World,* July 15, 1980.

Lee, Yvonne, and Rachel Parker. "Leader of the Pack." *Infoworld,* May 25, 1990, pp. 45–46.

Lombardi, John. "Wordstar 5.5: Grand Old Man Gets a New Hat and Cane." *Infoworld,* July 3, 1989, pp. 55–57.

Machrone, Bill. "Roots: The Evolution of Innovation." *PC Magazine,* May 26, 1987, pp. 166–74.

Meilach, Dona. "The New Generations of Word Processors." *Interface Age,* April 1984, pp. 25–26.

Picarille, Lisa. "WordStar Tries to Keep Up with the Times." *Infoworld,* December 2, 1991, p. 104.

Pompili, Tony. "WordPerfect for Windows Delay Sends Some Companies Shopping Elsewhere." *PC Week,* March 25, 1991, p. 15.

———. "WordPerfect Growth Stalls as Windows Effort Stumbles." *PC Week,* July 1, 1991, pp. 1, 12.

Rebello, Kathy. "The Glitch at WordPerfect." *Business Week,* May 17, 1993, pp. 90–91.

Rooney, Paula. "Windows WP Fight Gets Fierce." *PC Week,* March 23, 1992, pp. 43, 48.

———. "WP Duel Scars Smaller Companies." *PC Week,* June 22, 1992, p. 221.

"The Selling of Software." *Datamation,* April 15, 1984, pp. 125–28.

Strehlo, Christine. "What's So Special About WordPerfect?" *Personal Computing,* March 1988, p. 100–114.

Zachary, Pascal. "WordPerfect Ships Windows Version of Software, Heating Up Competition." *Wall Street Journal,* November 11, 1991, sec. B, p. 1.

SELECTED READINGS _____

Aaker, David, and George Day. "The Perils of High-Growth Markets." *Strategic Management Journal*, September–October 1986, pp. 409–21.

Andrews, Edmund. "When Imitation Isn't the Sincerest Form of Flattery." *New York Times*, August 5, 1990, sec. 4, p. E20.

————. "There's Cash in Mining the Courts." *New York Times*, November 9, 1992, p. D.2.

Angelmar, Reinhard. "Product Innovation: A Tool for Competitive Advantage." *European Journal of Operational Research*, 1990, pp. 182–89.

Ansoff, H. Igor, and John Stewart. "Strategies for a Technology-Based Business." *Harvard Business Review*, November–December 1967, pp. 71–83.

Atlas, James. "When an Original Idea Sounds Familiar." *New York Times*, July 28, 1991, p. 2.

Bain, Joe. *Barriers to New Competition*. Cambridge, Mass.: Harvard University Press, 1956.

Baldwin, William, and Gerald Childs. "The Fast Second and Rivalry in Research and Development." *Southern Economic Journal*, 1969, pp. 18–24.

Barzel, Yoram. "Optimal Timing of Innovations." *Review of Economics and Statistics*, August 1968, pp. 348–55.

Benedict, Daniel, "Imitation Can Be Flattering—and Illegal." *Venture*, April 1989, pp. 58, 60.

Biggadike, Ralph. *Corporate Diversification: Entry, Strategy and Performance*. Cambridge, Mass.: Harvard University Press, 1979.

————. "The Risky Business of Diversification." *Harvard Business Review*, May–June 1979, pp. 103–11.

Bond, Ronald, and David Lean. *Sales, Promotion, and Product Differentiation in Two Prescription Drug Markets*. Washington, D.C.: Federal Trade Commission, Bureau of Economics, February 1977.

Brown, Paul. "Beverages." *Forbes*, January 3, 1983, pp. 188–89.

Carpenter, Gregory. "Market Pioneering and Competitive Positioning Strategy." *Extrait Des Annales Des Telecommunications*, November–December 1987.

Carpenter, Gregory, and Kent Nakamoto. "Competitive Strategies for Late Entry

into a Market With a Dominant Brand," *Management Science,* October 1990, pp. 1268–78.

———. "Consumer Preference Formation and Pioneering Advantage." *Journal of Marketing Research,* August 1988, pp. 285–98.

Carte, Norman. "Patent Applications: Need and Timing Can Be as Critical as Validity." *High Technology Business,* December 1988, pp. 14–15.

Chatterjee, Rabikar, and Yoshi Sugita. "New Product Introduction Under Demand Uncertainty in Competitive Industries." *Managerial & Decision Economics,* February 1990, pp. 1–12.

Coleman, Henry, and John Vandenberg. "How to Follow the Leader." *Inc.,* July 1988, pp. 125–26.

Conrad, Cecilia. "The Advantages of Being First and Competition Between Firms." *International Journal of Industrial Organization,* 1983, pp. 354–64.

Cooper, Arnold, and Dan Schendel: "Strategic Responses to Technological Threats." *Business Horizons,* February 1976, pp. 61–69.

Cooper, R. G. "The Dimensions of Industrial New Product Success and Failure." *Journal of Marketing,* Summer 1979, pp. 93–103.

Crawford, C. Merle. "How Product Innovators Can Foreclose the Options of Adaptive Followers." *Journal of Consumer Marketing,* Fall 1988, pp. 17–24.

Dasgupta, Partha. "Patents, Priority, and Imitation or, the Economics of Races and Waiting Games." *Economic Journal,* March 1988, pp. 66–80.

Davidson, Hugh. "Why Most New Consumer Brands Fail." *Harvard Business Review,* March–April 1976, pp. 117–21.

Day, George, and Robin Wensley. "Assessing Advantage: A Framework for Diagnosing Competitive Superiority." *Journal of Marketing,* April 1988, pp. 1–20.

Dixit, Avinash. "The Role of Investment in Entry Deterence." *The Economics Journal,* March 1980, pp. 95–106.

Donnelly, James, Jr. "Competing When You're Not Number One." *Bank Marketing,* February 1990, pp. 36–37.

Dreyfuss, Joel. "How Japan Picks America's Brains." *Fortune,* December 21, 1987, pp. 79–89.

Economist editors. "Whose Ideas Is It Anyway?" *Economist,* November 12, 1988, pp. 73–74.

———. "Science and Technology: Who Are the Copy Cats Now?" *Economist,* May 20, 1989, pp. 91–94.

Falvey, Jack. "Follow the Leader." *Inc.,* July 1986, pp. 93–94.

Feder, Barnaby. "Formica: When a Household Name Becomes an Also-Ran," *New York Times,* August 12, 1989, p. 12.

Ferris, Patricia. "Knock-off . . . Knock-out? Brand Names vs. Generics." *Marketing News,* Fall 1990, p. 3.

Fershtman, Chaim; Vijay Mahajan; and Eitan Muller. "Market Share Pioneering Advantage: A Theoretical Approach." *Management Science,* August 1990, pp. 900–918.

Fortune editors. "An Inventor Won't Take It Lying Down." *Fortune,* April 22, 1991, pp. 229–30.

Freudenheim, Milt. "Now the Big Drug Makers Are Imitating Their Imitators." *New York Times*, September 20, 1992, p. 5.

Fujiki, Mikako. "Japan—Technology Licensing." *East Asian Executive Reports*, February 15, 1989, pp. 16–17.

Ghemawat, Pankaj. "Sustainable Advantages." *Harvard Business Review*, September–October 1986, pp. 53–58.

Glazer, A. "The Advantages of Being First." *American Economic Review*, June 1985, pp. 473–80.

Golder, Peter, and Gerard Tellis. *Do Pioneers Really Have Long-Term Advantages? A Historical Analysis.* Cambridge, Mass.: Marketing Science Institute, Report no. 92-124, September 1992.

————. "Pioneer Advantage: Marketing Logic or Marketing Legend?" *Journal of Marketing Research*, May 1993, pp. 158–70.

Grabowski, Henry, and John Vernon. "Pioneers, Imitators, and Generics: A Simulation Model of Schumpeterian Competition." *Quarterly Journal of Economics*, August 1987, pp. 491–525.

Green, Gerald. "A Lawyer's View: Design Patents—Infringements, Damages, and Profits." *Research and Development*, August 1984, p. 31.

Greshman, Michael. *Getting It Right the Second Time: How American Ingenuity Transformed 49 Marketing Failures Into Some of Our Most Successful Products.* Reading, Mass.: Addison-Wesley, 1990.

Gubernick, Lisa. "Step 1: Go to Lunch." *Forbes*, July 9, 1990, p. 104.

Hafner, Katherine. "The Knockoffs Head for a Knockdown Fight with IBM." *Business Week*, December 21, 1987, pp. 112–13.

Haines, Daniel; Rajan Chandran; and Arvind Parke. "Winning by Being the First to Market . . . Or Second?" *Journal of Consumer Marketing*, Winter 1989, pp. 63–69.

Hannon, Kerry. "Danger Zone." *Forbes*, November 2, 1987, pp. 54, 57.

Harris, John. "Your Taste Buds Won't Know, Your Pocketbook Will." *Forbes*, September 3, 1990, pp. 88–90.

Hauser, John, and Steven Shugan. "Defensive Marketing Strategies." *Marketing Science*, Fall 1983, pp. 319–60.

Heins, John. "Why Do Wild Things?" *Forbes*, May 5, 1986, pp. 96, 98.

Hutheesing, Nikhil. "The First Shall Be Last." *Forbes*, October 25, 1993, pp. 220–21.

Ingrassia, Lawrence. "In High-Tech Battles, Goliaths Usually Win by Outlasting Davids." *Wall Street Journal*, September 13, 1982, pp. 1, 19.

Jensen, Richard. "Adoption and Diffusion of an Innovation of Uncertain Profitability." *Journal of Economic Theory*, June 1982, pp. 182–93.

Kalish, Shlomo, and Gary Lilien. "A Market Entry Timing Model for New Technologies." *Management Science*, February 1986, pp. 194–202.

Kane, Chester. "Overcome the 'Me Too' Product Syndrome." *Journal of Business Strategy*, March–April 1989, pp. 14–16.

Katz, Michael, and Carl Shapiro. "R&D Rivalry with Licensing or Imitation." *American Economic Review*, June 1987, pp. 402–20.

Kerin, Roger; P. Rajan Varandarajan; and Robert Peterson. "First-Mover Advantage:

A Synthesis, Conceptual Framework, and Research Propositions. *Journal of Marketing,* October 1992, pp. 33–52.

Kinkead, Gwen. "A Me-Too Strategy That Paid Off." *Fortune,* August 27, 1979, pp. 86–88.

Koselka, Rita. "When a Partner Becomes a Competitor." *Forbes,* April 30, 1990, pp. 133–38.

Kremen-Bolton, Michele. "Imitation Versus Innovation: Lessons to be Learned from the Japanese." *Organizational Dynamics,* Winter 1993, p. 30.

Lambkin, Mary. "Order of Entry and Performance in New Markets." *Strategic Management Journal,* Summer 1988, pp. 127–40.

Lappen, Alyssa. "Step Aside, Superman." *Forbes,* February 6, 1989, pp. 124–26.

Levin, Doron. "Hot Wheels." *New York Times Magazine,* September 30, 1990, sec. 6, pp. 32ff.

Levin, Richard. "Appropiability, R&D Spending, and Technological Performance." *American Economic Review,* May 1988, pp. 424–28.

Levin, Richard; Alvin Klevorick; Richard Nelson; and Sidney Winter. "Appropriating the Returns from Industrial Research and Development." *Brookings Paper on Economic Activity,* 1987, pp. 783–820.

Levitt, Theodore. "Exploit the Product Life Cycle." *Harvard Business Review,* November–December 1965, pp. 81–94.

———. "Exploiting What Others Have." In *Marketing for Business Growth.* New York: McGraw-Hill, 1969, pp. 174–86.

———. *Innovation in Marketing.* New York: McGraw-Hill, 1962.

———. "Innovative Imitation." *Harvard Business Review,* September–October 1966, pp. 63–70.

Lieberman, Marvin, and David Montgomery. "First-Mover Advantages." *Strategic Management Journal,* Summer 1988, pp. 41–58.

Light, Larry. "New Lemons from the Auto Lot." *Business Week,* December 3, 1990, p. 148.

Lilien, Gary, and Eunsang Yoon. "The Timing of Competitive Market Entry: An Exploratory Study of New Industrial Products." *Management Science,* May 1990, pp. 568–85.

Link, Albert, and John Neufeld. "Innovation Versus Imitation: Investigating Alternative R&D Strategies." *Applied Economics,* December 1986, pp. 1359–63.

Lipman, Steven, and Kevin McCardle. "Does Cheaper, Faster or Better Imply Sooner in the Timing of Innovation Decisions?" *Management Science,* August 1987, pp. 1058–64.

Logan, William. "Don't Follow the Leaders." *Venture,* October 1986, pp. 35–40.

Lyons, James. "Smash the Competition," *Forbes,* September 3, 1990, p. 46.

MacMillan, Ian, and Mary McCaffery. "How Aggressive Innovation Can Help Your Company." *Journal of Business Strategy,* Spring 1982, pp. 115–19.

MacMillan, Ian; Mary McCaffery; and Gilles Van Wijk. "Competitors' Responses to Easily Imitated New Products: Exploring Commercial Banking Product Introductions." *Strategic Management Journal,* 1988, pp. 75–86.

Mansfield, Edwin. "How Rapidly Does New Industrial Technology Leak Out?" *Journal of Industrial Economics,* December 1985, pp. 217–23.

————. "Technical Change and the Rate of Imitation." *Econometrica,* October 1961, pp. 741–66.

Mansfield, Edwin; Mark Schwartz; and Samuel Wagner. "Imitation Costs and Patents: An Empirical Study." *The Economics Journal,* December 1981, pp. 907–918.

————. *The Production and Application of New Industrial Technology.* New York: W. W. Norton, 1977

————. *Research and Innovation in the Modern Corporation.* New York: W. W. Norton, 1971.

McCoy, Michael. "Chip Pirates: Beware the Law." *IEEE Spectrum,* July 1985, pp. 74–80.

Meeks, Fleming. "Shakespeare, Dickens & Hillegass." *Forbes,* October 30, 1989, pp. 206–9.

————. "So Sue Me." *Forbes,* November 28, 1988, pp. 72, 74.

Meltzer, Rachel. "Fending Off the Copycats." *Venture,* February 1989, pp. 62–63.

Michaelson, Peter. "The 1984 Semiconductor Chip Protection Act: A Comprehensive View." *Communications & the Law,* October 1986, pp. 23–55.

Miller, Cyndee. "Competitor Rips Beech-Nut Line." *Marketing News,* June 10, 1991, pp. 1, 12.

Mitchell, Will. "Dual Clocks: Entry Order Influences on Incumbent and Newcomer Market Share and Survival When Specialized Assets Retain Their Value." *Strategic Management Journal,* 1991.

————. "Whether and When? Probability and Timing of Incumbents' Entry into Emergent Industrial Subfields." *Administrative Science Quarterly,* 1989, pp. 208–30.

Moore, Michael; William Boulding; and Ronald Goodstein. "Pioneering and Market Share: Is Entry Time Endogenous and Does it Matter?" *Journal of Marketing Research,* February 1991, pp. 97–104.

Moskowitz, Daniel. "Companies Should Take Action Against Patent Infringement Charges." *Washington Post,* August 7, 1989, p. WB14.

Nelson, Richard, and Sidney Winter. *An Evolutionary Theory of Economic Change.* Cambridge, Mass.: Belknap Press of Harvard University Press, 1982.

Novak, Josephine. "Coping with Protecting an Invention." *New York Times,* October 8, 1988, p. 54.

Nussbaum, Bruce. "Design Patents: How the Courts Help the Copycats." *Business Week,* November 5, 1990, p. 105.

Olleros, Francisco-Javier. "Emerging Industries and the Burnout of Pioneers." *Journal of Product Innovation Management,* March 1986, pp. 5–18.

Onkvisit, Sak, and John Shaw. "Competition and Product Management: Can the Product Life Cycle Help?" *Business Horizons,* July–August 1986, pp. 51–62.

Orza, Vincent. "Copycats Keep an Eye on Independents." *Restaurant Management,* January 1988, pp. 17–18.

Paepke, C. Owen. "An Economic Interpretation of the Misappropriation Doctrine: Common Law Protection for Investments in Innovating." *High Technology Law Journal,* Spring 1987, pp. 55–89.

Park, C. Whan, and Daniel Smith. "Product Class Competitors as Sources of Inno-

vative Marketing Strategies." *Journal of Consumer Marketing,* Spring 1990, pp. 27–38.

Parry, Mark, and Frank Bass. "When to Lead or Follow? It Depends." *Marketing Letters,* 1989, pp. 187–98.

Porter, Michael. *Competitive Strategy.* New York: Free Press, 1980.

Reed, Richard, and Robert DeFillippi. "Casual Ambiguity, Barriers to Imitation, and Sustainable Competitive Advantage." *Academy of Management Review,* January 1990, pp. 88–102.

Robinson, William. "Product Innovation and Start-up Business Market Share Performance." *Management Science,* October 1990, pp. 1279–89.

———. "Sources of Market Pioneer Advantages: The Case of Industrial Goods Industries," *Journal of Marketing Research,* Vol. 25, no. 1, February 1988, pp. 87–94.

Robinson, William, and Claes Fornell. "Sources of Market Pioneer Advantages: The Case of Consumer Goods Industries." *Journal of Marketing Research,* August 1985, pp. 305–17.

Rosenberg, Nathan. "Why Do Firms Do Basic Research (With Their Own Money)?" *Research Policy,* April 1990, pp. 165–74.

Rosenberg, Nathan, and W. Edward Steinmueller. "Why Are Americans Such Poor Imitators?" *American Economics Review,* May 1988, pp. 229–34.

Rosenbloom, Richard, and Michael Cusumano. "Technological Pioneering and Competitive Advantage: The Birth of the VCR Industry." *California Management Review,* Summer 1987, pp. 51–76.

Rowland, Mary. "Tales of Triumph." *Working Woman,* February 1988, pp. 76–79.

Sands, Saul. "Innovate or Imitate?" *Management Review,* December 1979, pp. 44–46.

Schewe, Gerard. "Imitation as an Option of Successful Technology Management." Working paper, Institute of Business Administration, University of Kiel, 40, D-2300 Kiel, Germany.

Schifrin, Matthew. "The Case of Discount Diapers." *Forbes,* September 13, 1993, pp. 60–65.

Schine, Eric. "Clay Jacobson Calls It Patently Unfair." *Business Week,* August 19, 1991, p. 48.

Schmalensee, Richard. "Product Differentiation Advantages of Pioneering Brands." *American Economic Review,* Fall 1982, pp. 349–65.

Schmid, Robert, Jr. "Reverse Engineering a Service Product." *Planning Review,* September–October 1987, pp. 33–35.

Schmitz, James, Jr. "Imitation, Entrepreneurship, and Long-Run Growth." *Journal of Political Economy,* June 1989, pp. 721–39.

Schnaars, Steven. "When Entering Growth Markets, Are Pioneers Better Than Poachers?" *Business Horizons,* March–April 1986, pp. 27–36.

Schrage, Michael. "Beware the Innovation Protectionists." *Wall Street Journal,* January 14, 1991, p. A14.

Sheeran, Lisa. "Copycat and Mouse." *Inc.,* April 1986, pp. 123–24.

Sinclair, P. J. N. "The Economics of Imitation." *Scottish Journal of Political Economy,* May 1990, pp. 113–44.

Sloan, Pat. "Toiletries & Beauty Aids: Knock-offs Deliver Blows to Fragrance Market." *Advertising Age,* March 2, 1987, p. S14.

Smedinghoff, Thomas. "The Legalities of Reverse Engineering Software." *Systems/3X & AS World,* May 1990, pp. 8, 150.

Sullivan, Mary. *Brand Extension and Order of Entry.* Cambridge, Mass.: Marketing Science Institute, Report no. 91-105, March 1991.

Teece, David. "Capturing Value from Technological Innovation: Integration, Strategic Partnering, and Licensing Decisions." *Interfaces,* May–June 1988, pp. 46–61.

Thomas, Robert. "Timing—The Key to Market Entry." *Journal of Consumer Marketing,* Summer 1985, pp. 77–87.

Ulrich, William. "A Look at Re- and Reverse Engineering: Does Anyone Really Know the Difference?" *Computing Canada,* October 26, 1989, pp. 26, 31.

Urban, Glen; Theresa Carter; Steve Gaskin; and Zofia Mucha. "Market Share Rewards to Pioneering, Brands: An Empirical Analysis and Strategic Implications." *Management Science,* June 1986, pp. 645–59.

Urban, Glen; Theresa Carter; and Zofia Mucha. "Market Share Rewards to Pioneering Brands: An Exploratory Empirical Analysis." In *Strategic Marketing and Management,* ed. H. Thomas and D. Gardner. New York: John Wiley & Sons, 1985, pp. 239–52.

Vasilash, Gary. "Defining the Unknown Part." *Production,* February 1989, pp. 57–59.

Walbert, Laura. "Copycat." *Forbes,* May 18, 1987, pp. 92–93.

Wallace, Don. "Giant Killers: How to Fight the Big Guys and Win." *Success,* April 1990, pp. 36–41.

Wernerfelt, Birger, and Aneel Karnani. "Competitive Strategy Under Uncertainty." *Strategic Management Journal,* March–April 1987, pp. 187–94.

Westney, D. Eleanor. *Imitation and Innovation.* Cambridge, Mass.: Harvard University Press, 1988.

Whitten, Ira. *Brand Performance in the Cigarette Industry and the Advantage of Early Entry, 1913–1974.* Washington, D.C.: Federal Trade Commission, Bureau of Economics, 1979.

Woodruff, David. "A New Era for Auto Quality." *Business Week,* October 22, 1990, pp. 84–96.

WSJ editors. "Too Flattering." *Wall Street Journal,* October 29, 1987, p. 35.

Yip, George. "Gateways to Entry." *Harvard Business Review,* September–October 1982, pp. 85–92.

Yoon, Eunsang, and Gary Lilien. "New Industrial Product Performance: The Effects of Market Characteristics and Strategy." *Journal of Product Innovation Management,* September 1985, pp. 134–44.

Ziegler, Charles. "Innovation and the Imitative Entrepreneur." *Journal of Economic Behavior & Organization,* June 1985, pp. 103–21.

Zwarun, Suzanne. "Parrying Unkind Cuts: The Battle Is On." *Canadian Business,* February 1987, pp. 21–24.

ACKNOWLEDGMENTS _____

A commuter who descends the stairs into New York's Pennsylvania Station is often confronted with a bevy of street vendors hawking their wares. For a while, one particularly creative vendor loudly proclaimed that he was selling "original imitations" of Mont Blanc's coveted ballpoint pen. He wanted to make sure that his wares would not be confused with the cheap knockoffs sold by other unscrupulous vendors. His pens were special. So were some of the people who helped me with this book.

Writing a book on imitation actually required a great deal of original research. Much of the material is simply not catalogued in a simple, easy-to-find way. Because of cultural biases, many firms are reluctant to talk about or publicize their experiences. We had to dig deep to find the facts. My research assistant, Tamoghna Chattopadhyay, was particularly helpful. Over the course of more than a year, he scoured the literature with incredible skill and diligence. Kyriacos Kousis, my other assistant, was equally helpful in finding obscure materials. My secretaries, Ada Perez and Eileen Goldberg, were also supportive. Bob Wallace, my editor at The Free Press, and Elena Vega, assistant editor, offered constructive comments and fine editorial support. Finally, my wife Gail and two sons, Paul and John, each helped immeasurably, largely by giving me the free time to concentrate on the project. I could not have written this book without them. To me, the people who helped were neither imitations nor "original imitations." In every case I received the help of true originals, and I deeply appreciate it.

INDEX _____